WOLF GIRL AND BLACK PRINCE

2

STORY & ART BY

Ayuko Hatta

CONTENTS

VOLUME

2

STORY

High schooler Erika Shinohara loves to be the center of attention but has no dating experience whatsoever. So when her friends Marin and Tezuka start bragging about their boyfriends, she doesn't hesitate to spin a fantastical tale of romance—complete with a fake boyfriend—to fit in. When the pair begin to grow suspicious of Erika, she snaps a picture of a hot guy she sees on the street to use an evidence. Her plan quickly goes awry, however, when she finds out that hot guy is her schoolmate Kyoya Sata!

Backed into a corner, Erika asks Kyoya to pretend to be her boyfriend. Unfortunately for Erika, though Kyoya has the looks of a prince, deep down he's actually a blackhearted sadist! Kyoya has one demand in exchange for the favor, and in a moment of weakness Erika accepts. She has to become Kyoya's dog (aka a servant, in Kyoya's twisted words)…

Shortly after summer vacation ends, Erika goes to look after Kyoya, who is stuck at home with a cold. Kyoya is so weak from fever that all he can do is spit venom. When he realizes that Erika's intentions are pure, however, he offers his sincere gratitude. Never having seen such a genuine side of Kyoya before, Erika finds her heart is all aflutter!

CHECK OUT
WOLF GIRL AND BLACK
PRINCE VOLUME 1
FOR ALL THE
JUICY DETAILS!

In this warmhearted romantic comedy, mistaken identity leads to a blossoming romance between two boys.

My Love Mix-Up!

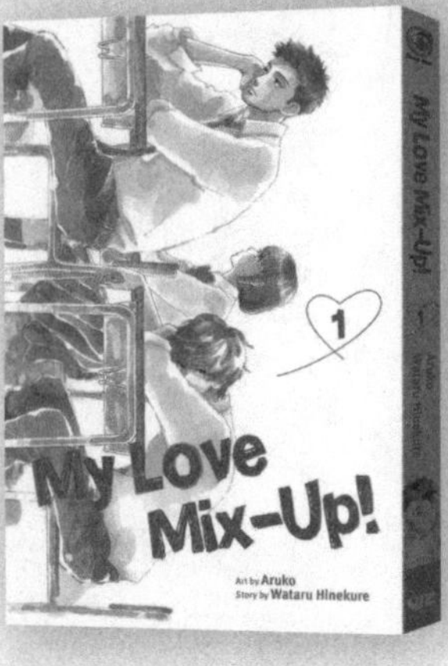

My Love Mix-Up!
1
Art by Aruko
Story by Wataru Hinekure

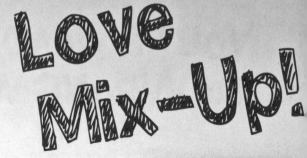

Art by **Aruko**
Story by **Wataru Hinekure**

Aoki has a crush on Hashimoto, the girl in the seat next to him in class. But he despairs when he borrows her eraser and sees she's written the name of another boy—Ida—on it. To make matters more confusing, Ida sees him holding that very eraser and thinks Aoki has a crush on him!

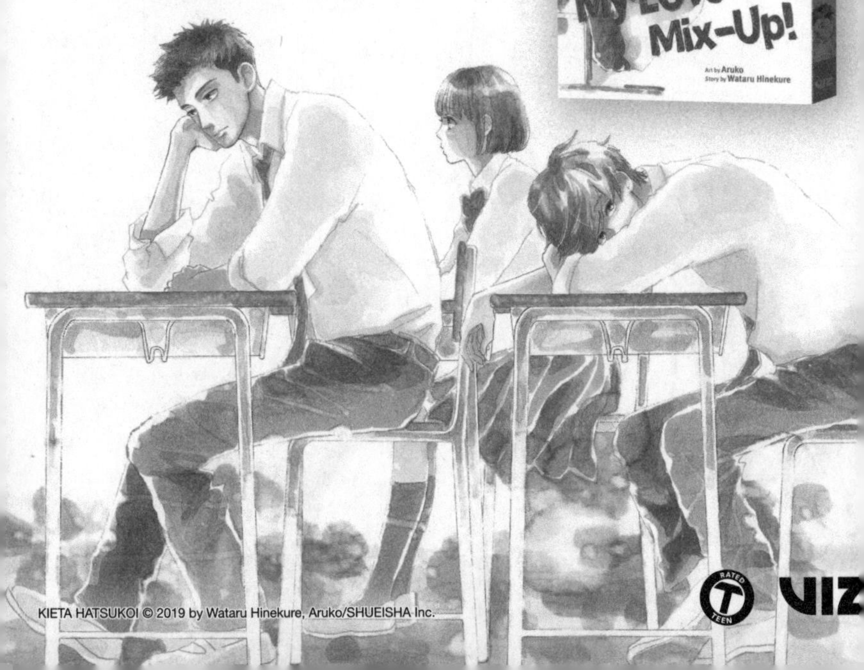

DROP IT! GOOD, GOOD!

YOU'RE READING THE WRONG WAY!

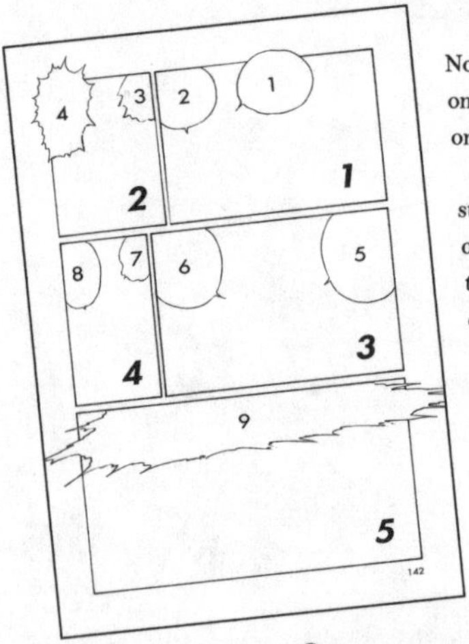
1
2
3
4
5
6
7
8
9
1
2
3
4
5
142

Now, watch me and listen up! I'm only explaining this once. To read *Wolf Girl and Black Prince* in its intended order, you need to flip it over and start again.

Wolf Girl and Black Prince reads from right to left, starting in the upper-right corner, to preserve the original Japanese orientation of the work. That means that the action, sound effects, and word balloons are completely reversed from English order.

You got all that? That's a good pooch! Now, spin around three times, shake, and give me a "woof."

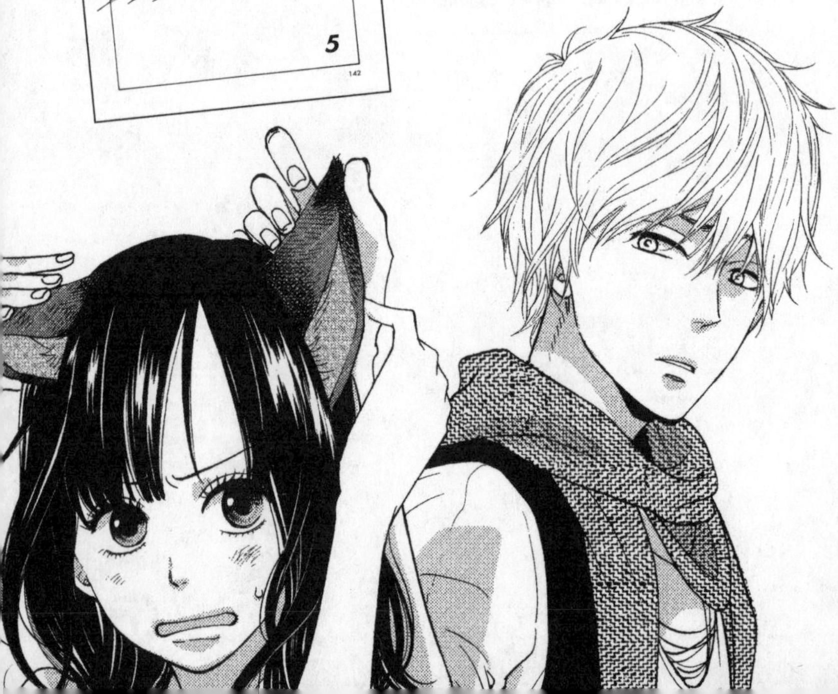

NOT YOUR IDOL

story and art by **aoi makino**

AFTER THAT DAY, SHE STOPPED BEING A GIRL...

In the wake of an assault, Nina Kamiyama, a former idol in the group Pure Club, shuns her femininity and starts dressing as a boy. At high school she keeps to herself, but fellow student Hikaru Horiuchi realizes who she is. What secrets is she keeping? The shocking drama starts.

A psychological suspense series about a girl who has given up her life as an idol after being assaulted by a fan.

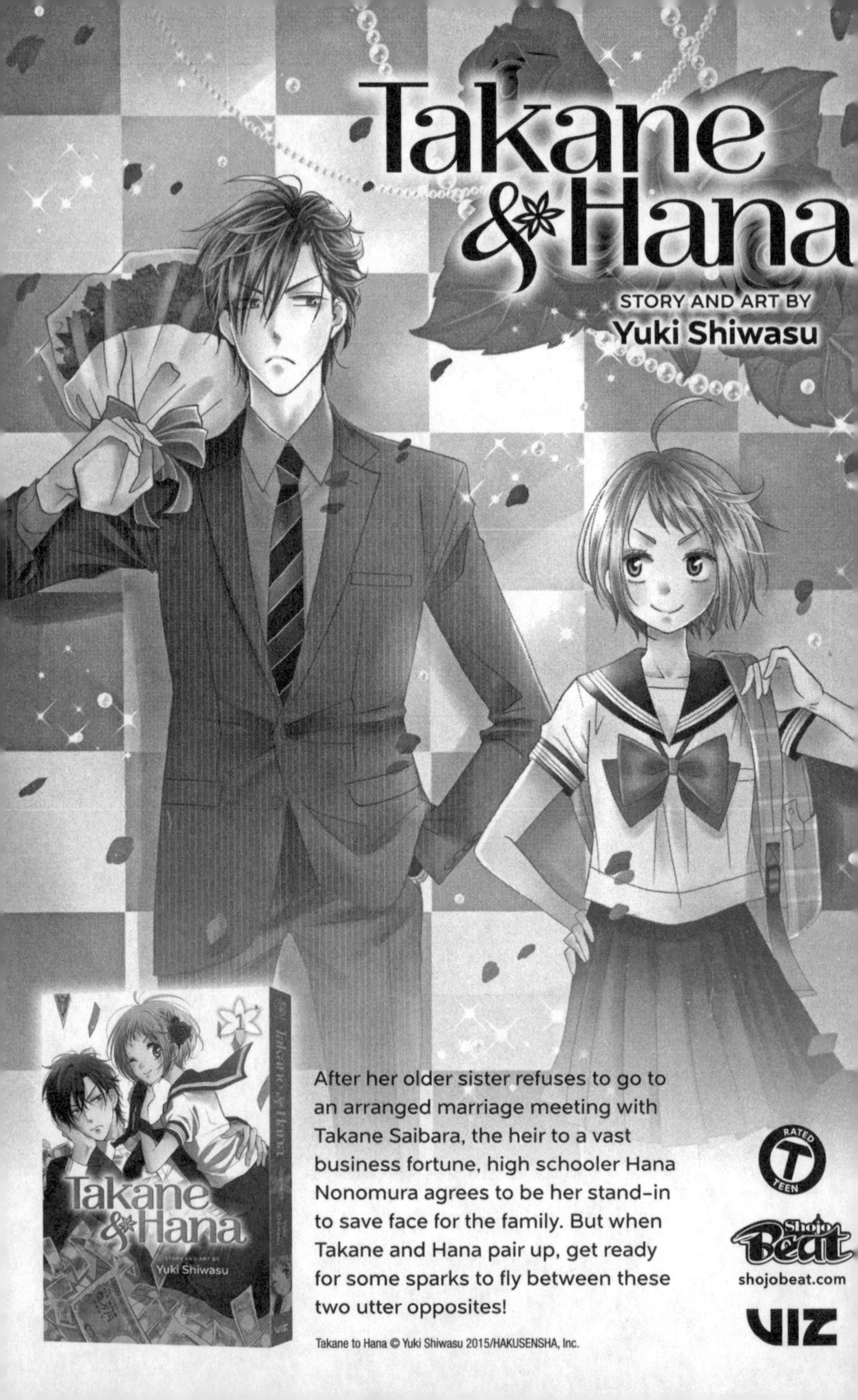
Takane & Hana
STORY AND ART BY
Yuki Shiwasu
After her older sister refuses to go to an arranged marriage meeting with Takane Saibara, the heir to a vast business fortune, high schooler Hana Nonomura agrees to be her stand-in to save face for the family. But when Takane and Hana pair up, get ready for some sparks to fly between these two utter opposites!
RATED T TEEN
Shojo Beat
shojobeat.com
VIZ
Takane to Hana © Yuki Shiwasu 2015/HAKUSENSHA, Inc.

THE YOUNG MASTER'S REVENGE

When Leo was a young boy, he had his pride torn to shreds by Tenma, a girl from a wealthy background who was always getting him into trouble. Now, years after his father's successful clothing business has made him the heir to a fortune, he searches out Tenma to enact a dastardly plan—he'll get his revenge by making her fall in love with him!

RATED TEEN

VIZ
viz.com

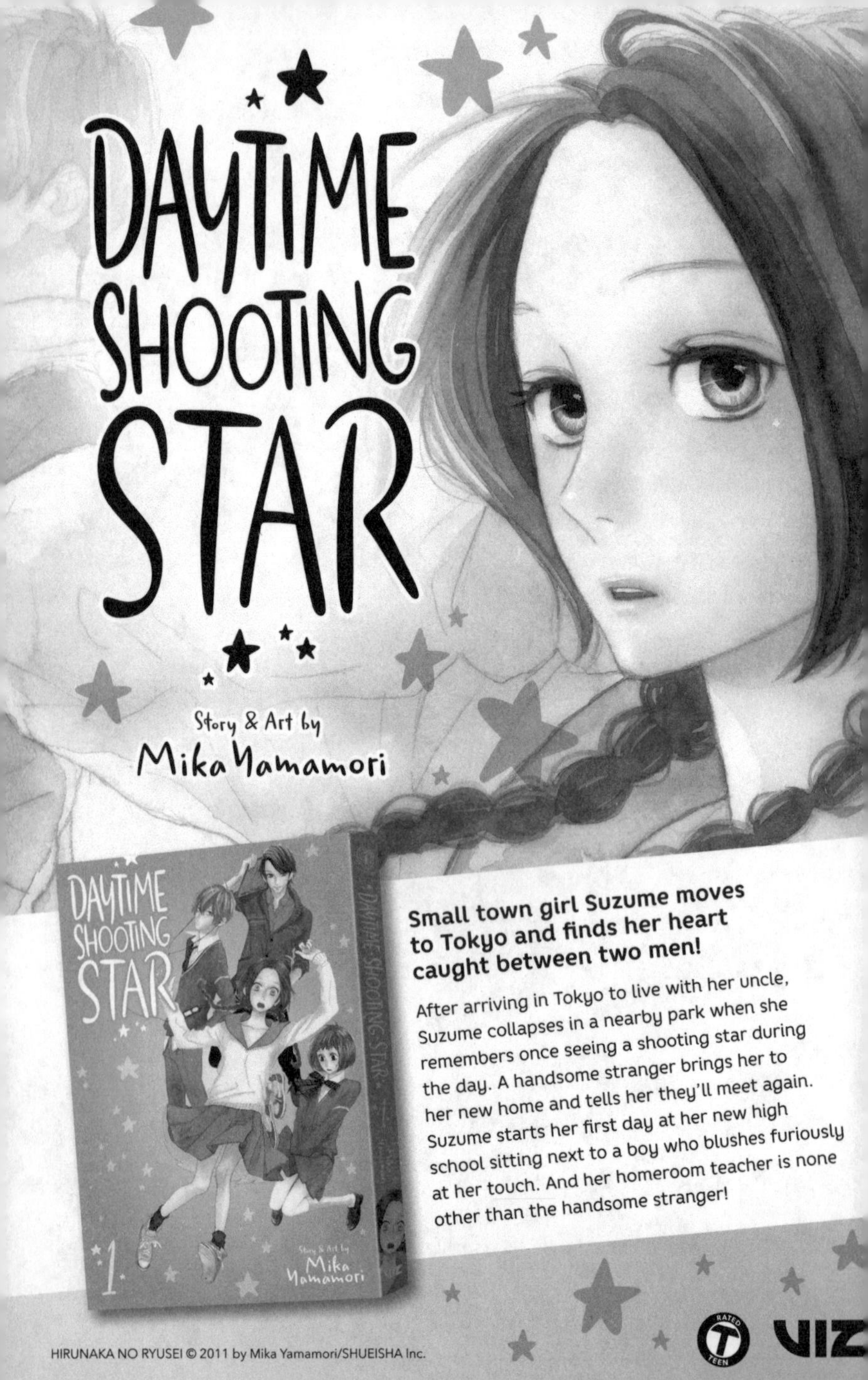
DAYTIME SHOOTING STAR
Story & Art by
Mika Yamamori
DAYTIME SHOOTING STAR
1
Story & Art by
Mika Yamamori
Small town girl Suzume moves to Tokyo and finds her heart caught between two men!
After arriving in Tokyo to live with her uncle, Suzume collapses in a nearby park when she remembers once seeing a shooting star during the day. A handsome stranger brings her to her new home and tells her they'll meet again. Suzume starts her first day at her new high school sitting next to a boy who blushes furiously at her touch. And her homeroom teacher is none other than the handsome stranger!
RATED T TEEN
VIZ

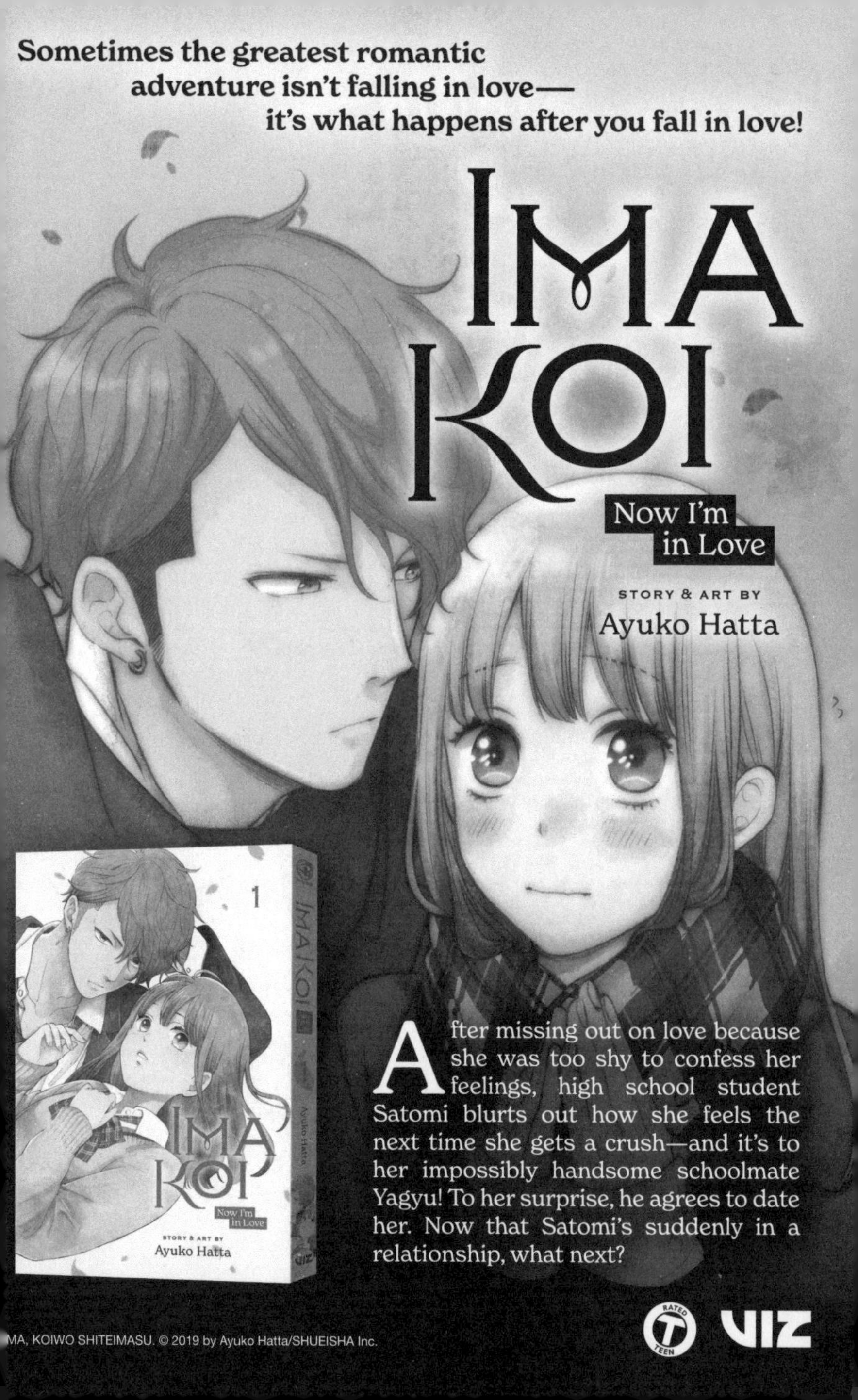

Sometimes the greatest romantic adventure isn't falling in love—it's what happens after you fall in love!
IMA KOI
Now I'm in Love
STORY & ART BY
Ayuko Hatta
1
IMA KOI
IMA KOI
Now I'm in Love
STORY & ART BY
Ayuko Hatta
After missing out on love because she was too shy to confess her feelings, high school student Satomi blurts out how she feels the next time she gets a crush—and it's to her impossibly handsome schoolmate Yagyu! To her surprise, he agrees to date her. Now that Satomi's suddenly in a relationship, what next?
RATED T TEEN
VIZ
MA, KOIWO SHITEIMASU. © 2019 by Ayuko Hatta/SHUEISHA Inc.

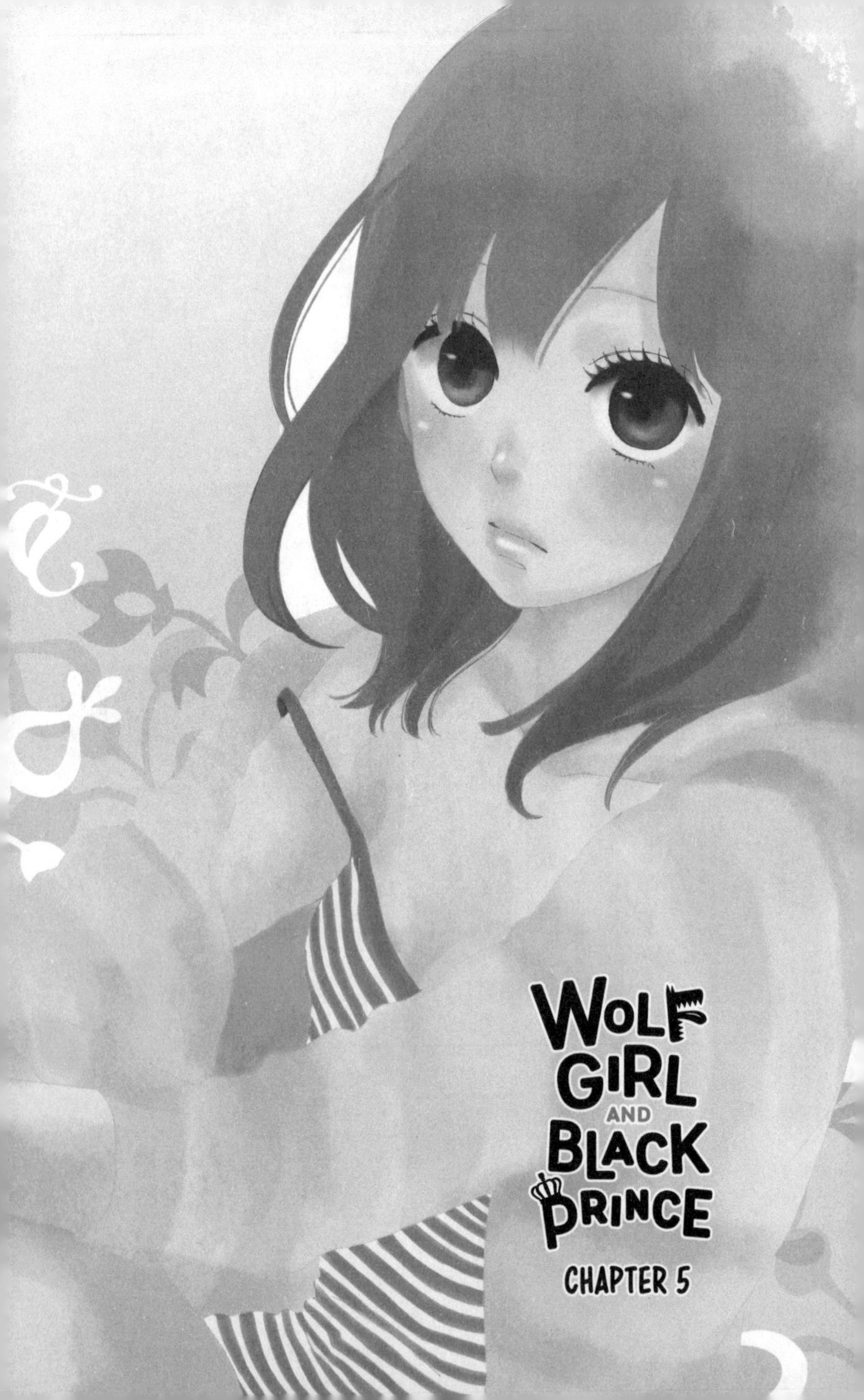
WOLF GIRL AND BLACK PRINCE
CHAPTER 5

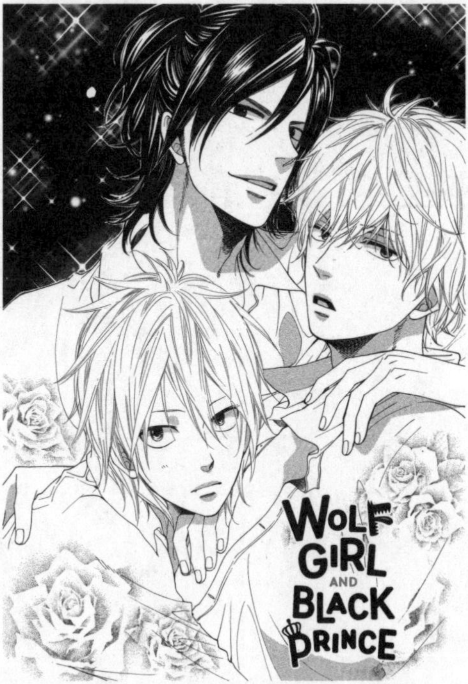
WOLF
GIRL
AND
BLACK
PRINCE

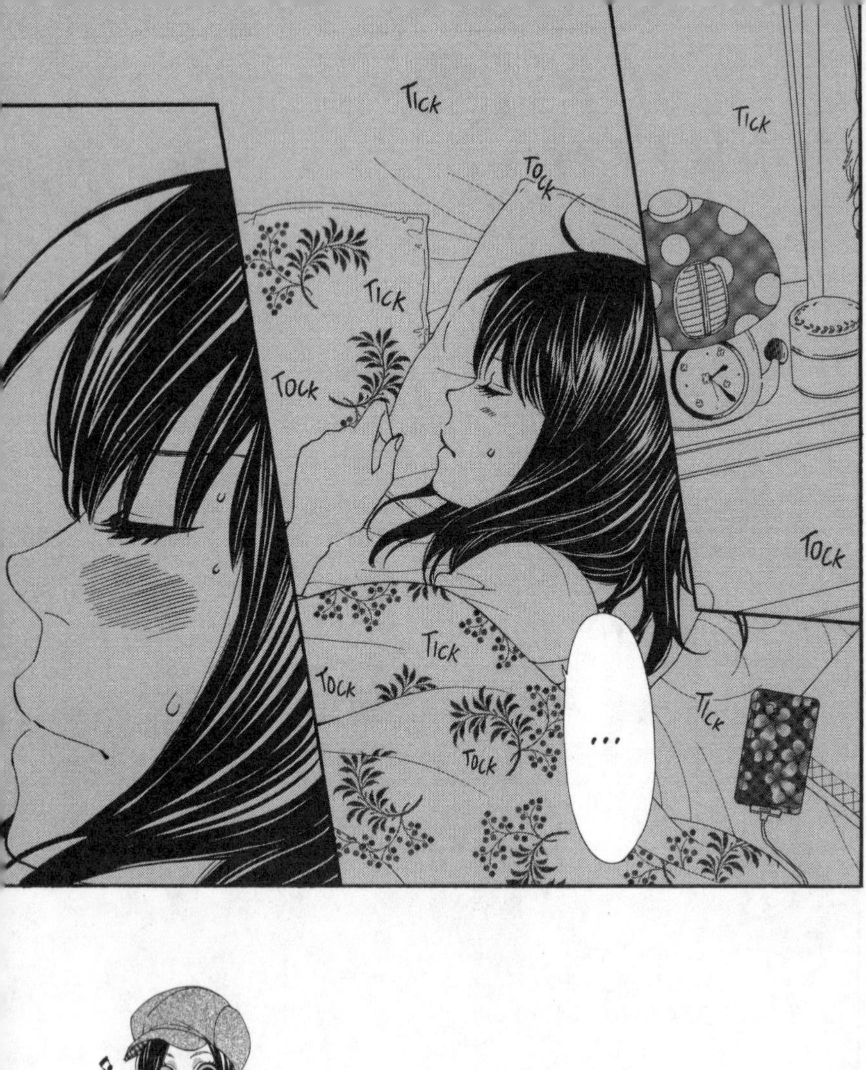
TICK
TOCK
TICK
TOCK
TICK
TOCK
TICK
...
TICK
TOCK
TOCK

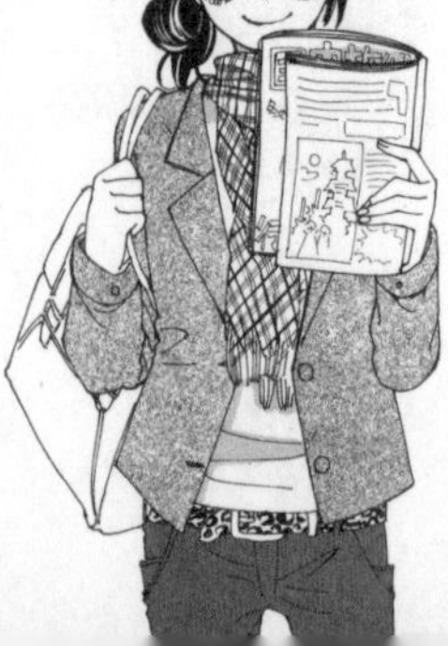

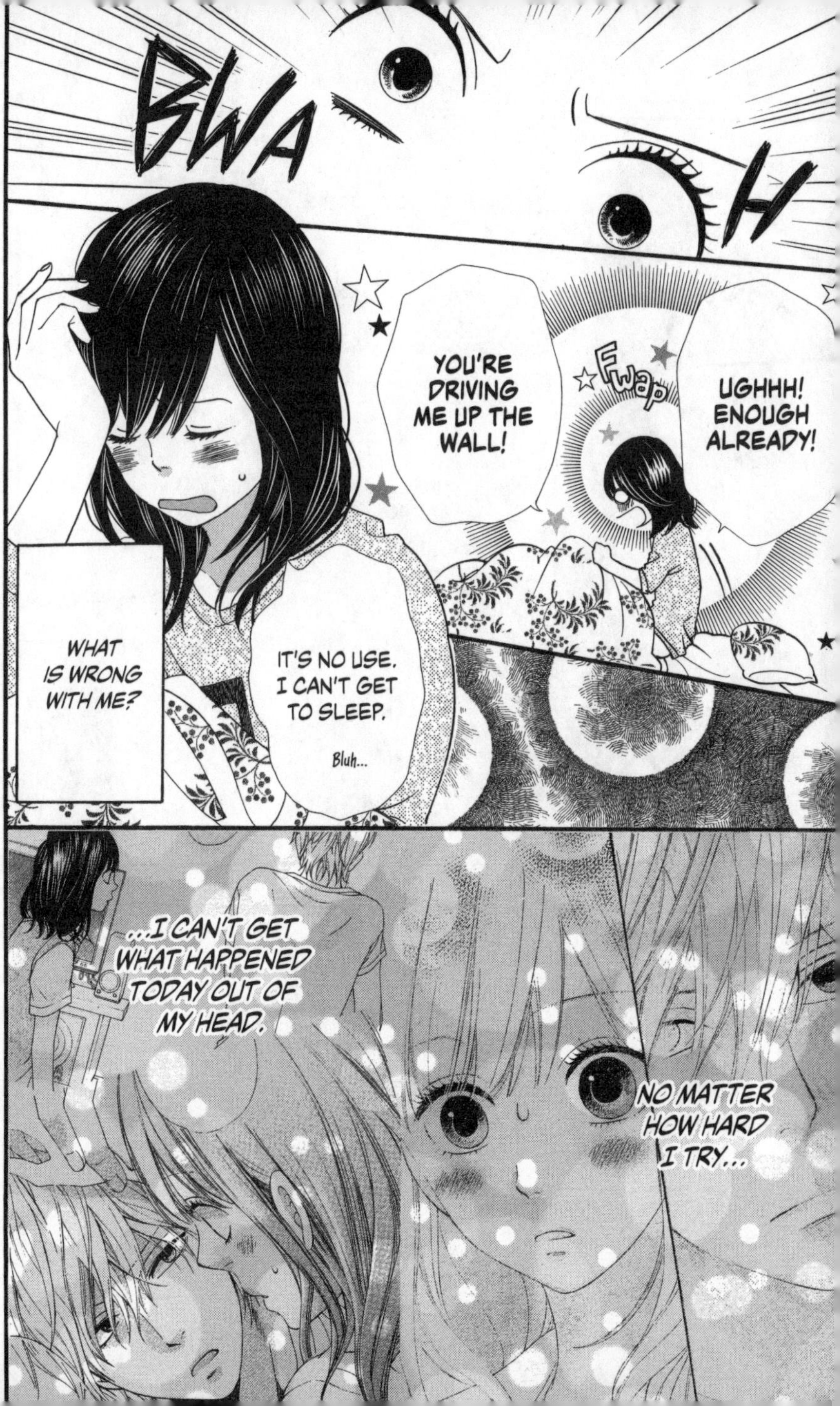
BWAH
UGHHH! ENOUGH ALREADY!
Fwap
YOU'RE DRIVING ME UP THE WALL!
IT'S NO USE. I CAN'T GET TO SLEEP.
Bluh...
WHAT IS WRONG WITH ME?
NO MATTER HOW HARD I TRY...
...I CAN'T GET WHAT HAPPENED TODAY OUT OF MY HEAD.

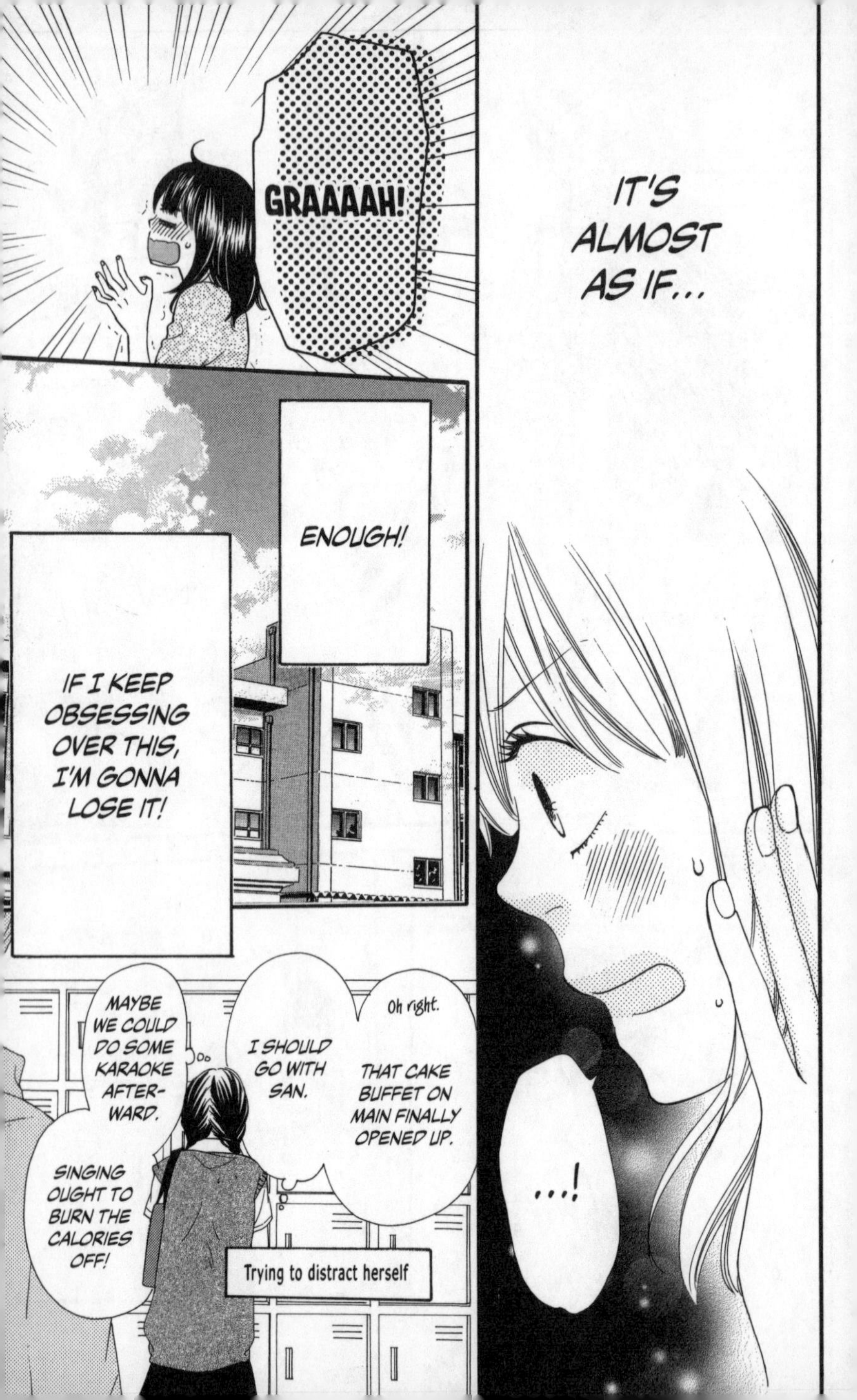
IT'S ALMOST AS IF...
...!
GRAAAAH!
ENOUGH!
IF I KEEP OBSESSING OVER THIS, I'M GONNA LOSE IT!
Oh right.
THAT CAKE BUFFET ON MAIN FINALLY OPENED UP.
I SHOULD GO WITH SAN.
MAYBE WE COULD DO SOME KARAOKE AFTER-WARD.
SINGING OUGHT TO BURN THE CALORIES OFF!
Trying to distract herself

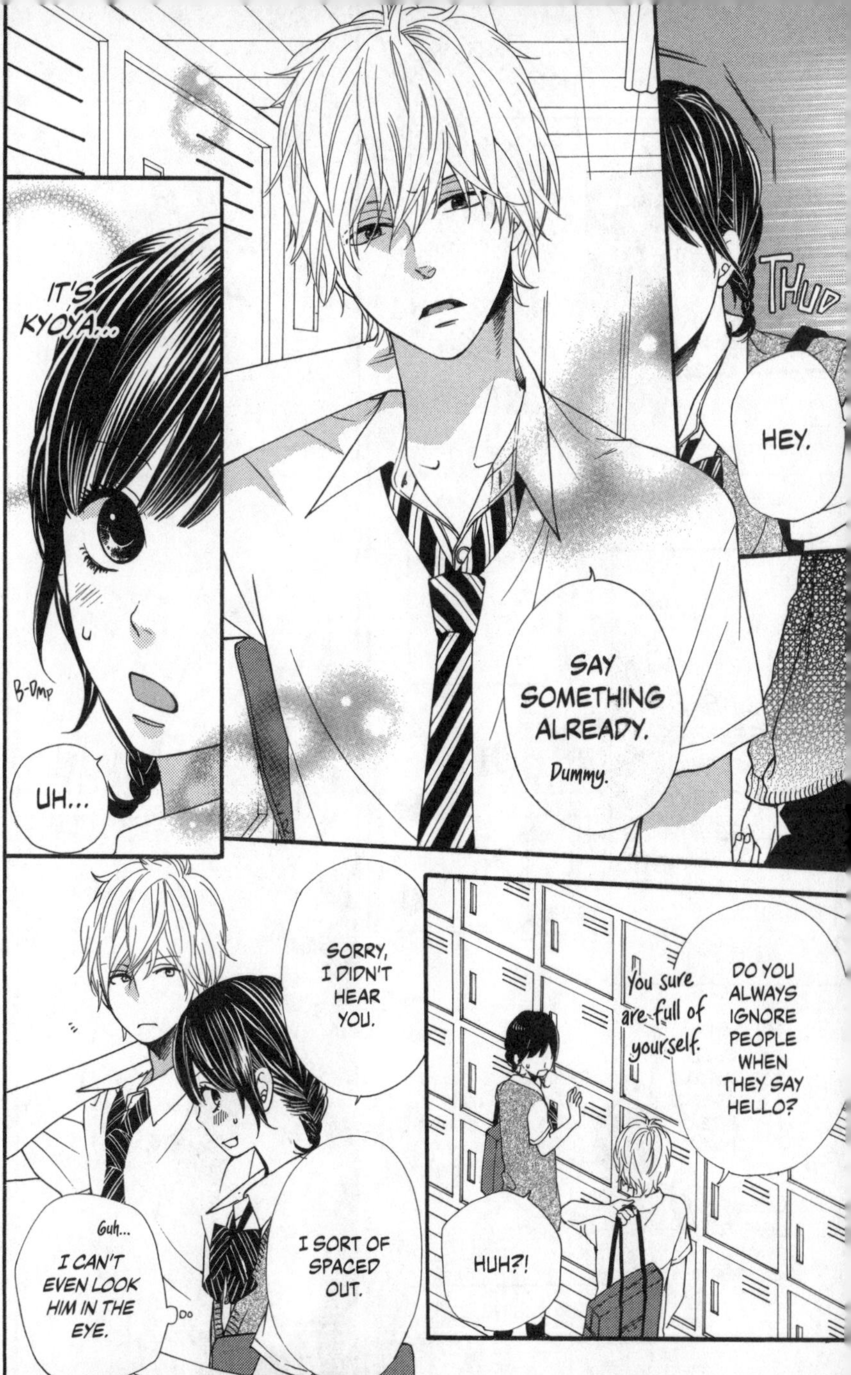
THUD
HEY.
SAY SOMETHING ALREADY.
Dummy.
IT'S KYOYA...
B-DMP
UH...
DO YOU ALWAYS IGNORE PEOPLE WHEN THEY SAY HELLO?
You sure are full of yourself.
HUH?!
SORRY, I DIDN'T HEAR YOU.
I SORT OF SPACED OUT.
Guh...
I CAN'T EVEN LOOK HIM IN THE EYE.

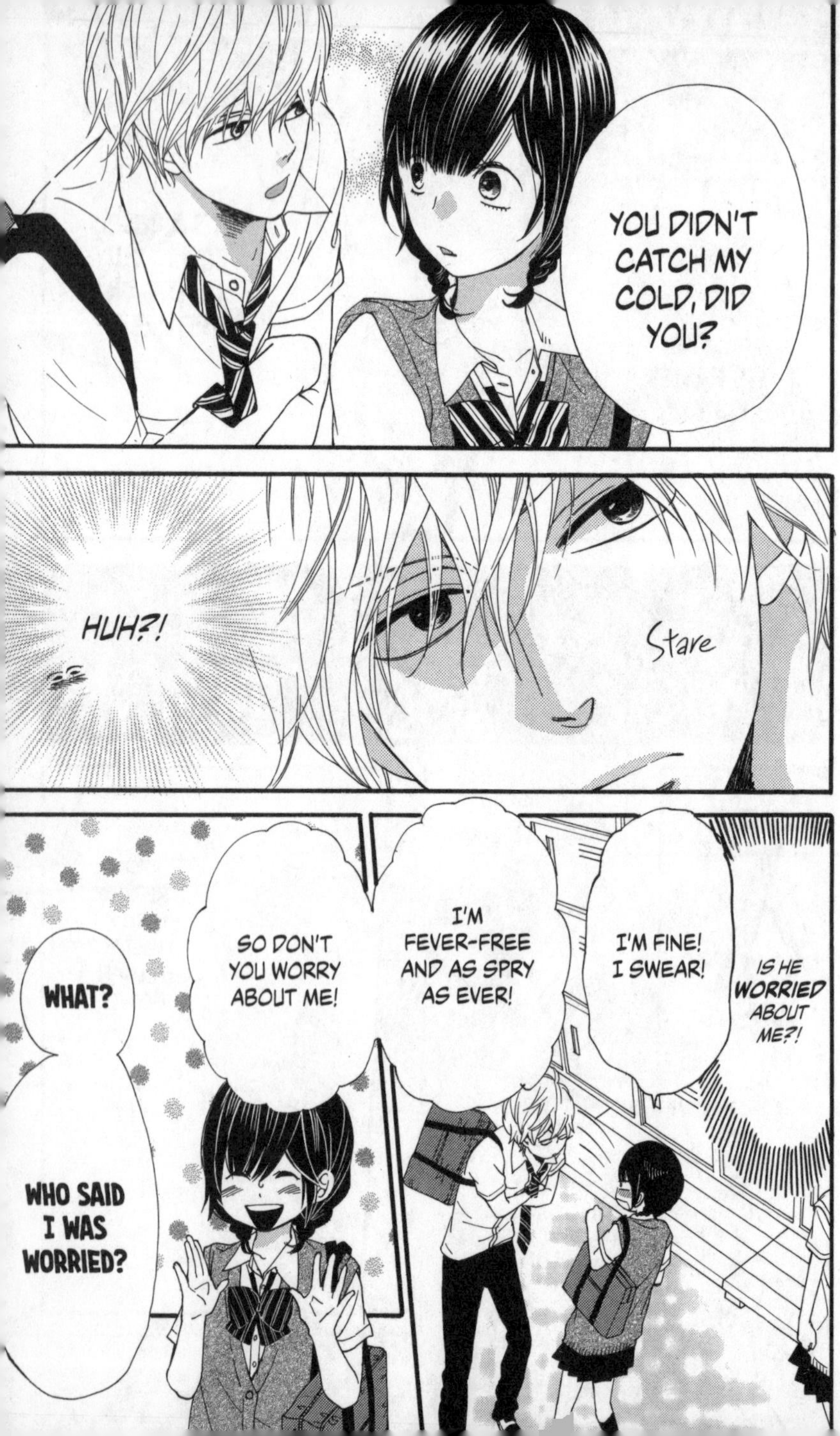
YOU DIDN'T CATCH MY COLD, DID YOU?
Stare
HUH?!
IS HE WORRIED ABOUT ME?!
I'M FINE! I SWEAR!
I'M FEVER-FREE AND AS SPRY AS EVER!
SO DON'T YOU WORRY ABOUT ME!
WHAT?
WHO SAID I WAS WORRIED?

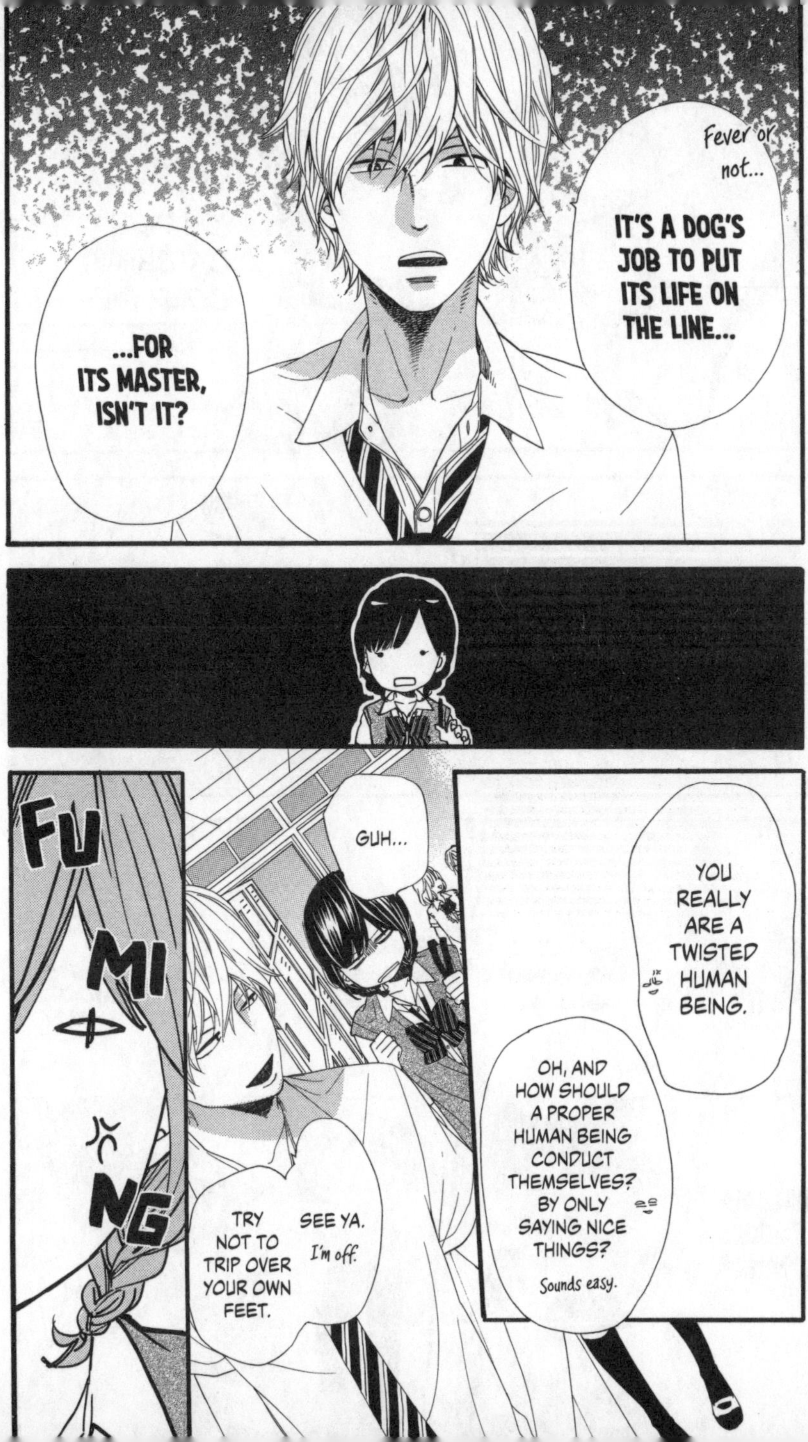
Fever or not...
IT'S A DOG'S JOB TO PUT ITS LIFE ON THE LINE...
...FOR ITS MASTER, ISN'T IT?
YOU REALLY ARE A TWISTED HUMAN BEING.
OH, AND HOW SHOULD A PROPER HUMAN BEING CONDUCT THEMSELVES? BY ONLY SAYING NICE THINGS?
Sounds easy.
GUH...
SEE YA.
I'm off.
TRY NOT TO TRIP OVER YOUR OWN FEET.
FUMING

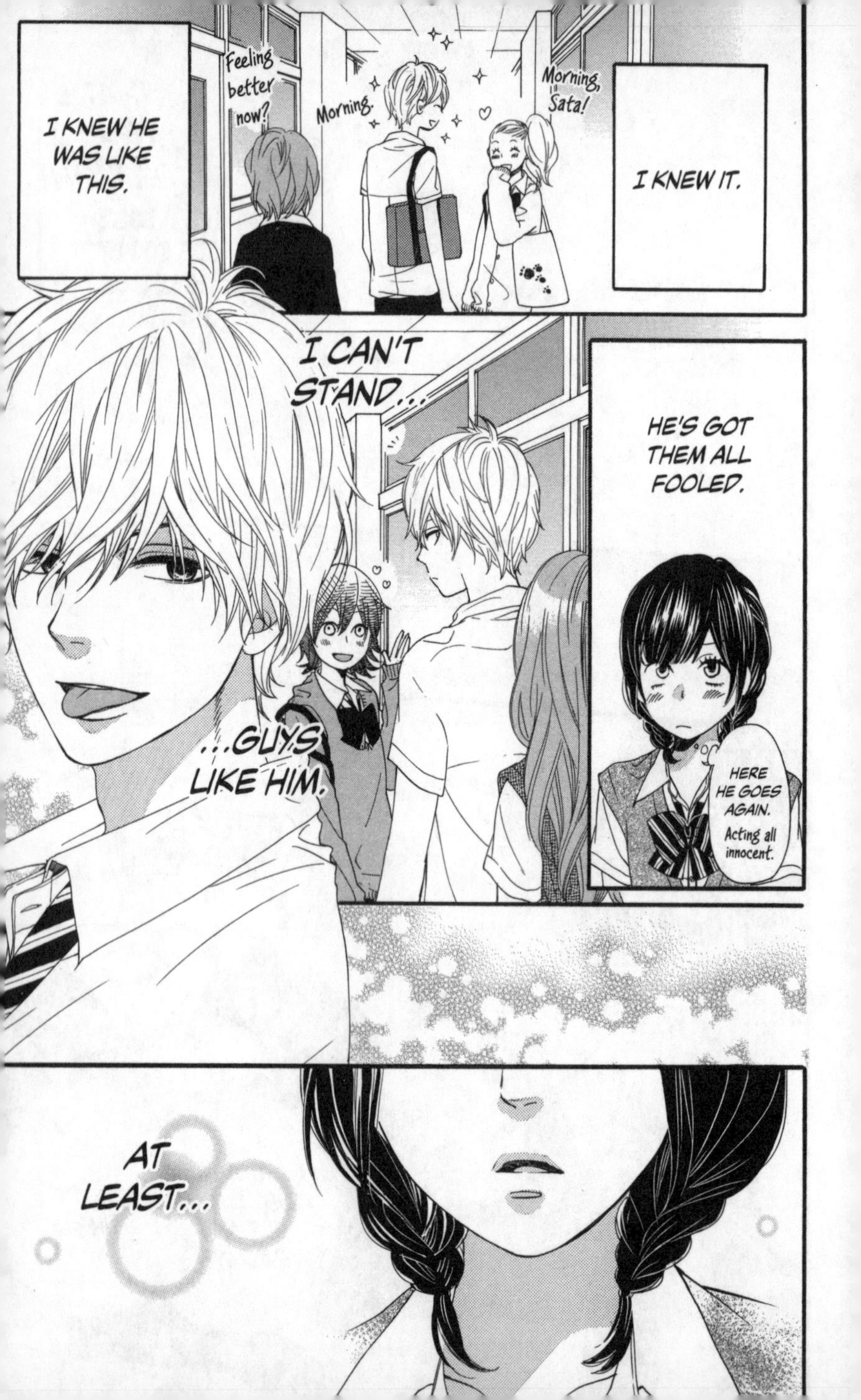

I KNEW IT.
Morning, Sata!
Morning.
Feeling better now?
I KNEW HE WAS LIKE THIS.
HE'S GOT THEM ALL FOOLED.
HERE HE GOES AGAIN. Acting all innocent.
I CAN'T STAND...
...GUYS LIKE HIM.
AT LEAST...

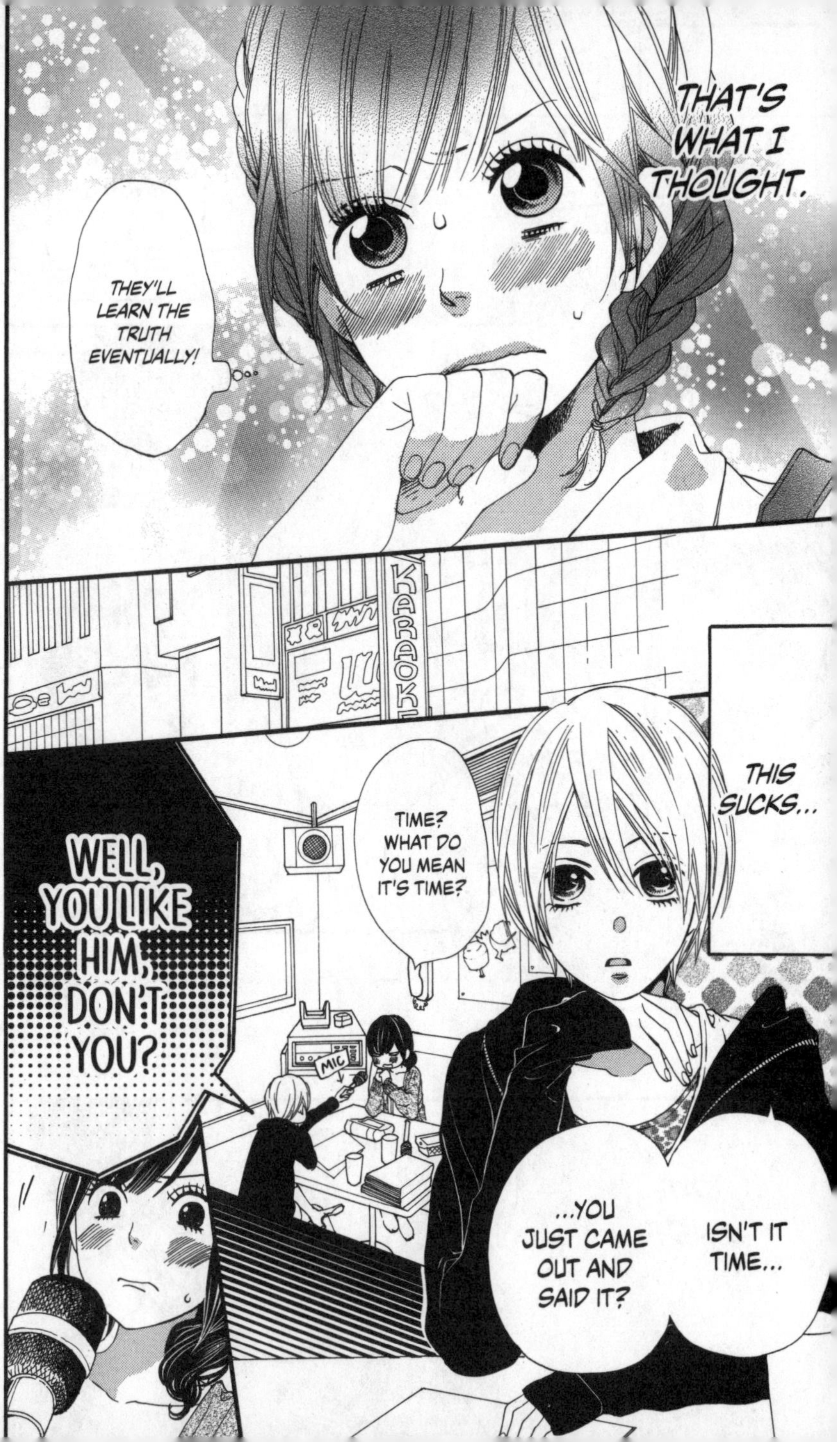
THAT'S WHAT I THOUGHT.
THEY'LL LEARN THE TRUTH EVENTUALLY!
KARAOKE
THIS SUCKS...
ISN'T IT TIME...
...YOU JUST CAME OUT AND SAID IT?
TIME? WHAT DO YOU MEAN IT'S TIME?
MIC
WELL, YOU LIKE HIM, DON'T YOU?

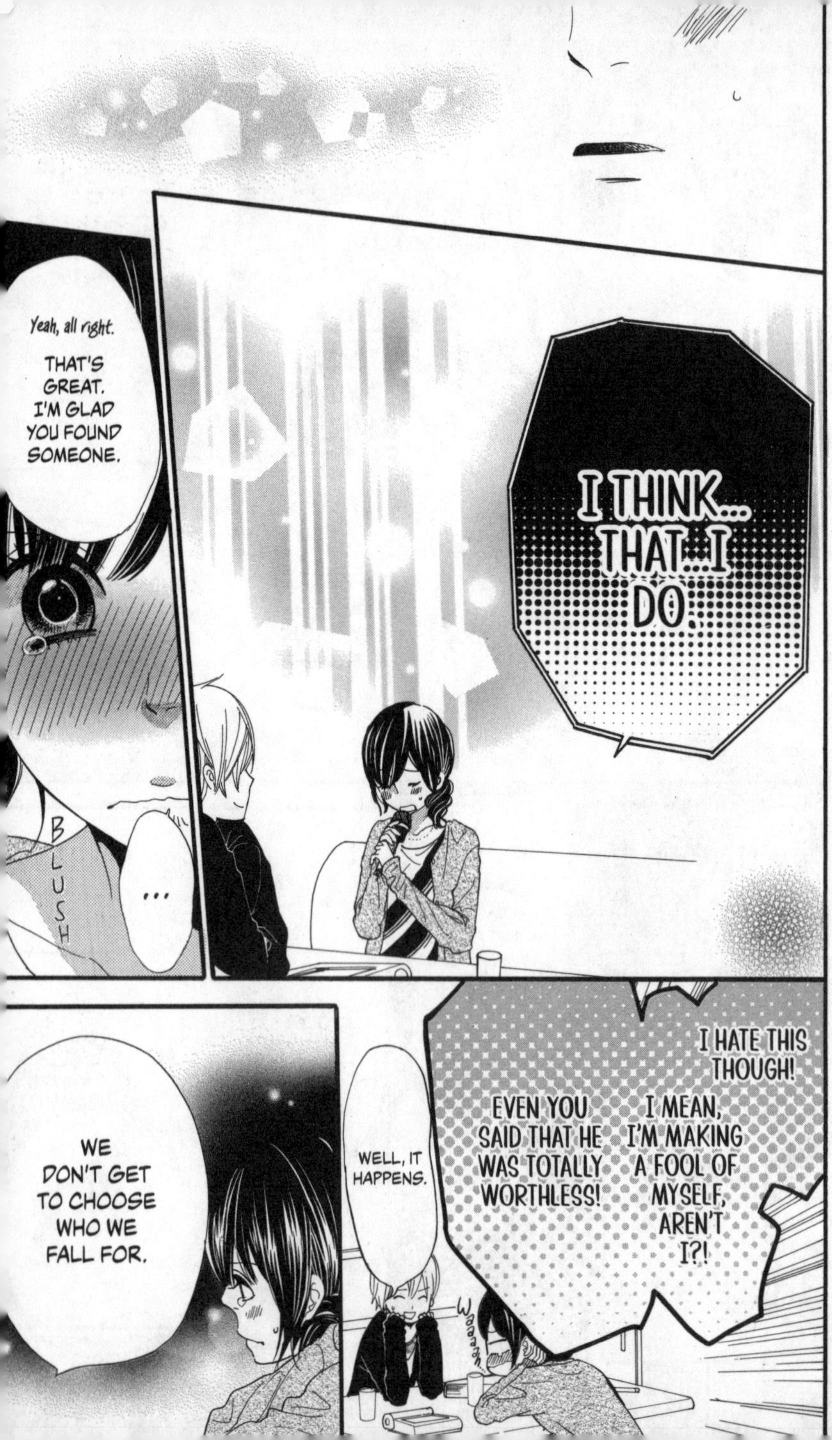
I THINK... THAT...I DO.
Yeah, all right.
THAT'S GREAT. I'M GLAD YOU FOUND SOMEONE.
BLUSH
...
I HATE THIS THOUGH!
I MEAN, I'M MAKING A FOOL OF MYSELF, AREN'T I?!
EVEN YOU SAID THAT HE WAS TOTALLY WORTHLESS!
WELL, IT HAPPENS.
WE DON'T GET TO CHOOSE WHO WE FALL FOR.

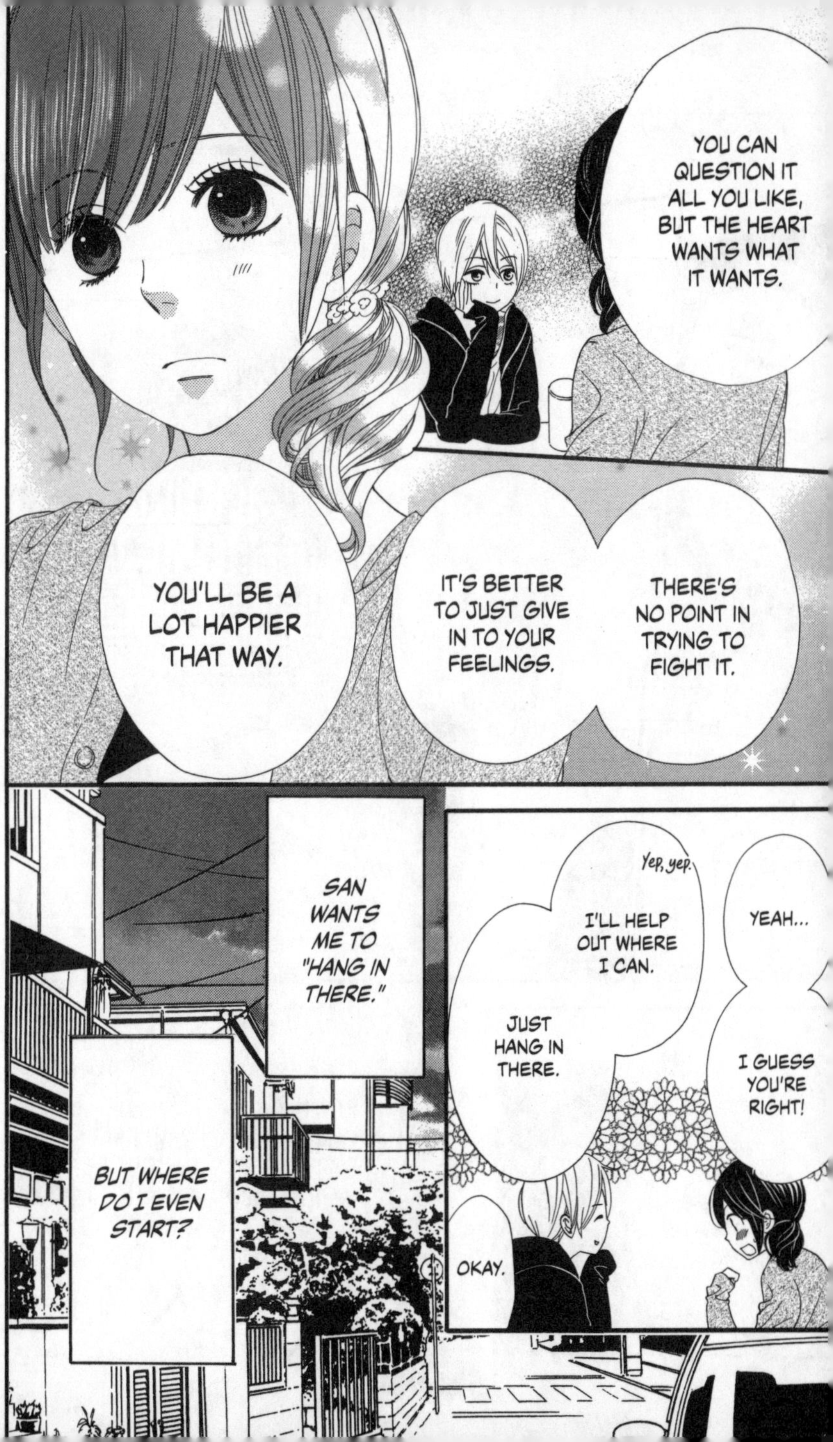
YOU CAN QUESTION IT ALL YOU LIKE, BUT THE HEART WANTS WHAT IT WANTS.
THERE'S NO POINT IN TRYING TO FIGHT IT.
IT'S BETTER TO JUST GIVE IN TO YOUR FEELINGS.
YOU'LL BE A LOT HAPPIER THAT WAY.
YEAH...
I GUESS YOU'RE RIGHT!
Yep, yep.
I'LL HELP OUT WHERE I CAN.
JUST HANG IN THERE.
OKAY.
SAN WANTS ME TO "HANG IN THERE."
BUT WHERE DO I EVEN START?

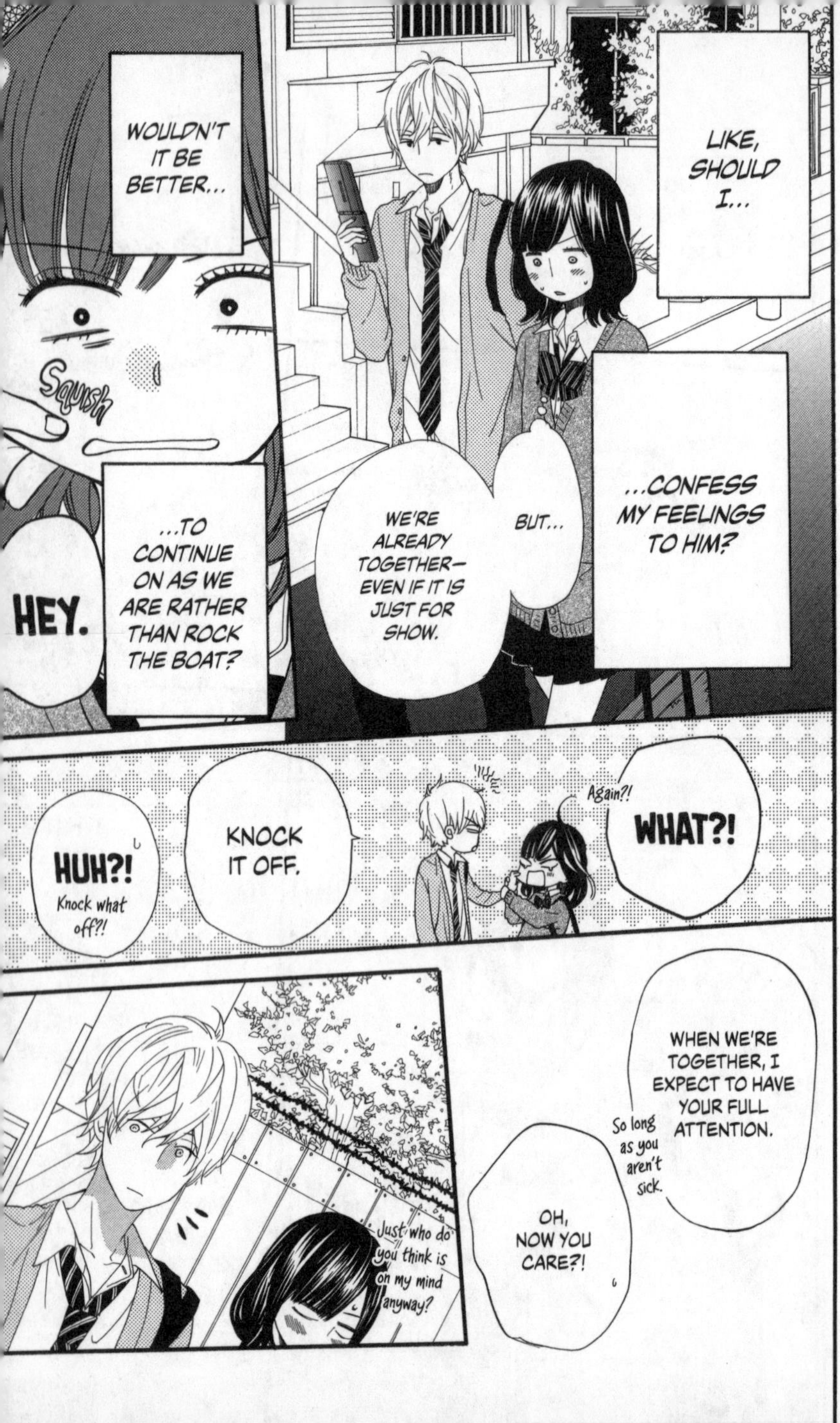

LIKE, SHOULD I...
...CONFESS MY FEELINGS TO HIM?
BUT...
WE'RE ALREADY TOGETHER— EVEN IF IT IS JUST FOR SHOW.
WOULDN'T IT BE BETTER...
...TO CONTINUE ON AS WE ARE RATHER THAN ROCK THE BOAT?
Squish
HEY.
WHAT?!
Again?!
KNOCK IT OFF.
HUH?!
Knock what off?!
WHEN WE'RE TOGETHER, I EXPECT TO HAVE YOUR FULL ATTENTION.
So long as you aren't sick.
OH, NOW YOU CARE?!
Just who do you think is on my mind anyway?

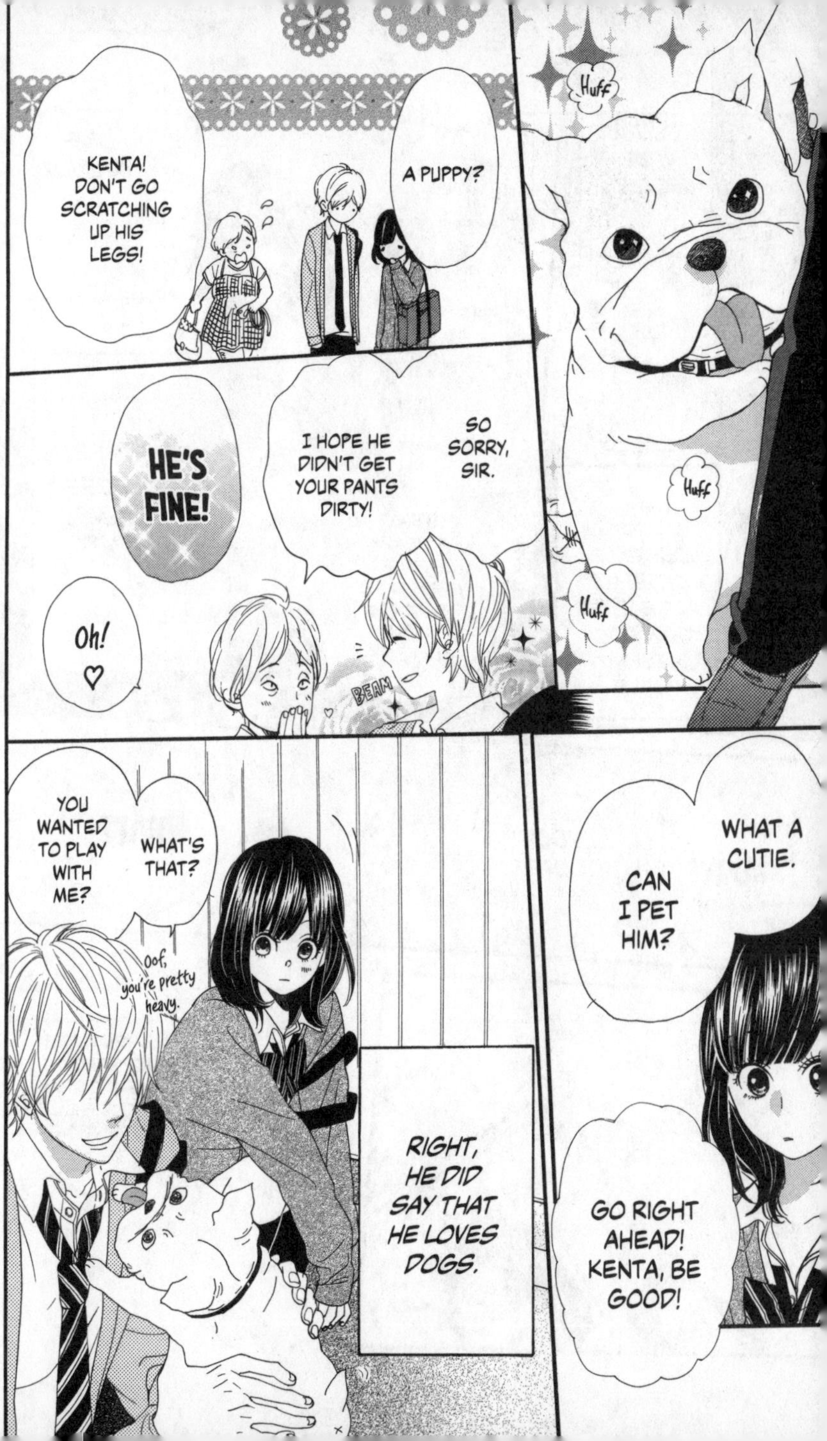
Huff
Huff
Huff
A PUPPY?
KENTA! DON'T GO SCRATCHING UP HIS LEGS!
SO SORRY, SIR.
I HOPE HE DIDN'T GET YOUR PANTS DIRTY!
HE'S FINE!
Oh! ♡
BEAM
WHAT A CUTIE.
CAN I PET HIM?
GO RIGHT AHEAD! KENTA, BE GOOD!
WHAT'S THAT?
YOU WANTED TO PLAY WITH ME?
Oof, you're pretty heavy.
RIGHT, HE DID SAY THAT HE LOVES DOGS.

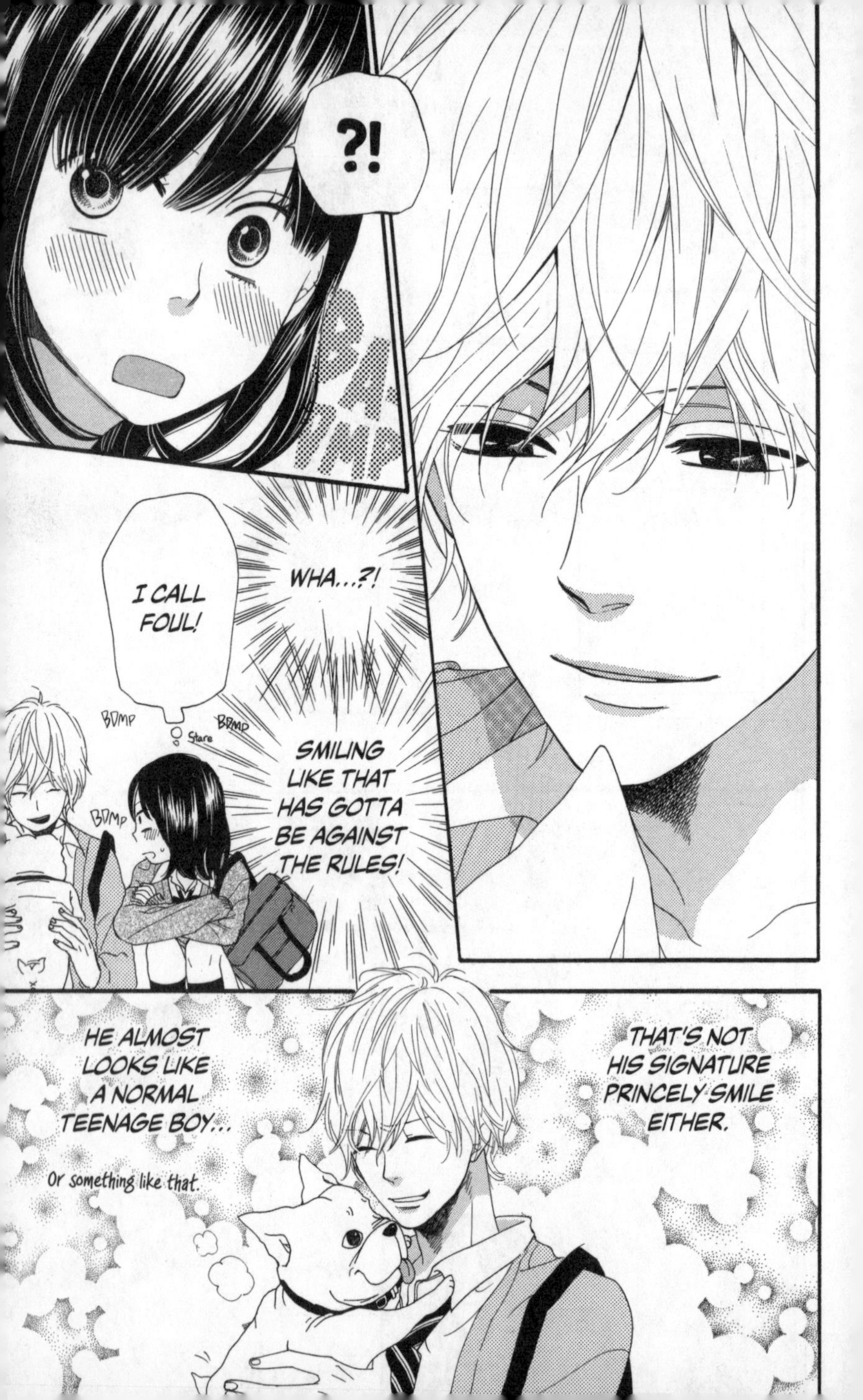
?!
BA-DUMP
WHA...?!
I CALL FOUL!
BDMP
Stare
BDMP
BDMP
SMILING LIKE THAT HAS GOTTA BE AGAINST THE RULES!
THAT'S NOT HIS SIGNATURE PRINCELY SMILE EITHER.
HE ALMOST LOOKS LIKE A NORMAL TEENAGE BOY...
Or something like that.

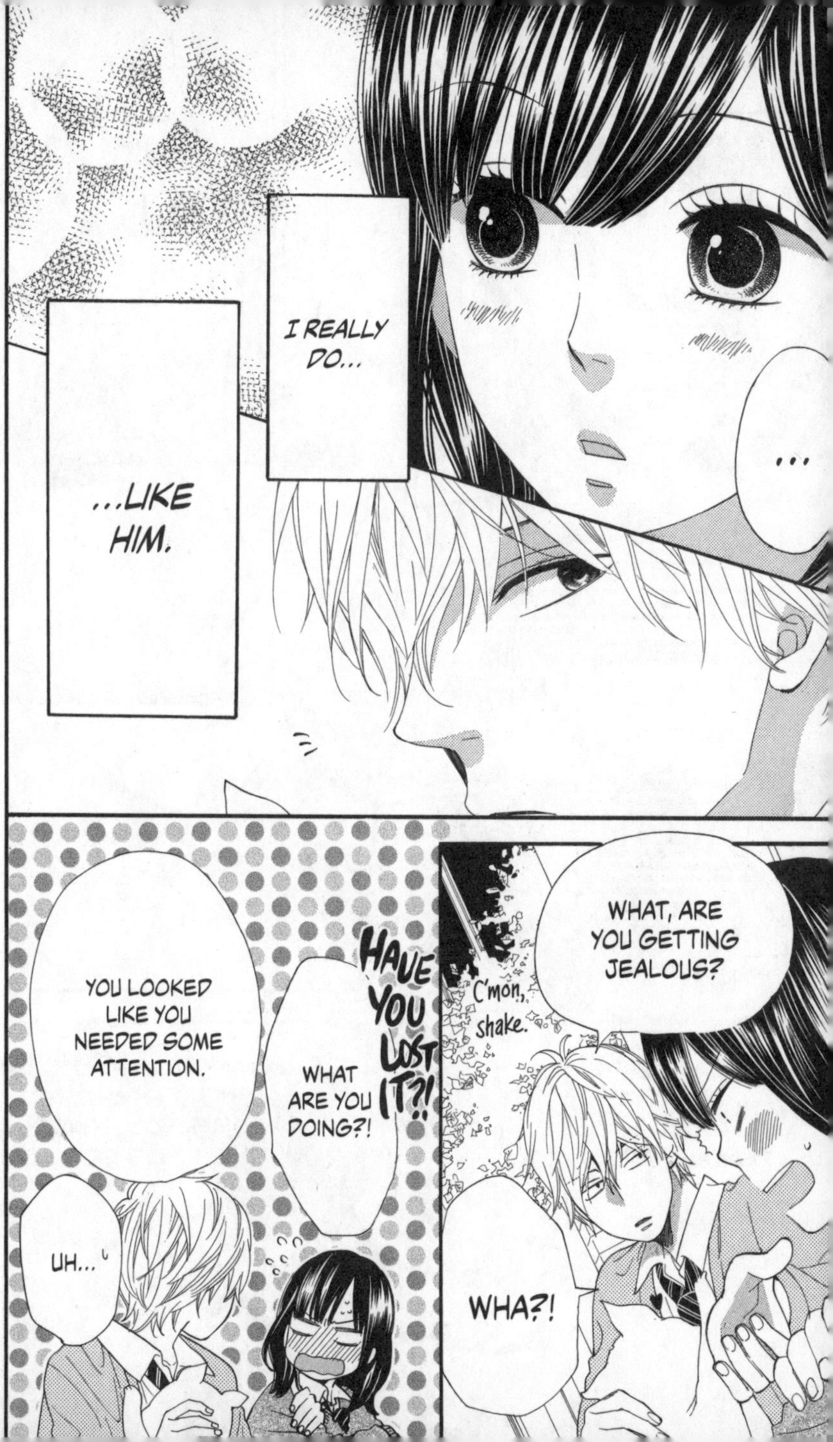
...
I REALLY DO...
...LIKE HIM.
WHAT, ARE YOU GETTING JEALOUS?
C'mon, shake.
WHA?!
HAVE YOU LOST IT?!
WHAT ARE YOU DOING?!
YOU LOOKED LIKE YOU NEEDED SOME ATTENTION.
UH...

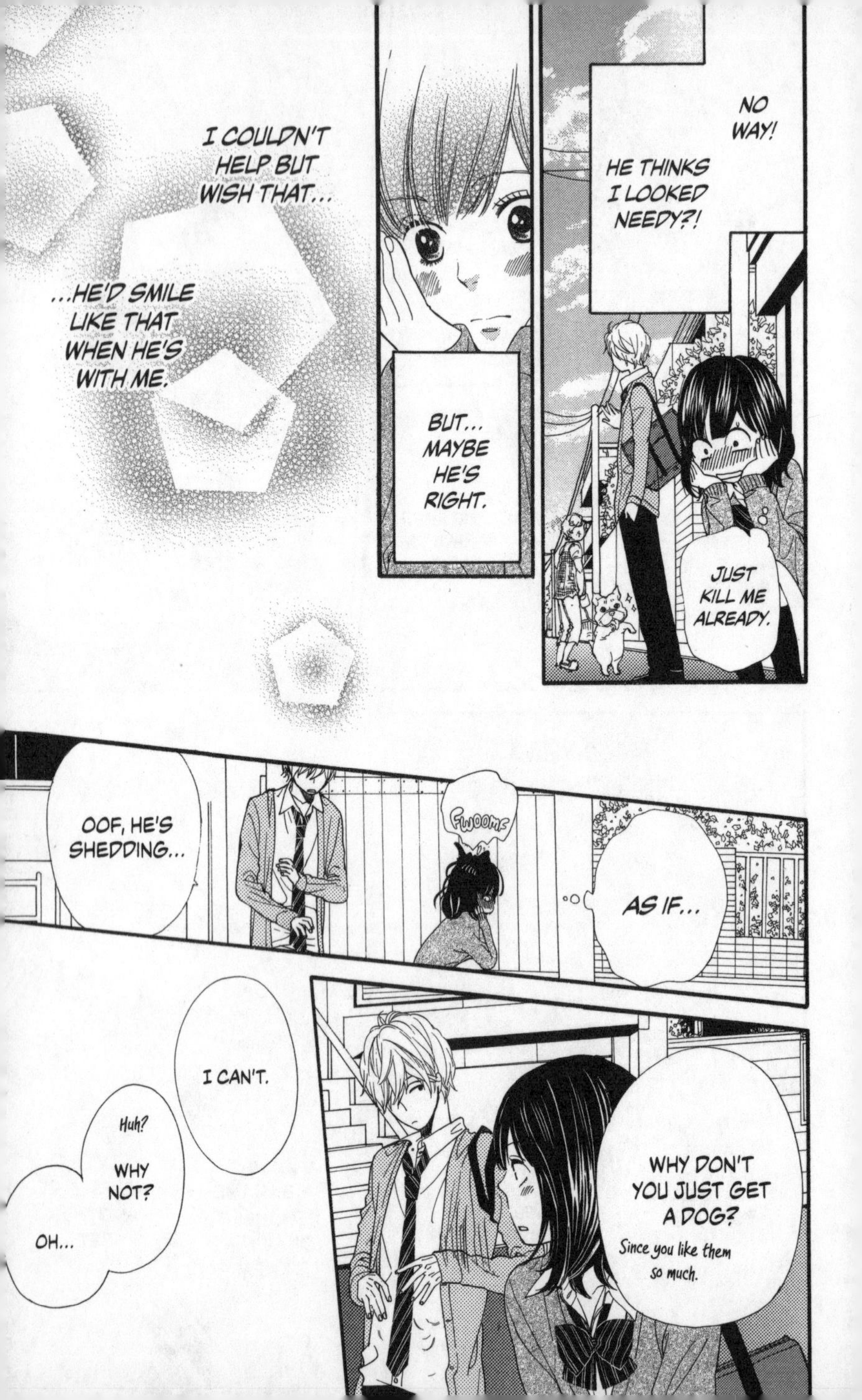
NO WAY!
HE THINKS I LOOKED NEEDY?!
JUST KILL ME ALREADY.
BUT... MAYBE HE'S RIGHT.
I COULDN'T HELP BUT WISH THAT...
...HE'D SMILE LIKE THAT WHEN HE'S WITH ME.
AS IF...
FWOOMF
OOF, HE'S SHEDDING...
WHY DON'T YOU JUST GET A DOG? Since you like them so much.
I CAN'T.
Huh? WHY NOT?
OH...

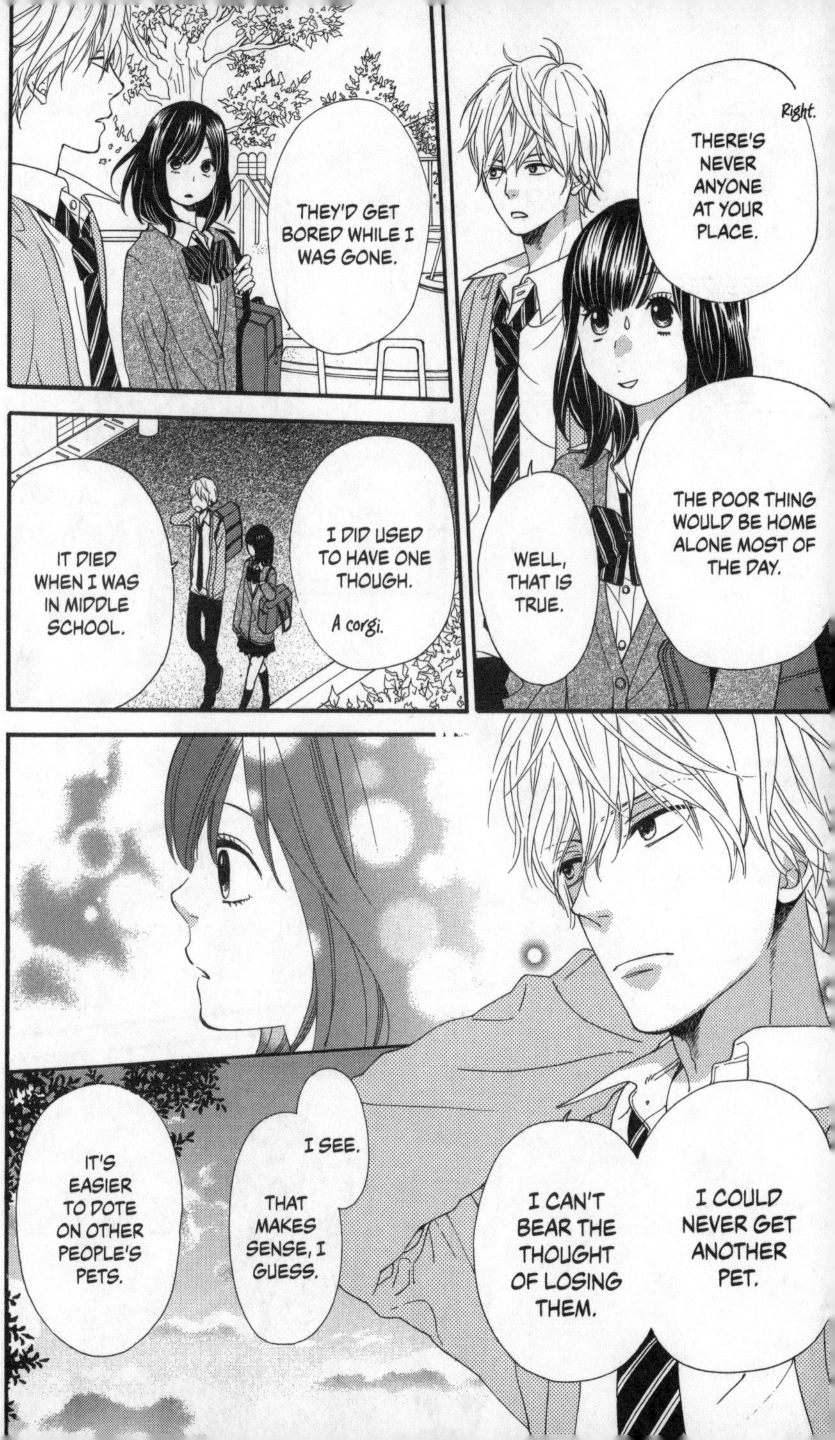
Right.
THERE'S NEVER ANYONE AT YOUR PLACE.
THE POOR THING WOULD BE HOME ALONE MOST OF THE DAY.
WELL, THAT IS TRUE.
THEY'D GET BORED WHILE I WAS GONE.
I DID USED TO HAVE ONE THOUGH.
A corgi.
IT DIED WHEN I WAS IN MIDDLE SCHOOL.
I COULD NEVER GET ANOTHER PET.
I CAN'T BEAR THE THOUGHT OF LOSING THEM.
I SEE.
THAT MAKES SENSE, I GUESS.
IT'S EASIER TO DOTE ON OTHER PEOPLE'S PETS.

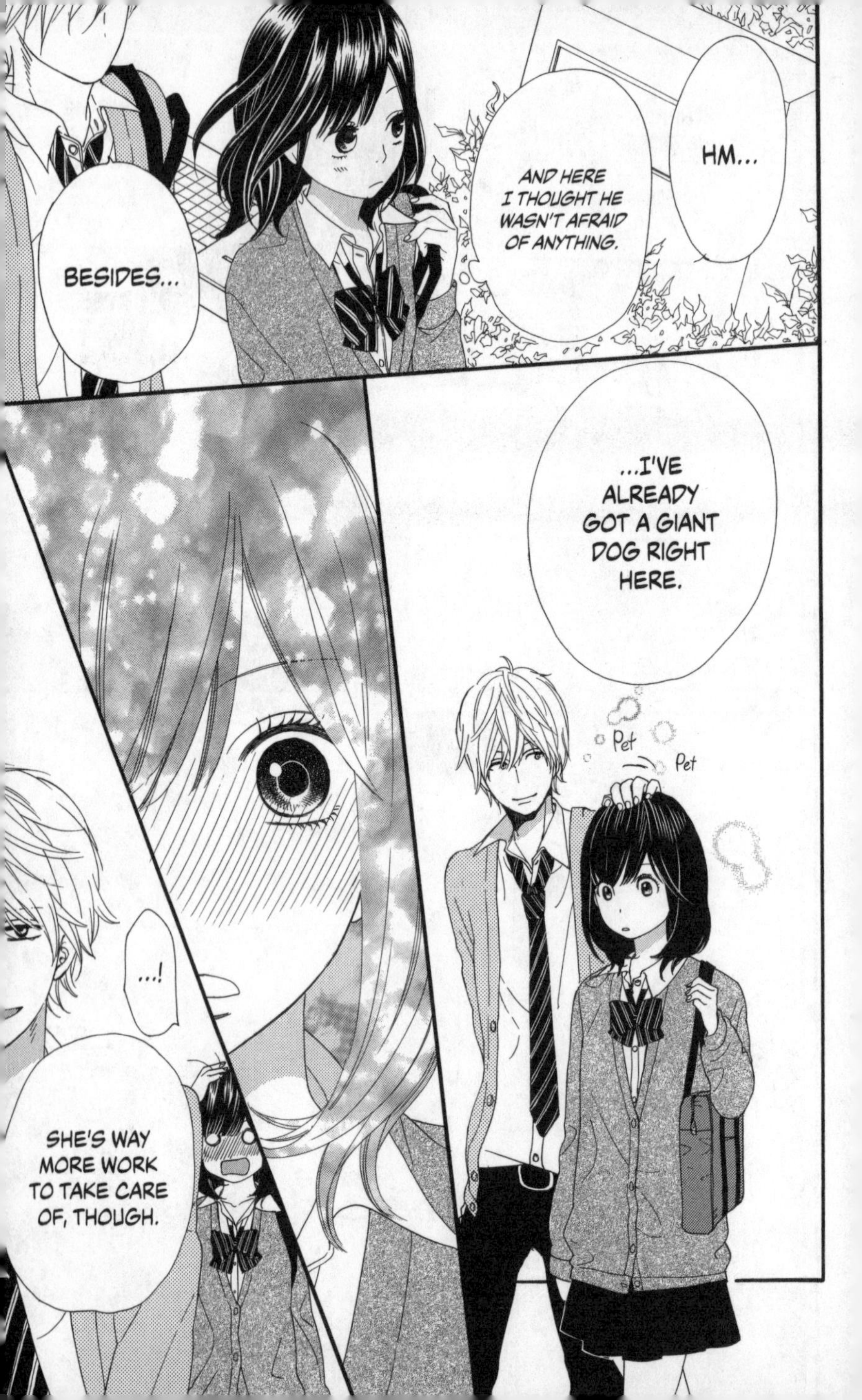
HM...
AND HERE I THOUGHT HE WASN'T AFRAID OF ANYTHING.
BESIDES...
...I'VE ALREADY GOT A GIANT DOG RIGHT HERE.
Pet
Pet
...!
SHE'S WAY MORE WORK TO TAKE CARE OF, THOUGH.

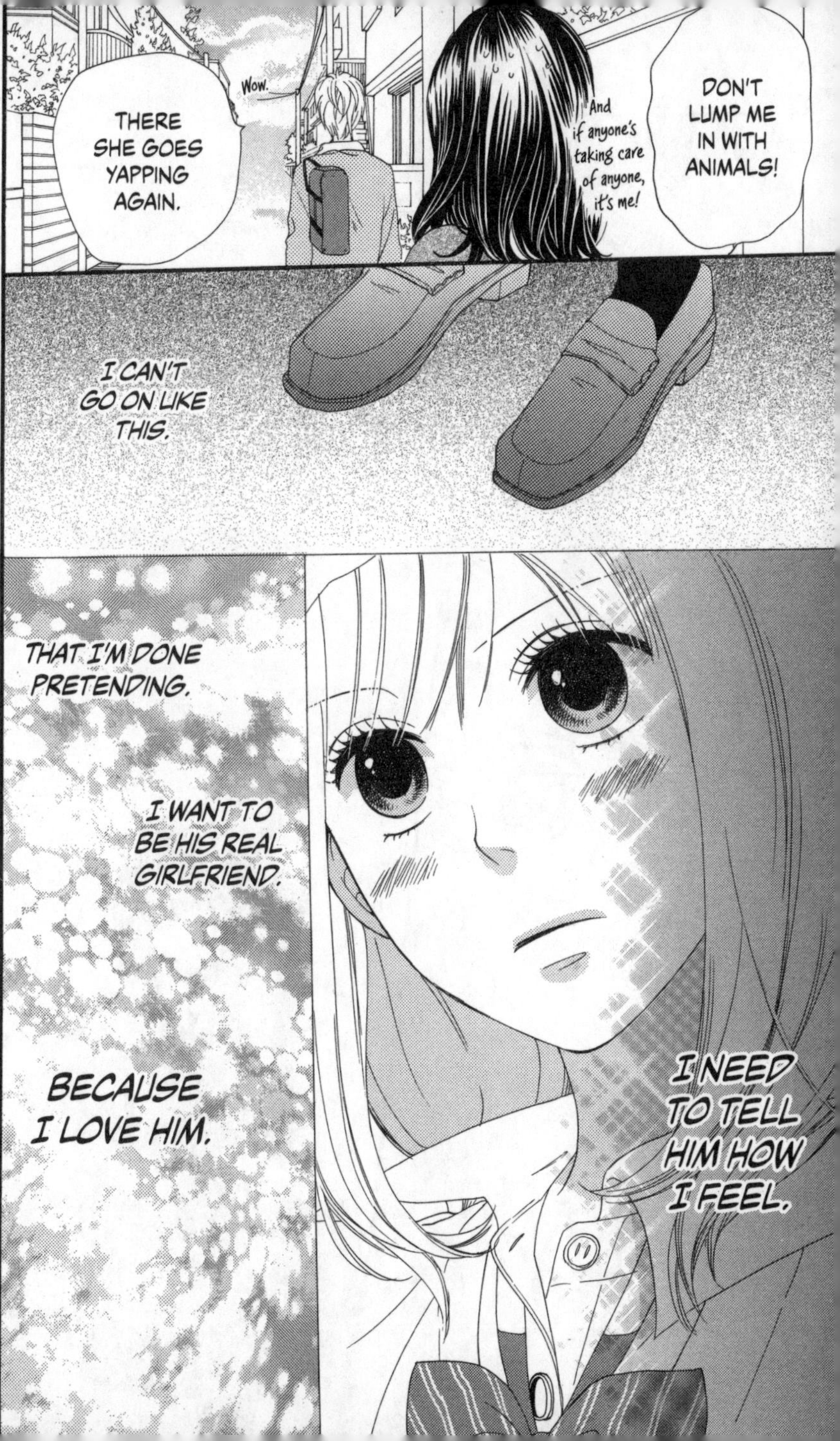
DON'T LUMP ME IN WITH ANIMALS!
And if anyone's taking care of anyone, it's me!
Wow.
THERE SHE GOES YAPPING AGAIN.
I CAN'T GO ON LIKE THIS.
I NEED TO TELL HIM HOW I FEEL.
THAT I'M DONE PRETENDING.
I WANT TO BE HIS REAL GIRLFRIEND.
BECAUSE I LOVE HIM.

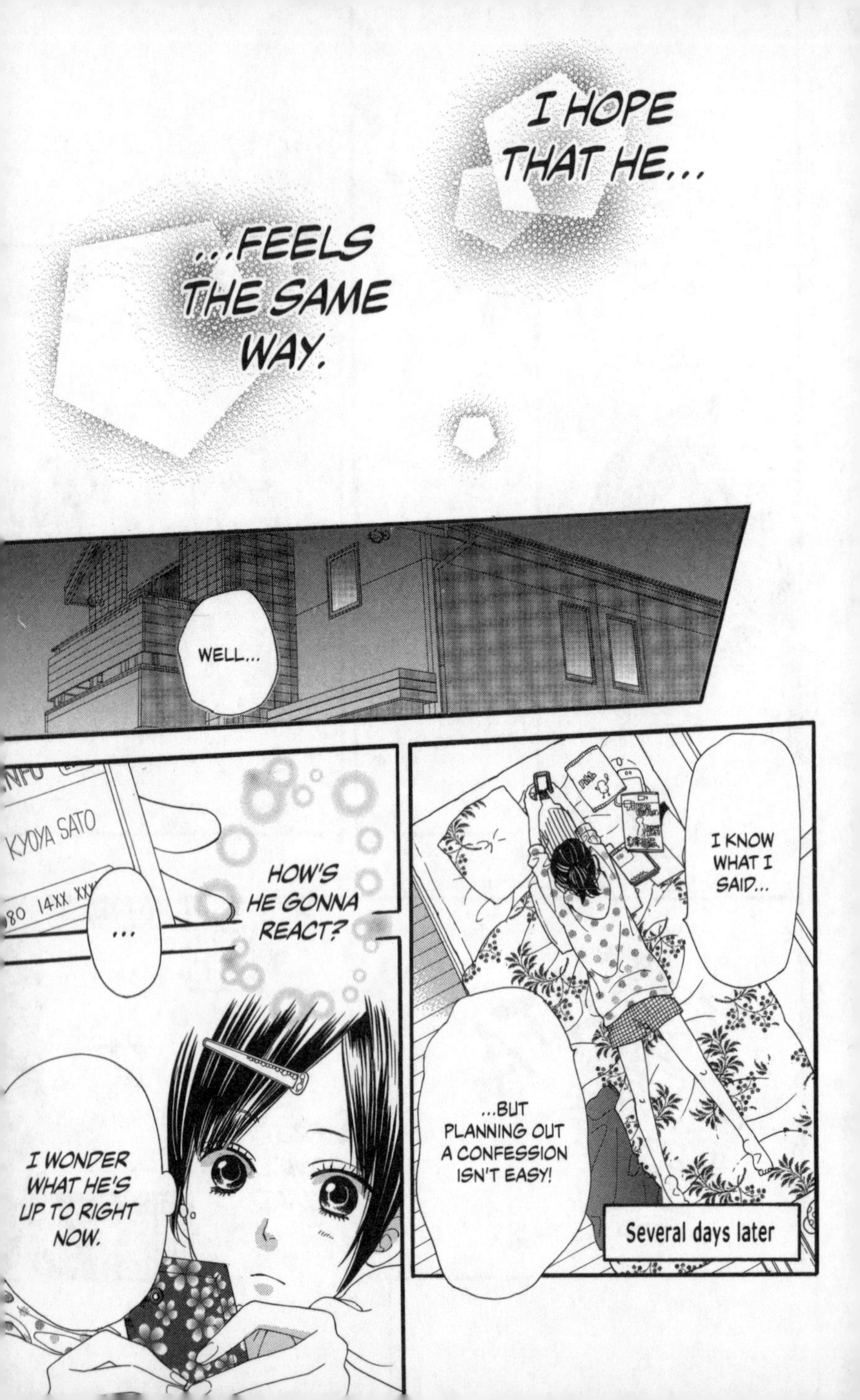
I HOPE THAT HE...
...FEELS THE SAME WAY.
WELL...
I KNOW WHAT I SAID...
...BUT PLANNING OUT A CONFESSION ISN'T EASY!
Several days later
KYOYA SATO
HOW'S HE GONNA REACT?
...
I WONDER WHAT HE'S UP TO RIGHT NOW.

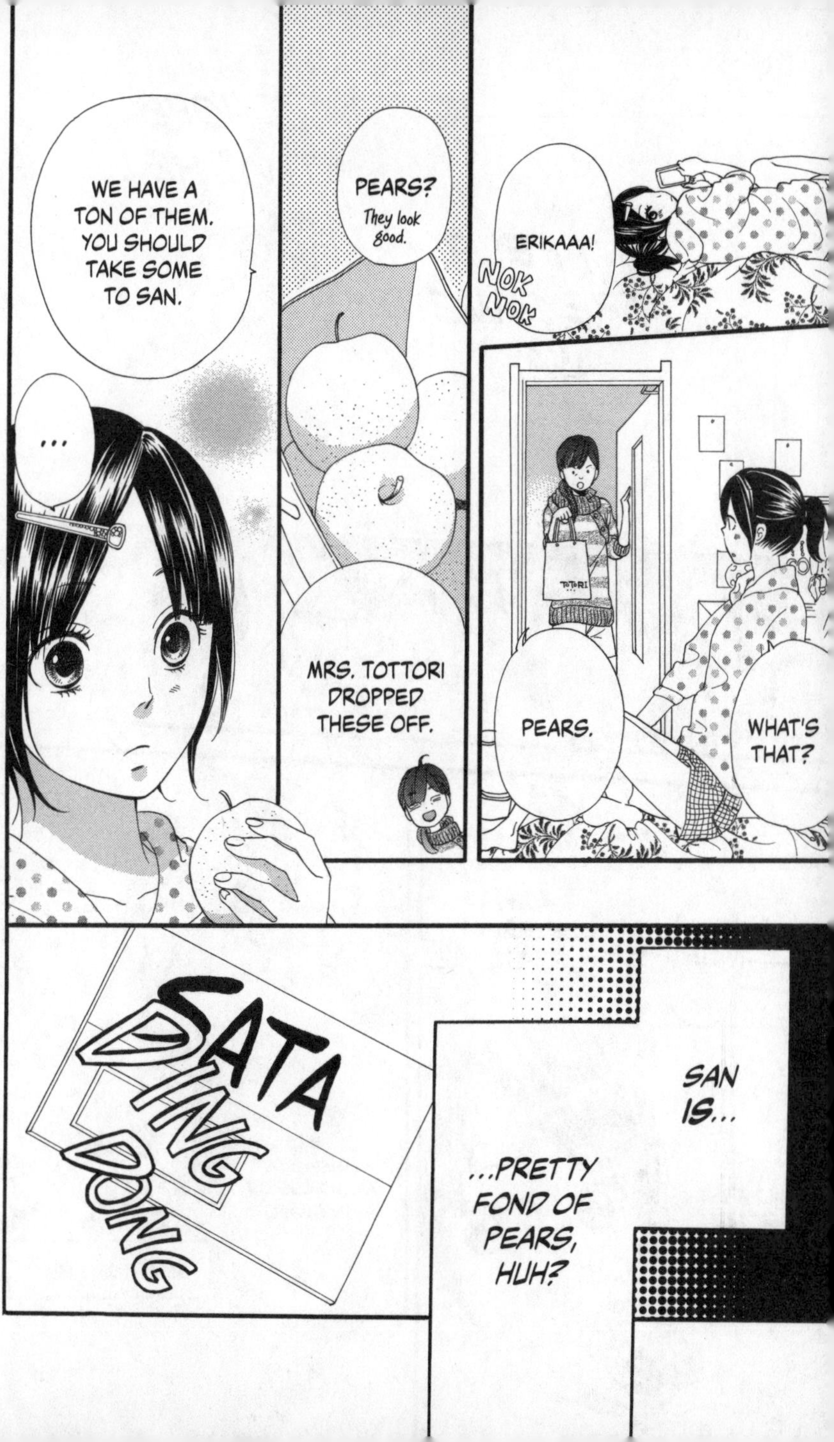
ERIKAAA!
NOK NOK
WHAT'S THAT?
PEARS.
PEARS? They look good.
MRS. TOTTORI DROPPED THESE OFF.
WE HAVE A TON OF THEM. YOU SHOULD TAKE SOME TO SAN.
...
SAN IS...
...PRETTY FOND OF PEARS, HUH?
SATA
DING DONG

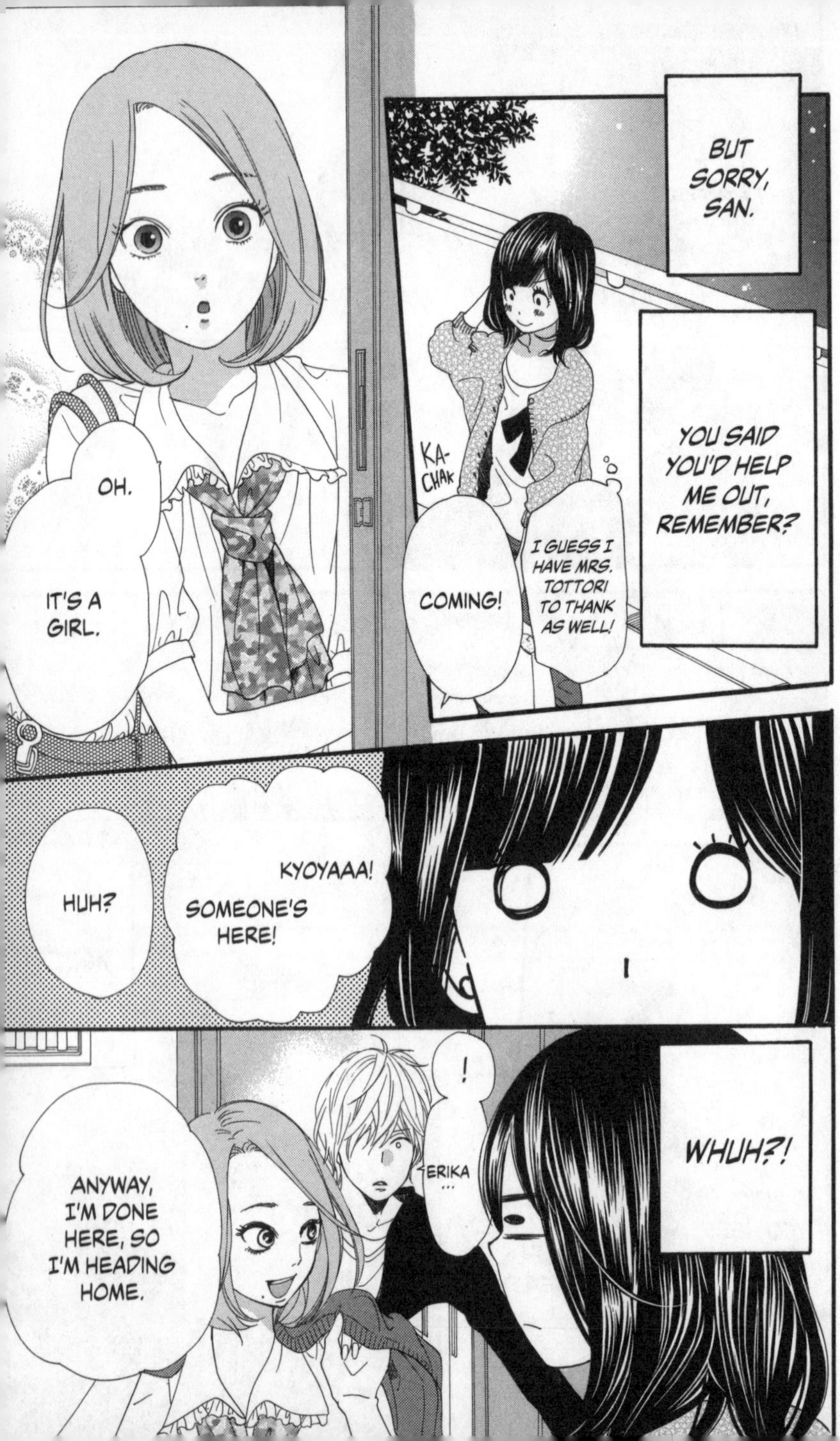
BUT SORRY, SAN.
YOU SAID YOU'D HELP ME OUT, REMEMBER?
I GUESS I HAVE MRS. TOTTORI TO THANK AS WELL!
COMING!
KA-CHAK
OH.
IT'S A GIRL.
KYOYAAA! SOMEONE'S HERE!
HUH?
WHUH?!
!
ERIKA...
ANYWAY, I'M DONE HERE, SO I'M HEADING HOME.

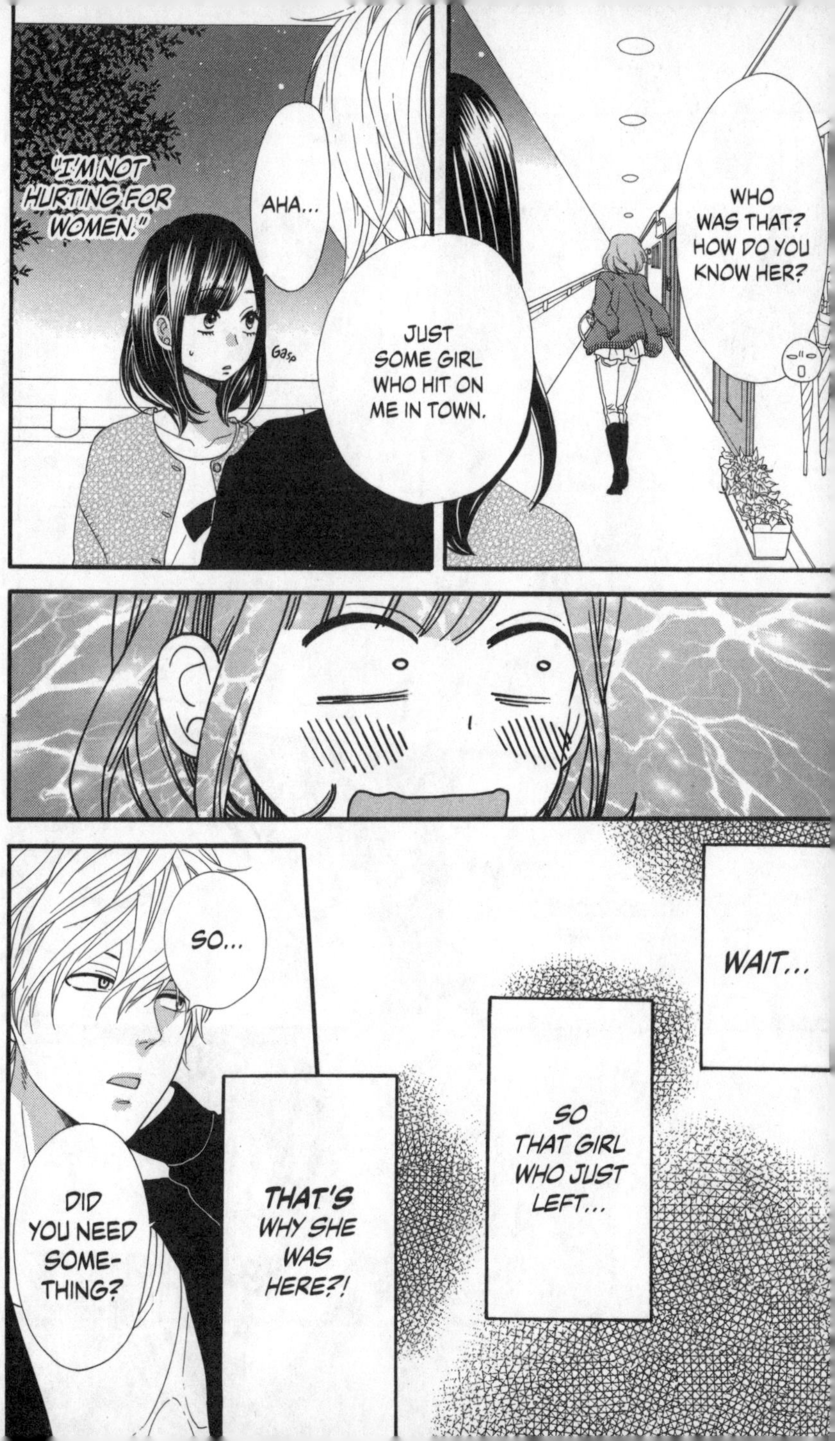
WHO WAS THAT? HOW DO YOU KNOW HER?
JUST SOME GIRL WHO HIT ON ME IN TOWN.
AHA...
Gasp
"I'M NOT HURTING FOR WOMEN."
WAIT...
SO THAT GIRL WHO JUST LEFT...
THAT'S WHY SHE WAS HERE?!
SO...
DID YOU NEED SOME-THING?

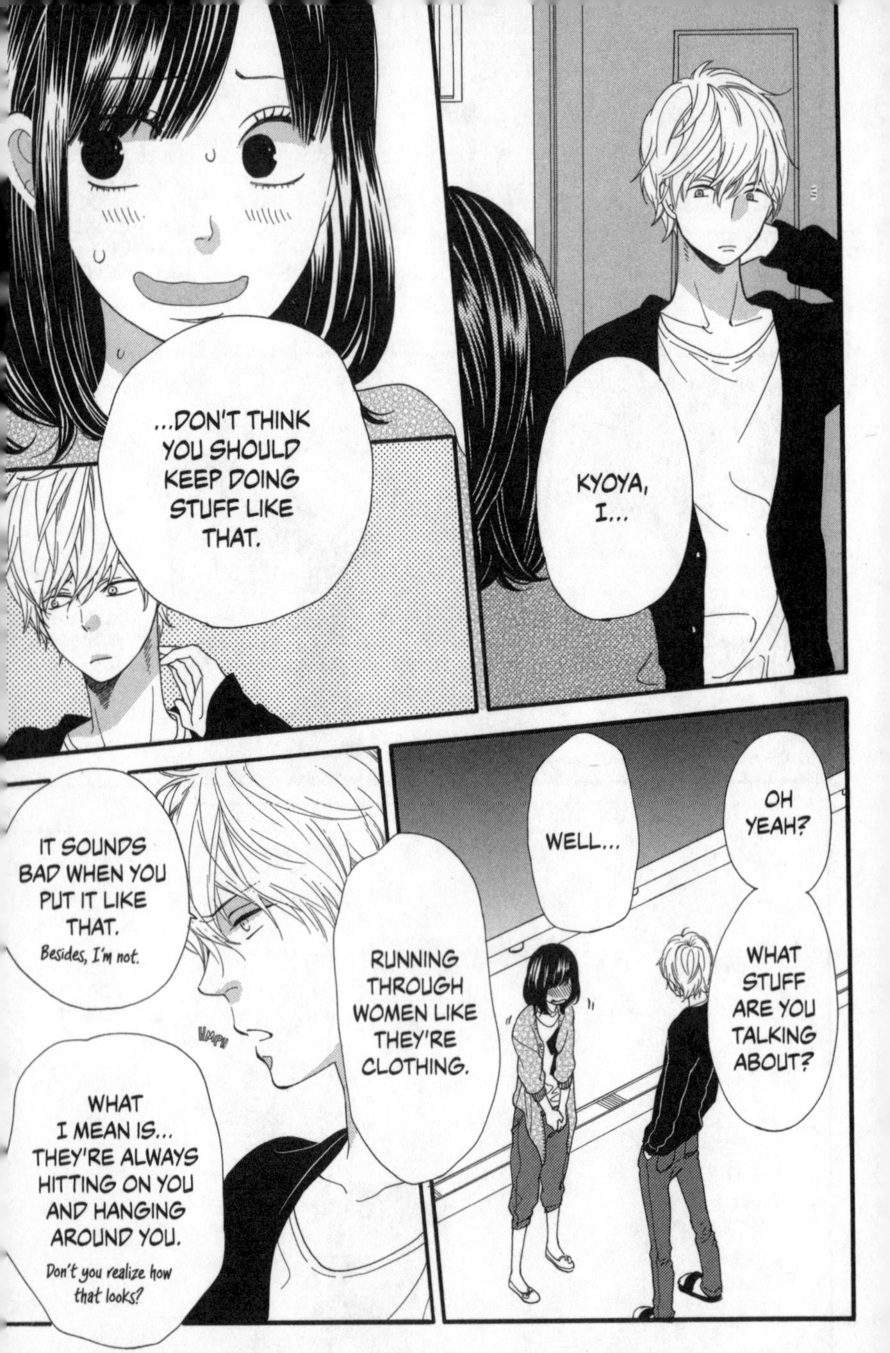
KYOYA, I...
...DON'T THINK YOU SHOULD KEEP DOING STUFF LIKE THAT.
OH YEAH?
WHAT STUFF ARE YOU TALKING ABOUT?
WELL...
RUNNING THROUGH WOMEN LIKE THEY'RE CLOTHING.
IT SOUNDS BAD WHEN YOU PUT IT LIKE THAT.
Besides, I'm not.
HMPH
WHAT I MEAN IS... THEY'RE ALWAYS HITTING ON YOU AND HANGING AROUND YOU.
Don't you realize how that looks?

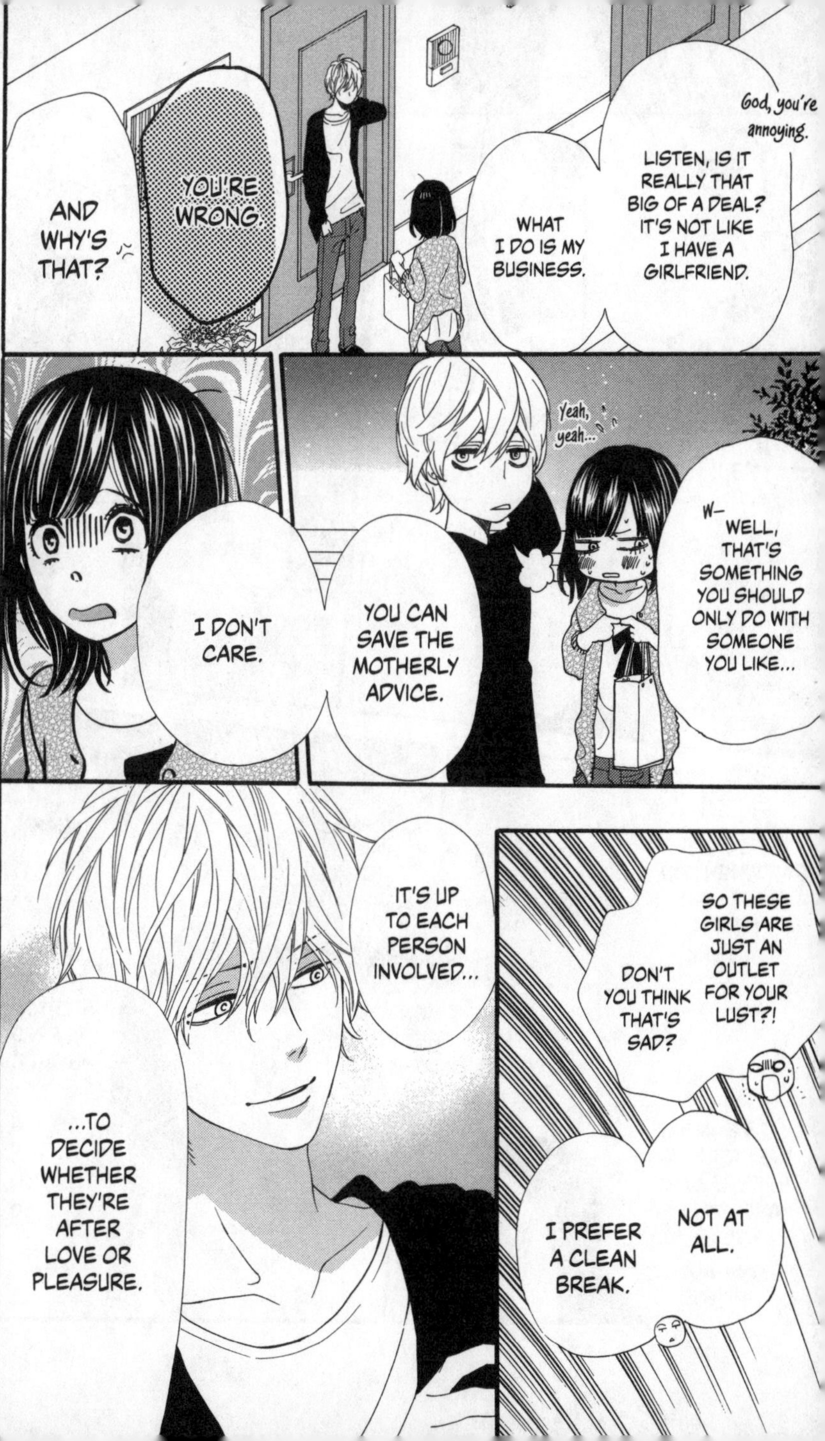
God, you're annoying.
LISTEN, IS IT REALLY THAT BIG OF A DEAL? IT'S NOT LIKE I HAVE A GIRLFRIEND.
WHAT I DO IS MY BUSINESS.
YOU'RE WRONG.
AND WHY'S THAT?
W— WELL, THAT'S SOMETHING YOU SHOULD ONLY DO WITH SOMEONE YOU LIKE...
Yeah, yeah...
YOU CAN SAVE THE MOTHERLY ADVICE.
I DON'T CARE.
SO THESE GIRLS ARE JUST AN OUTLET FOR YOUR LUST?!
DON'T YOU THINK THAT'S SAD?
NOT AT ALL.
I PREFER A CLEAN BREAK.
IT'S UP TO EACH PERSON INVOLVED...
...TO DECIDE WHETHER THEY'RE AFTER LOVE OR PLEASURE.

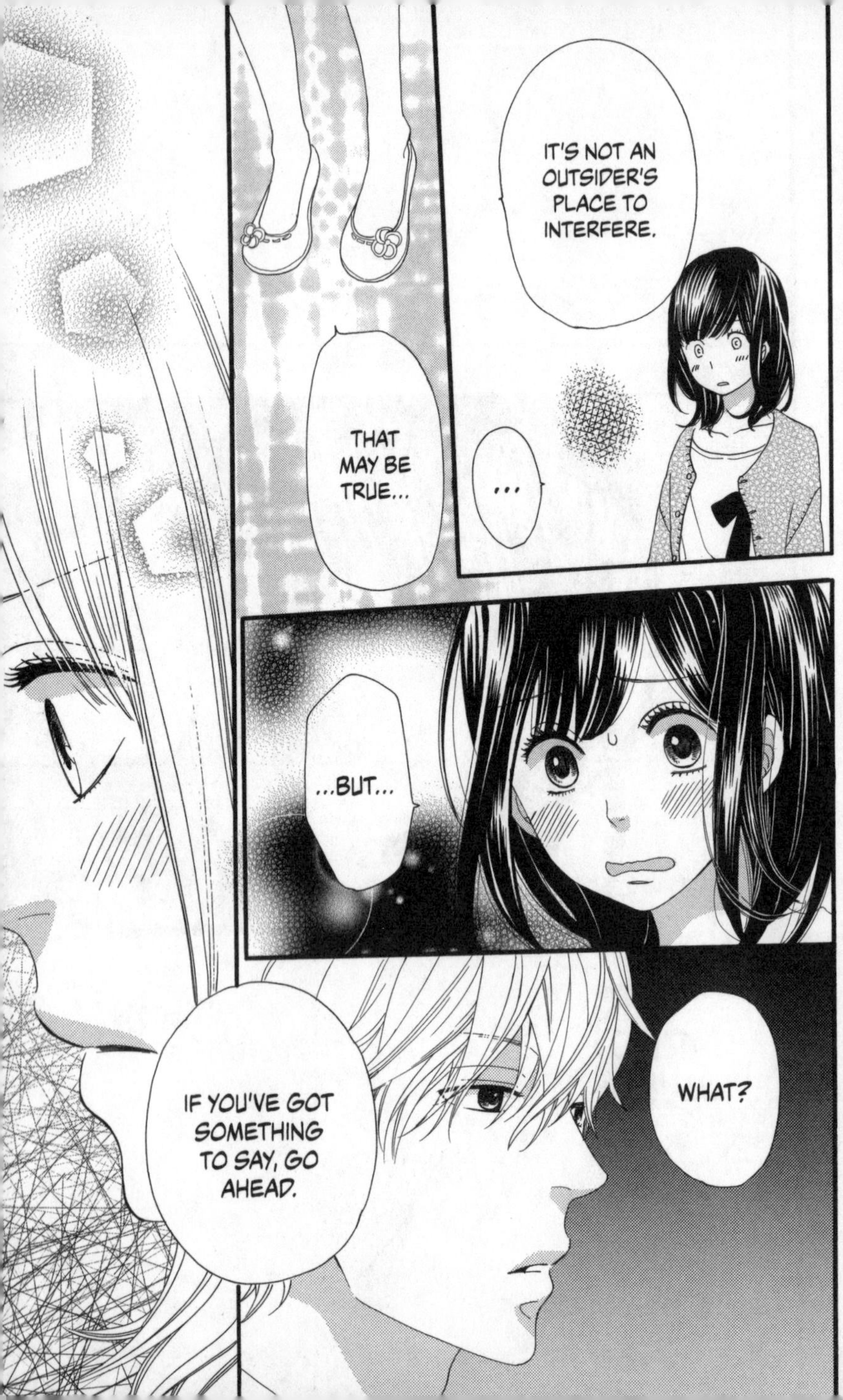
IT'S NOT AN OUTSIDER'S PLACE TO INTERFERE.
...
THAT MAY BE TRUE...
...BUT...
WHAT?
IF YOU'VE GOT SOMETHING TO SAY, GO AHEAD.

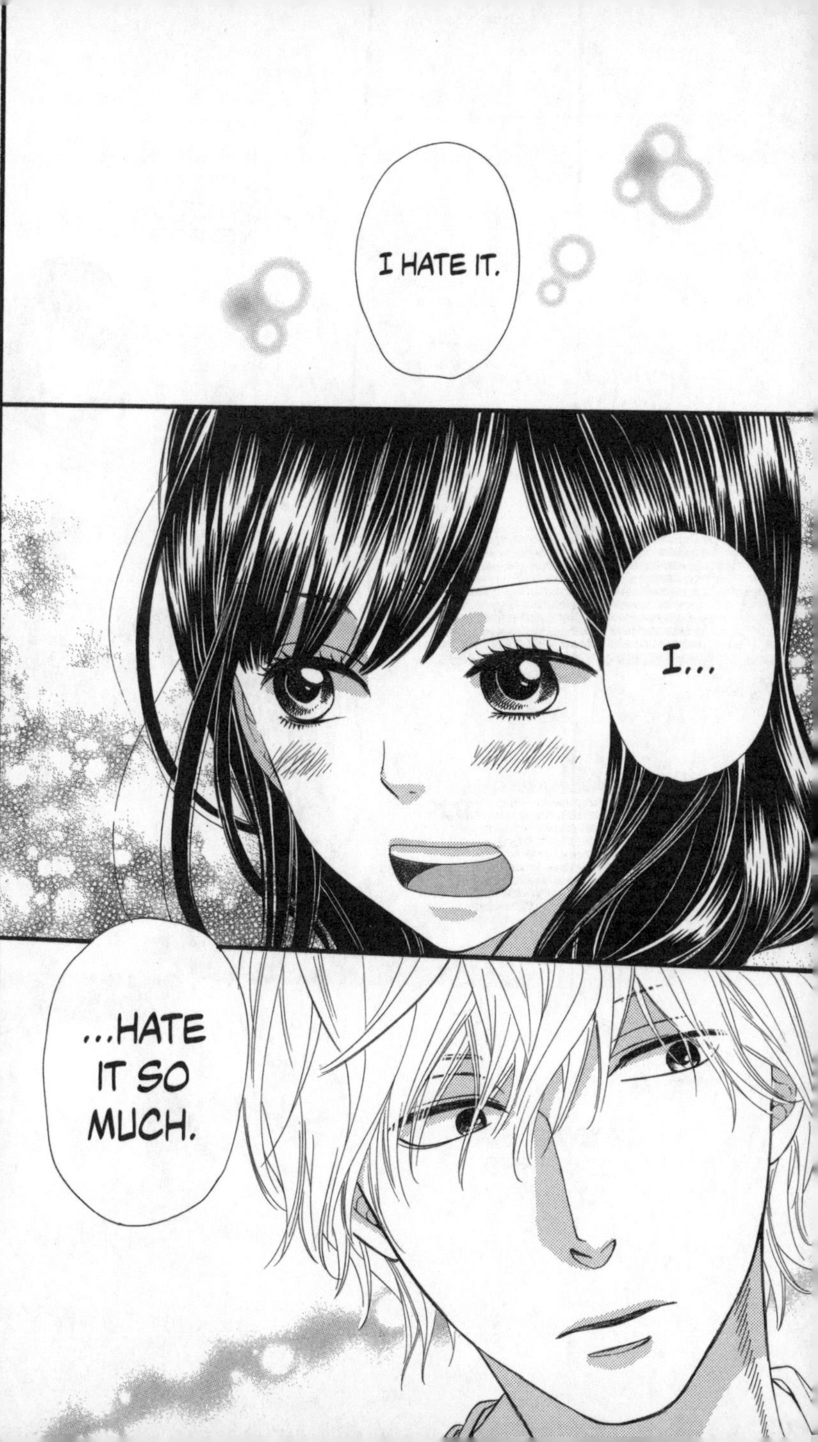
I HATE IT.
I...
...HATE IT SO MUCH.

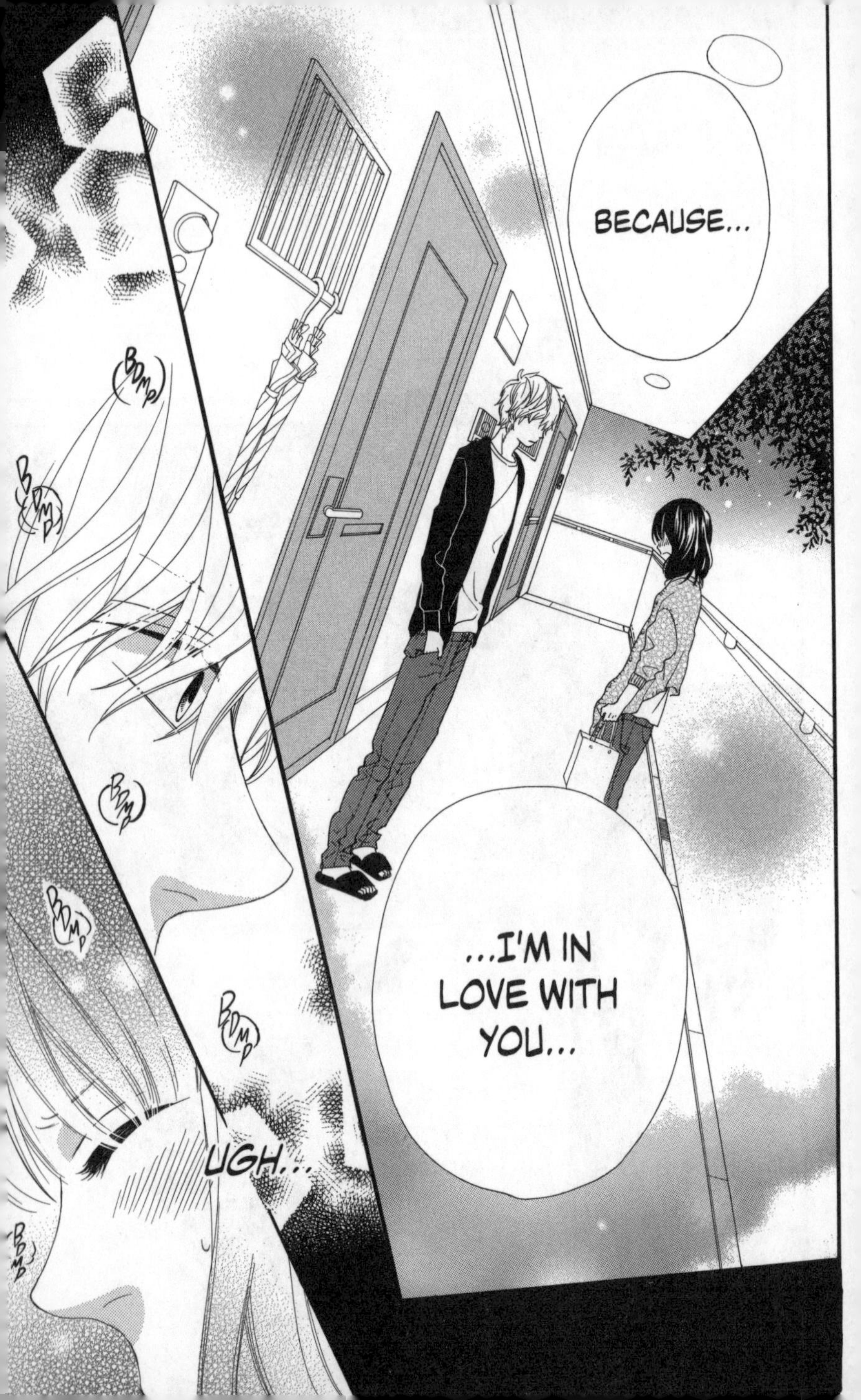
BECAUSE...
...I'M IN LOVE WITH YOU...
BDMP
BDMP
BDMP
BDMP
BDMP
UGH...
BDMP

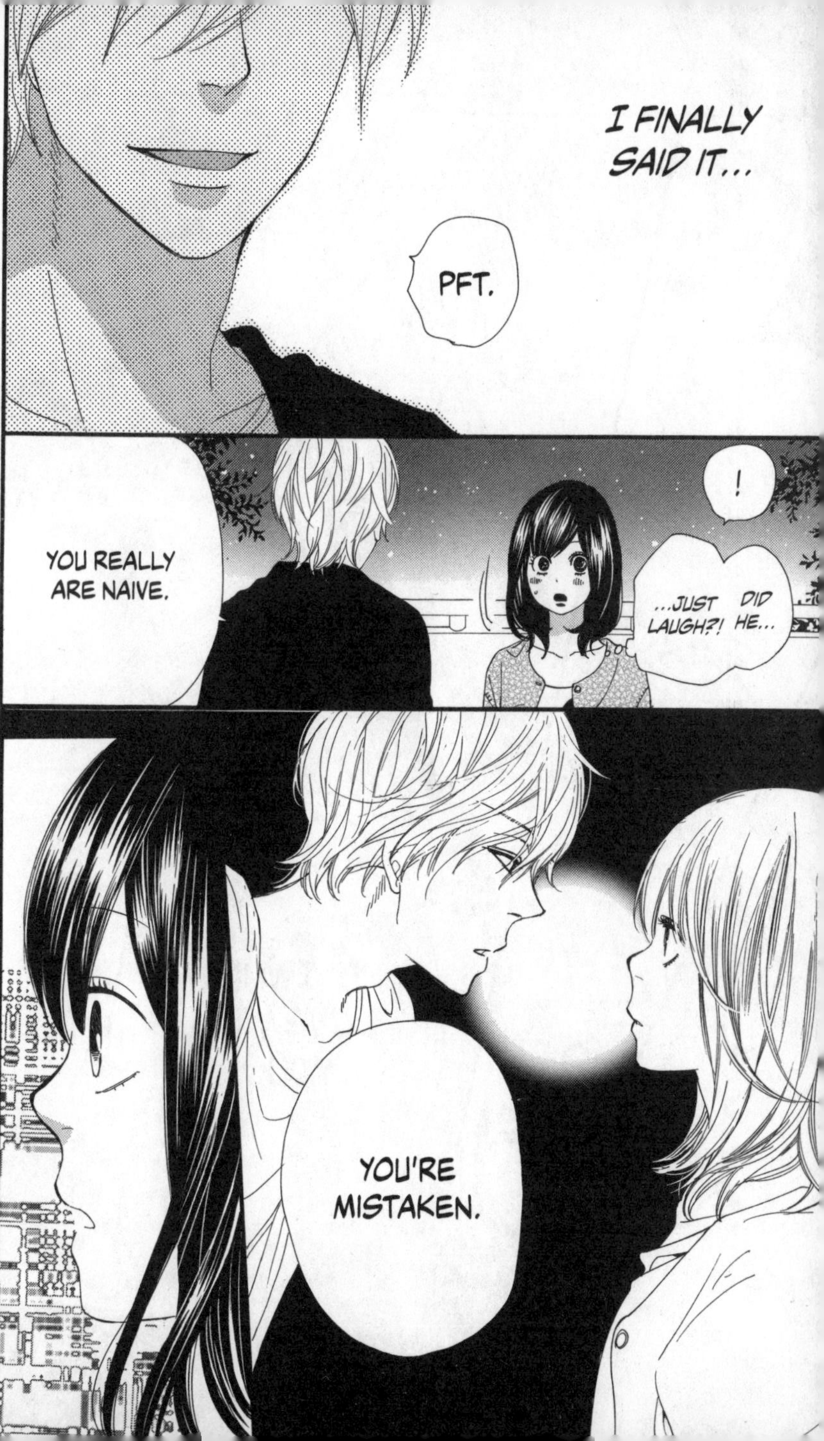
I FINALLY SAID IT...
PFT.
!
DID HE... ...JUST LAUGH?!
YOU REALLY ARE NAIVE.
YOU'RE MISTAKEN.

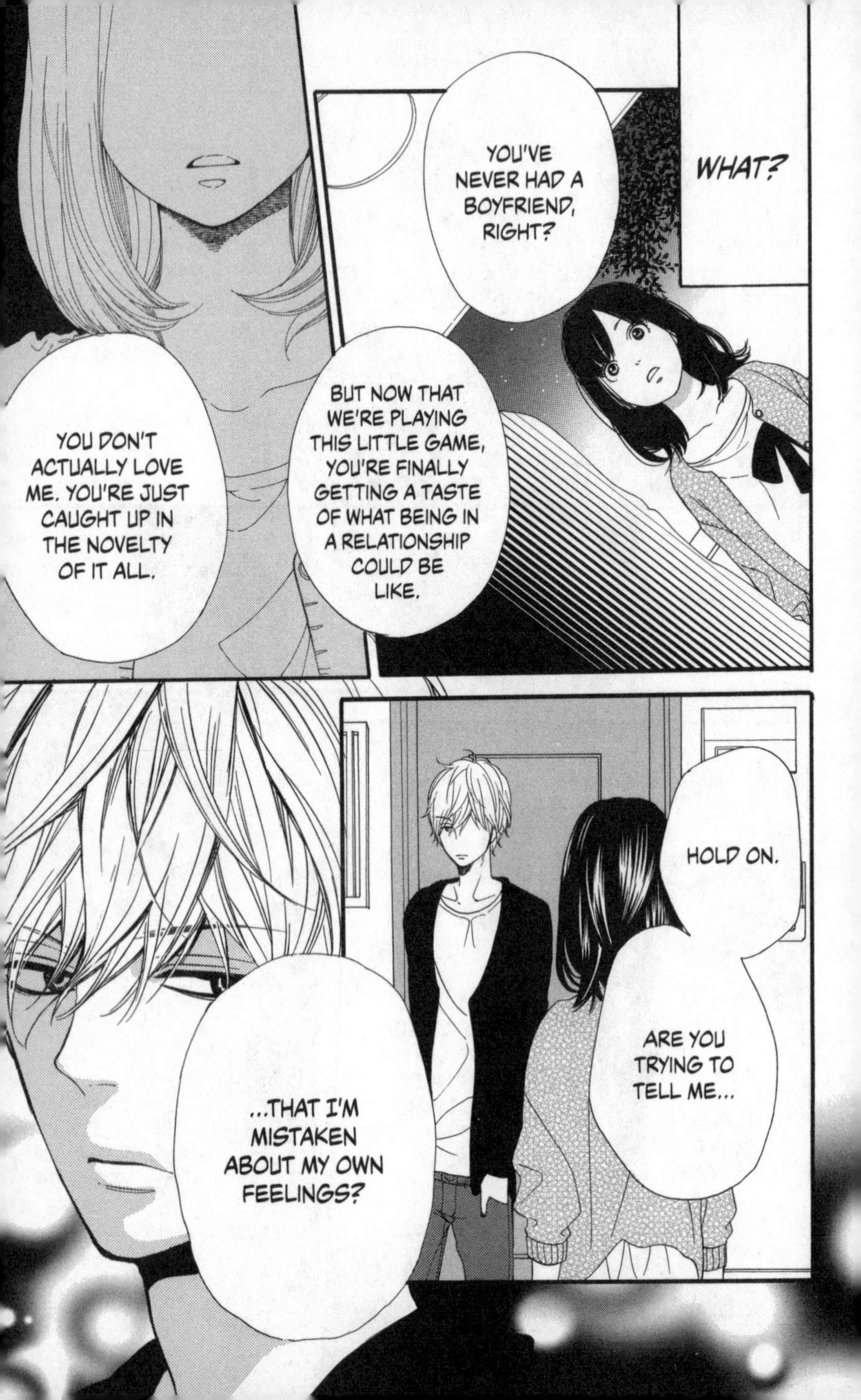
WHAT?
YOU'VE NEVER HAD A BOYFRIEND, RIGHT?
BUT NOW THAT WE'RE PLAYING THIS LITTLE GAME, YOU'RE FINALLY GETTING A TASTE OF WHAT BEING IN A RELATIONSHIP COULD BE LIKE.
YOU DON'T ACTUALLY LOVE ME. YOU'RE JUST CAUGHT UP IN THE NOVELTY OF IT ALL.
HOLD ON.
ARE YOU TRYING TO TELL ME...
...THAT I'M MISTAKEN ABOUT MY OWN FEELINGS?

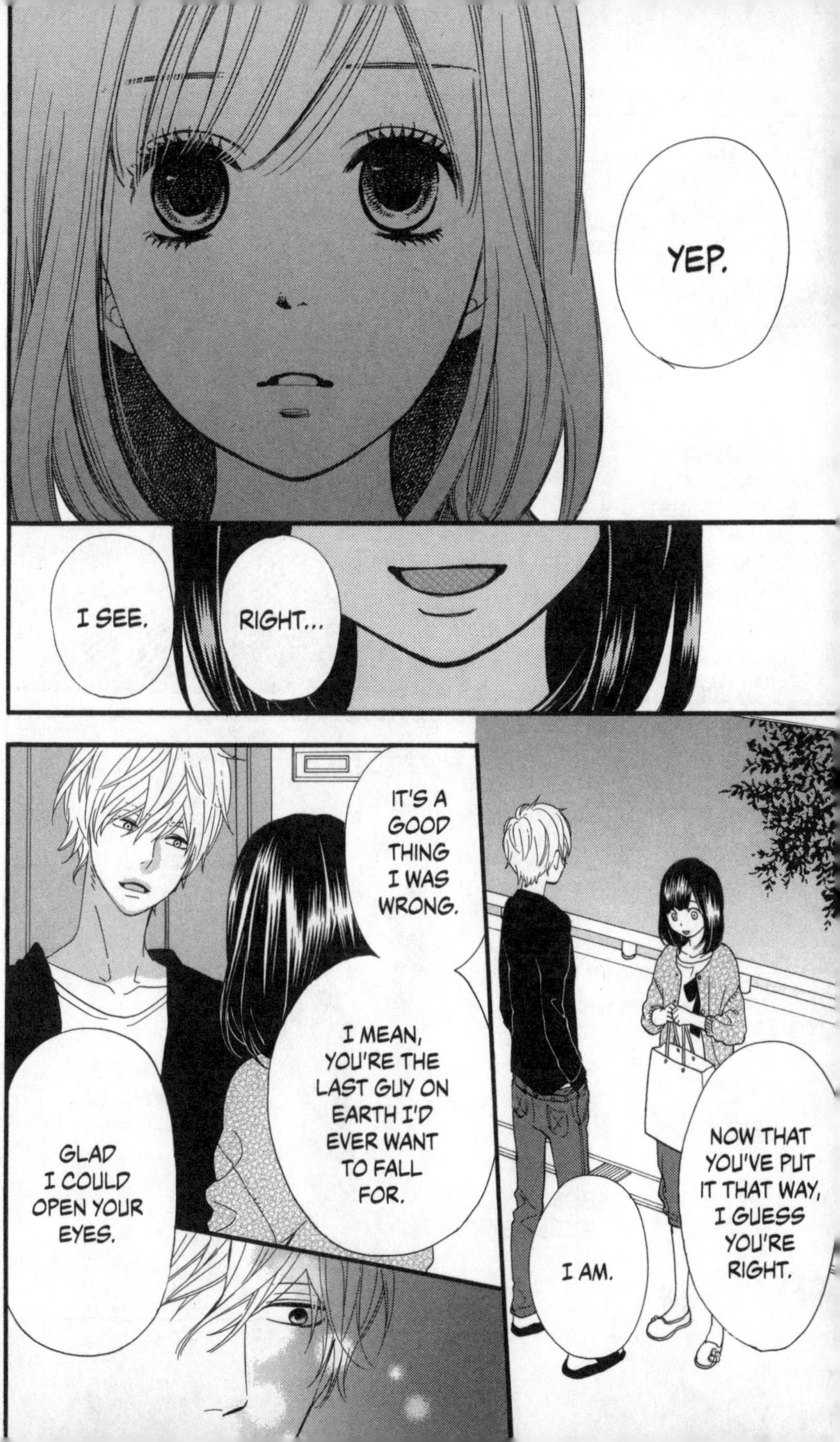
YEP.
RIGHT...
I SEE.
NOW THAT YOU'VE PUT IT THAT WAY, I GUESS YOU'RE RIGHT.
I AM.
IT'S A GOOD THING I WAS WRONG.
I MEAN, YOU'RE THE LAST GUY ON EARTH I'D EVER WANT TO FALL FOR.
GLAD I COULD OPEN YOUR EYES.

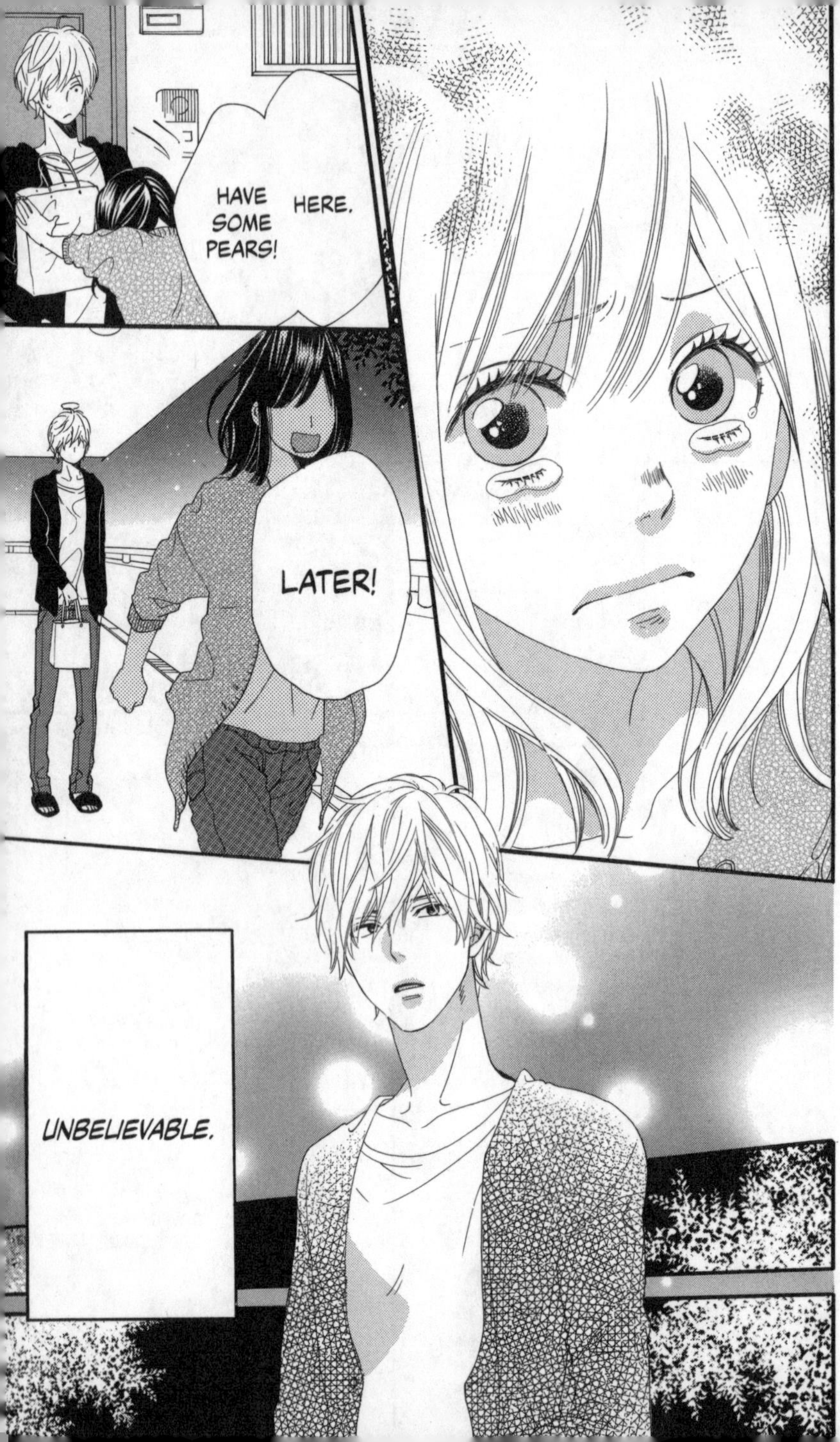
HERE.
HAVE SOME PEARS!
LATER!
UNBELIEVABLE.

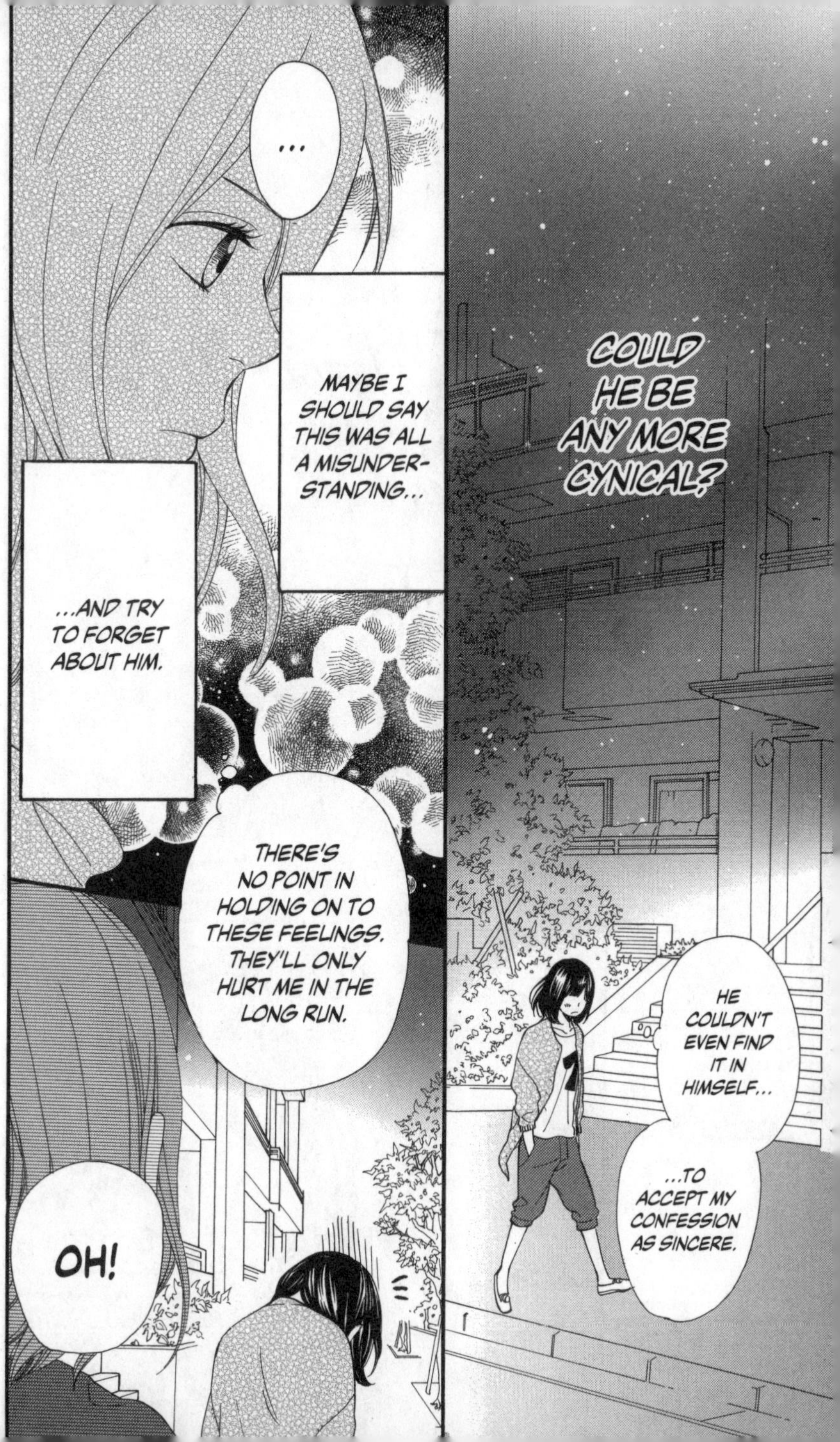
COULD HE BE ANY MORE CYNICAL?
HE COULDN'T EVEN FIND IT IN HIMSELF...
...TO ACCEPT MY CONFESSION AS SINCERE.
...
MAYBE I SHOULD SAY THIS WAS ALL A MISUNDER-STANDING...
...AND TRY TO FORGET ABOUT HIM.
THERE'S NO POINT IN HOLDING ON TO THESE FEELINGS. THEY'LL ONLY HURT ME IN THE LONG RUN.
OH!

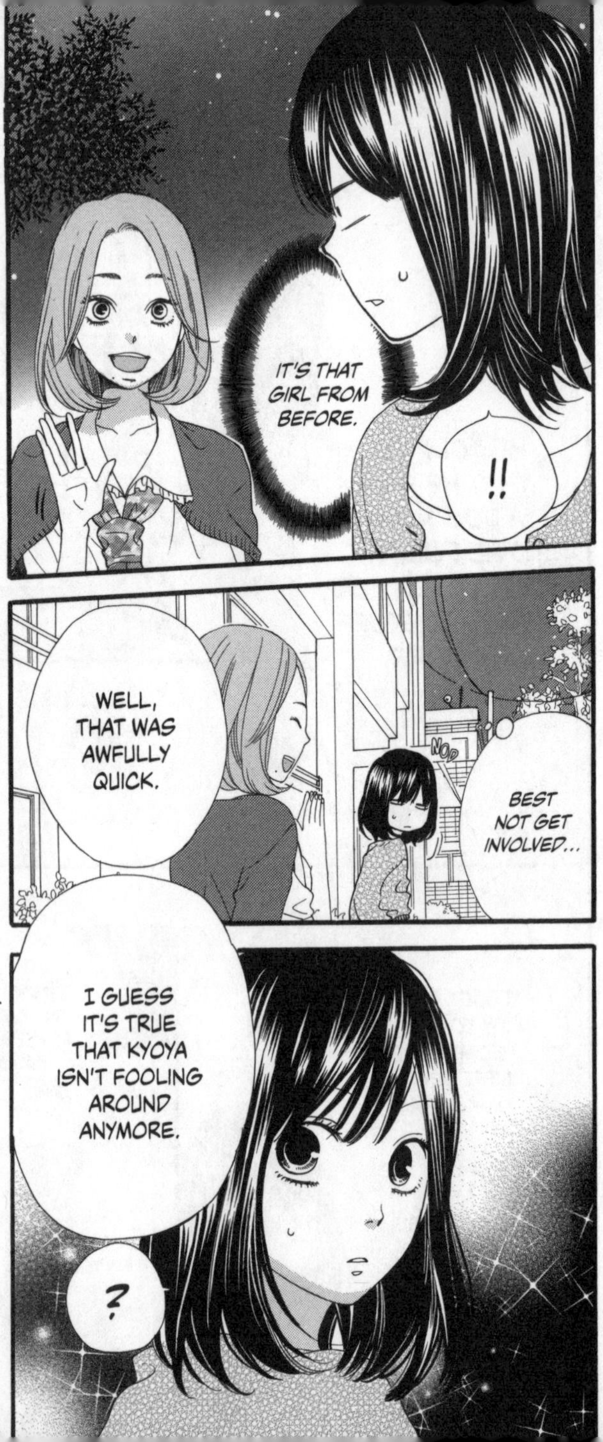
IT'S THAT GIRL FROM BEFORE.
!!
WELL, THAT WAS AWFULLY QUICK.
NOD
BEST NOT GET INVOLVED...
I GUESS IT'S TRUE THAT KYOYA ISN'T FOOLING AROUND ANYMORE.
?

Hey there! ☆

Hello, hello! It's volume 2. Can you believe it? This isn't just amazing, it's super amazing! I'm so excited. How's everyone been doing lately? Winter is on the horizon, so I'm full of energy. But emotionally, I've been feeling a tad sentimental now that the days are getting shorter. And trying to put on a happy face just makes me feel worse. But I always perk back up eventually.

It's December now, which means Christmas is coming. I even managed to fit a Christmas story in here. Not that I have any good memories of Christmas. Or any particularly bad ones either. All I'm looking forward to is eating cake. Though I do enjoy the festive atmosphere that overtakes the town.

I love round things. You know those round Christmas ornaments you can find in shops?

I never have a tree, but I always end up buying a bunch of ornaments for some pointless reason. I have nowhere to hang them, so they're basically junk. And yet, I still buy them. Round things are just so cute, aren't they? The baubles on hair ties make me super happy. I love marbles too. I get so excited just looking at them. They're almost like Dragon Balls. I wanna collect them all.

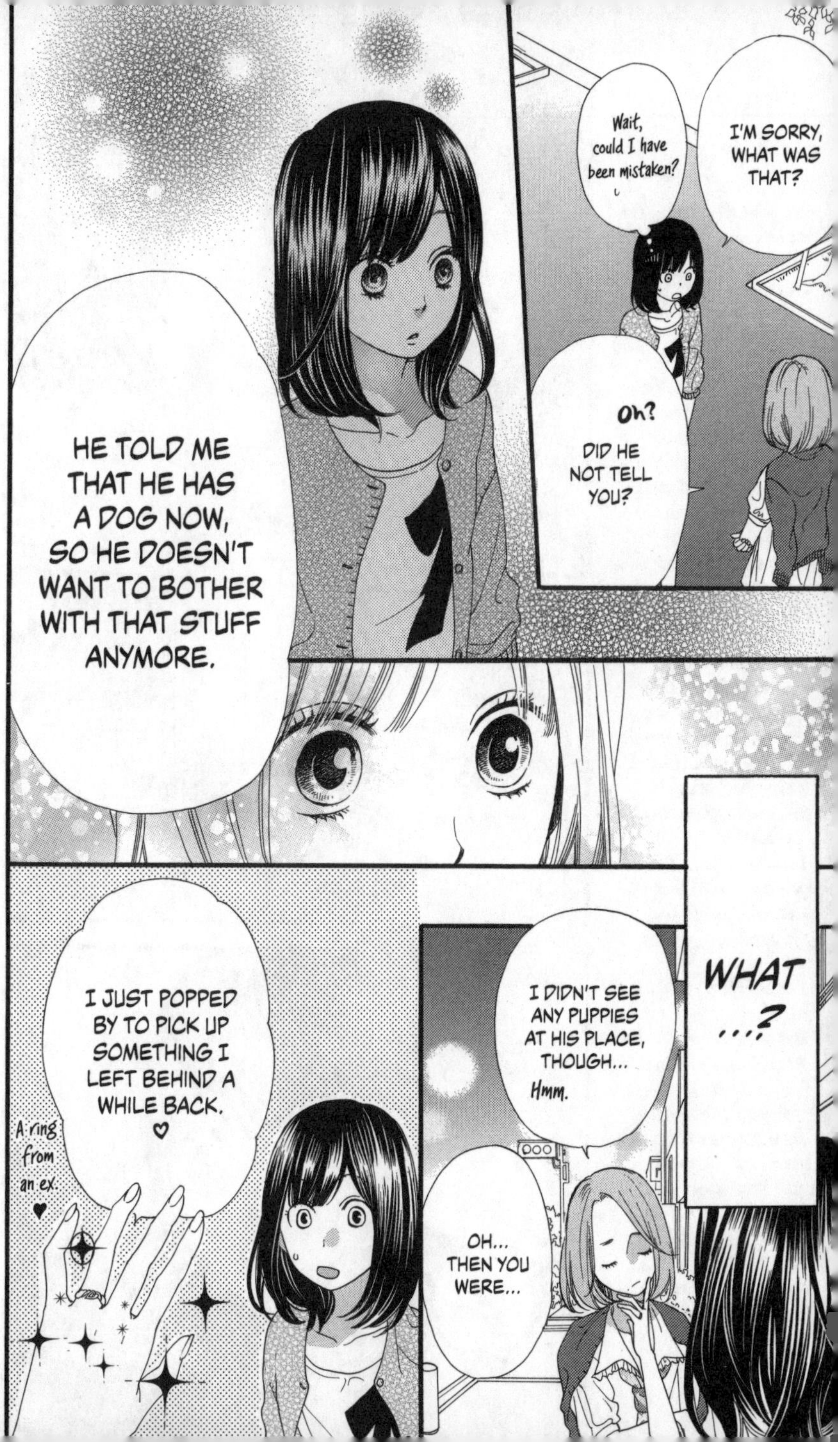
I'M SORRY, WHAT WAS THAT?
Wait, could I have been mistaken?
Oh?
DID HE NOT TELL YOU?
HE TOLD ME THAT HE HAS A DOG NOW, SO HE DOESN'T WANT TO BOTHER WITH THAT STUFF ANYMORE.
WHAT ...?
I DIDN'T SEE ANY PUPPIES AT HIS PLACE, THOUGH...
Hmm.
OH... THEN YOU WERE...
I JUST POPPED BY TO PICK UP SOMETHING I LEFT BEHIND A WHILE BACK. ♡
A ring from an ex. ♥

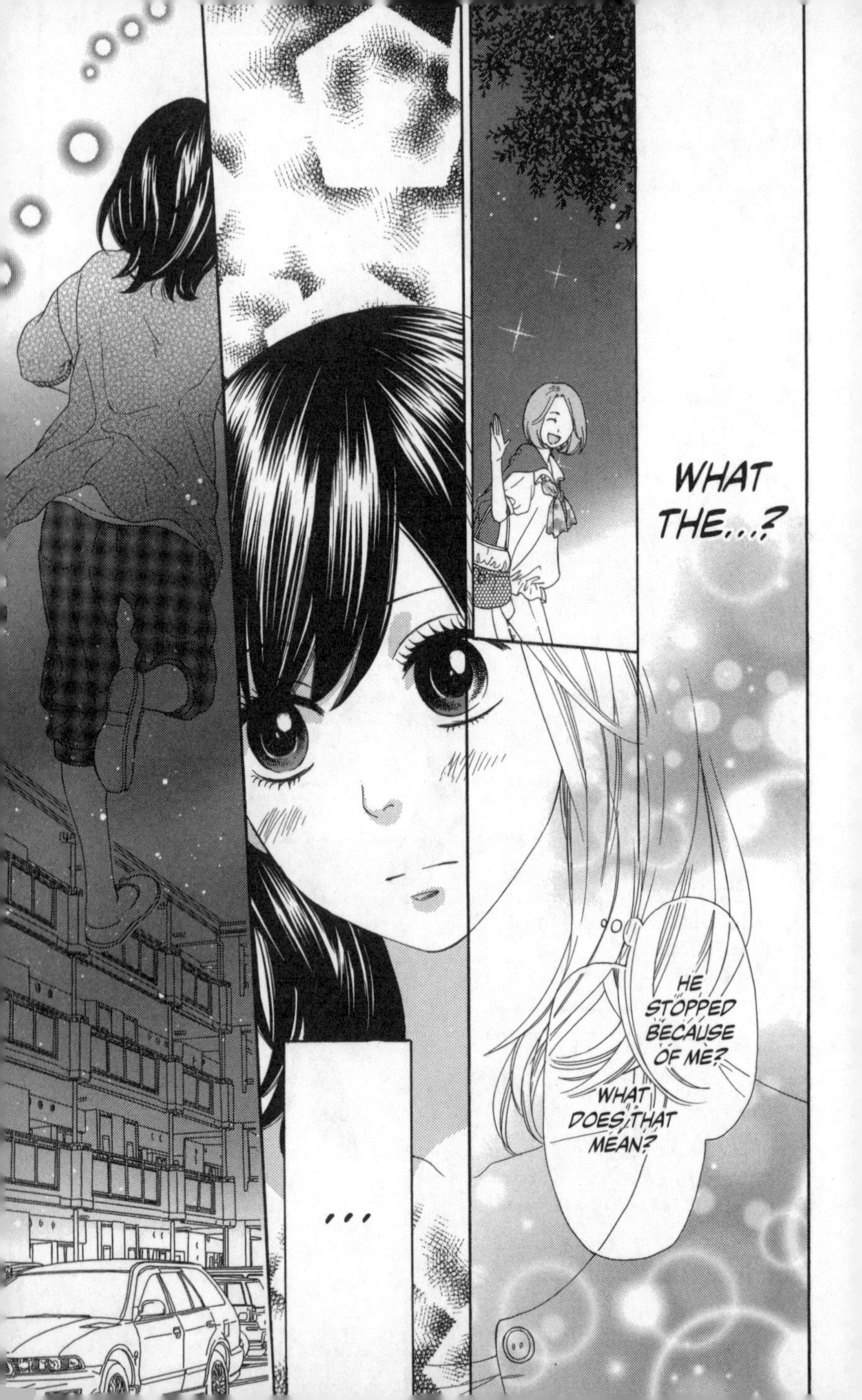
WHAT THE...?
HE STOPPED BECAUSE OF ME?
WHAT DOES THAT MEAN?
...

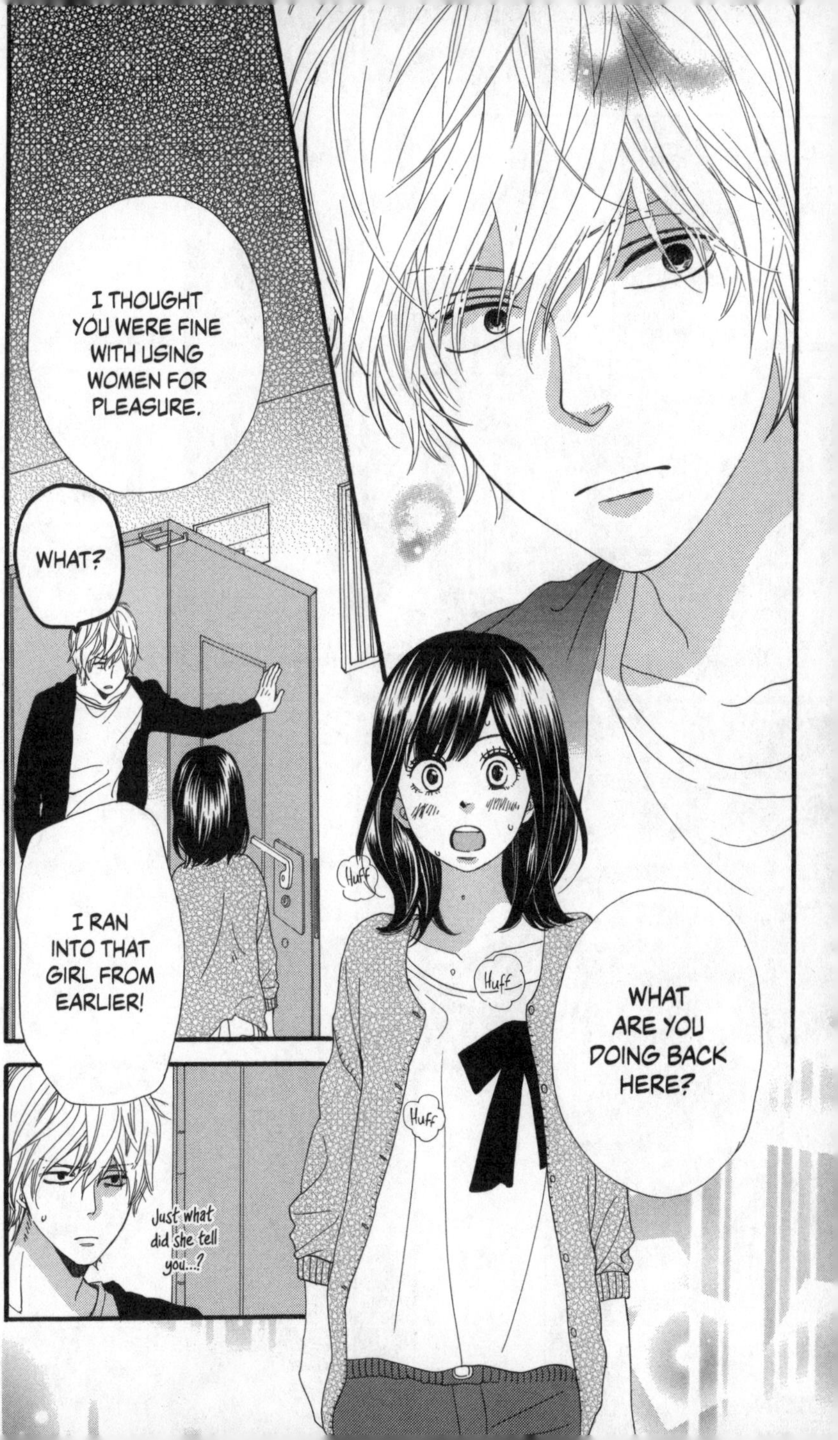
Huff
Huff
Huff
WHAT ARE YOU DOING BACK HERE?
I THOUGHT YOU WERE FINE WITH USING WOMEN FOR PLEASURE.
WHAT?
I RAN INTO THAT GIRL FROM EARLIER!
Just what did she tell you...?

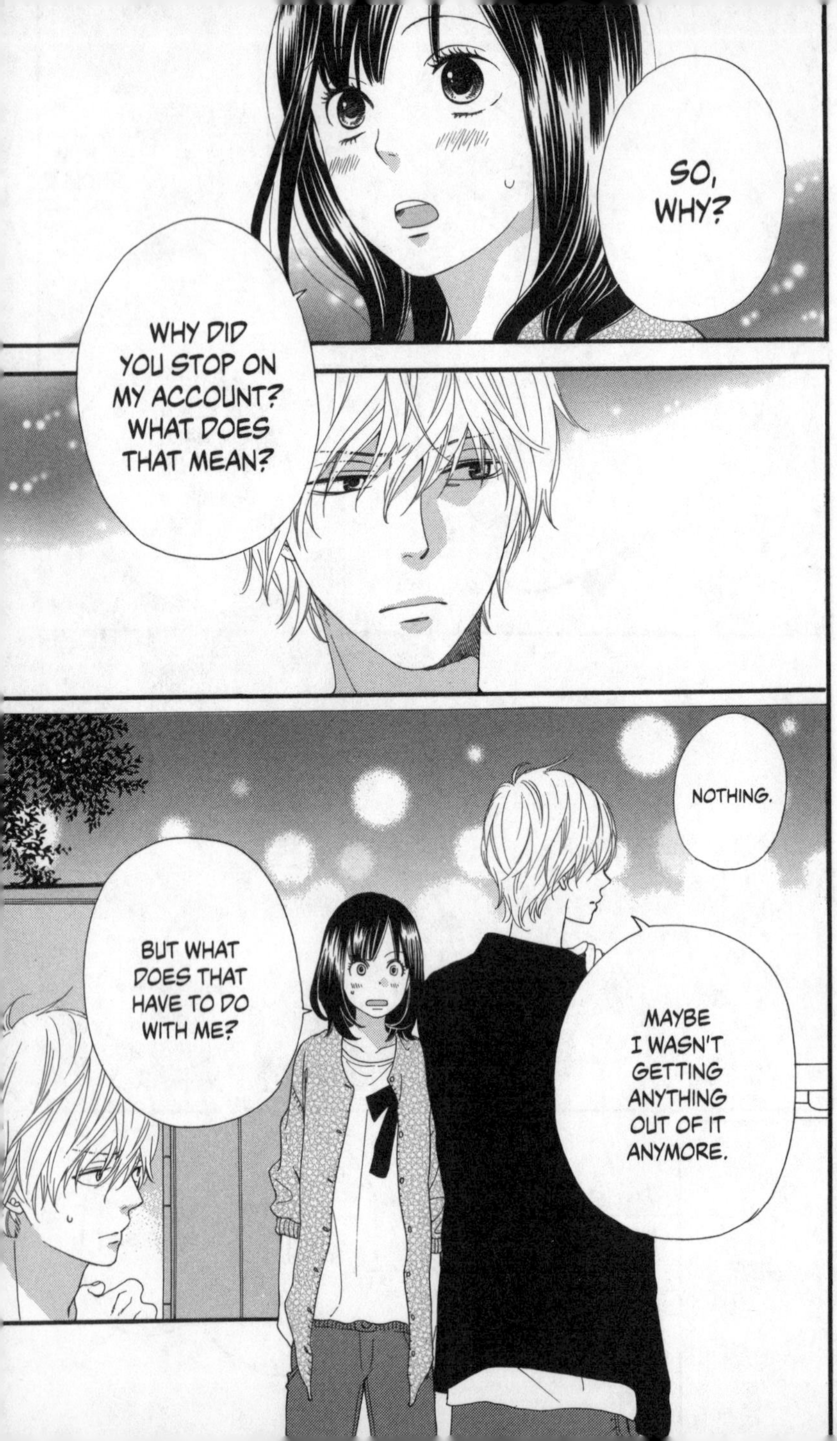
SO, WHY?
WHY DID YOU STOP ON MY ACCOUNT? WHAT DOES THAT MEAN?
NOTHING.
MAYBE I WASN'T GETTING ANYTHING OUT OF IT ANYMORE.
BUT WHAT DOES THAT HAVE TO DO WITH ME?

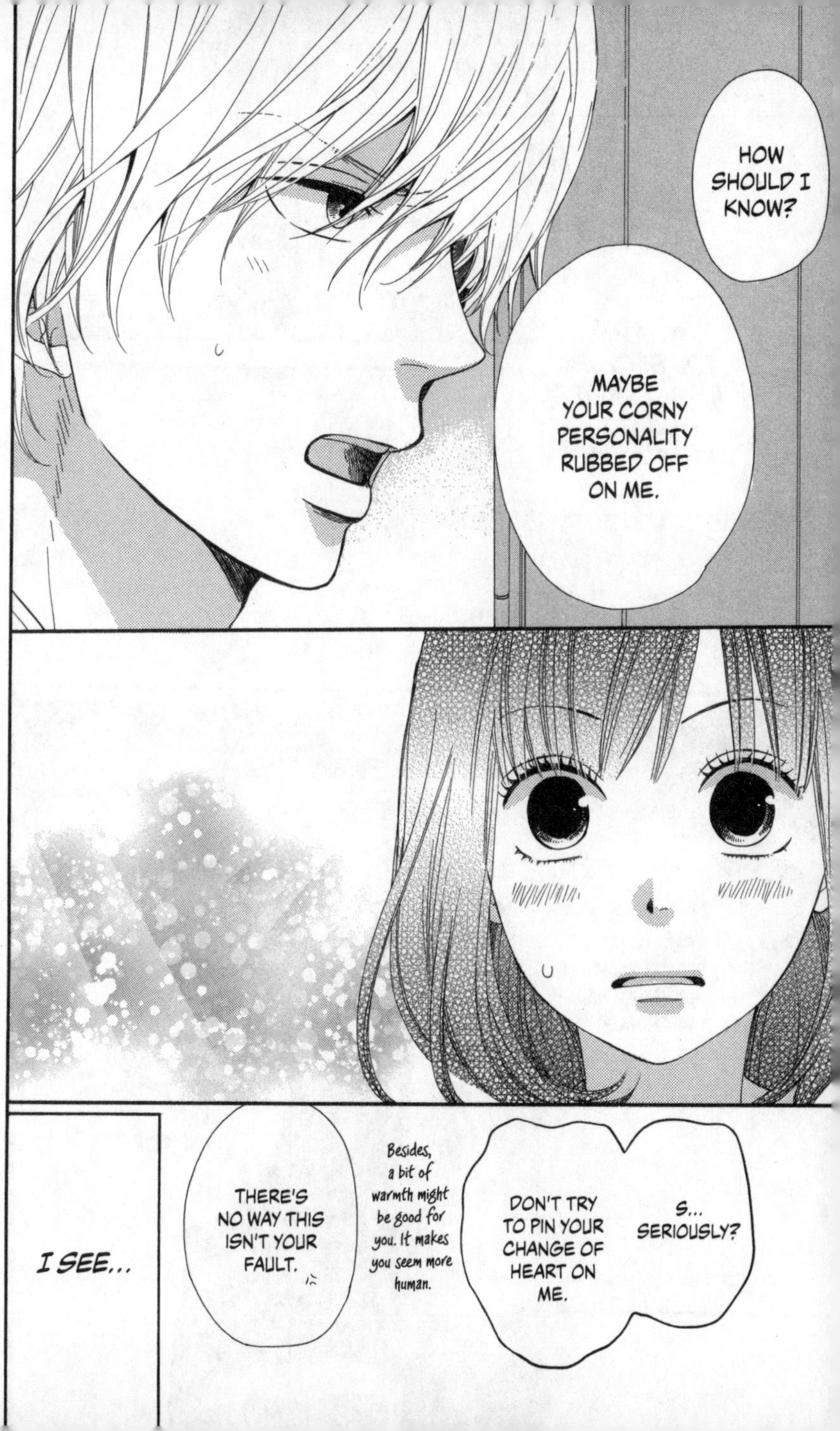
HOW SHOULD I KNOW?
MAYBE YOUR CORNY PERSONALITY RUBBED OFF ON ME.
S... SERIOUSLY?
DON'T TRY TO PIN YOUR CHANGE OF HEART ON ME.
Besides, a bit of warmth might be good for you. It makes you seem more human.
THERE'S NO WAY THIS ISN'T YOUR FAULT.
I SEE...

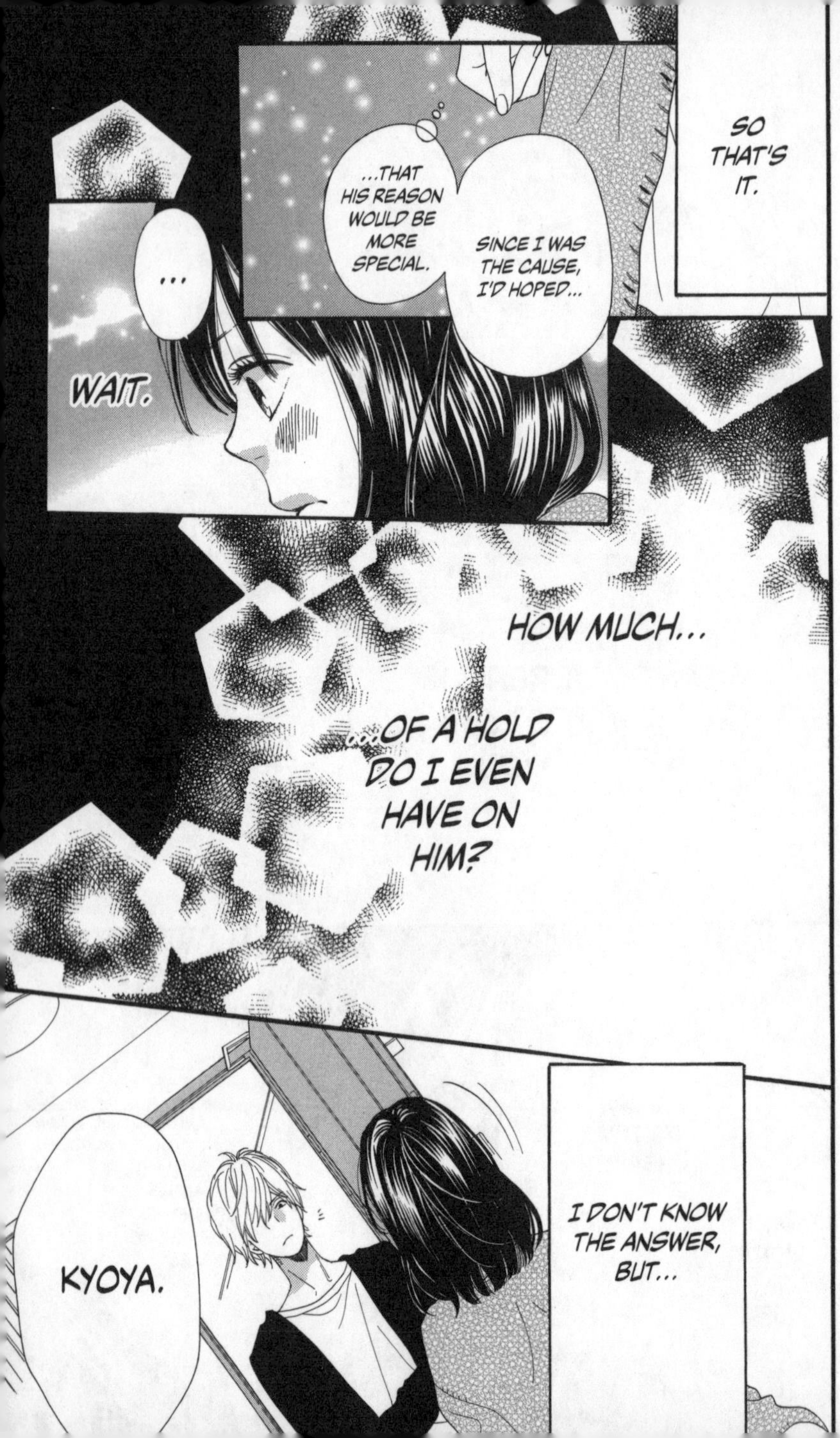
SO THAT'S IT.
SINCE I WAS THE CAUSE, I'D HOPED...
...THAT HIS REASON WOULD BE MORE SPECIAL.
...
WAIT.
HOW MUCH...
...OF A HOLD DO I EVEN HAVE ON HIM?
I DON'T KNOW THE ANSWER, BUT...
KYOYA.

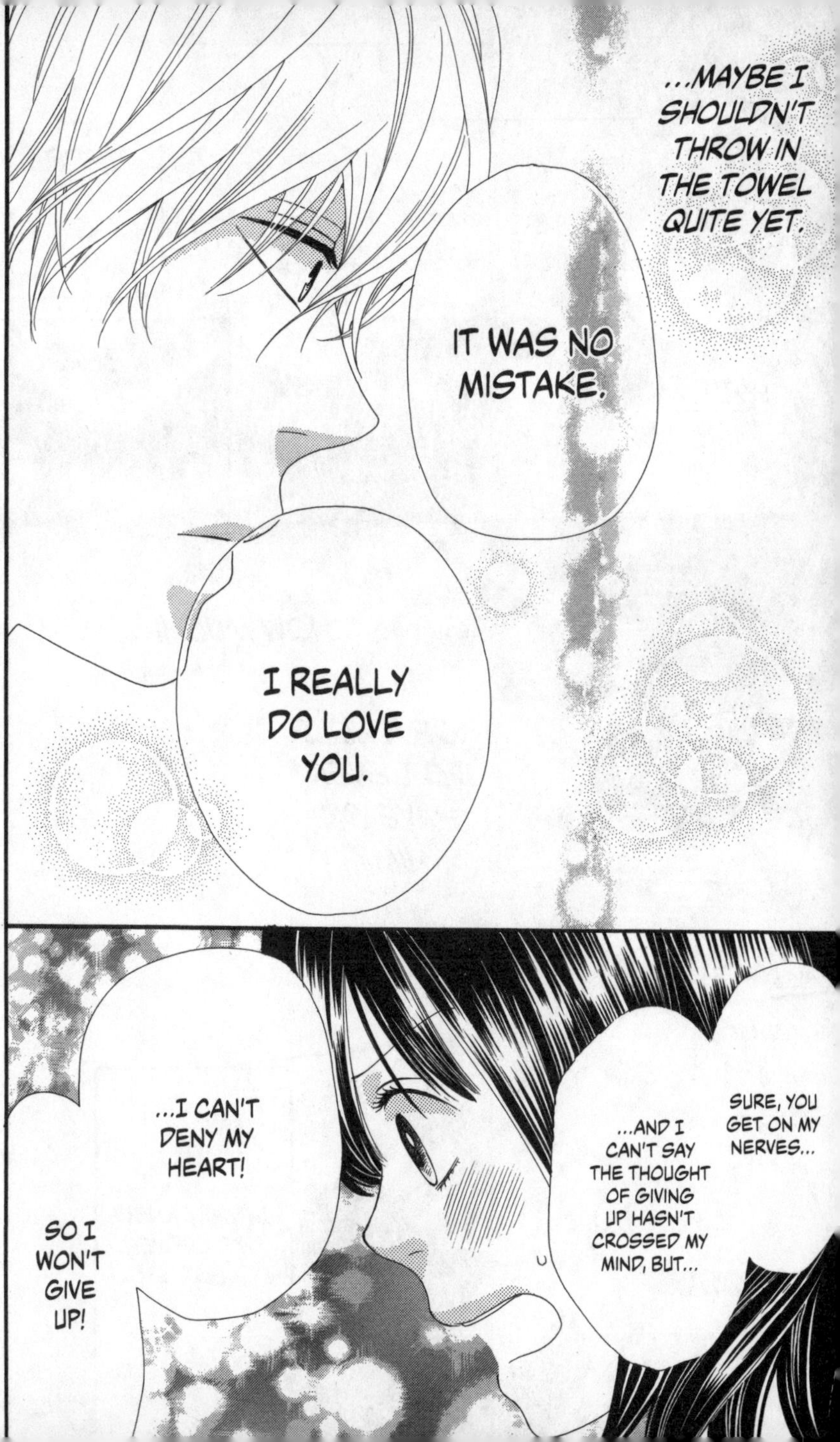
...MAYBE I SHOULDN'T THROW IN THE TOWEL QUITE YET.
IT WAS NO MISTAKE.
I REALLY DO LOVE YOU.
SURE, YOU GET ON MY NERVES...
...AND I CAN'T SAY THE THOUGHT OF GIVING UP HASN'T CROSSED MY MIND, BUT...
...I CAN'T DENY MY HEART!
SO I WON'T GIVE UP!

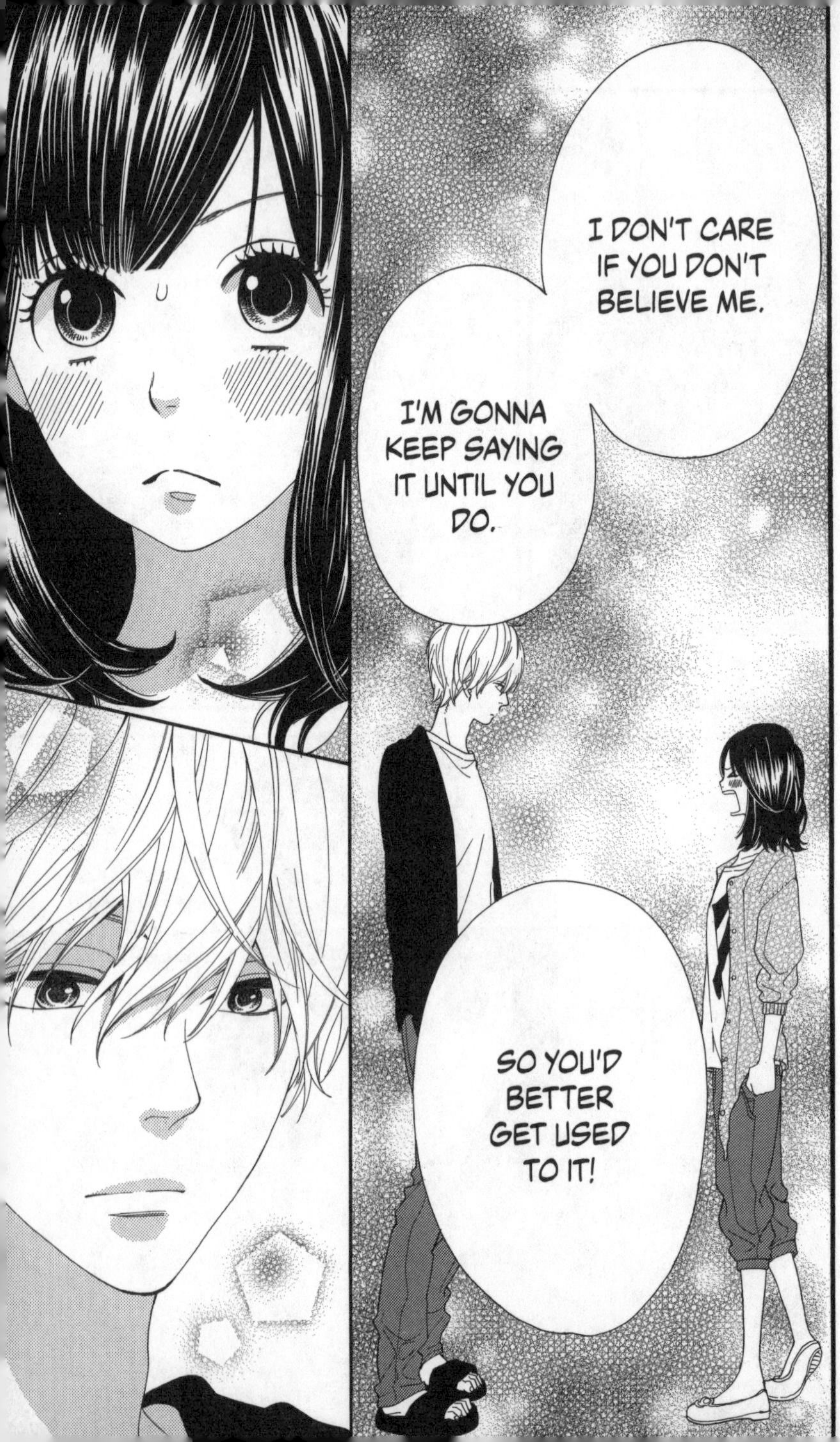
I DON'T CARE IF YOU DON'T BELIEVE ME.
I'M GONNA KEEP SAYING IT UNTIL YOU DO.
SO YOU'D BETTER GET USED TO IT!

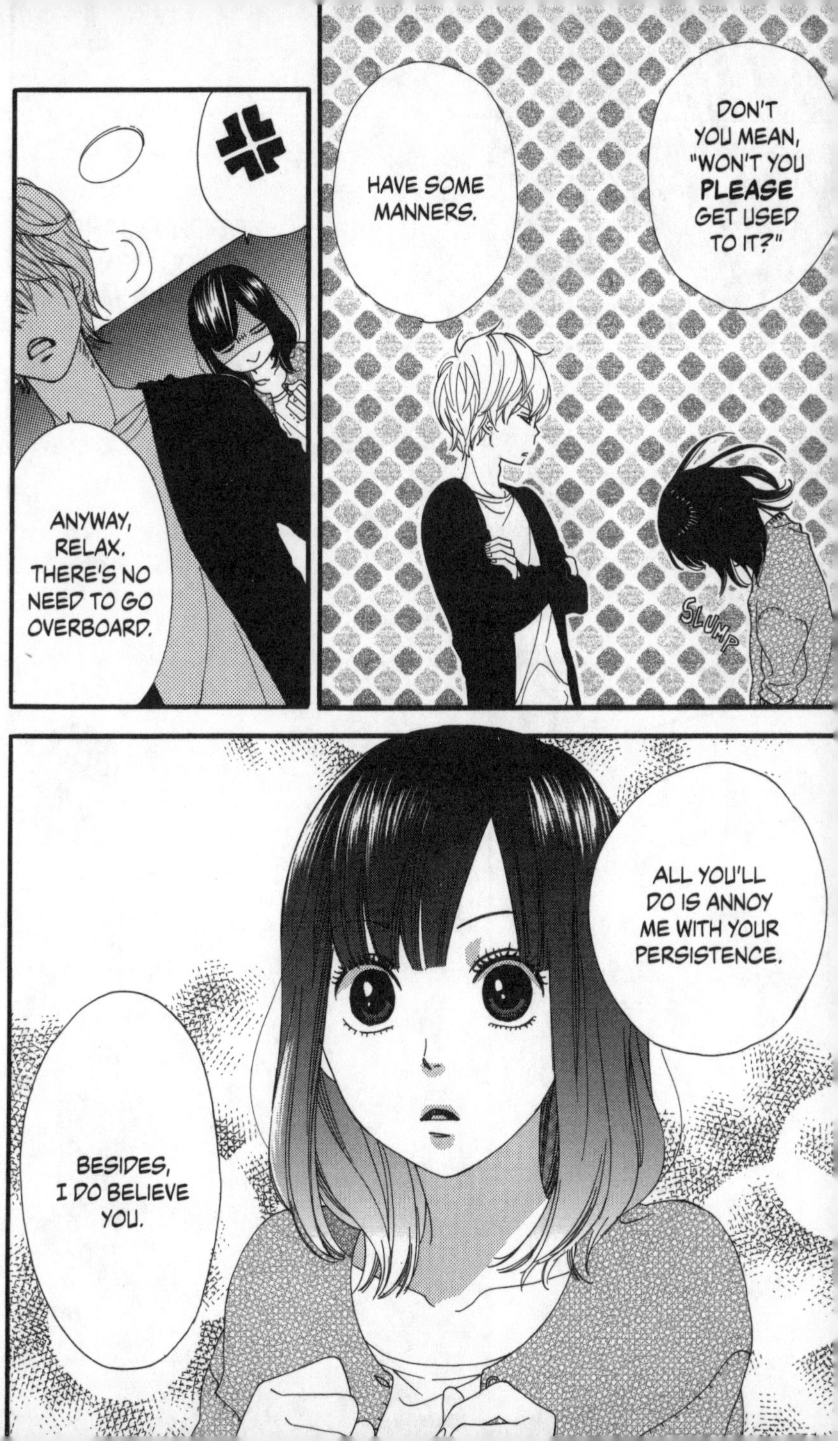
DON'T YOU MEAN, "WON'T YOU **PLEASE** GET USED TO IT?"
HAVE SOME MANNERS.
SLUMP
ANYWAY, RELAX. THERE'S NO NEED TO GO OVERBOARD.
ALL YOU'LL DO IS ANNOY ME WITH YOUR PERSISTENCE.
BESIDES, I DO BELIEVE YOU.

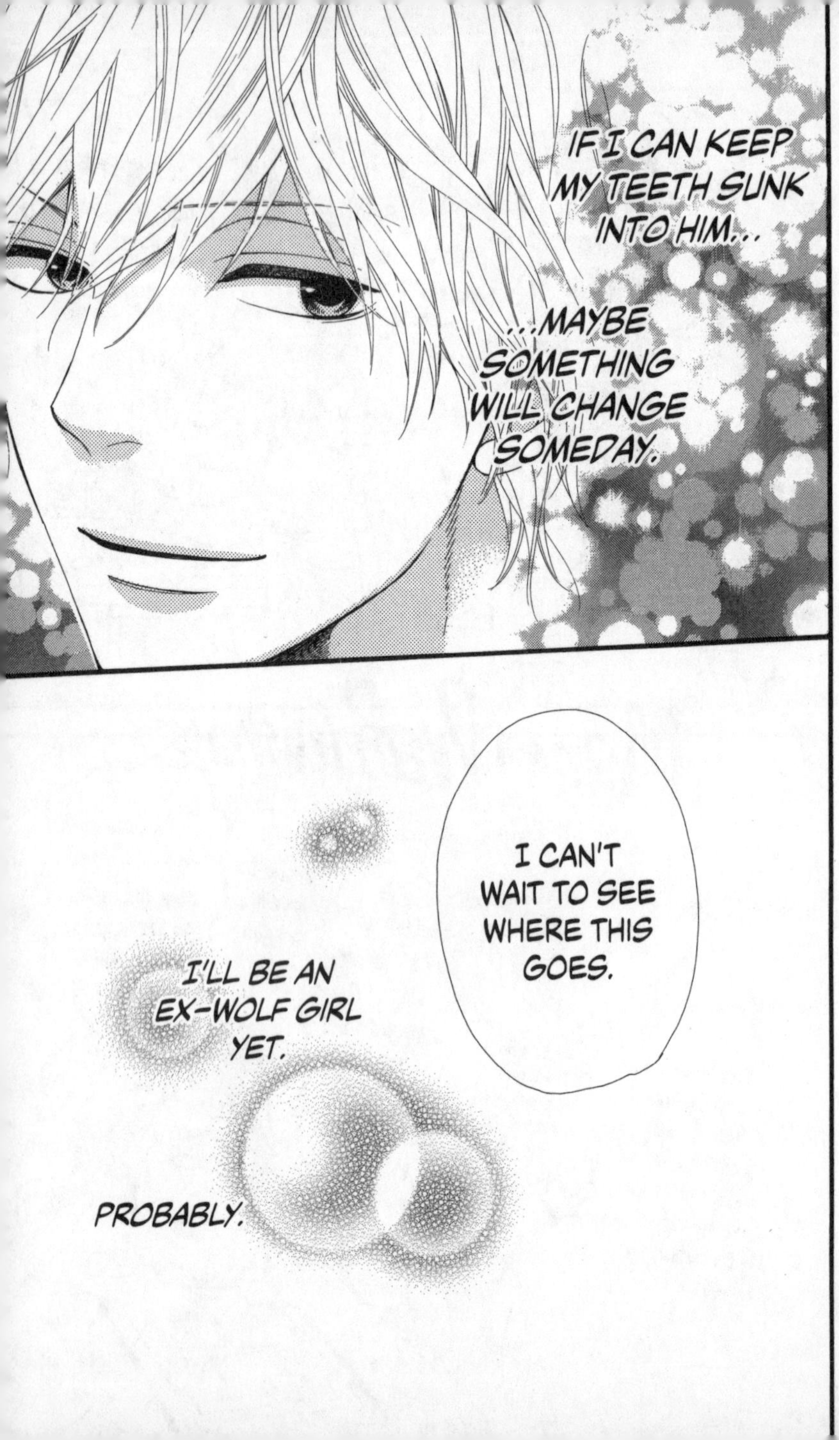
IF I CAN KEEP MY TEETH SUNK INTO HIM...
...MAYBE SOMETHING WILL CHANGE SOMEDAY.
I CAN'T WAIT TO SEE WHERE THIS GOES.
I'LL BE AN EX-WOLF GIRL YET.
PROBABLY.

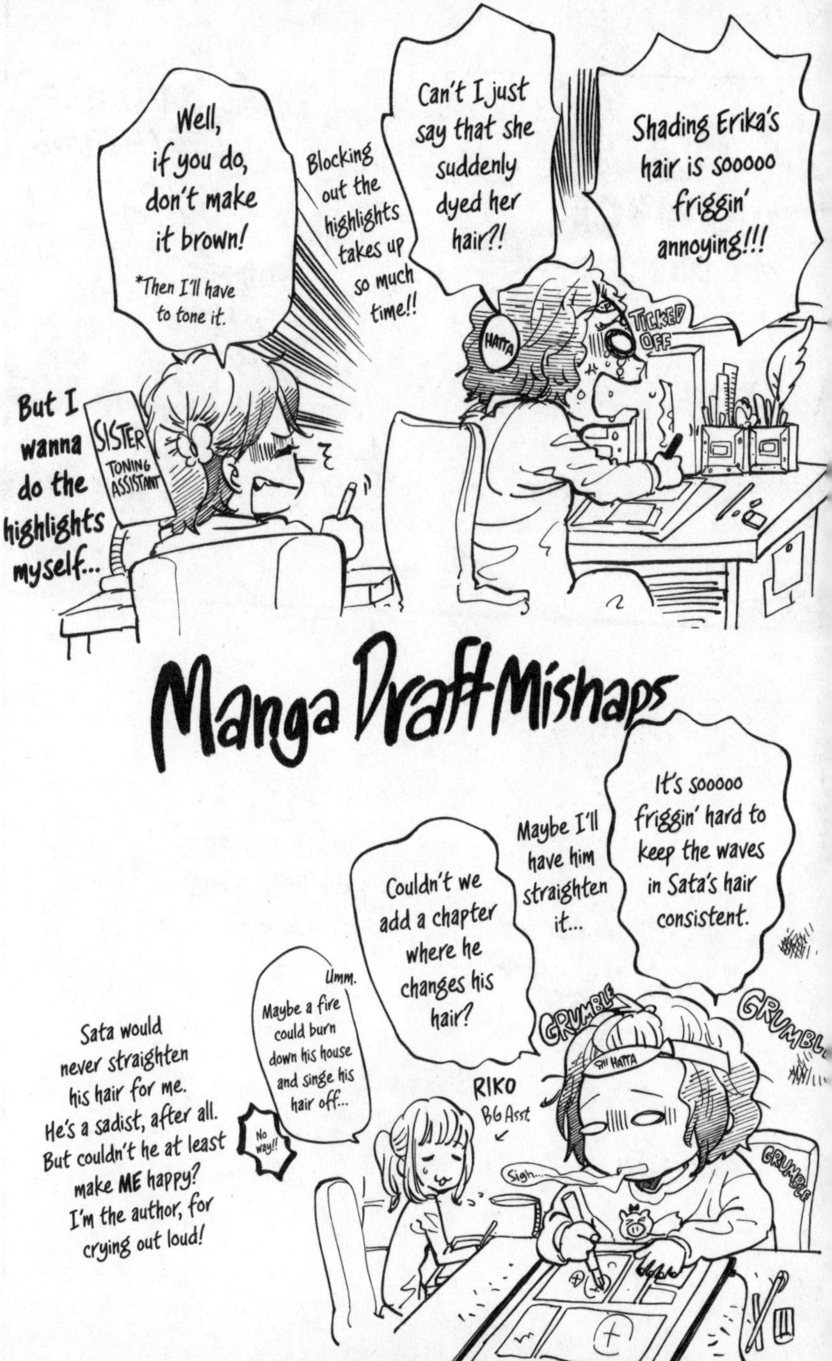
Shading Erika's hair is sooooo friggin' annoying!!!
Can't I just say that she suddenly dyed her hair?!
Blocking out the highlights takes up so much time!!
TICKED OFF
HATTA
Well, if you do, don't make it brown!
*Then I'll have to tone it.
SISTER TONING ASSISTANT
But I wanna do the highlights myself...
Manga Draft Mishaps
It's sooooo friggin' hard to keep the waves in Sata's hair consistent.
Maybe I'll have him straighten it...
Couldn't we add a chapter where he changes his hair?
GRUMBLE
GRUMBLE
HATTA
Umm.
Maybe a fire could burn down his house and singe his hair off...
RIKO
BG Asst.
No way!!
GRUMBLE
Sigh...
Sata would never straighten his hair for me. He's a sadist, after all. But couldn't he at least make ME happy? I'm the author, for crying out loud!

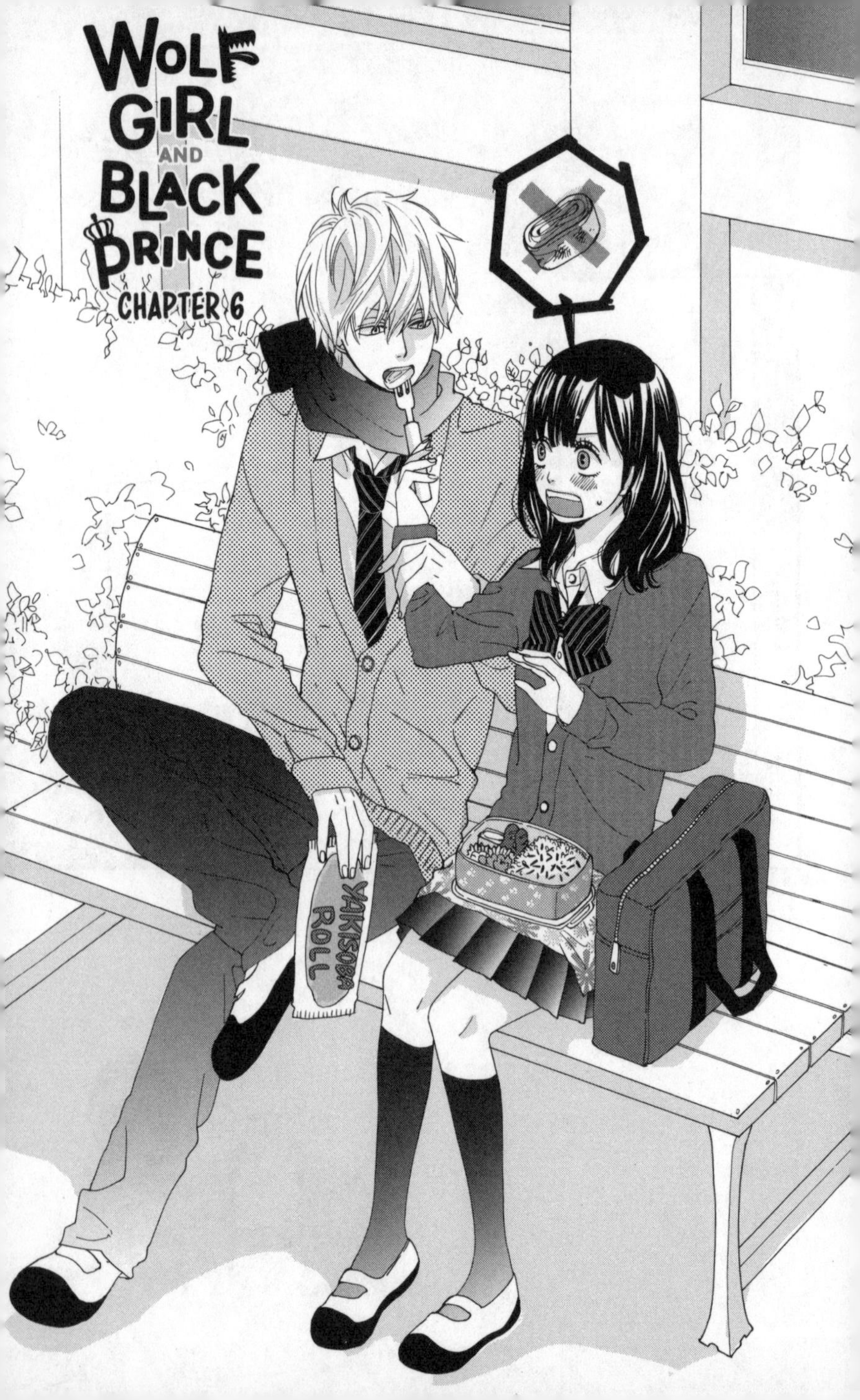
WOLF GIRL AND BLACK PRINCE
CHAPTER 6
YAKISOBA ROLL

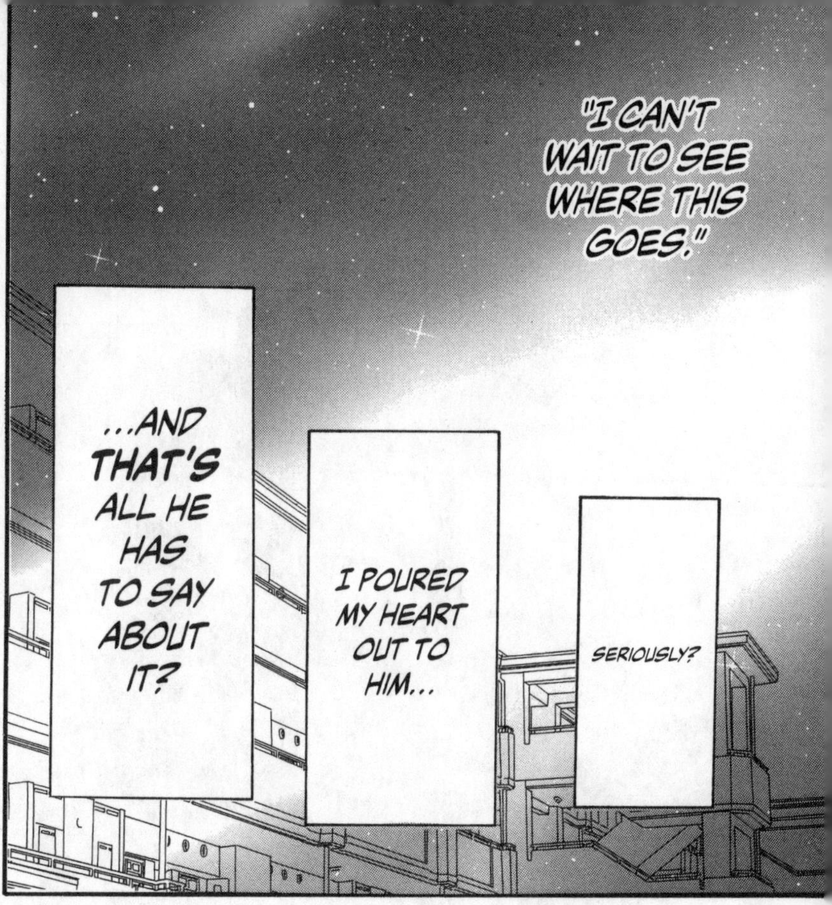
"I CAN'T WAIT TO SEE WHERE THIS GOES."
SERIOUSLY?
I POURED MY HEART OUT TO HIM...
...AND THAT'S ALL HE HAS TO SAY ABOUT IT?

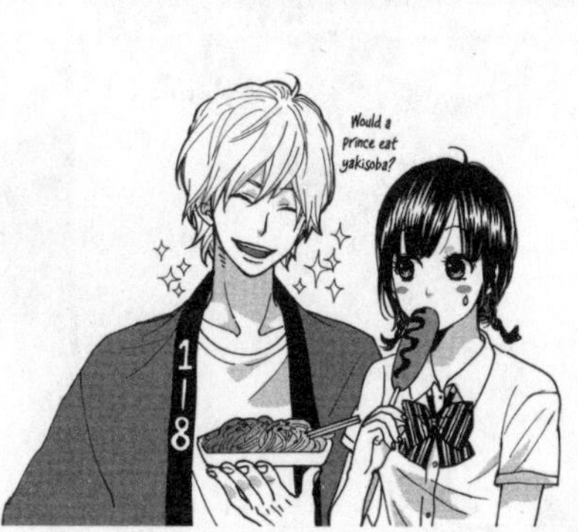
Would a prince eat yakisoba?

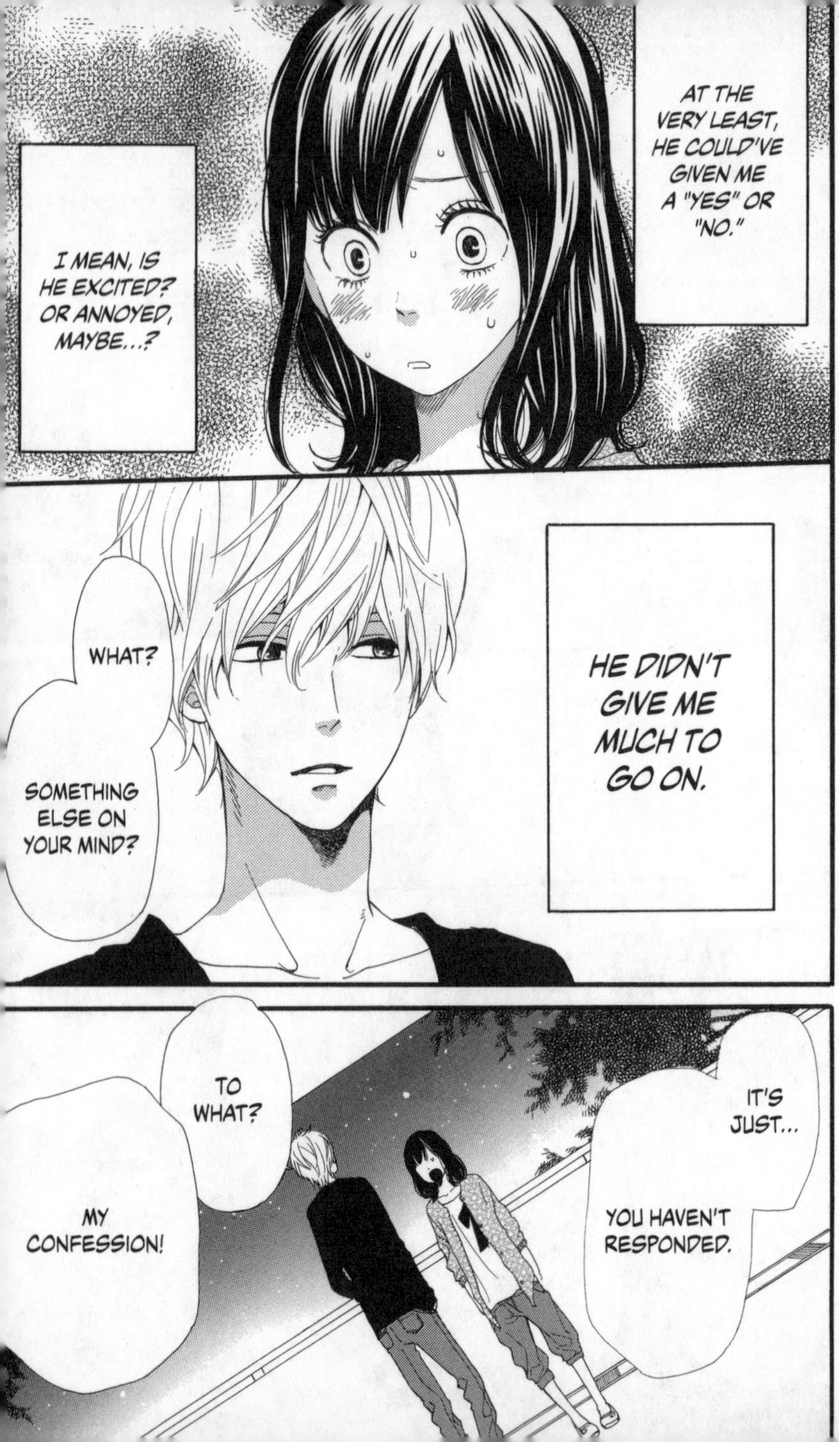
AT THE VERY LEAST, HE COULD'VE GIVEN ME A "YES" OR "NO."
I MEAN, IS HE EXCITED? OR ANNOYED, MAYBE...?
HE DIDN'T GIVE ME MUCH TO GO ON.
WHAT?
SOMETHING ELSE ON YOUR MIND?
IT'S JUST...
YOU HAVEN'T RESPONDED.
TO WHAT?
MY CONFESSION!

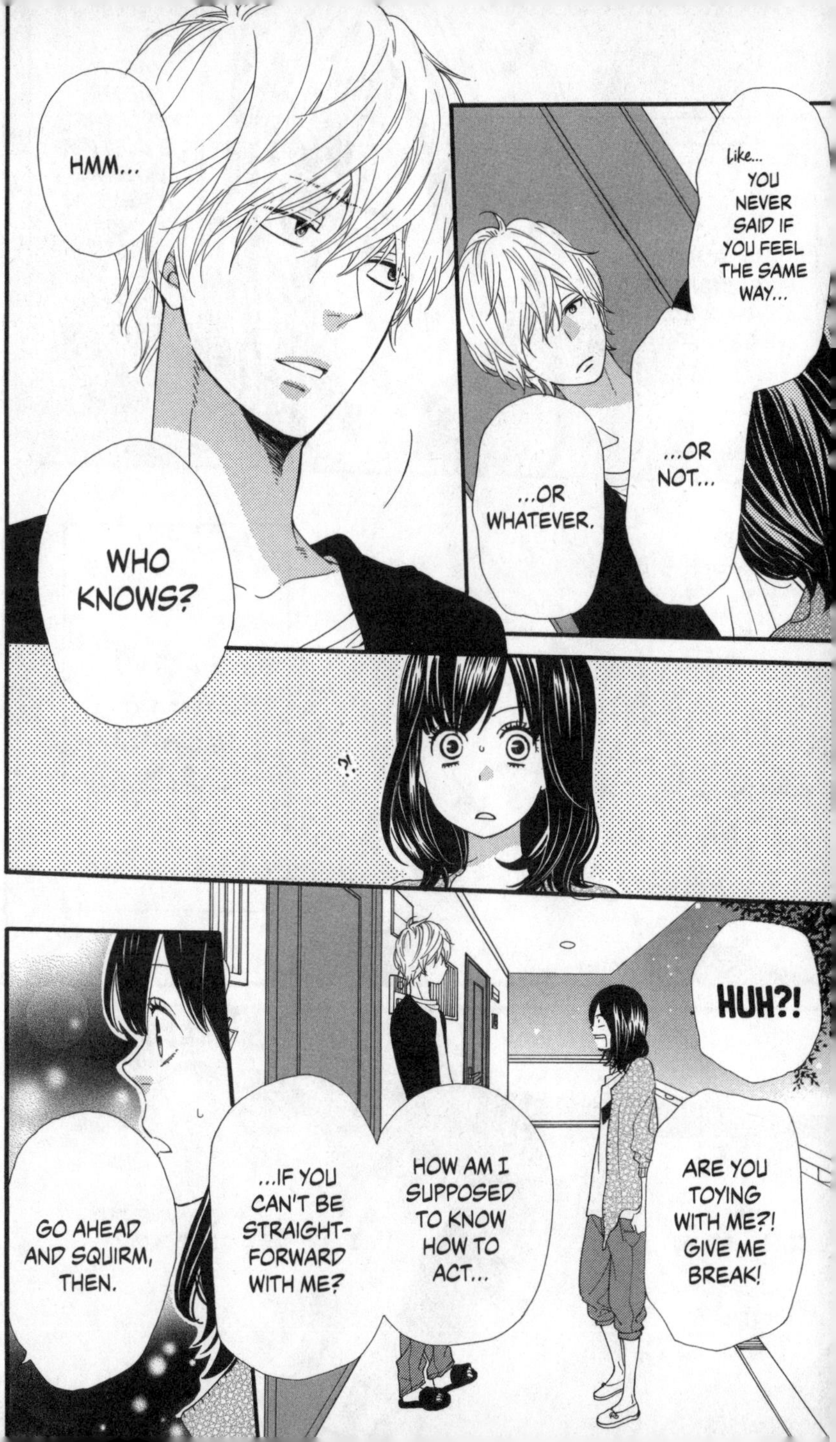
Like... YOU NEVER SAID IF YOU FEEL THE SAME WAY...
...OR NOT...
...OR WHATEVER.
HMM...
WHO KNOWS?
?!
HUH?!
ARE YOU TOYING WITH ME?! GIVE ME BREAK!
HOW AM I SUPPOSED TO KNOW HOW TO ACT...
...IF YOU CAN'T BE STRAIGHT-FORWARD WITH ME?
GO AHEAD AND SQUIRM, THEN.

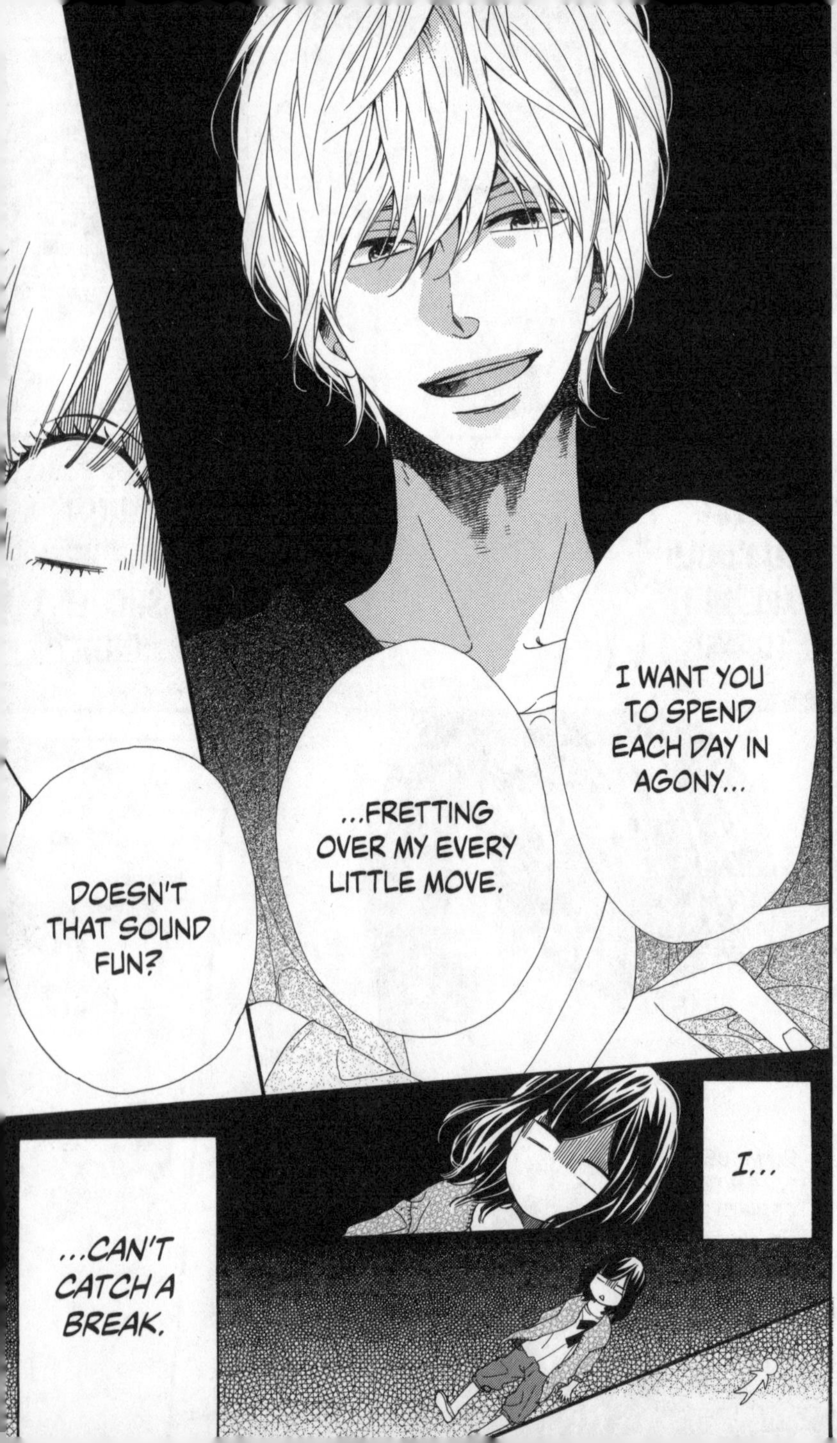
I WANT YOU TO SPEND EACH DAY IN AGONY...
...FRETTING OVER MY EVERY LITTLE MOVE.
DOESN'T THAT SOUND FUN?
I...
...CAN'T CATCH A BREAK.

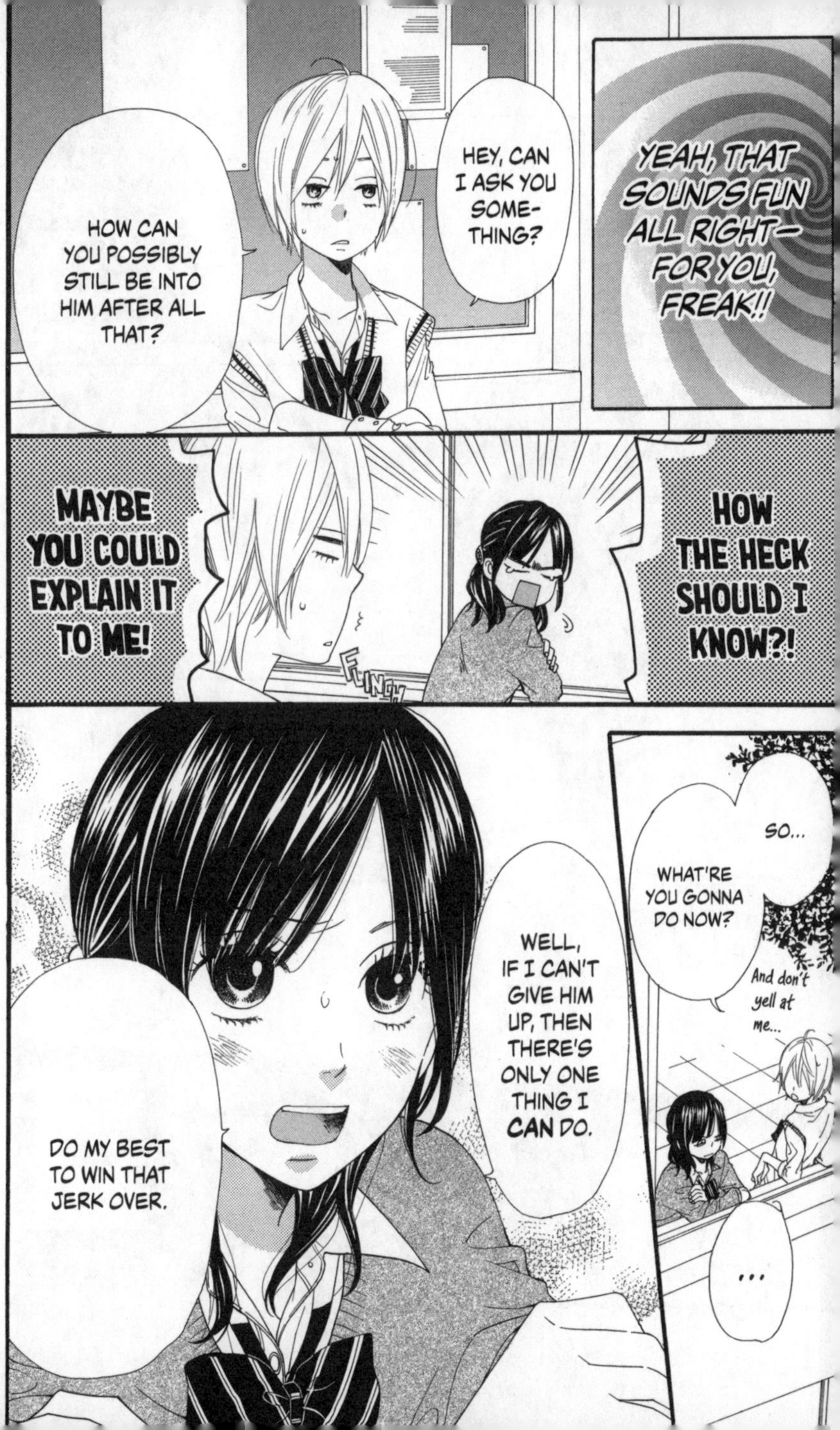
YEAH, THAT SOUNDS FUN ALL RIGHT— FOR YOU, FREAK!!
HEY, CAN I ASK YOU SOME-THING?
HOW CAN YOU POSSIBLY STILL BE INTO HIM AFTER ALL THAT?
HOW THE HECK SHOULD I KNOW?!
FLINCH
MAYBE YOU COULD EXPLAIN IT TO ME!
SO...
WHAT'RE YOU GONNA DO NOW?
And don't yell at me...
...
WELL, IF I CAN'T GIVE HIM UP, THEN THERE'S ONLY ONE THING I CAN DO.
DO MY BEST TO WIN THAT JERK OVER.

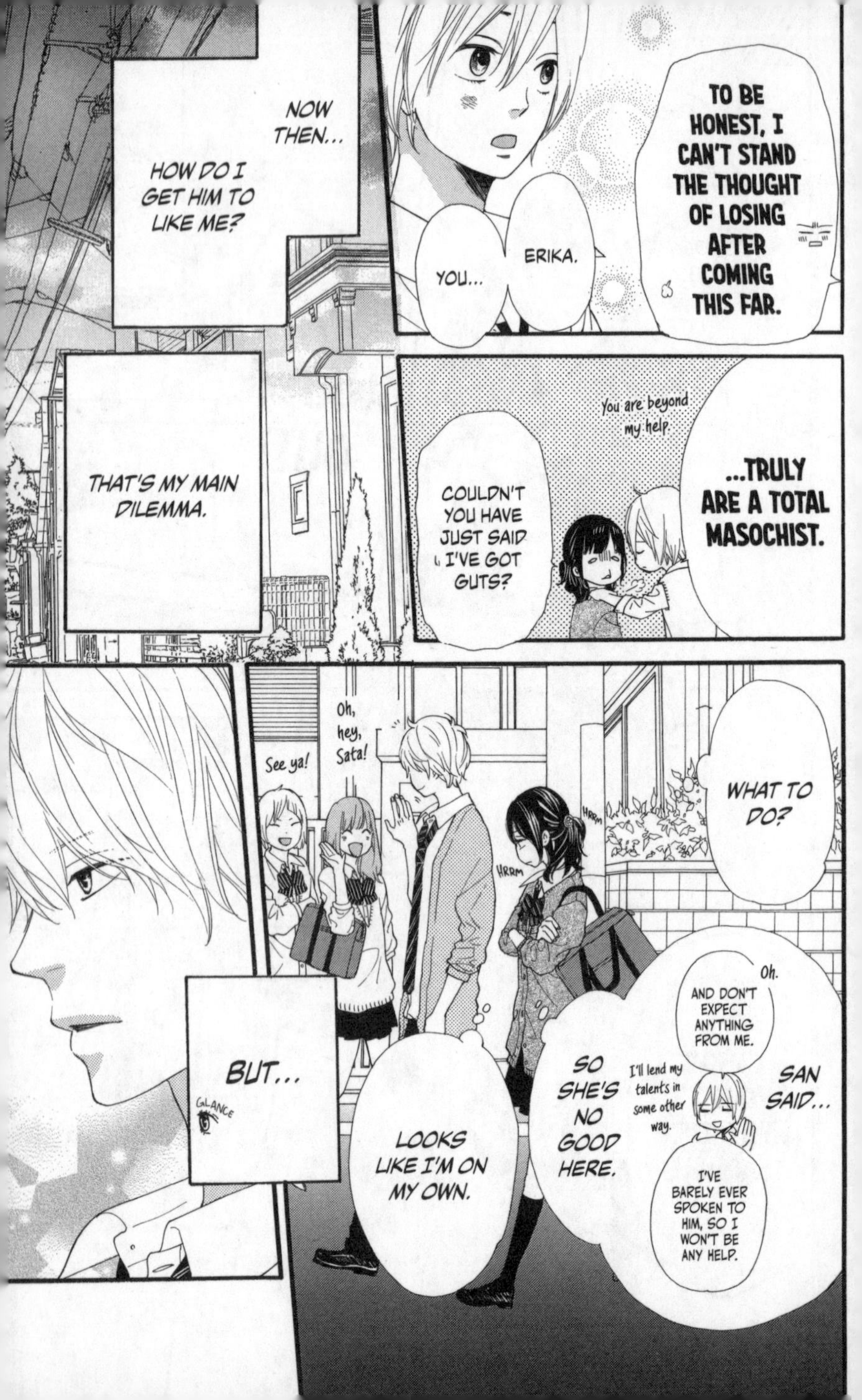
TO BE HONEST, I CAN'T STAND THE THOUGHT OF LOSING AFTER COMING THIS FAR.
ERIKA.
YOU...
...TRULY ARE A TOTAL MASOCHIST.
You are beyond my help.
COULDN'T YOU HAVE JUST SAID I'VE GOT GUTS?
NOW THEN...
HOW DO I GET HIM TO LIKE ME?
THAT'S MY MAIN DILEMMA.
WHAT TO DO?
HRRM
HRRM
Oh, hey, Sata!
See ya!
SAN SAID...
Oh.
AND DON'T EXPECT ANYTHING FROM ME.
I'll lend my talents in some other way.
I'VE BARELY EVER SPOKEN TO HIM, SO I WON'T BE ANY HELP.
SO SHE'S NO GOOD HERE.
LOOKS LIKE I'M ON MY OWN.
BUT...
GLANCE

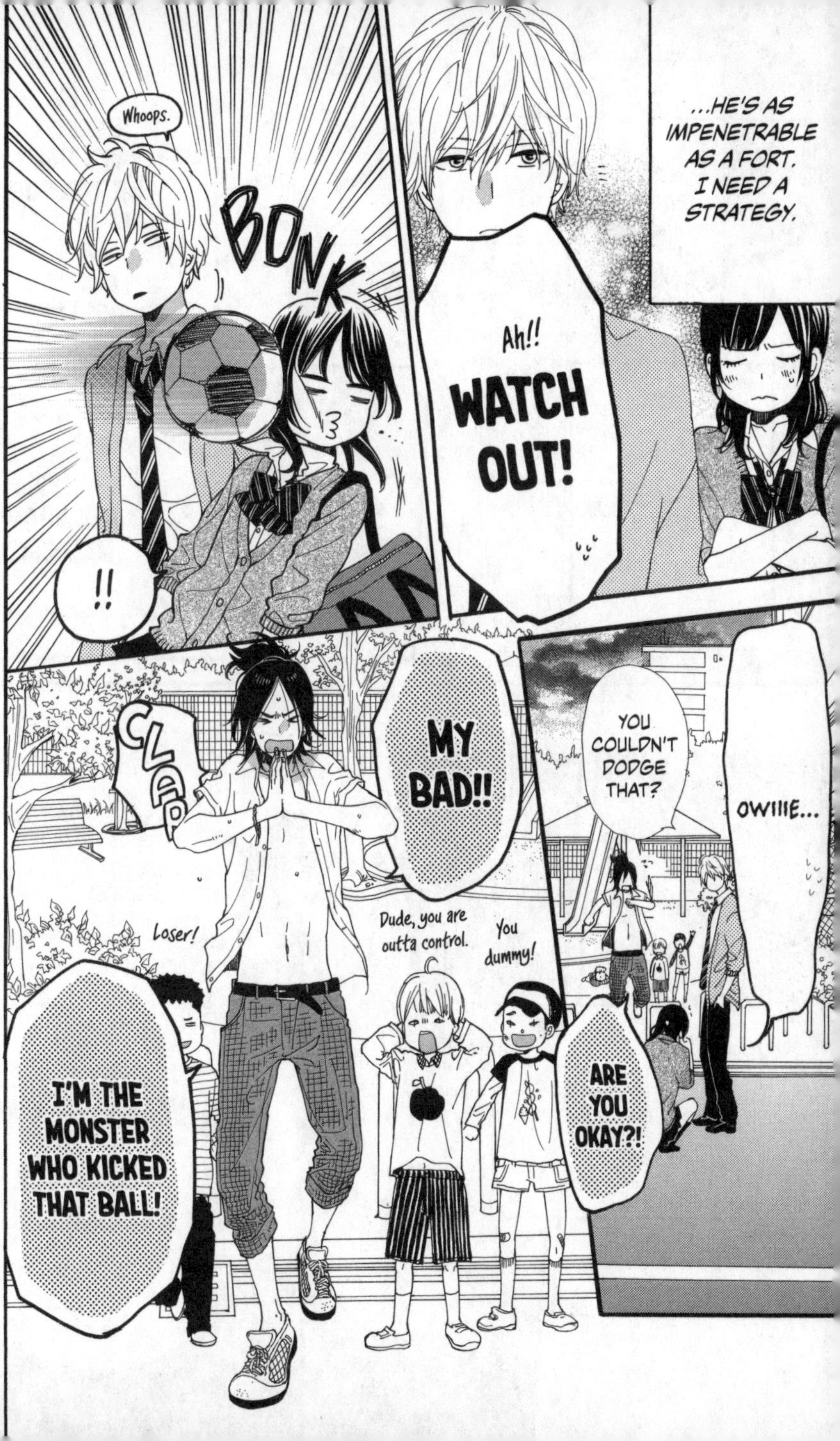
...HE'S AS IMPENETRABLE AS A FORT. I NEED A STRATEGY.
Ah!!
WATCH OUT!
Whoops.
BONK
!!
OWIIIE...
YOU COULDN'T DODGE THAT?
ARE YOU OKAY?!
MY BAD!!
CLAP
You dummy!
Dude, you are outta control.
Loser!
I'M THE MONSTER WHO KICKED THAT BALL!

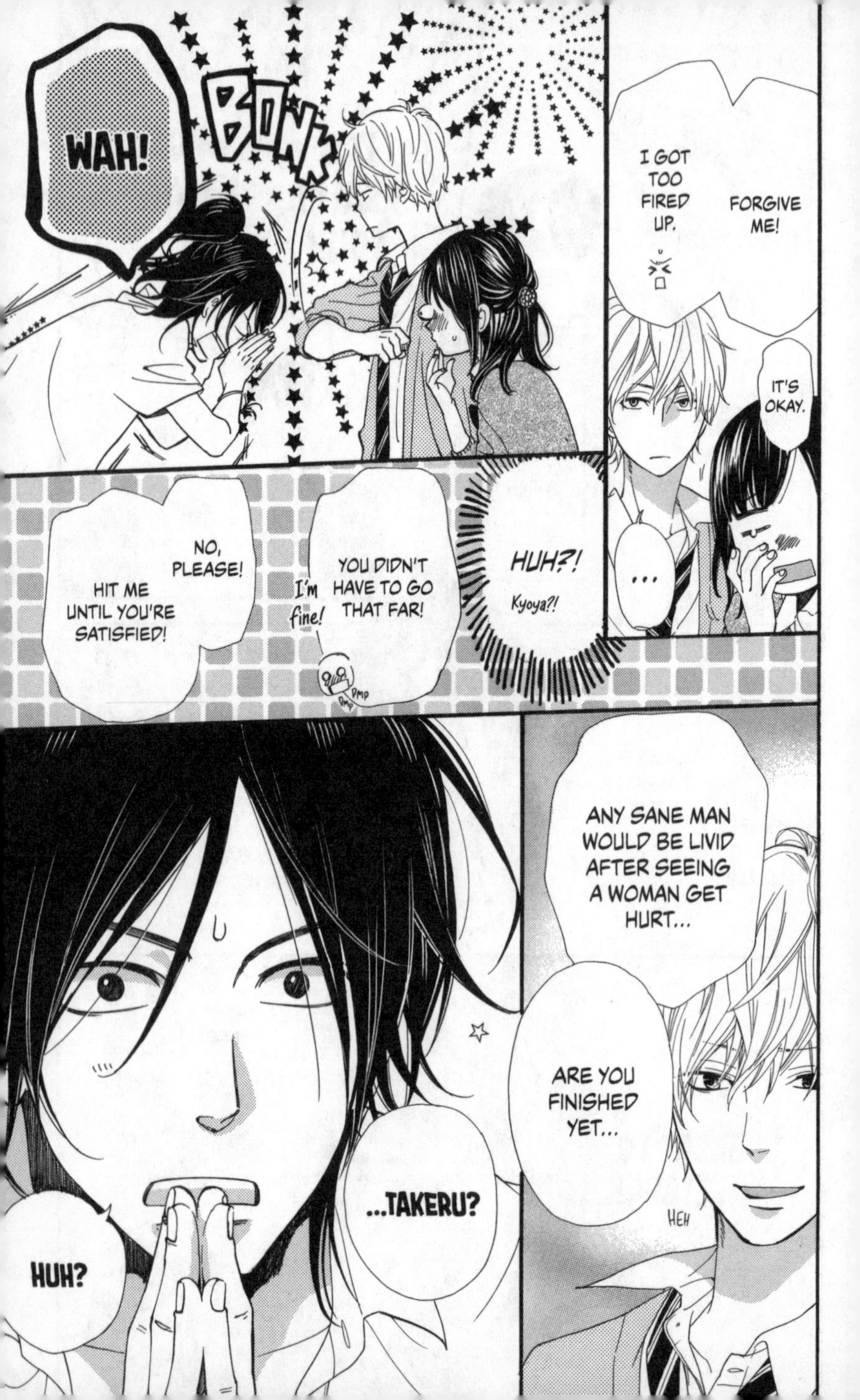
I GOT TOO FIRED UP. FORGIVE ME!
IT'S OKAY.
...
BONK
WAH!
HUH?!
Kyoya?!
YOU DIDN'T HAVE TO GO THAT FAR!
I'm fine!
DMP DMP
NO, PLEASE!
HIT ME UNTIL YOU'RE SATISFIED!
ANY SANE MAN WOULD BE LIVID AFTER SEEING A WOMAN GET HURT...
ARE YOU FINISHED YET...
HEH
...TAKERU?
HUH?

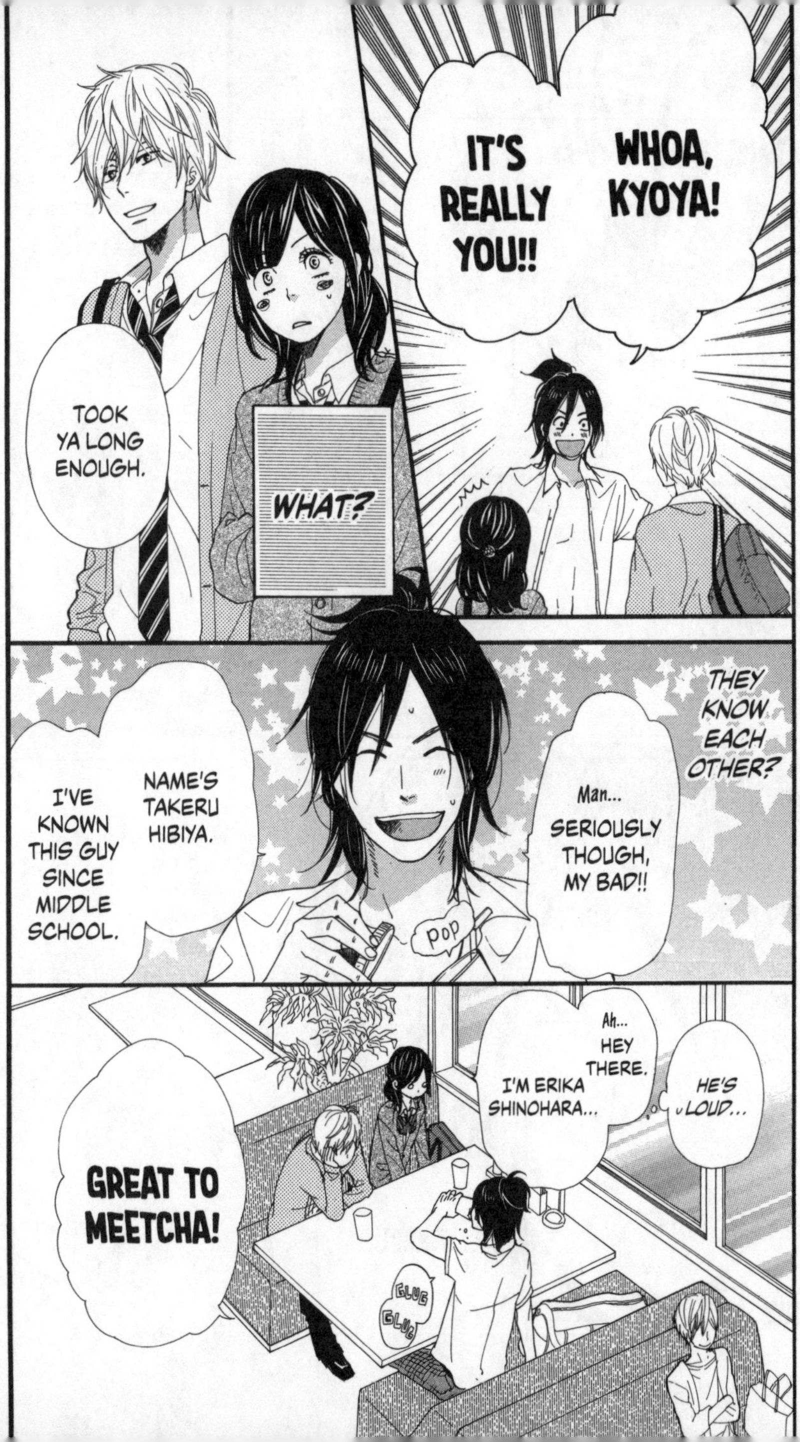
WHOA, KYOYA!
IT'S REALLY YOU!!
TOOK YA LONG ENOUGH.
WHAT?
THEY KNOW EACH OTHER?
Man... SERIOUSLY THOUGH, MY BAD!!
pop
NAME'S TAKERU HIBIYA.
I'VE KNOWN THIS GUY SINCE MIDDLE SCHOOL.
HE'S LOUD...
Ah... HEY THERE.
I'M ERIKA SHINOHARA...
GLUG GLUG
GREAT TO MEETCHA!

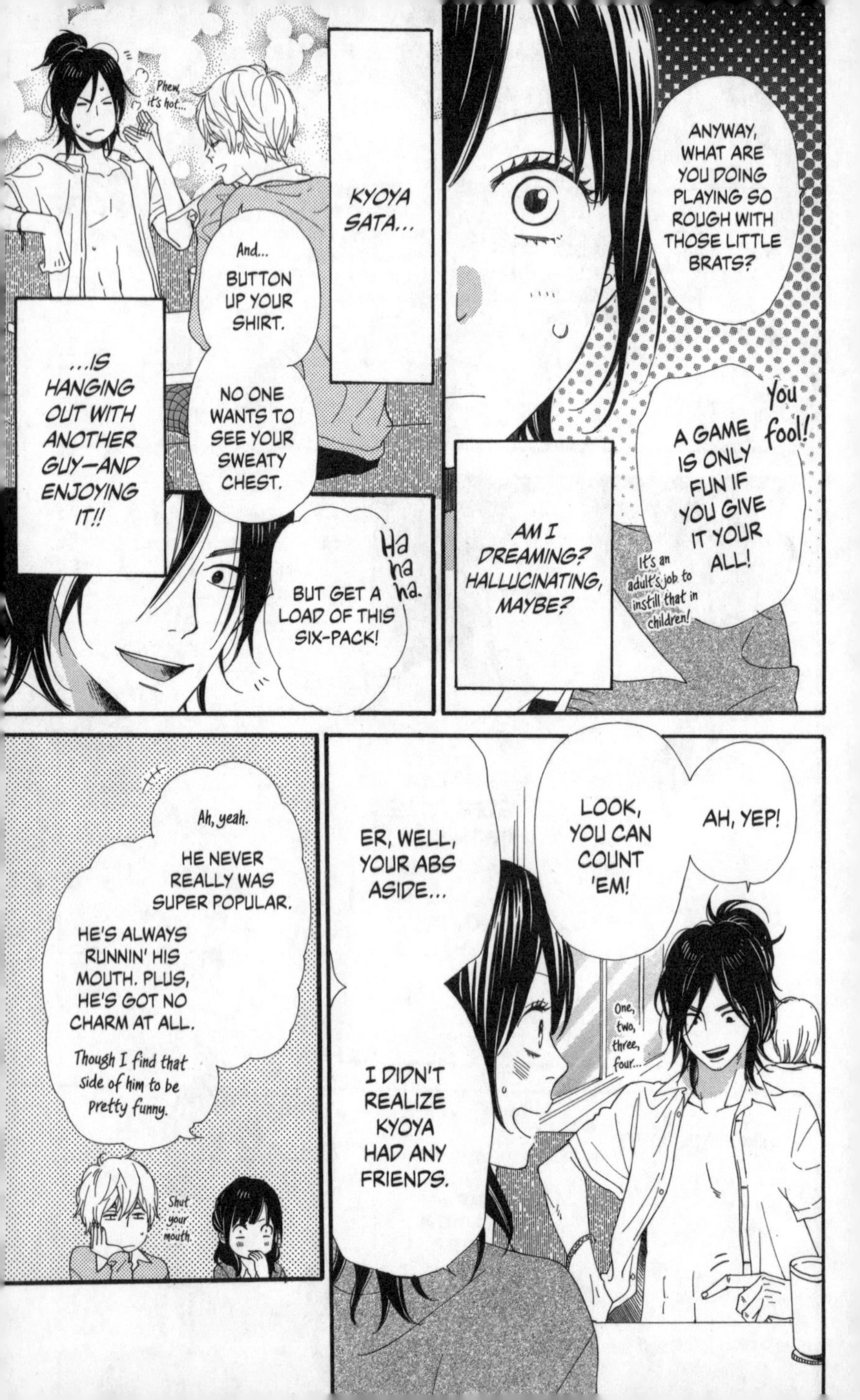
ANYWAY, WHAT ARE YOU DOING PLAYING SO ROUGH WITH THOSE LITTLE BRATS?
You fool!
A GAME IS ONLY FUN IF YOU GIVE IT YOUR ALL!
It's an adult's job to instill that in children!
AM I DREAMING? HALLUCINATING, MAYBE?
KYOYA SATA...
Ha ha ha.
BUT GET A LOAD OF THIS SIX-PACK!
Phew, it's hot...
And... BUTTON UP YOUR SHIRT.
NO ONE WANTS TO SEE YOUR SWEATY CHEST.
...IS HANGING OUT WITH ANOTHER GUY—AND ENJOYING IT!!
AH, YEP!
LOOK, YOU CAN COUNT 'EM!
One, two, three, four...
ER, WELL, YOUR ABS ASIDE...
I DIDN'T REALIZE KYOYA HAD ANY FRIENDS.
Ah, yeah.
HE NEVER REALLY WAS SUPER POPULAR.
HE'S ALWAYS RUNNIN' HIS MOUTH. PLUS, HE'S GOT NO CHARM AT ALL.
Though I find that side of him to be pretty funny.
Shut your mouth.

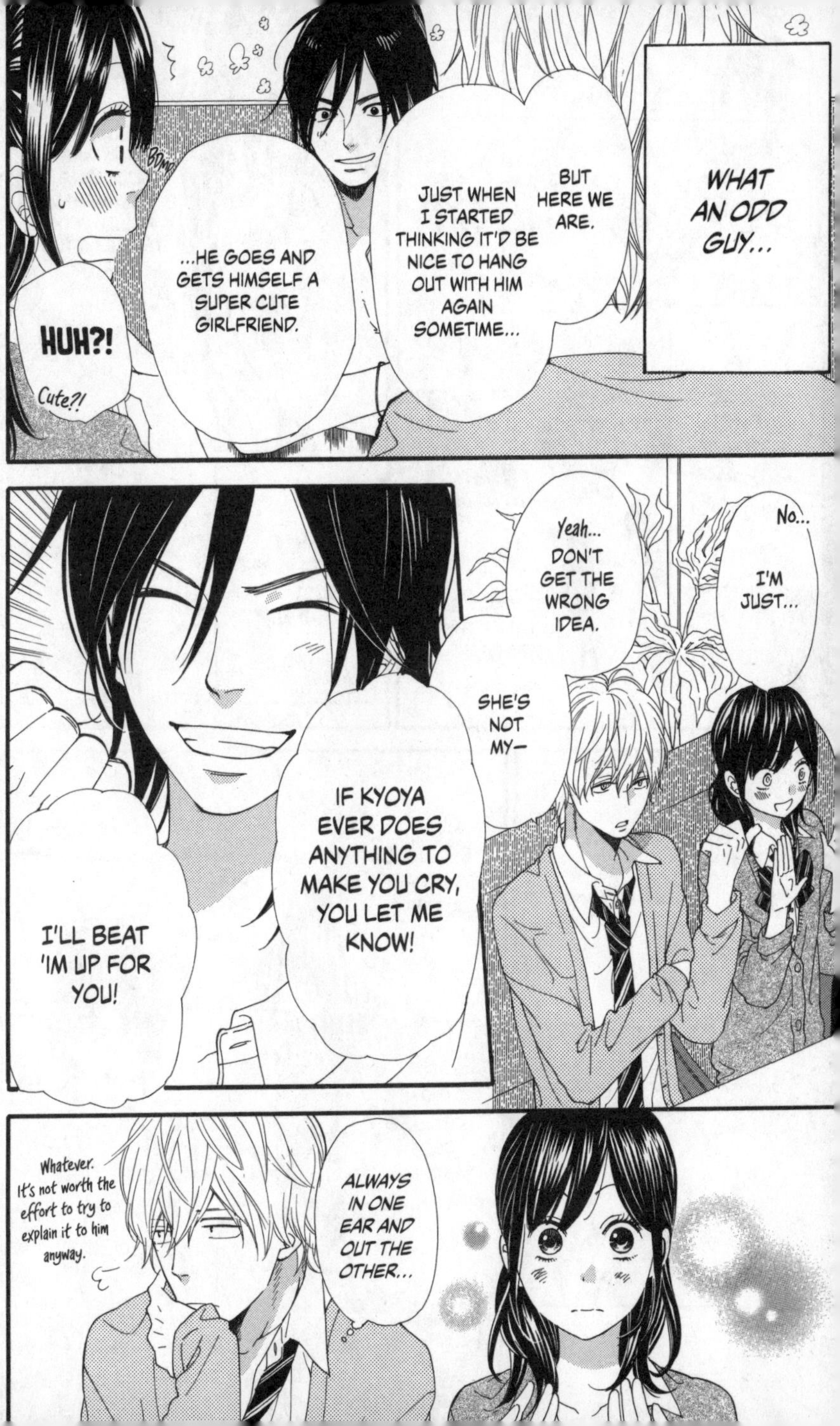
WHAT AN ODD GUY...
BUT HERE WE ARE.
JUST WHEN I STARTED THINKING IT'D BE NICE TO HANG OUT WITH HIM AGAIN SOMETIME...
...HE GOES AND GETS HIMSELF A SUPER CUTE GIRLFRIEND.
BDMP
HUH?!
Cute?!
No...
I'M JUST...
Yeah... DON'T GET THE WRONG IDEA.
SHE'S NOT MY—
IF KYOYA EVER DOES ANYTHING TO MAKE YOU CRY, YOU LET ME KNOW!
I'LL BEAT 'IM UP FOR YOU!
ALWAYS IN ONE EAR AND OUT THE OTHER...
Whatever. It's not worth the effort to try to explain it to him anyway.

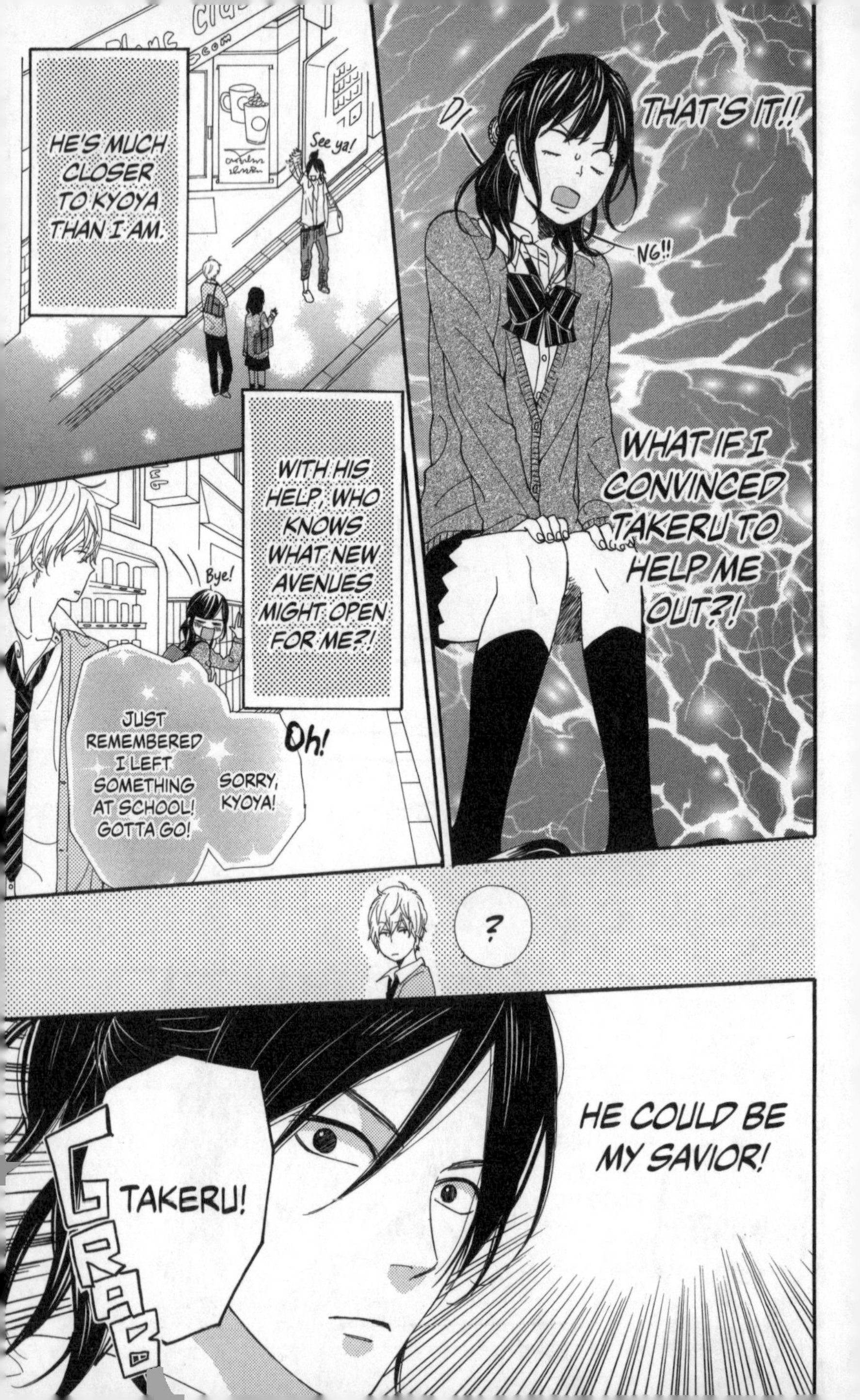
D!
THAT'S IT!!
NG!!
WHAT IF I CONVINCED TAKERU TO HELP ME OUT?!
HE'S MUCH CLOSER TO KYOYA THAN I AM.
See ya!
WITH HIS HELP, WHO KNOWS WHAT NEW AVENUES MIGHT OPEN FOR ME?!
Oh!
Bye!
SORRY, KYOYA! JUST REMEMBERED I LEFT SOMETHING AT SCHOOL! GOTTA GO!
?
HE COULD BE MY SAVIOR!
TAKERU!
GRAB

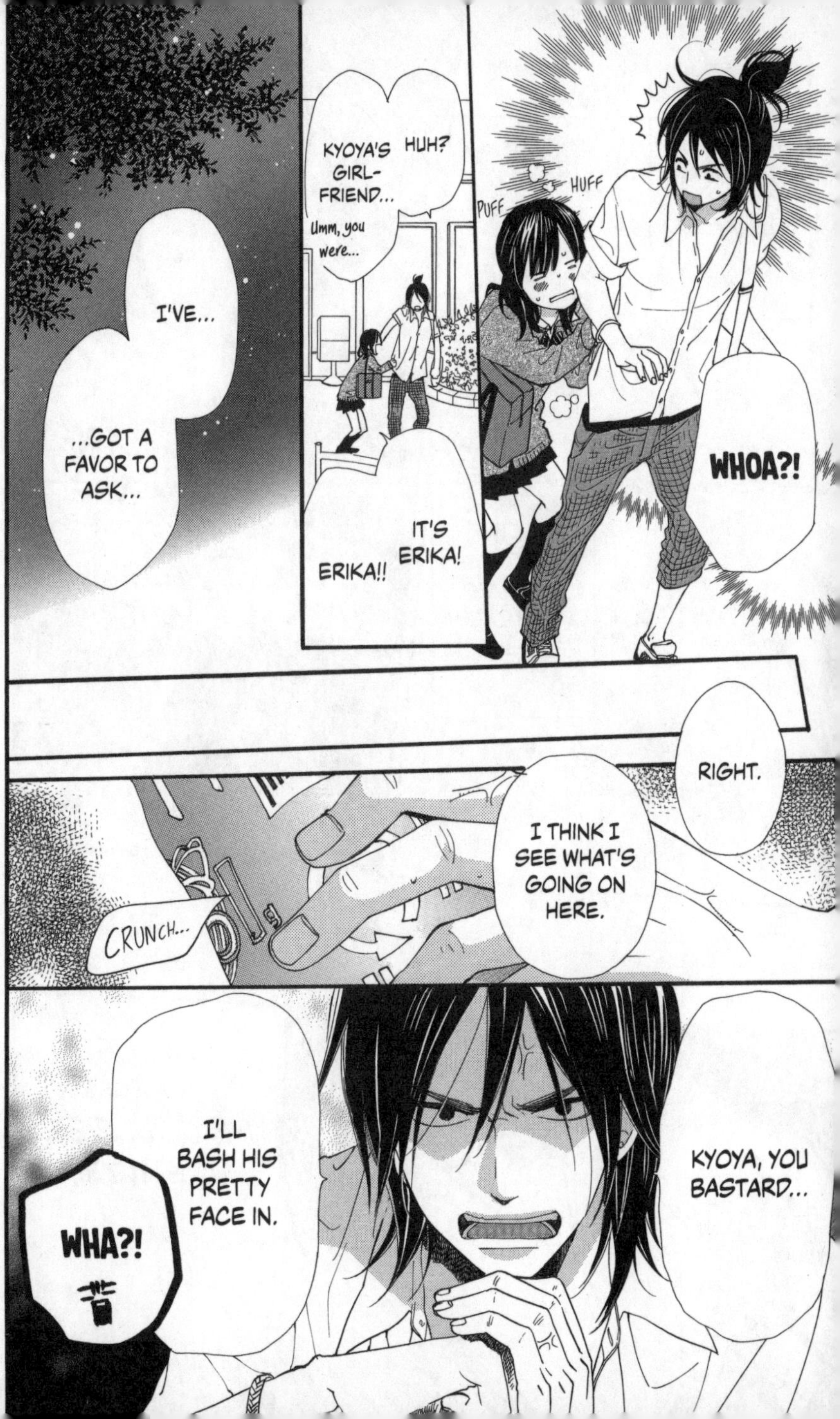
WHOA?!
HUFF
PUFF
HUH?
KYOYA'S GIRL-FRIEND...
Umm, you were...
IT'S ERIKA!
ERIKA!!
I'VE...
...GOT A FAVOR TO ASK...
RIGHT.
I THINK I SEE WHAT'S GOING ON HERE.
CRUNCH...
KYOYA, YOU BASTARD...
I'LL BASH HIS PRETTY FACE IN.
WHA?!

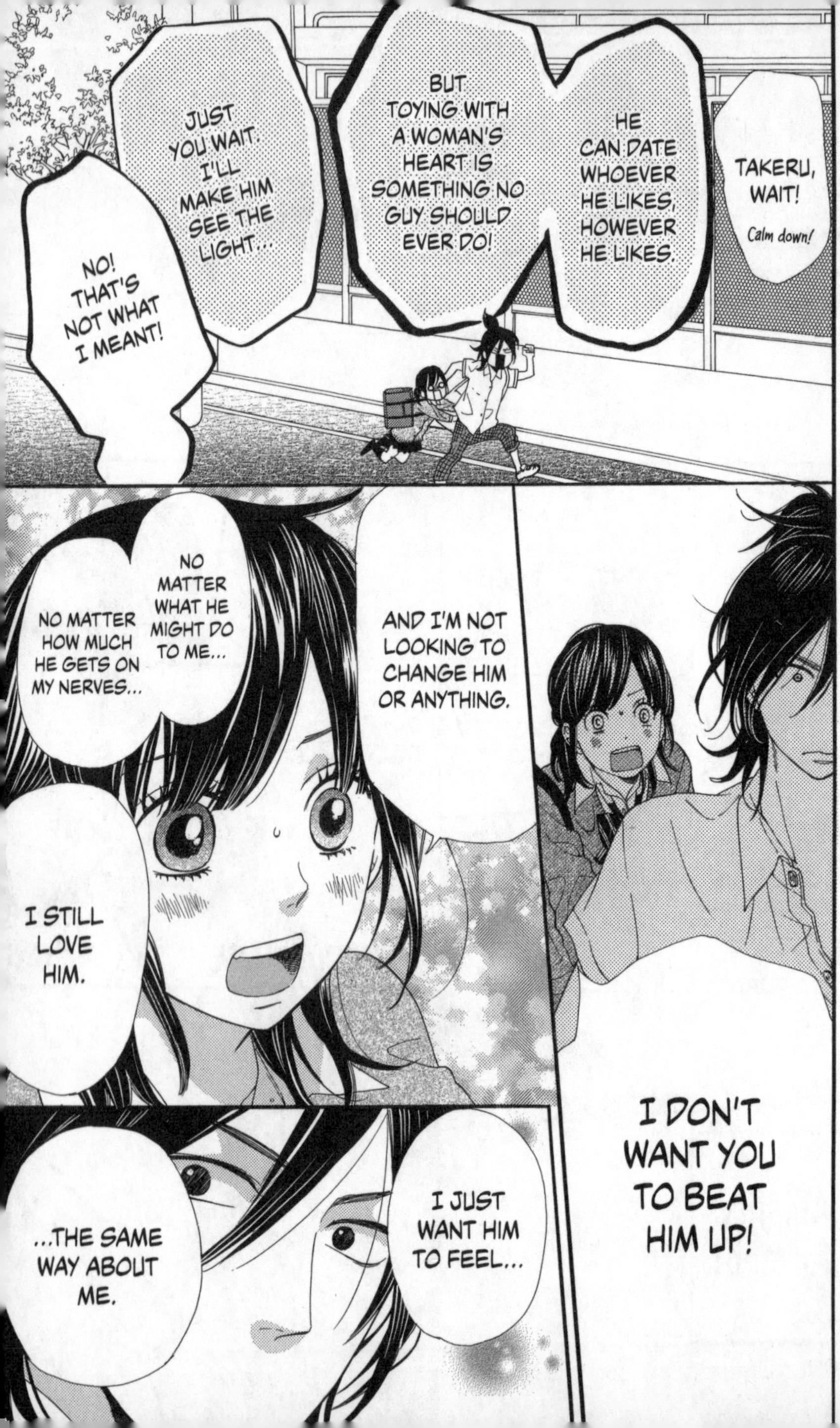
TAKERU, WAIT!
Calm down!
HE CAN DATE WHOEVER HE LIKES, HOWEVER HE LIKES.
BUT TOYING WITH A WOMAN'S HEART IS SOMETHING NO GUY SHOULD EVER DO!
JUST YOU WAIT. I'LL MAKE HIM SEE THE LIGHT...
NO! THAT'S NOT WHAT I MEANT!
I DON'T WANT YOU TO BEAT HIM UP!
AND I'M NOT LOOKING TO CHANGE HIM OR ANYTHING.
NO MATTER WHAT HE MIGHT DO TO ME...
NO MATTER HOW MUCH HE GETS ON MY NERVES...
I STILL LOVE HIM.
I JUST WANT HIM TO FEEL...
...THE SAME WAY ABOUT ME.

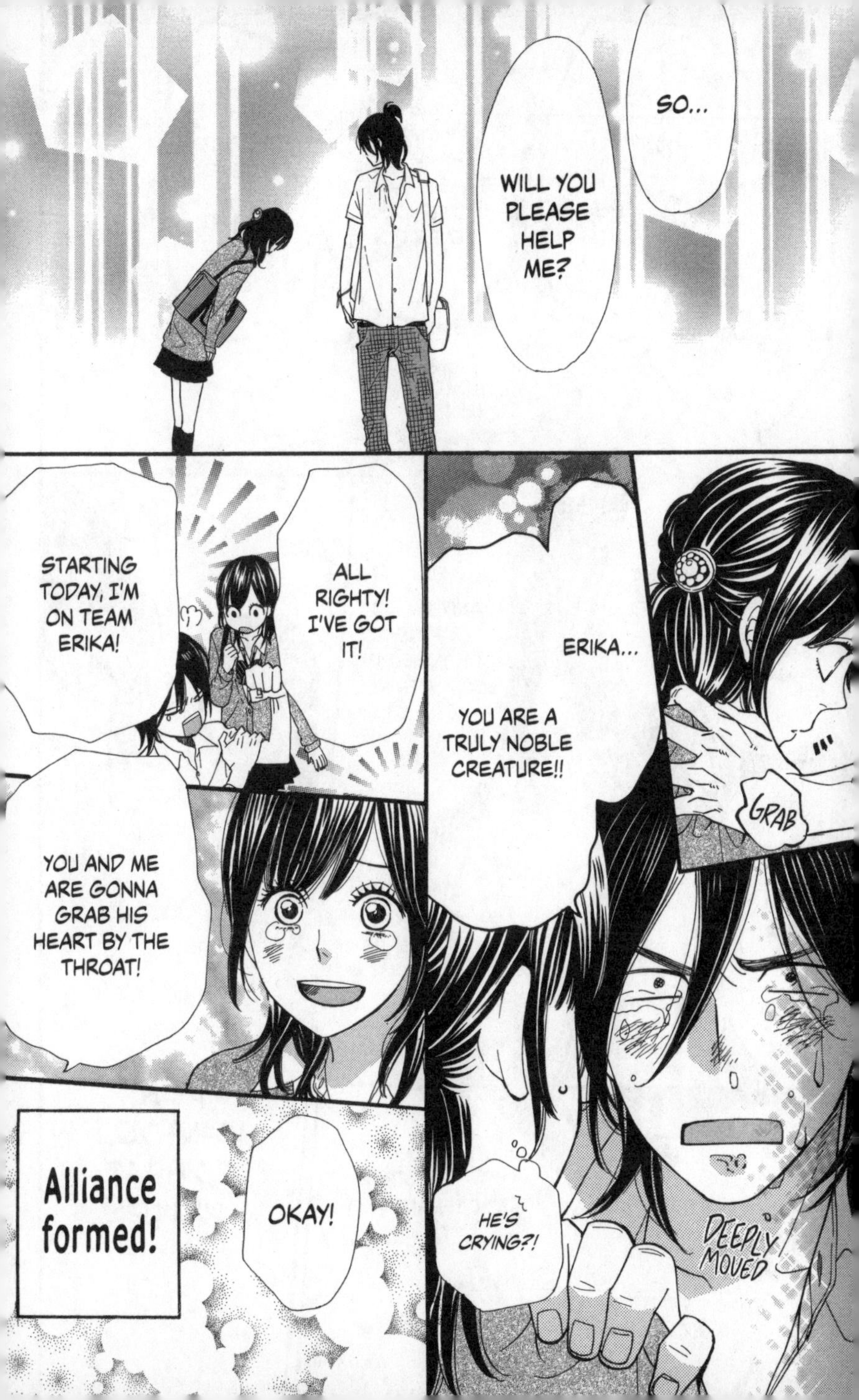
SO...
WILL YOU PLEASE HELP ME?
GRAB
ERIKA...
YOU ARE A TRULY NOBLE CREATURE!!
DEEPLY MOVED
HE'S CRYING?!
ALL RIGHTY! I'VE GOT IT!
STARTING TODAY, I'M ON TEAM ERIKA!
YOU AND ME ARE GONNA GRAB HIS HEART BY THE THROAT!
OKAY!
Alliance formed!

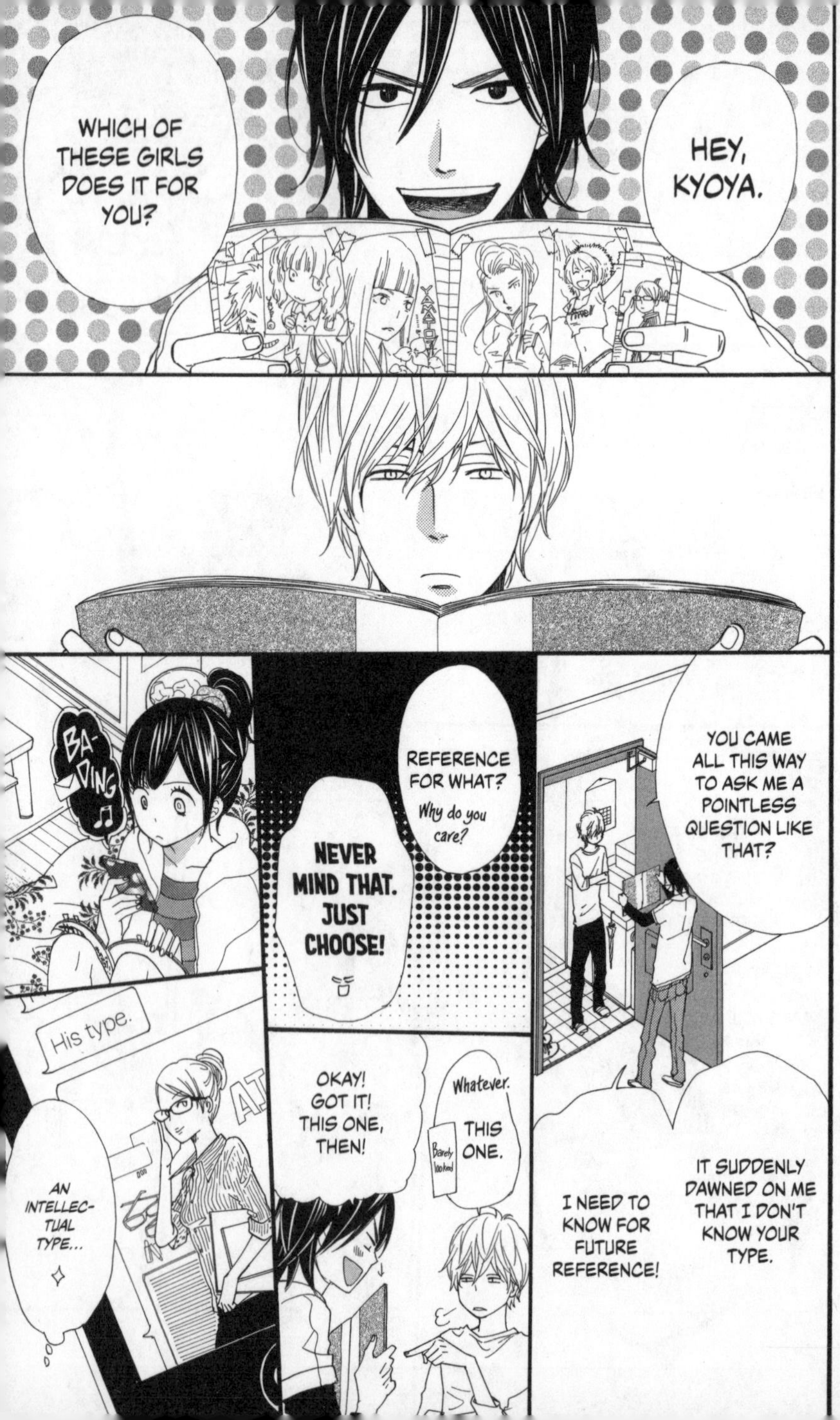
HEY, KYOYA.
WHICH OF THESE GIRLS DOES IT FOR YOU?
YOU CAME ALL THIS WAY TO ASK ME A POINTLESS QUESTION LIKE THAT?
IT SUDDENLY DAWNED ON ME THAT I DON'T KNOW YOUR TYPE.
I NEED TO KNOW FOR FUTURE REFERENCE!
REFERENCE FOR WHAT? Why do you care?
NEVER MIND THAT. JUST CHOOSE!
BA-DING♫
Whatever. THIS ONE.
Barely looked
OKAY! GOT IT! THIS ONE, THEN!
His type.
AN INTELLEC-TUAL TYPE...

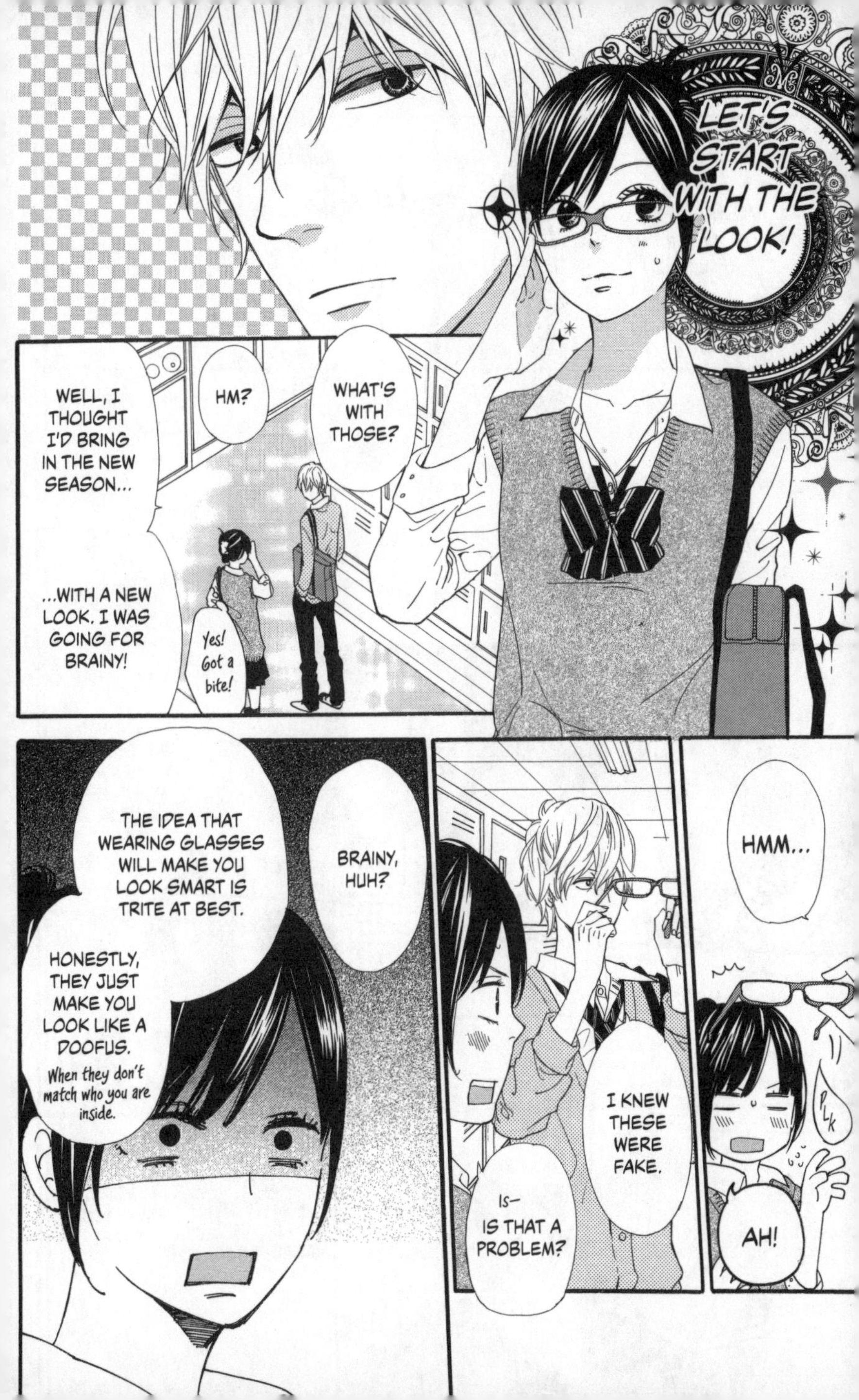
LET'S START WITH THE LOOK!
WHAT'S WITH THOSE?
HM?
WELL, I THOUGHT I'D BRING IN THE NEW SEASON...
...WITH A NEW LOOK. I WAS GOING FOR BRAINY!
Yes! Got a bite!
HMM...
PLK
AH!
I KNEW THESE WERE FAKE.
IS— IS THAT A PROBLEM?
BRAINY, HUH?
THE IDEA THAT WEARING GLASSES WILL MAKE YOU LOOK SMART IS TRITE AT BEST.
HONESTLY, THEY JUST MAKE YOU LOOK LIKE A DOOFUS.
When they don't match who you are inside.

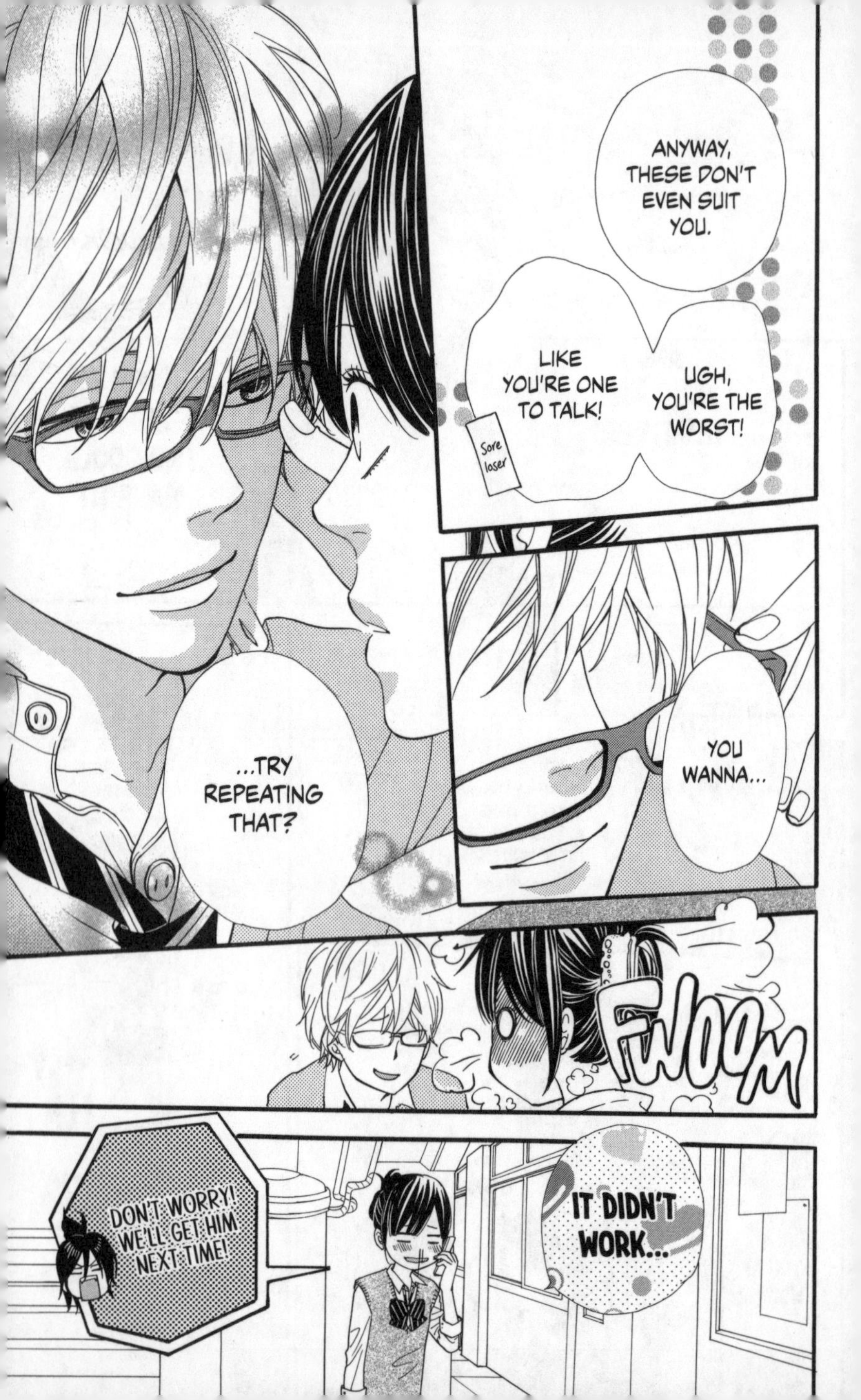
ANYWAY, THESE DON'T EVEN SUIT YOU.
UGH, YOU'RE THE WORST!
LIKE YOU'RE ONE TO TALK!
Sore loser
YOU WANNA...
...TRY REPEATING THAT?
FWOOM
IT DIDN'T WORK...
DON'T WORRY! WE'LL GET HIM NEXT TIME!

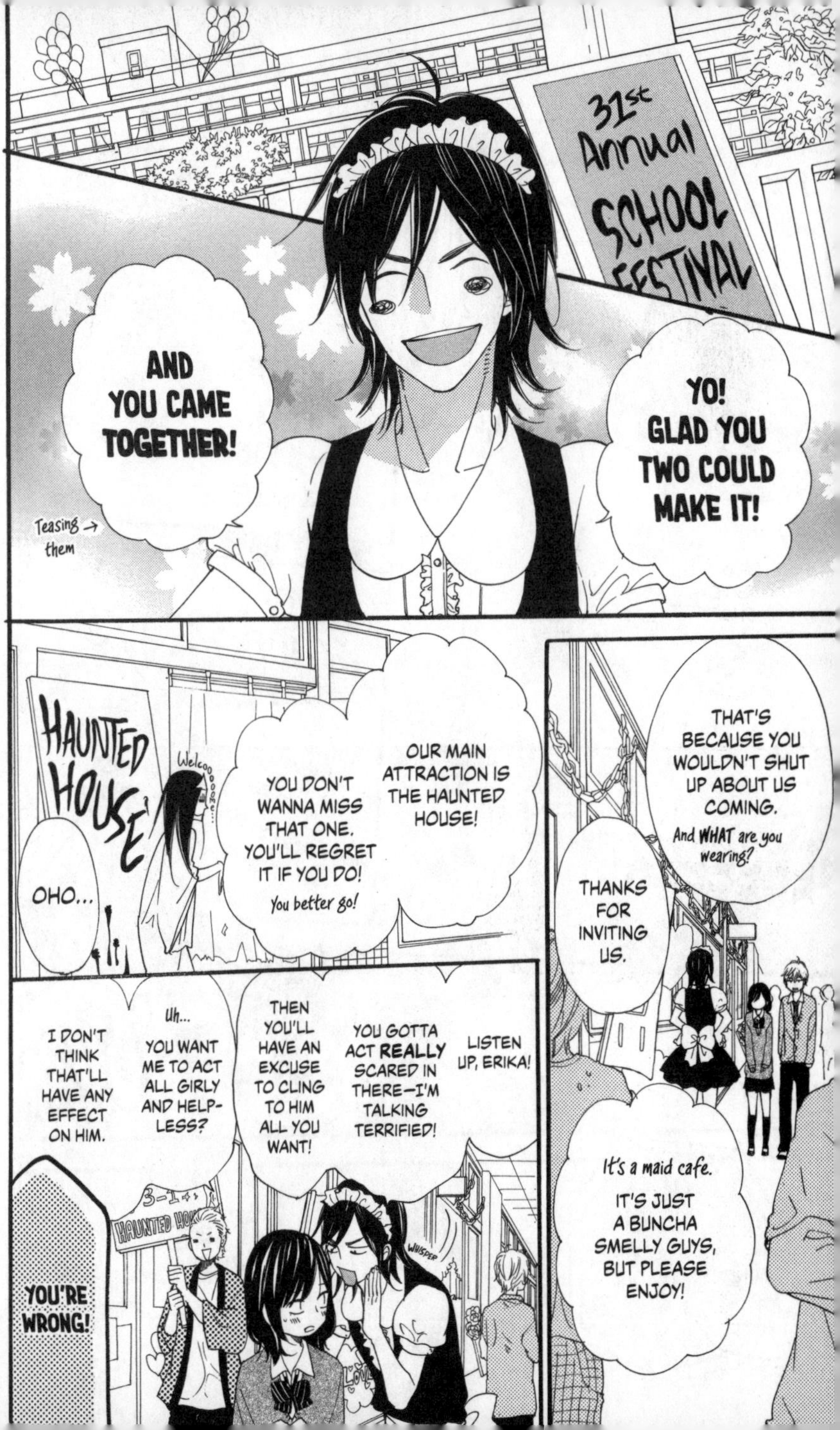
31st Annual SCHOOL FESTIVAL
YO! GLAD YOU TWO COULD MAKE IT!
AND YOU CAME TOGETHER!
Teasing → them
THAT'S BECAUSE YOU WOULDN'T SHUT UP ABOUT US COMING.
And WHAT are you wearing?
THANKS FOR INVITING US.
It's a maid cafe.
IT'S JUST A BUNCHA SMELLY GUYS, BUT PLEASE ENJOY!
OUR MAIN ATTRACTION IS THE HAUNTED HOUSE!
YOU DON'T WANNA MISS THAT ONE. YOU'LL REGRET IT IF YOU DO!
You better go!
HAUNTED HOUSE
Welcoooooome...
OHO...
LISTEN UP, ERIKA!
YOU GOTTA ACT REALLY SCARED IN THERE—I'M TALKING TERRIFIED!
THEN YOU'LL HAVE AN EXCUSE TO CLING TO HIM ALL YOU WANT!
Uh...
YOU WANT ME TO ACT ALL GIRLY AND HELP-LESS?
I DON'T THINK THAT'LL HAVE ANY EFFECT ON HIM.
WHISPER
3-1
HAUNTED HO
YOU'RE WRONG!

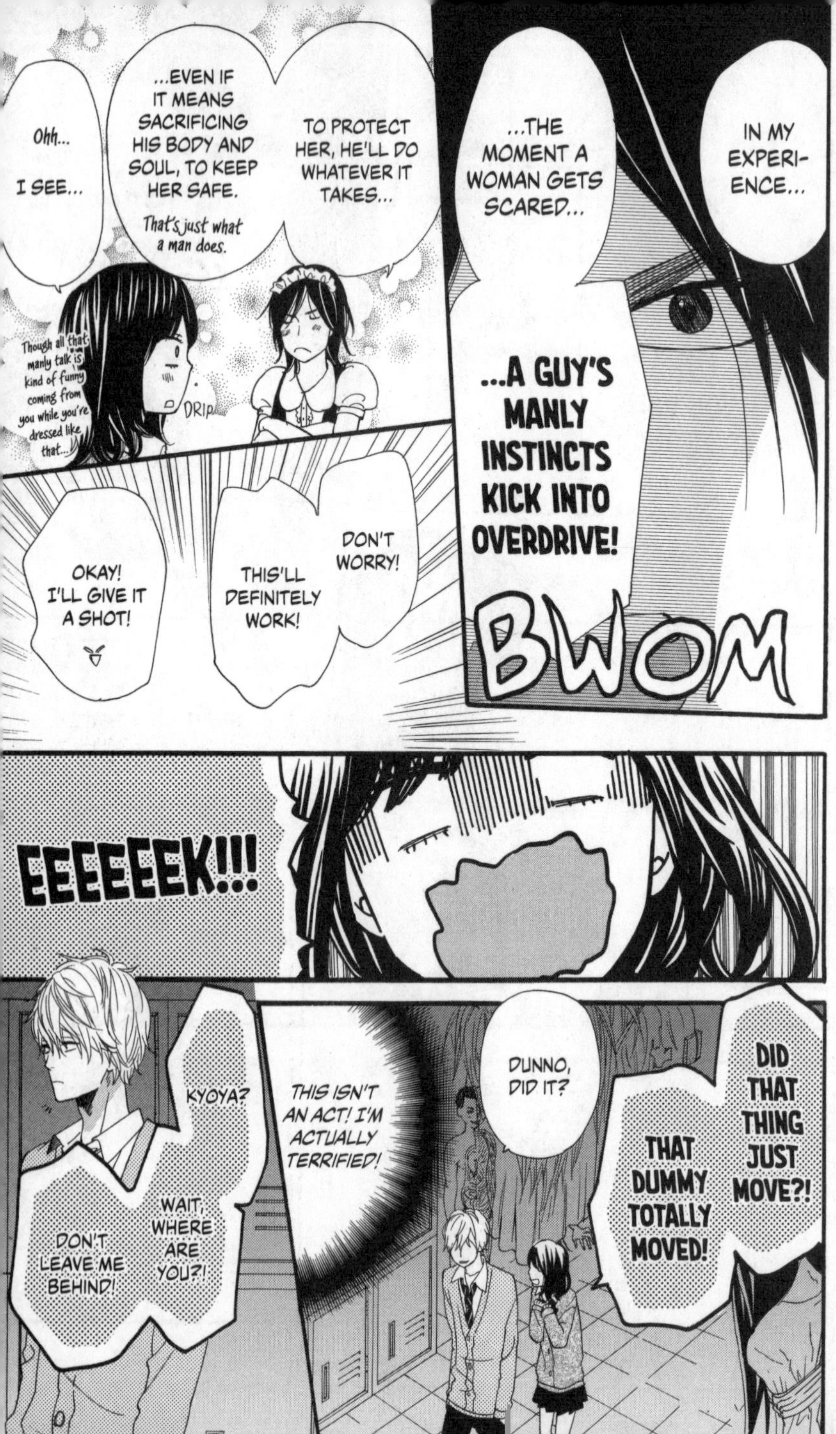
IN MY EXPERIENCE...
...THE MOMENT A WOMAN GETS SCARED...
...A GUY'S MANLY INSTINCTS KICK INTO OVERDRIVE!
BWOM
TO PROTECT HER, HE'LL DO WHATEVER IT TAKES...
...EVEN IF IT MEANS SACRIFICING HIS BODY AND SOUL, TO KEEP HER SAFE.
That's just what a man does.
Ohh... I SEE...
Though all that manly talk is kind of funny coming from you while you're dressed like that...
DRIP
DON'T WORRY!
THIS'LL DEFINITELY WORK!
OKAY! I'LL GIVE IT A SHOT!
EEEEEEK!!!
DID THAT THING JUST MOVE?!
THAT DUMMY TOTALLY MOVED!
DUNNO, DID IT?
THIS ISN'T AN ACT! I'M ACTUALLY TERRIFIED!
KYOYA?
WAIT, WHERE ARE YOU?!
DON'T LEAVE ME BEHIND!

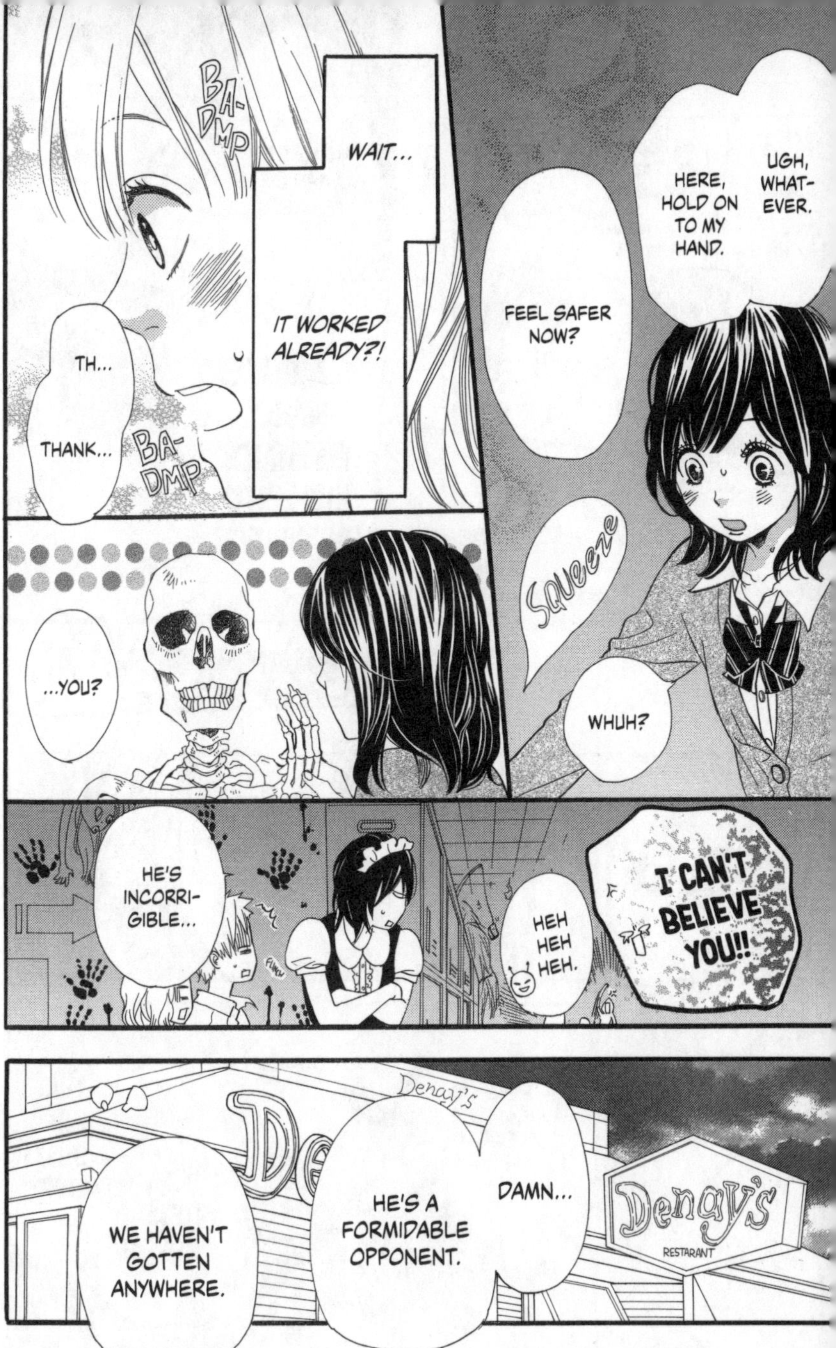
UGH, WHAT-EVER.
HERE, HOLD ON TO MY HAND.
FEEL SAFER NOW?
Squeeze
WHUH?
BA-DMP
WAIT...
IT WORKED ALREADY?!
TH...
THANK...
BA-DMP
...YOU?
I CAN'T BELIEVE YOU!!
HEH HEH HEH.
HE'S INCORRIGIBLE...
Denay's
RESTARANT
DAMN...
HE'S A FORMIDABLE OPPONENT.
WE HAVEN'T GOTTEN ANYWHERE.

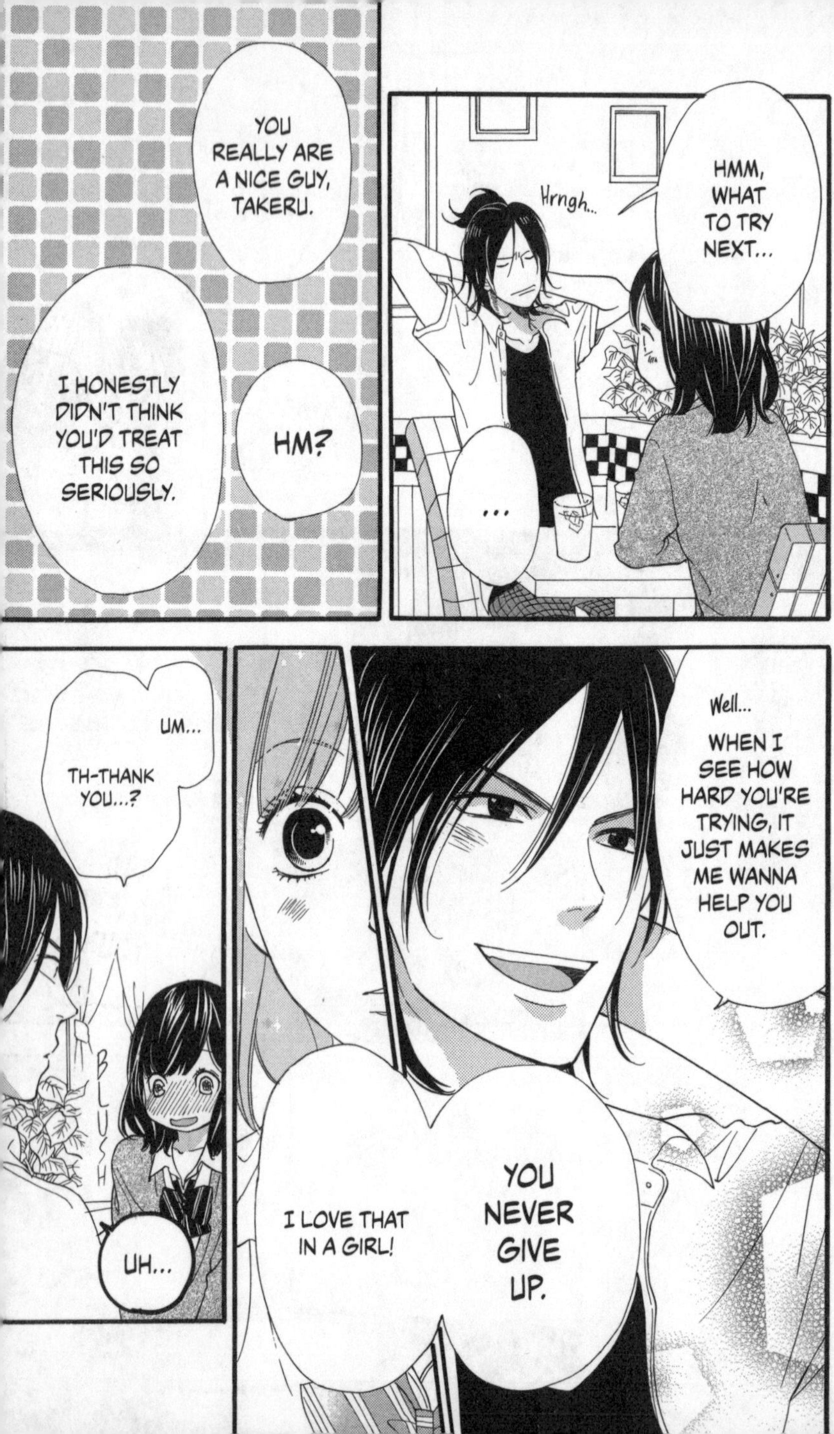
HMM, WHAT TO TRY NEXT...
Hrngh...
...
YOU REALLY ARE A NICE GUY, TAKERU.
HM?
I HONESTLY DIDN'T THINK YOU'D TREAT THIS SO SERIOUSLY.
Well...
WHEN I SEE HOW HARD YOU'RE TRYING, IT JUST MAKES ME WANNA HELP YOU OUT.
YOU NEVER GIVE UP.
I LOVE THAT IN A GIRL!
UM...
TH-THANK YOU...?
BLUSH
UH...

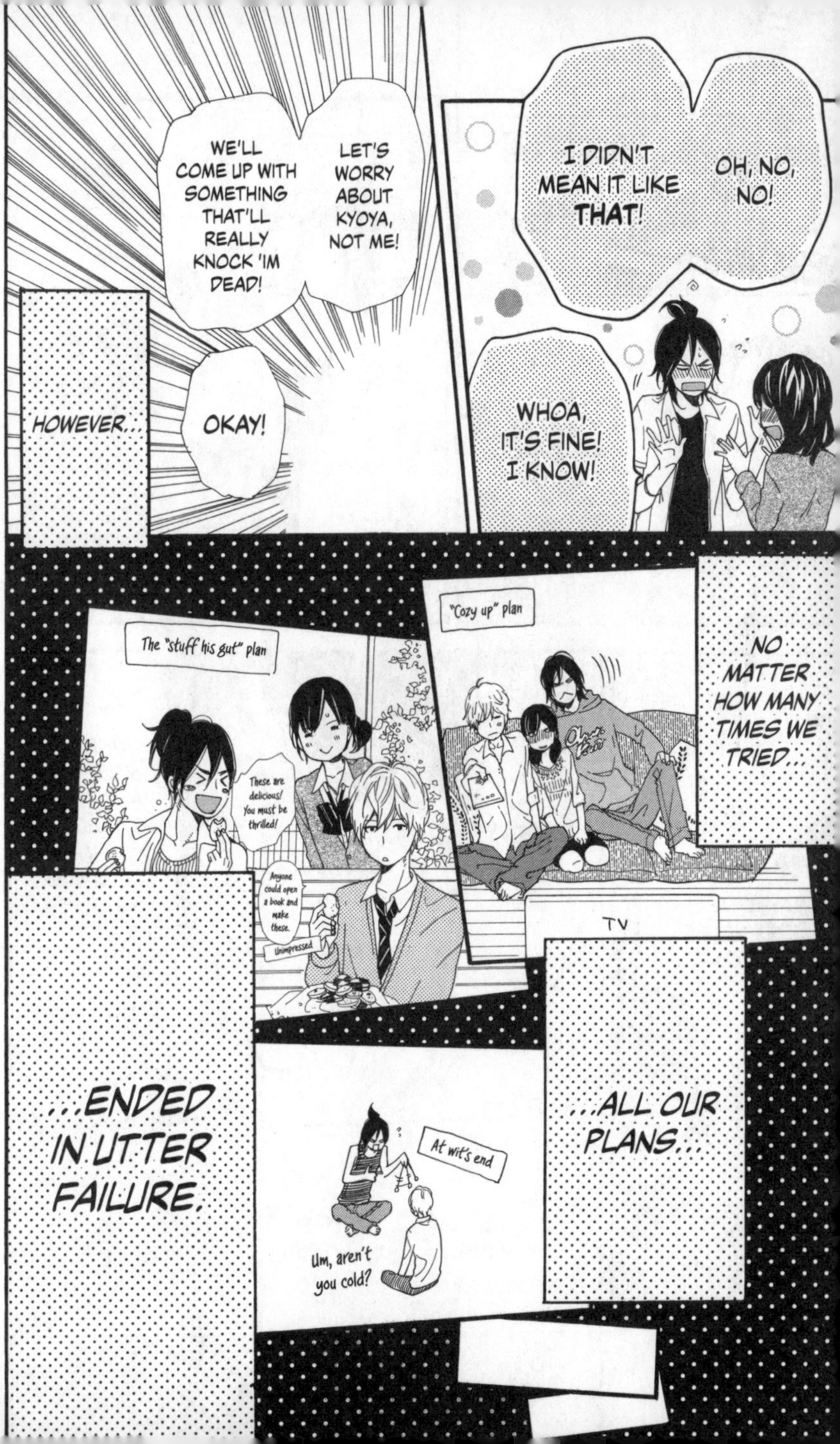
OH, NO, NO!
I DIDN'T MEAN IT LIKE THAT!
WHOA, IT'S FINE! I KNOW!
LET'S WORRY ABOUT KYOYA, NOT ME!
WE'LL COME UP WITH SOMETHING THAT'LL REALLY KNOCK 'IM DEAD!
OKAY!
HOWEVER...
NO MATTER HOW MANY TIMES WE TRIED...
"Cozy up" plan
TV
The "stuff his gut" plan
These are delicious! You must be thrilled!
Anyone could open a book and make these.
Unimpressed
...ALL OUR PLANS...
At wit's end
Um, aren't you cold?
...ENDED IN UTTER FAILURE.

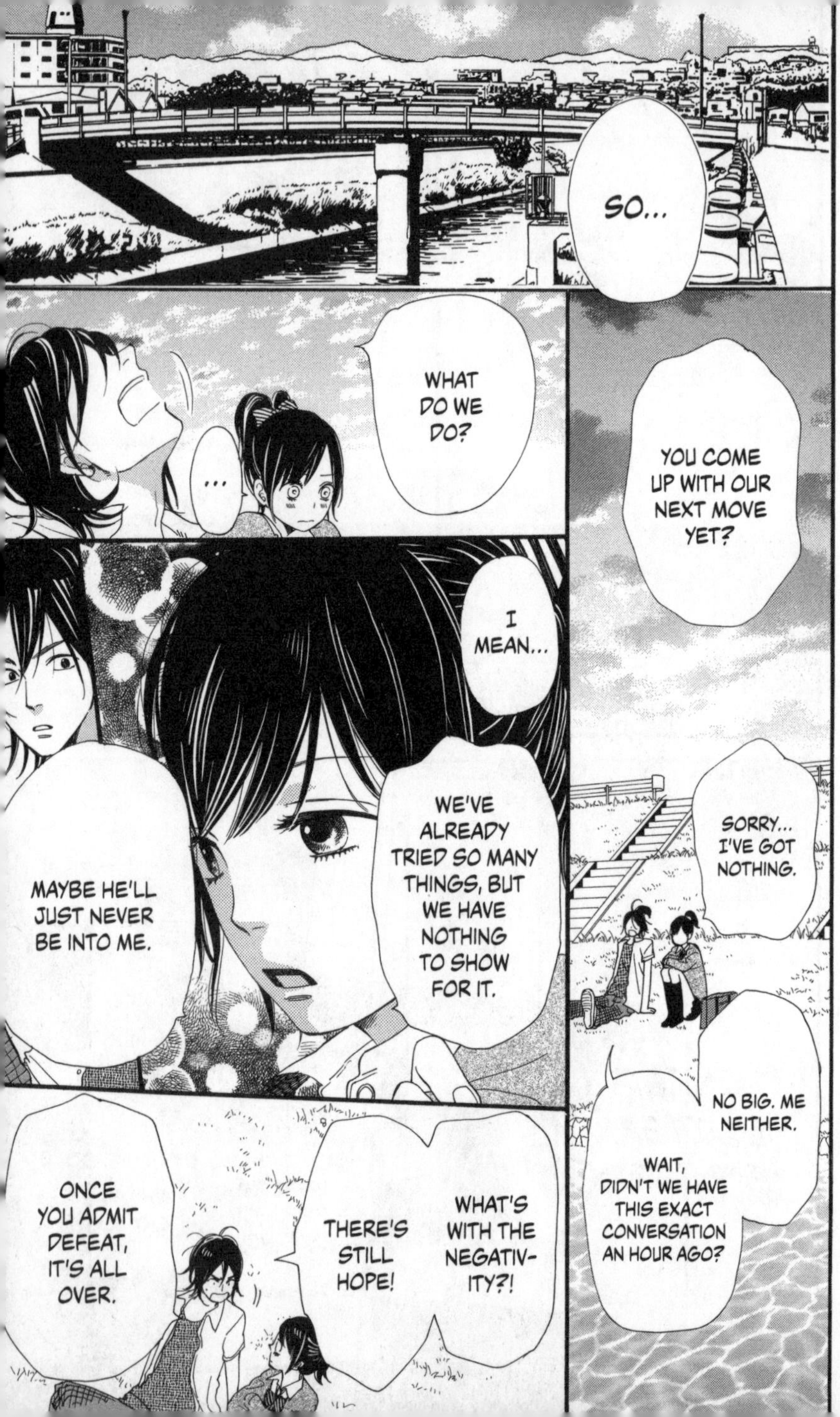
SO...
YOU COME UP WITH OUR NEXT MOVE YET?
SORRY... I'VE GOT NOTHING.
NO BIG. ME NEITHER.
WAIT, DIDN'T WE HAVE THIS EXACT CONVERSATION AN HOUR AGO?
WHAT DO WE DO?
...
I MEAN...
WE'VE ALREADY TRIED SO MANY THINGS, BUT WE HAVE NOTHING TO SHOW FOR IT.
MAYBE HE'LL JUST NEVER BE INTO ME.
WHAT'S WITH THE NEGATIV-ITY?!
THERE'S STILL HOPE!
ONCE YOU ADMIT DEFEAT, IT'S ALL OVER.

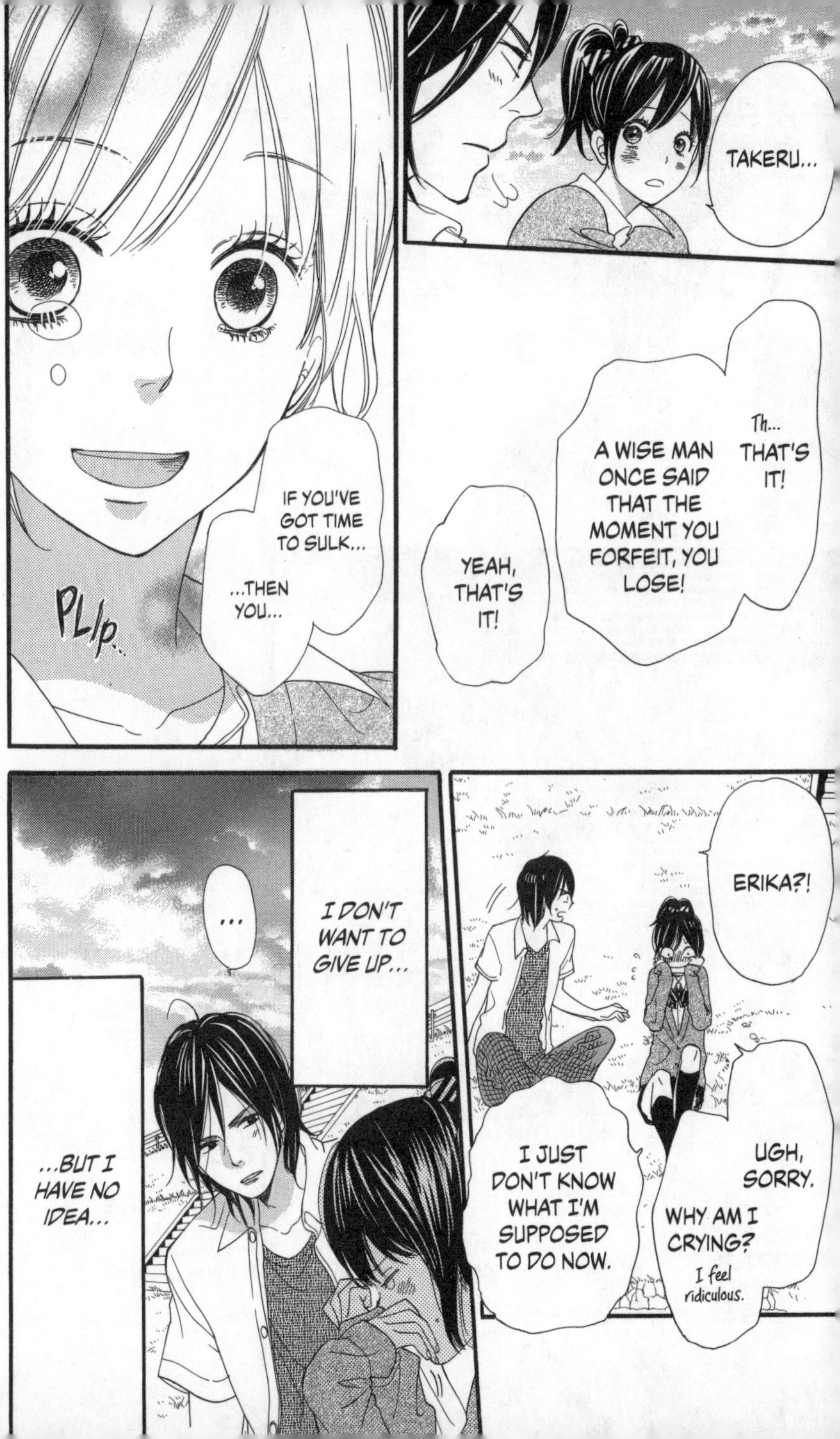
TAKERU...
Th... THAT'S IT!
A WISE MAN ONCE SAID THAT THE MOMENT YOU FORFEIT, YOU LOSE!
YEAH, THAT'S IT!
IF YOU'VE GOT TIME TO SULK...
...THEN YOU...
PLIP...
ERIKA?!
UGH, SORRY.
WHY AM I CRYING?
I feel ridiculous.
I JUST DON'T KNOW WHAT I'M SUPPOSED TO DO NOW.
I DON'T WANT TO GIVE UP...
...
...BUT I HAVE NO IDEA...

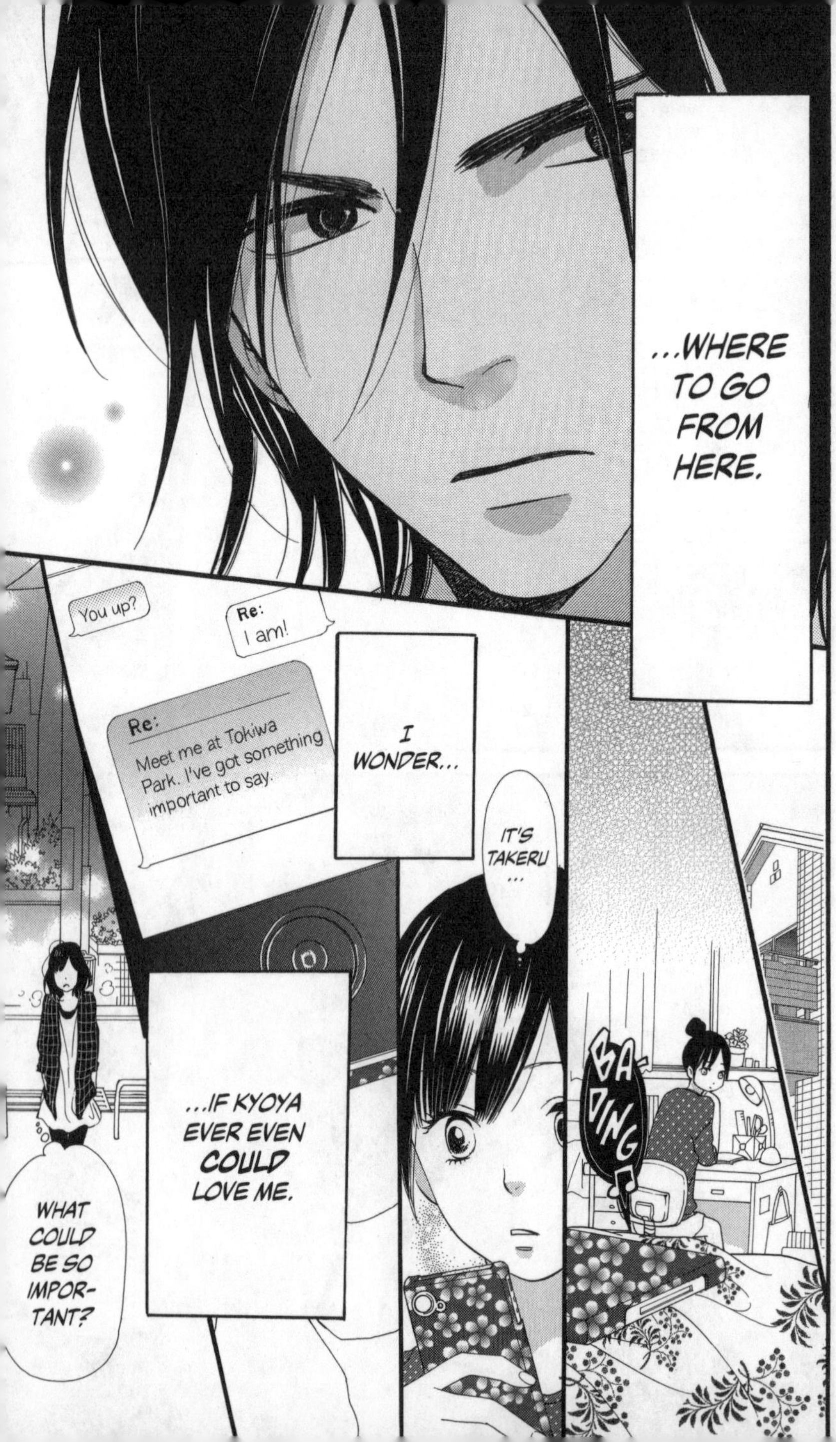
...WHERE TO GO FROM HERE.
BA-DING!
IT'S TAKERU...
I WONDER...
You up?
Re: I am!
Re: Meet me at Tokiwa Park. I've got something important to say.
...IF KYOYA EVER EVEN COULD LOVE ME.
WHAT COULD BE SO IMPORTANT?

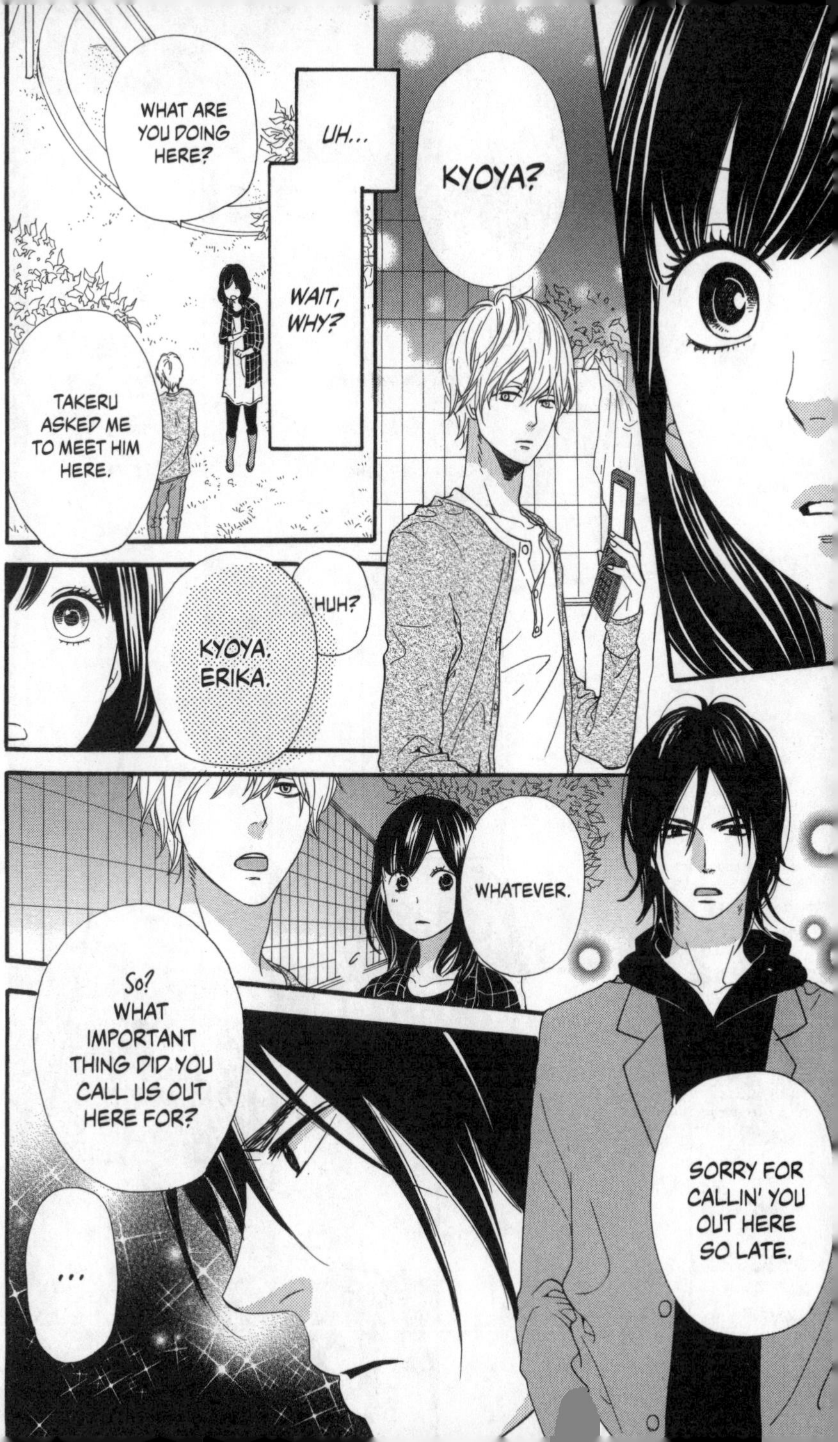
KYOYA?
UH...
WAIT, WHY?
WHAT ARE YOU DOING HERE?
TAKERU ASKED ME TO MEET HIM HERE.
HUH?
KYOYA. ERIKA.
SORRY FOR CALLIN' YOU OUT HERE SO LATE.
WHATEVER.
So? WHAT IMPORTANT THING DID YOU CALL US OUT HERE FOR?
...

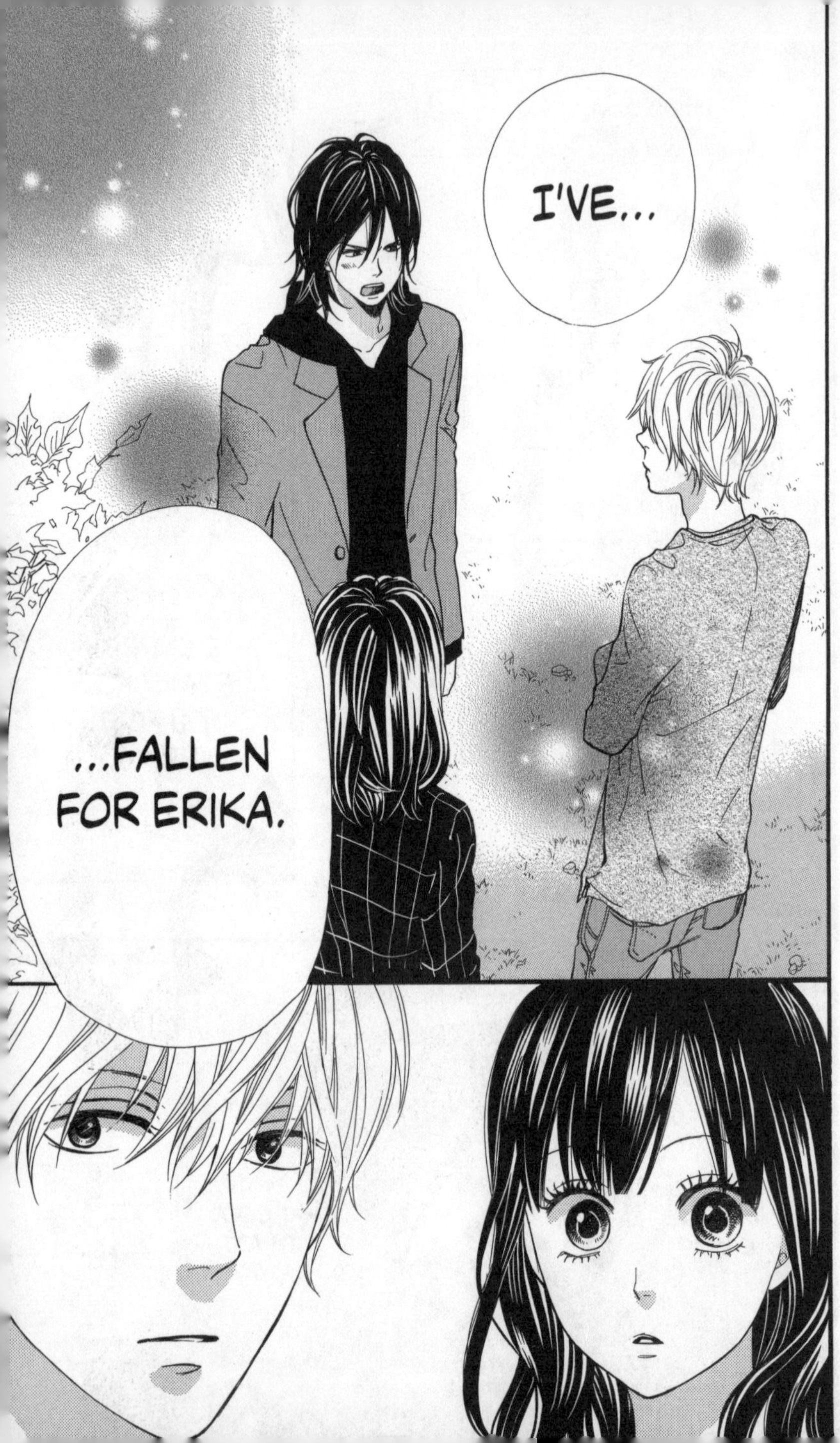
I'VE...
...FALLEN FOR ERIKA.

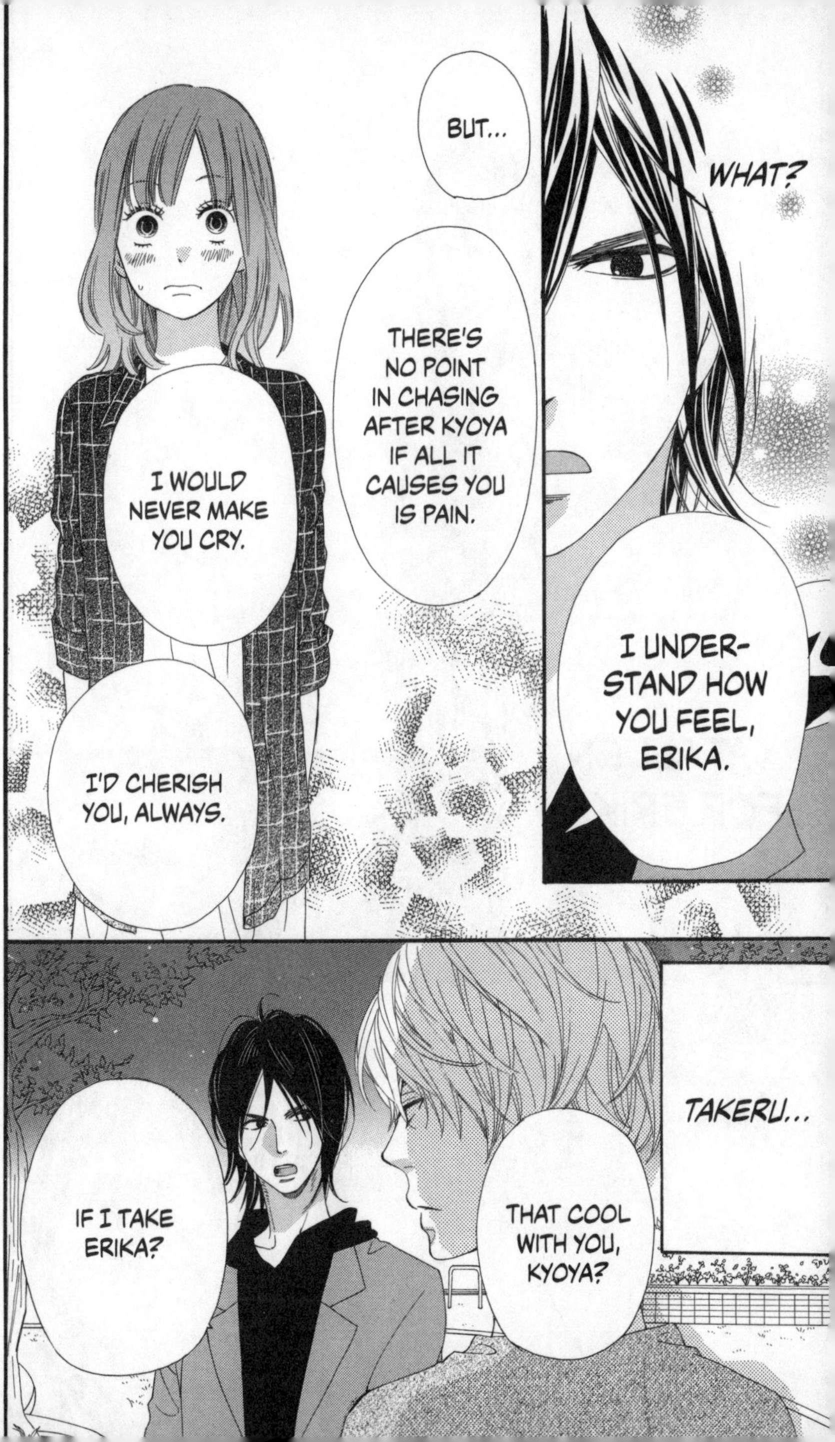
WHAT?
I UNDERSTAND HOW YOU FEEL, ERIKA.
BUT...
THERE'S NO POINT IN CHASING AFTER KYOYA IF ALL IT CAUSES YOU IS PAIN.
I WOULD NEVER MAKE YOU CRY.
I'D CHERISH YOU, ALWAYS.
TAKERU...
THAT COOL WITH YOU, KYOYA?
IF I TAKE ERIKA?

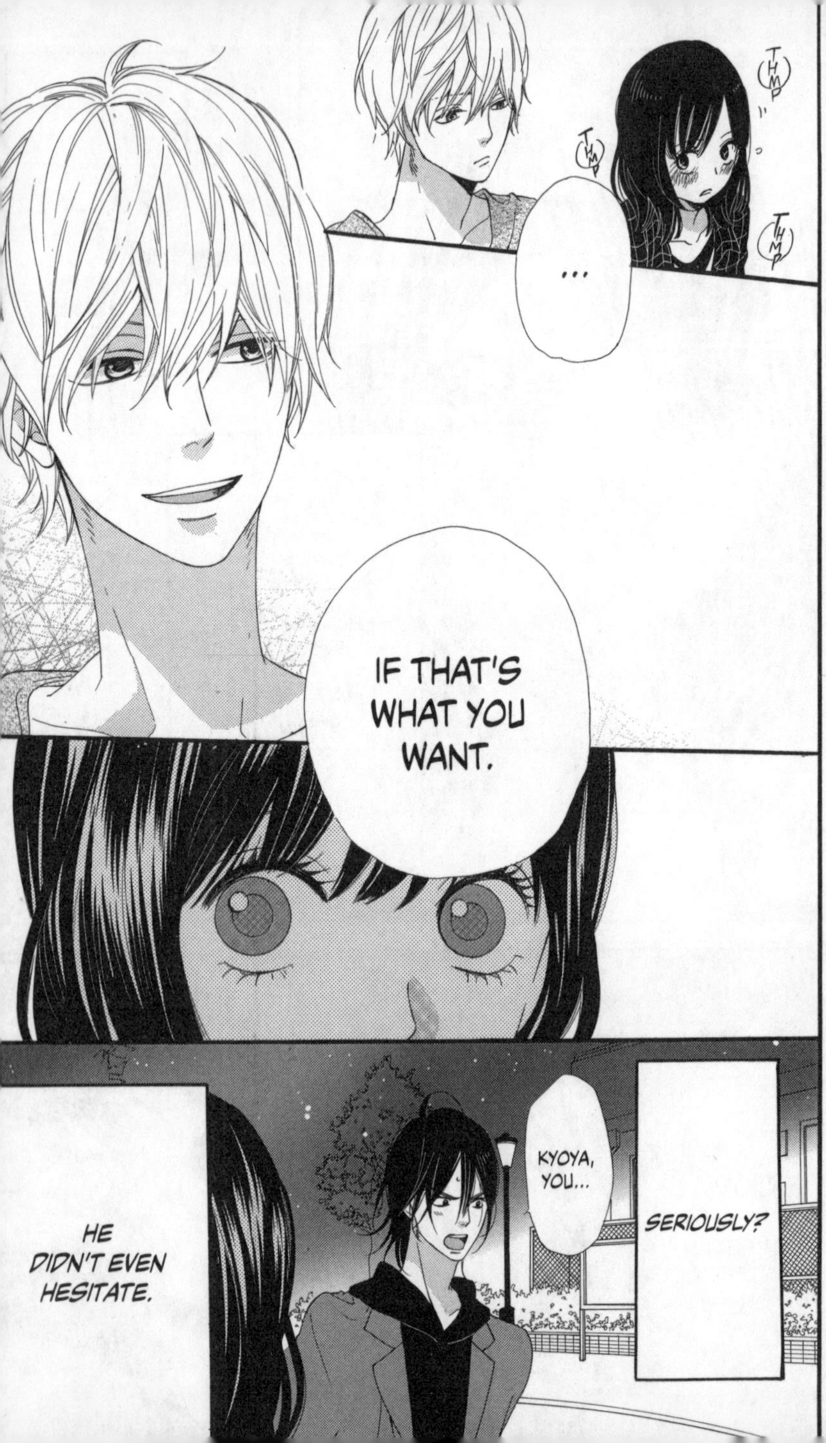
THMP
THMP
...
THMP
IF THAT'S WHAT YOU WANT.
SERIOUSLY?
KYOYA, YOU...
HE DIDN'T EVEN HESITATE.

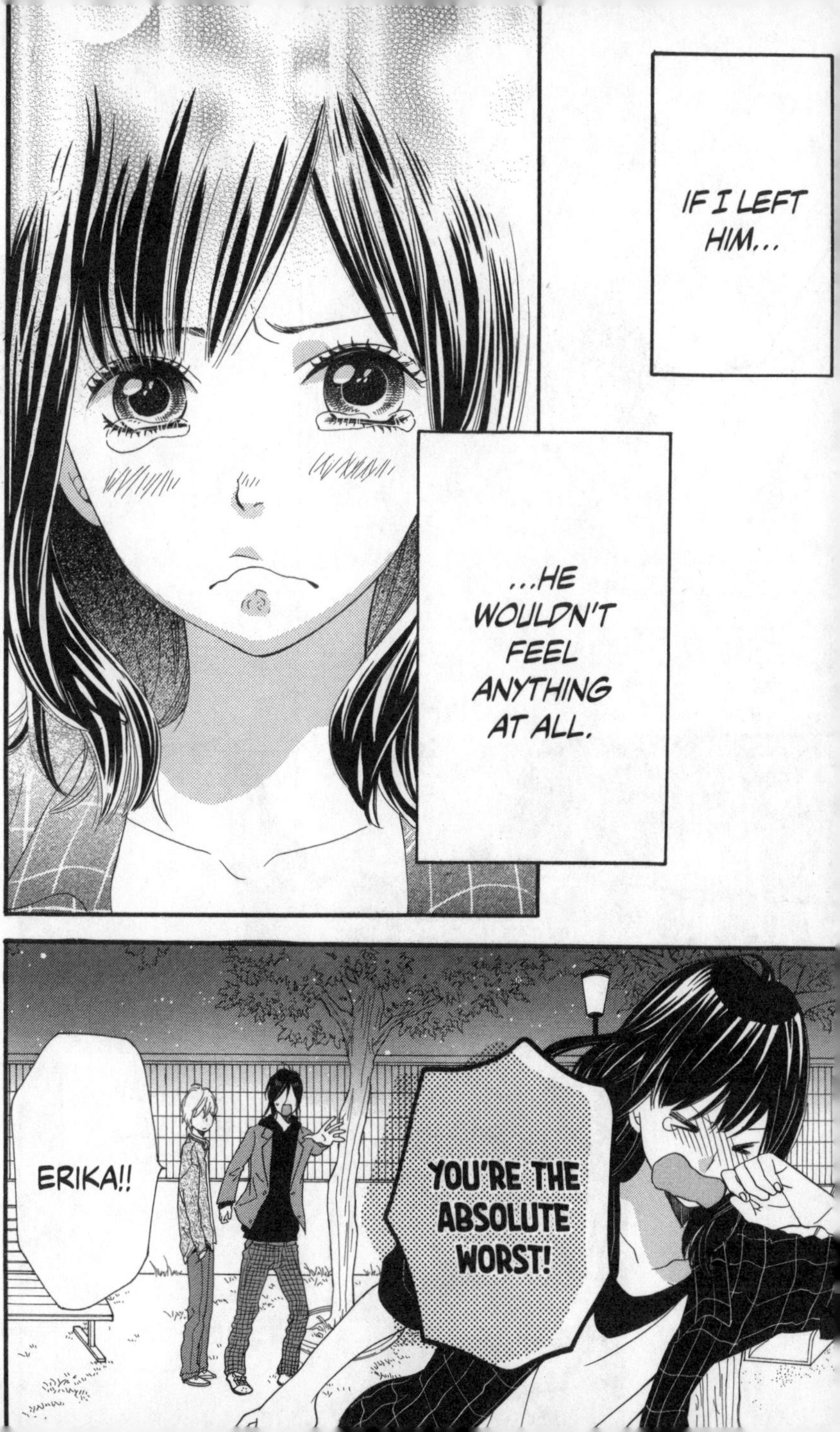
IF I LEFT HIM...
...HE WOULDN'T FEEL ANYTHING AT ALL.
YOU'RE THE ABSOLUTE WORST!
ERIKA!!

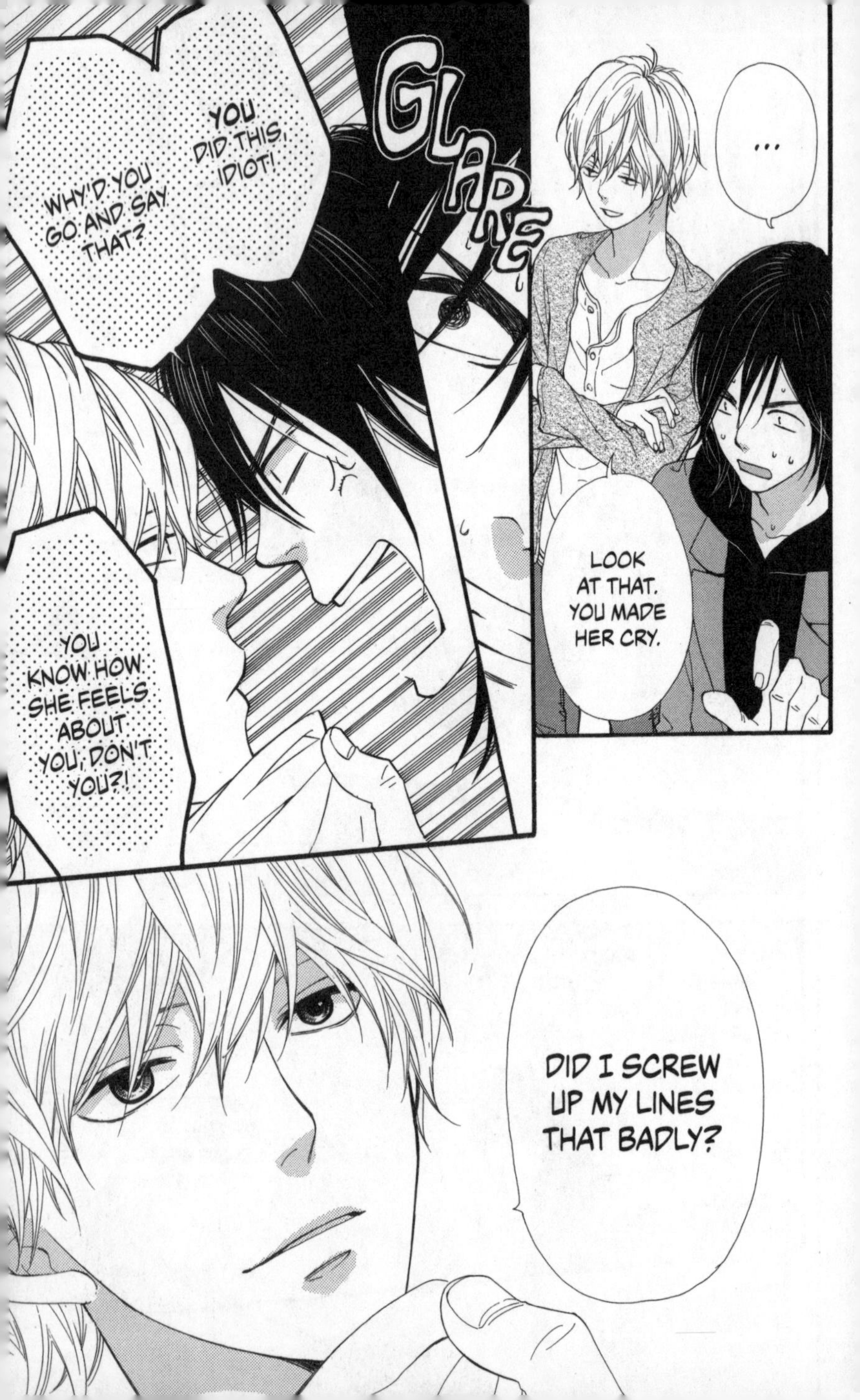
...
LOOK AT THAT. YOU MADE HER CRY.
GLARE
YOU DID THIS, IDIOT!
WHY'D YOU GO AND SAY THAT?
YOU KNOW HOW SHE FEELS ABOUT YOU, DON'T YOU?!
DID I SCREW UP MY LINES THAT BADLY?

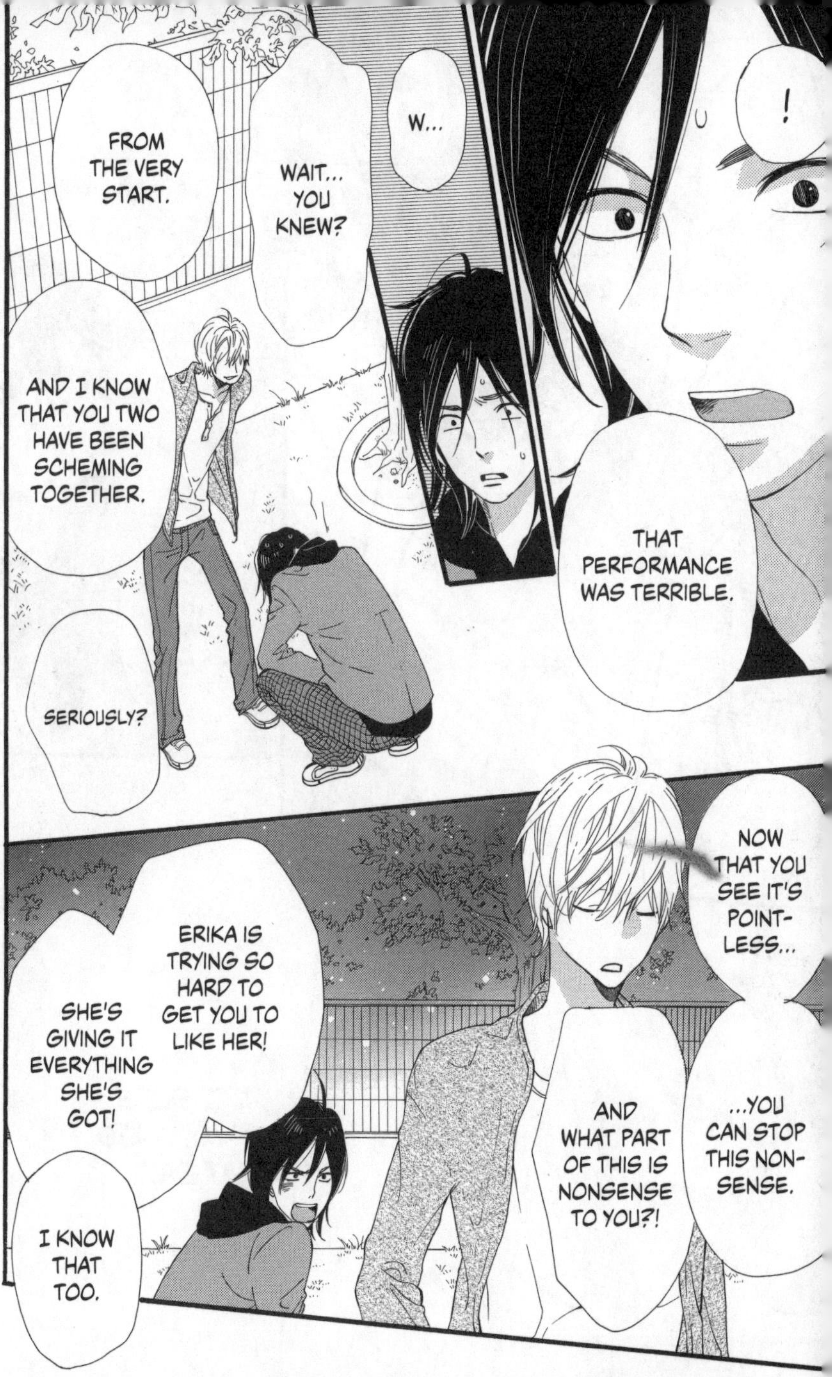
!
THAT PERFORMANCE WAS TERRIBLE.
W...
WAIT... YOU KNEW?
FROM THE VERY START.
AND I KNOW THAT YOU TWO HAVE BEEN SCHEMING TOGETHER.
SERIOUSLY?
NOW THAT YOU SEE IT'S POINT-LESS...
...YOU CAN STOP THIS NON-SENSE.
AND WHAT PART OF THIS IS NONSENSE TO YOU?!
ERIKA IS TRYING SO HARD TO GET YOU TO LIKE HER!
SHE'S GIVING IT EVERYTHING SHE'S GOT!
I KNOW THAT TOO.

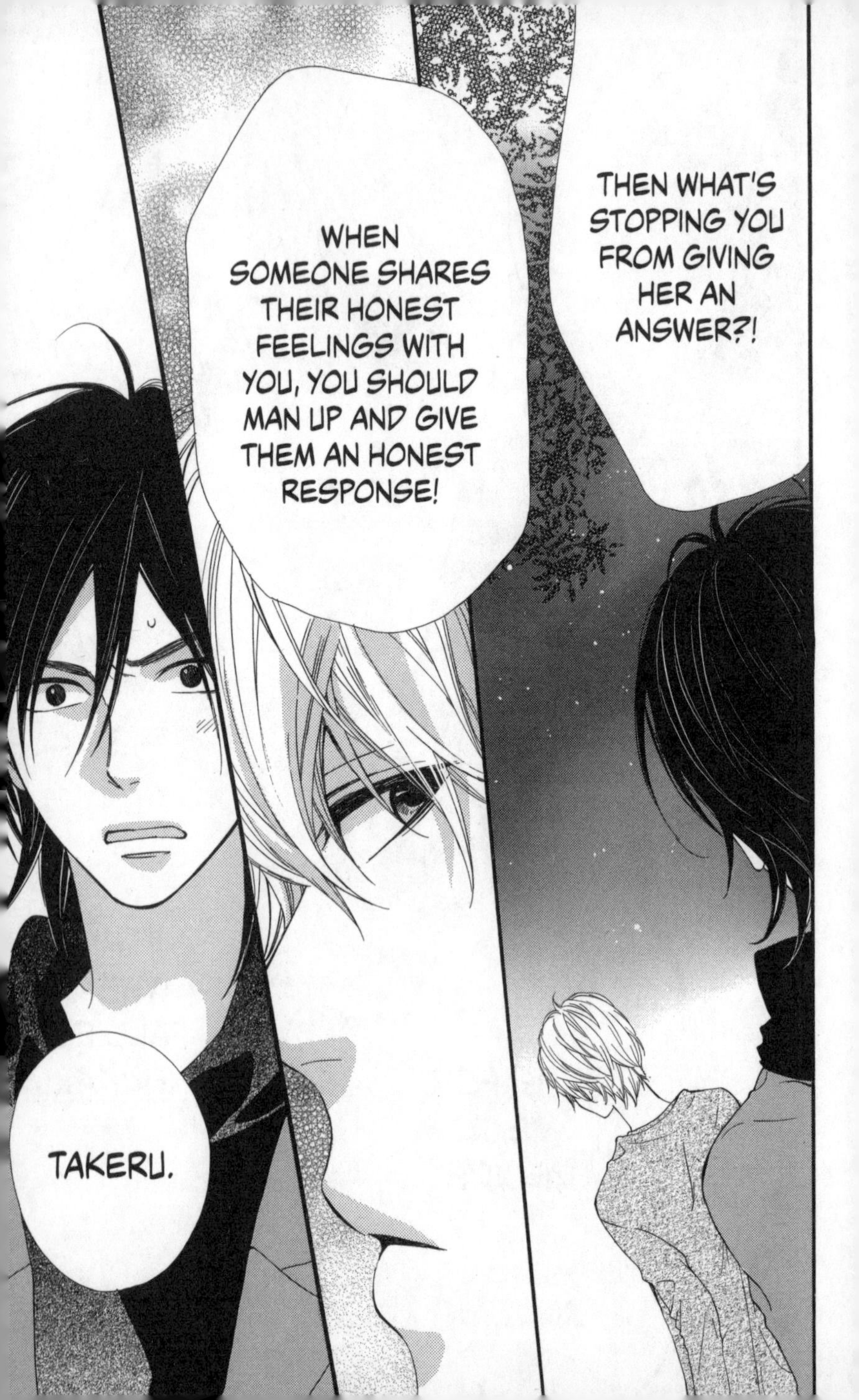
THEN WHAT'S STOPPING YOU FROM GIVING HER AN ANSWER?!
WHEN SOMEONE SHARES THEIR HONEST FEELINGS WITH YOU, YOU SHOULD MAN UP AND GIVE THEM AN HONEST RESPONSE!
TAKERU.

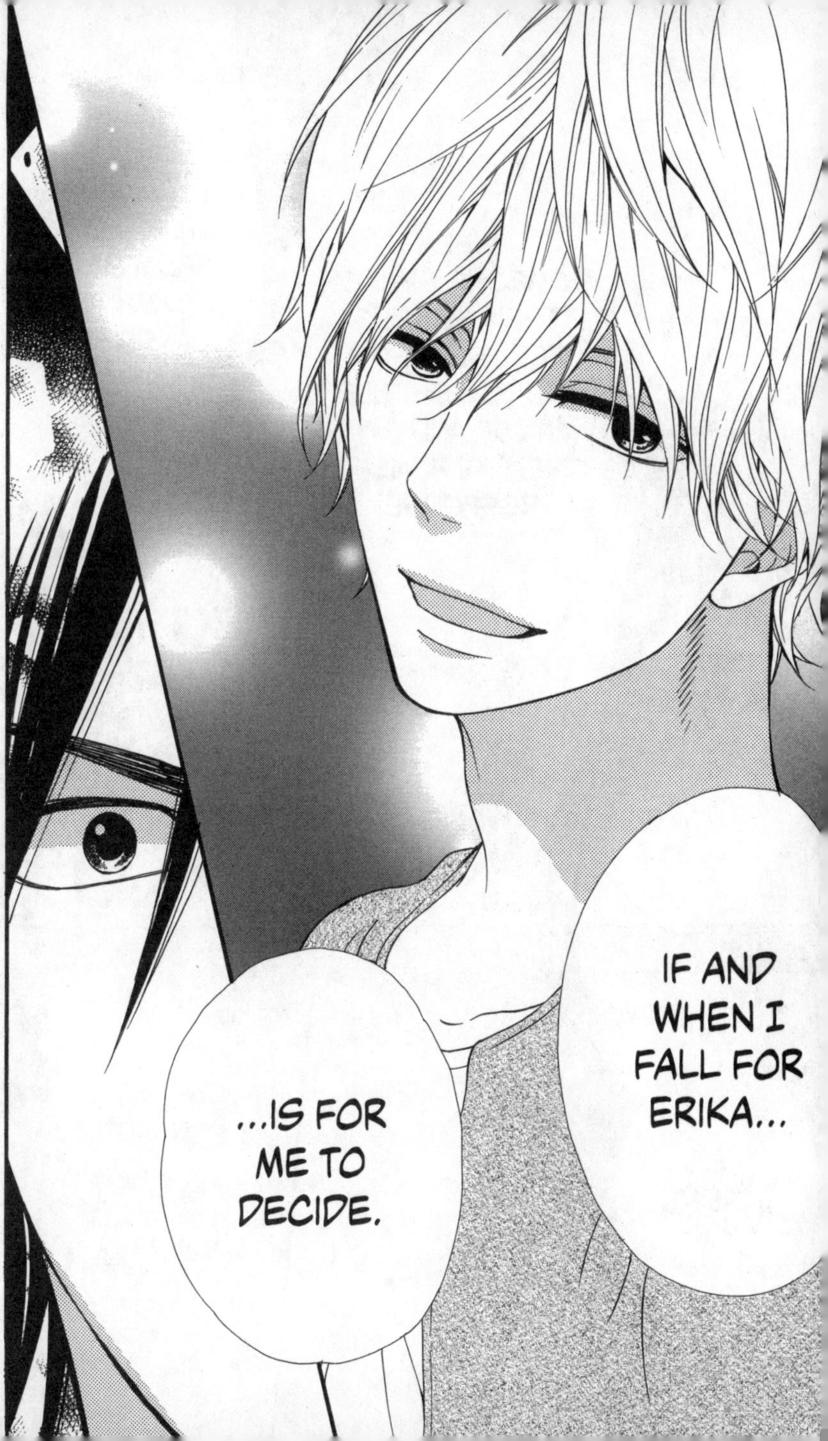
IF AND WHEN I FALL FOR ERIKA...
...IS FOR ME TO DECIDE.

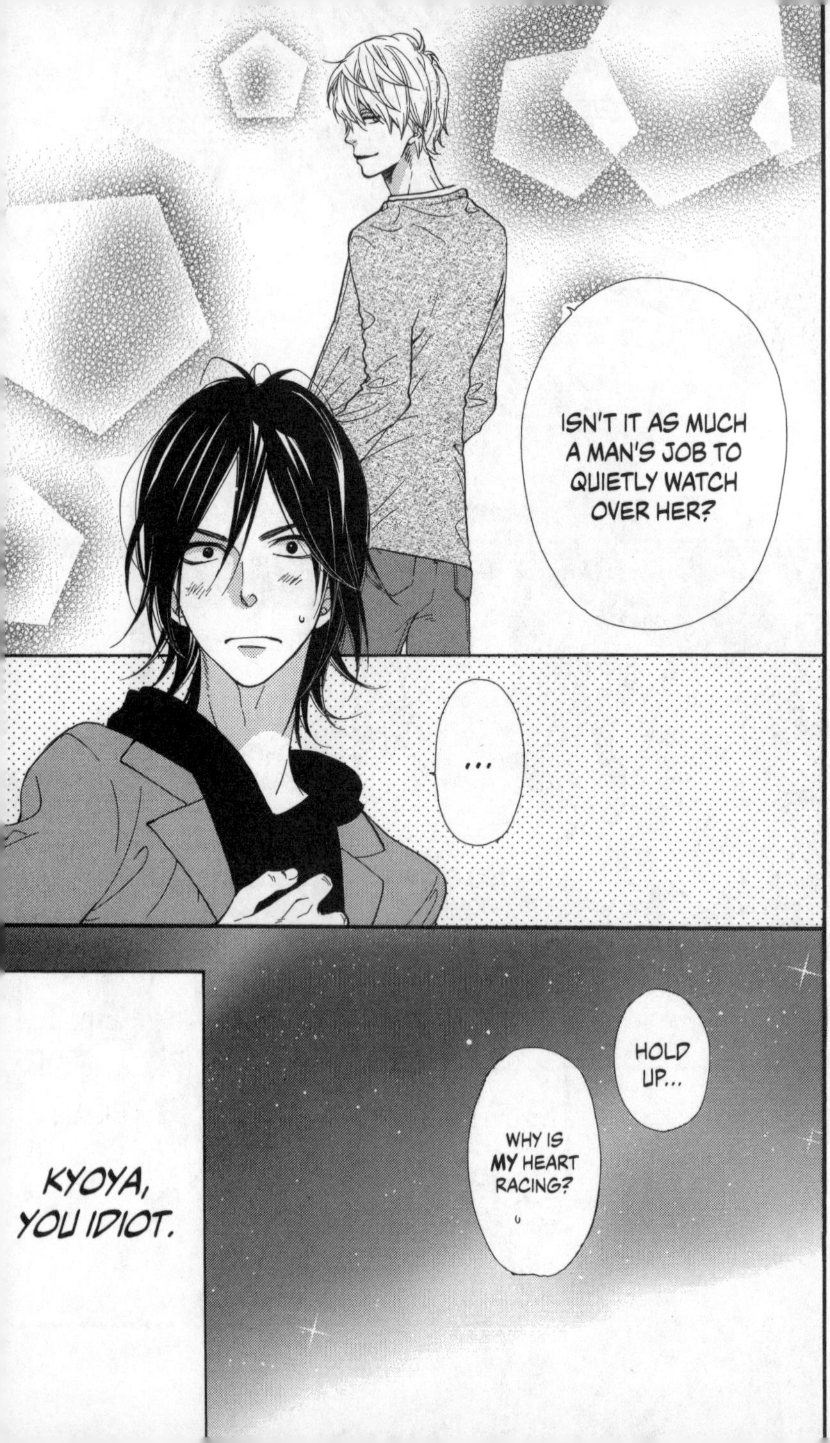
ISN'T IT AS MUCH A MAN'S JOB TO QUIETLY WATCH OVER HER?
...
HOLD UP...
WHY IS MY HEART RACING?
KYOYA, YOU IDIOT.

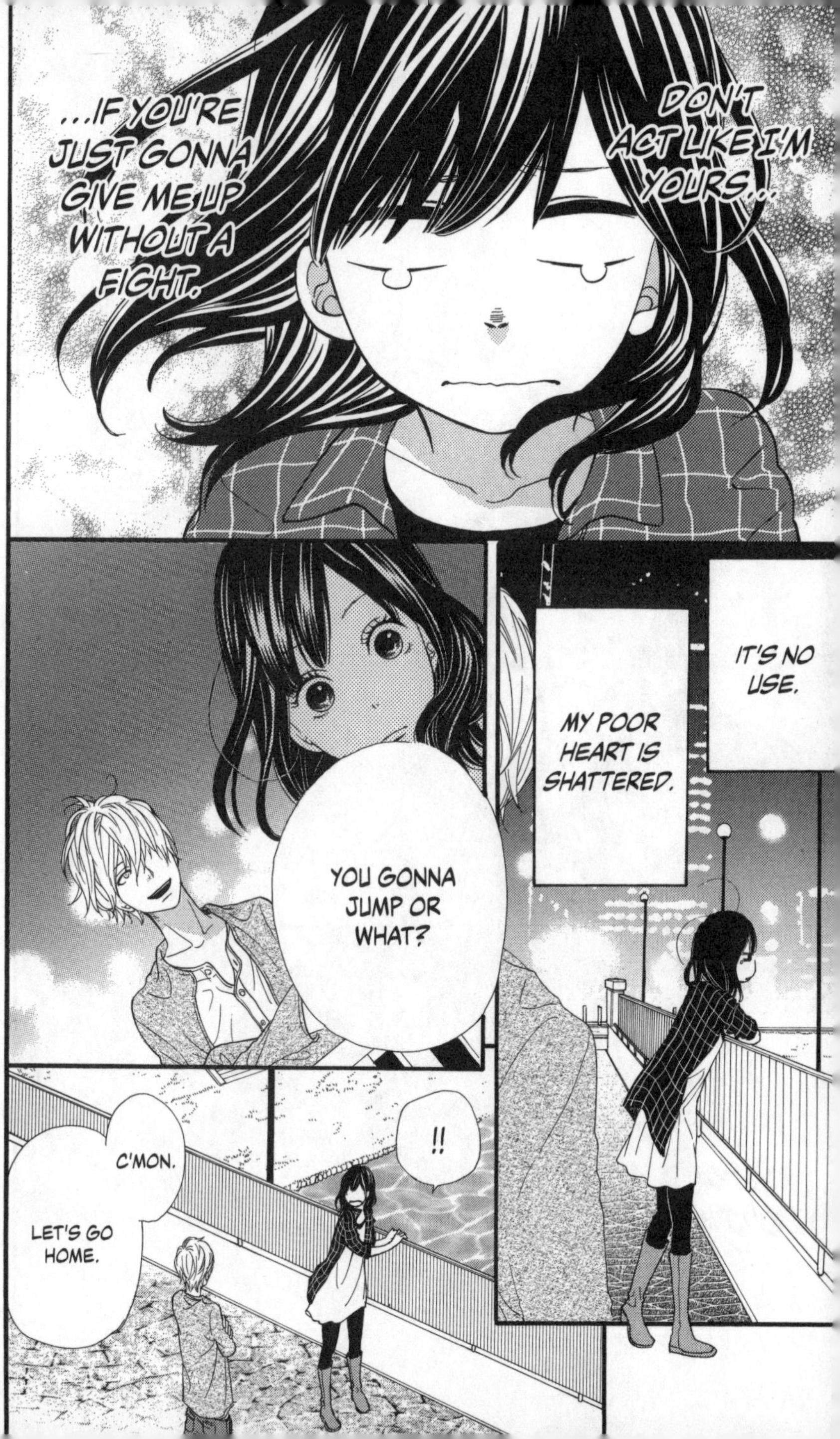
DON'T ACT LIKE I'M YOURS...
...IF YOU'RE JUST GONNA GIVE ME UP WITHOUT A FIGHT.
IT'S NO USE.
MY POOR HEART IS SHATTERED.
YOU GONNA JUMP OR WHAT?
!!
C'MON.
LET'S GO HOME.

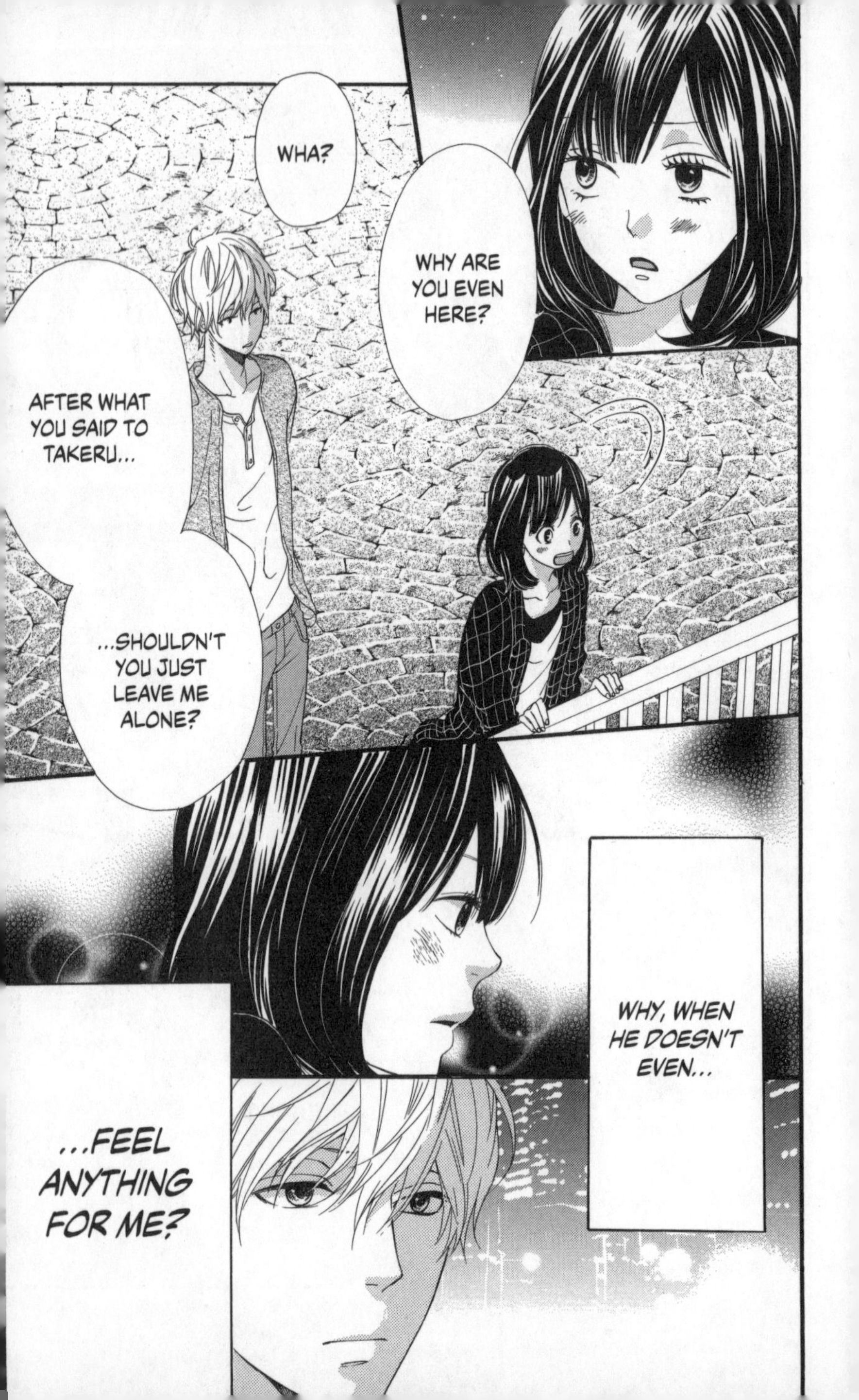
WHA?
WHY ARE YOU EVEN HERE?
AFTER WHAT YOU SAID TO TAKERU...
...SHOULDN'T YOU JUST LEAVE ME ALONE?
WHY, WHEN HE DOESN'T EVEN...
...FEEL ANYTHING FOR ME?

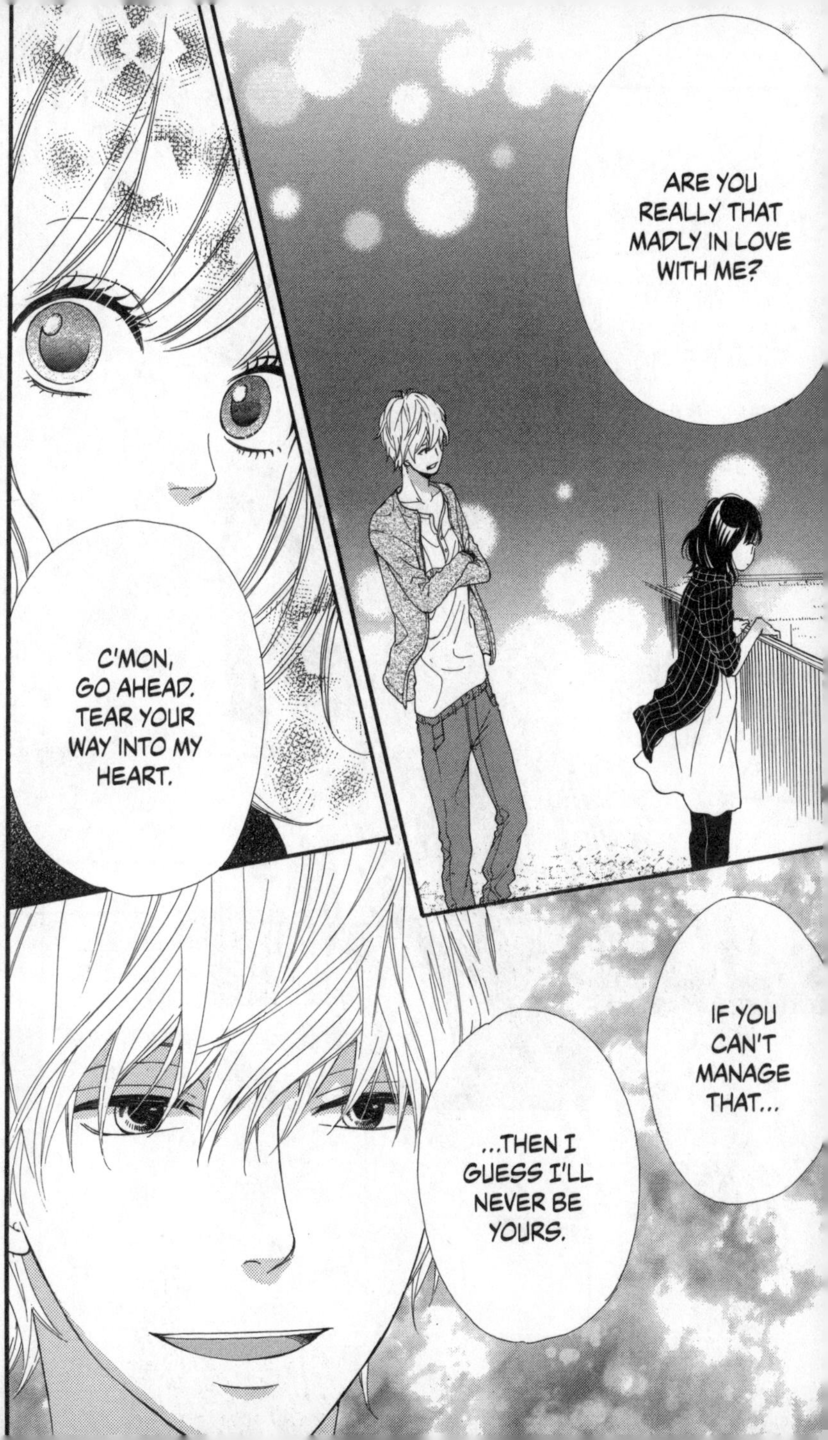
ARE YOU REALLY THAT MADLY IN LOVE WITH ME?
C'MON, GO AHEAD. TEAR YOUR WAY INTO MY HEART.
IF YOU CAN'T MANAGE THAT...
...THEN I GUESS I'LL NEVER BE YOURS.

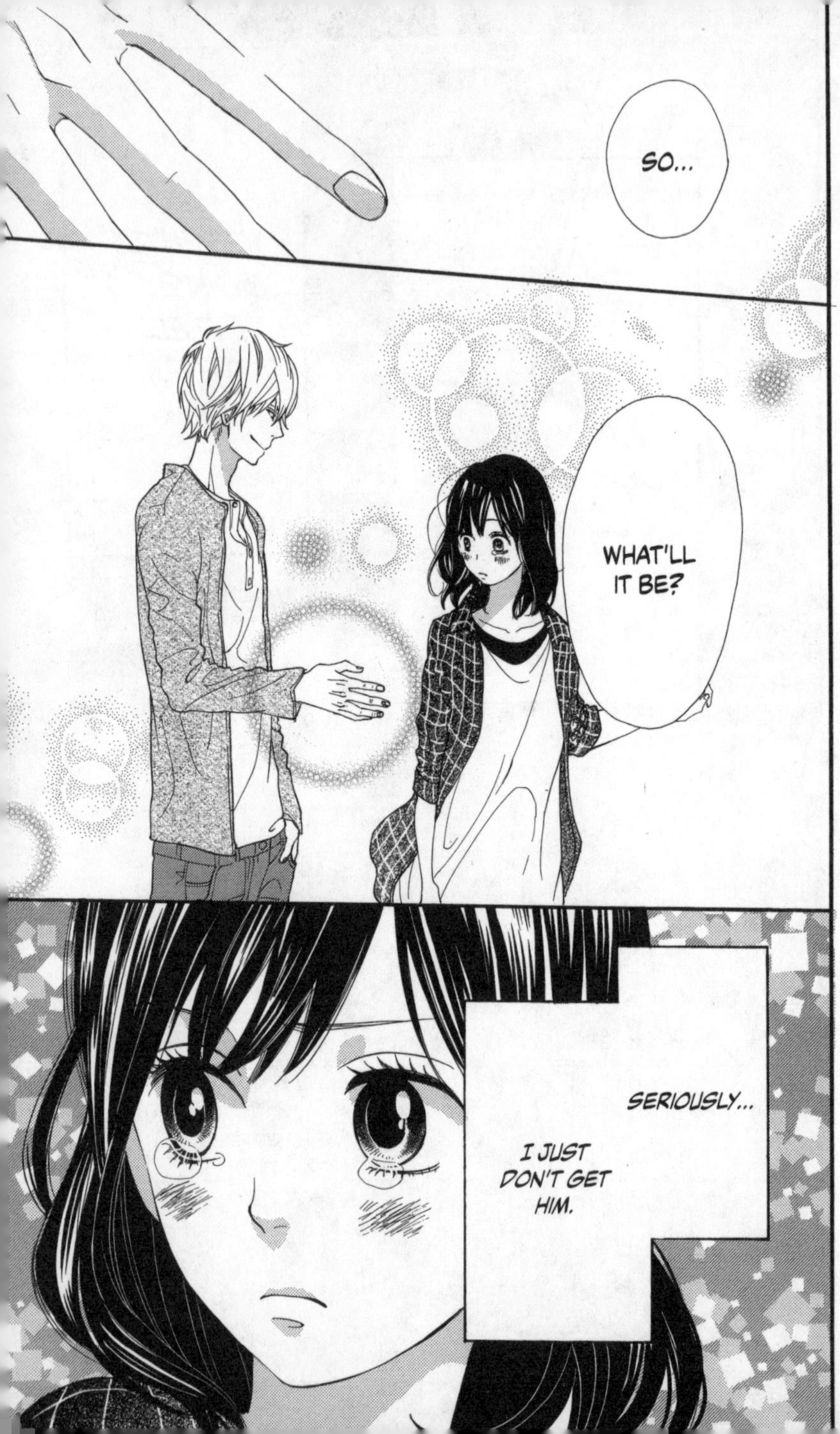
SO...
WHAT'LL IT BE?
SERIOUSLY...
I JUST DON'T GET HIM.

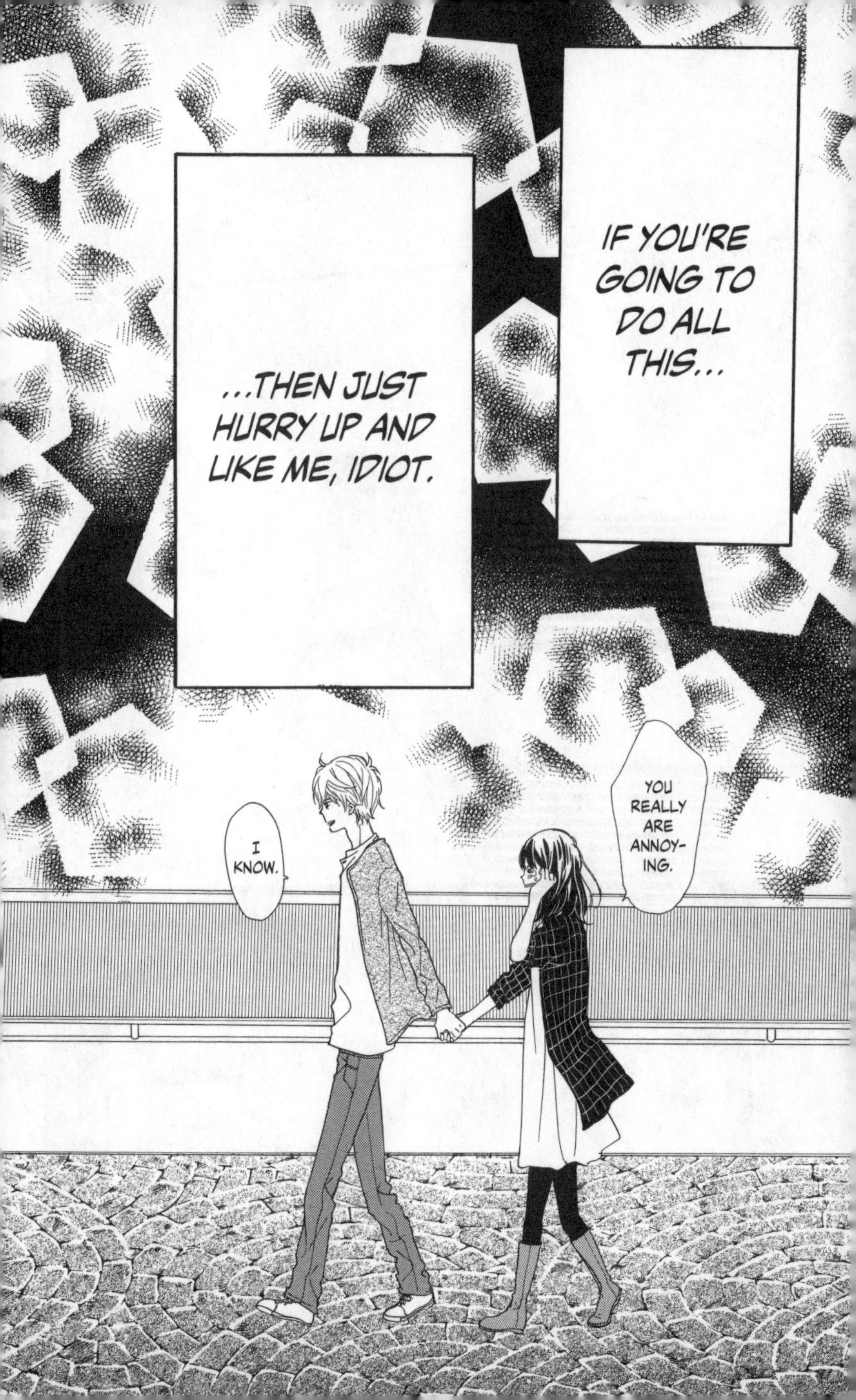
IF YOU'RE GOING TO DO ALL THIS...
...THEN JUST HURRY UP AND LIKE ME, IDIOT.
YOU REALLY ARE ANNOY-ING.
I KNOW.

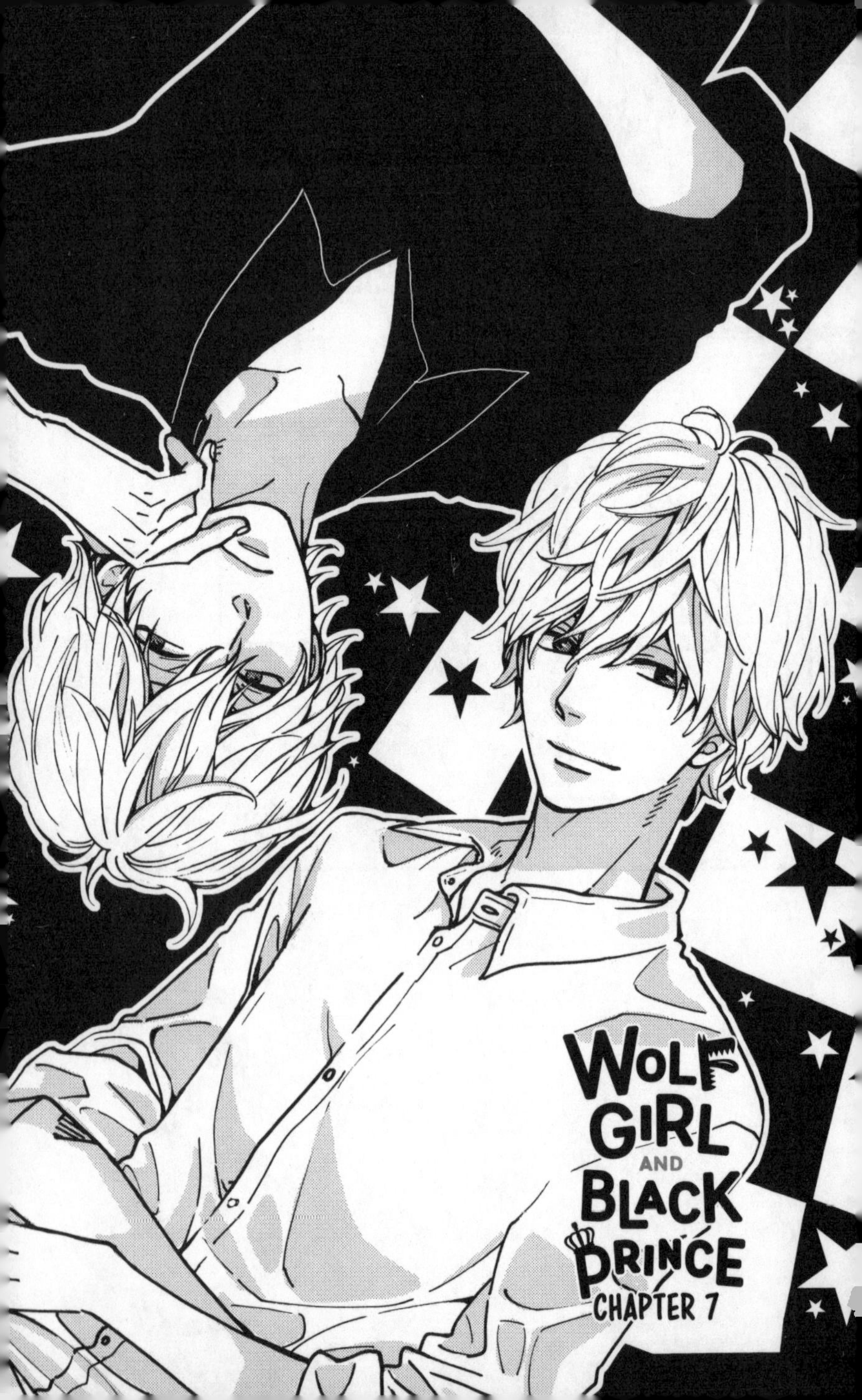
WOLF GIRL AND BLACK PRINCE
CHAPTER 7

REALLY
YOU ARE
ANNOY-
ING

REALLY TH
MADLY IN LO
WITH ME?

OR...

SO...
WHAT **AM**
I TO HIM?

AM I REALLY
NOTHING
MORE THAN
A DOG?

DOES
HE FEEL
AT LEAST
A LITTLE
SOMETHING
FOR ME?

IF Y
CA
MAN
THA

...THEN I
GUESS I'LL
NEVER BE
YOURS.

C'MON,
GO AHEAD.

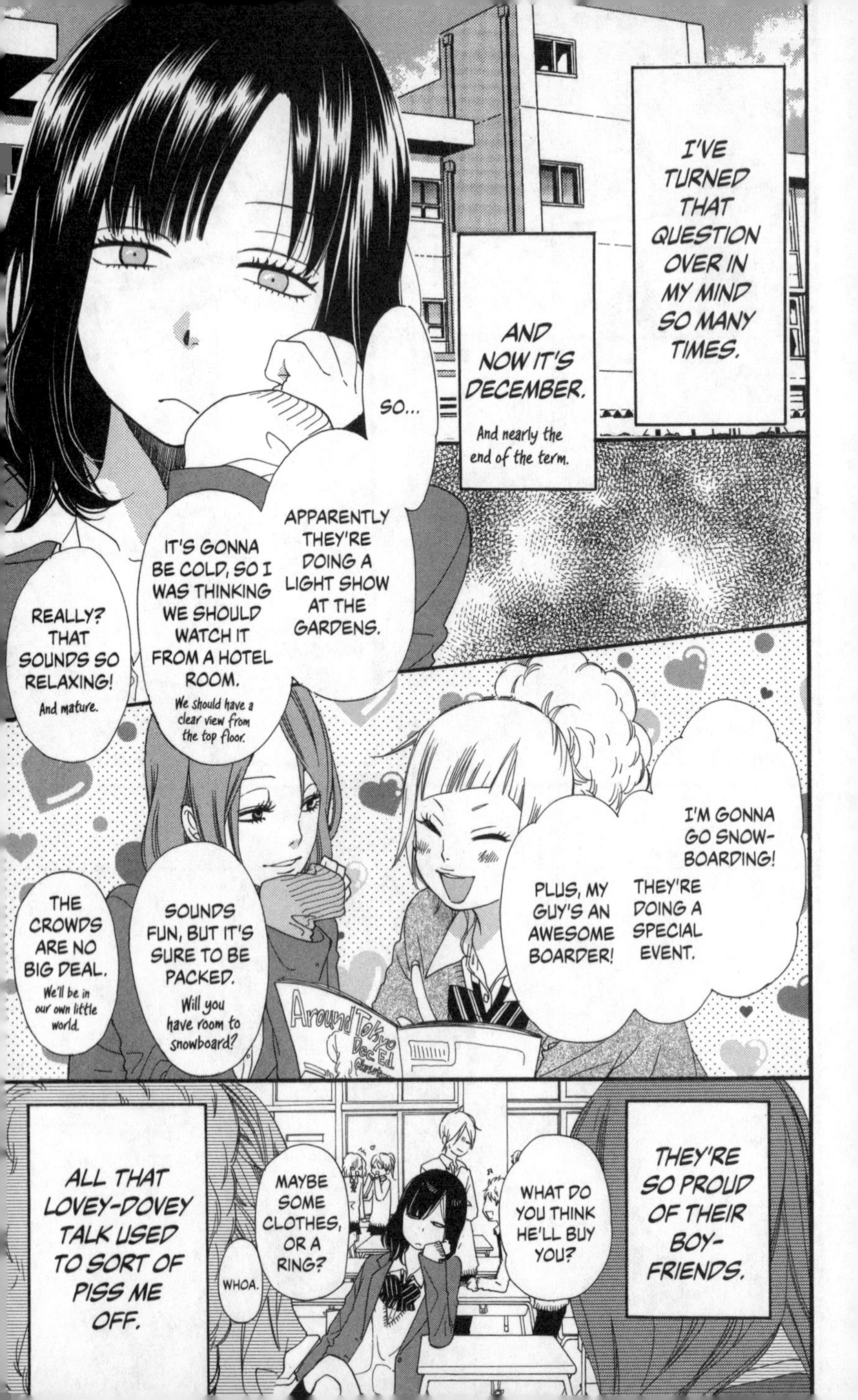
I'VE TURNED THAT QUESTION OVER IN MY MIND SO MANY TIMES.
AND NOW IT'S DECEMBER.
And nearly the end of the term.
SO...
APPARENTLY THEY'RE DOING A LIGHT SHOW AT THE GARDENS.
IT'S GONNA BE COLD, SO I WAS THINKING WE SHOULD WATCH IT FROM A HOTEL ROOM.
We should have a clear view from the top floor.
REALLY? THAT SOUNDS SO RELAXING!
And mature.
I'M GONNA GO SNOW-BOARDING!
THEY'RE DOING A SPECIAL EVENT.
PLUS, MY GUY'S AN AWESOME BOARDER!
SOUNDS FUN, BUT IT'S SURE TO BE PACKED.
Will you have room to snowboard?
THE CROWDS ARE NO BIG DEAL.
We'll be in our own little world.
Around Tokyo Dec Ed
THEY'RE SO PROUD OF THEIR BOY-FRIENDS.
WHAT DO YOU THINK HE'LL BUY YOU?
MAYBE SOME CLOTHES, OR A RING?
WHOA.
ALL THAT LOVEY-DOVEY TALK USED TO SORT OF PISS ME OFF.

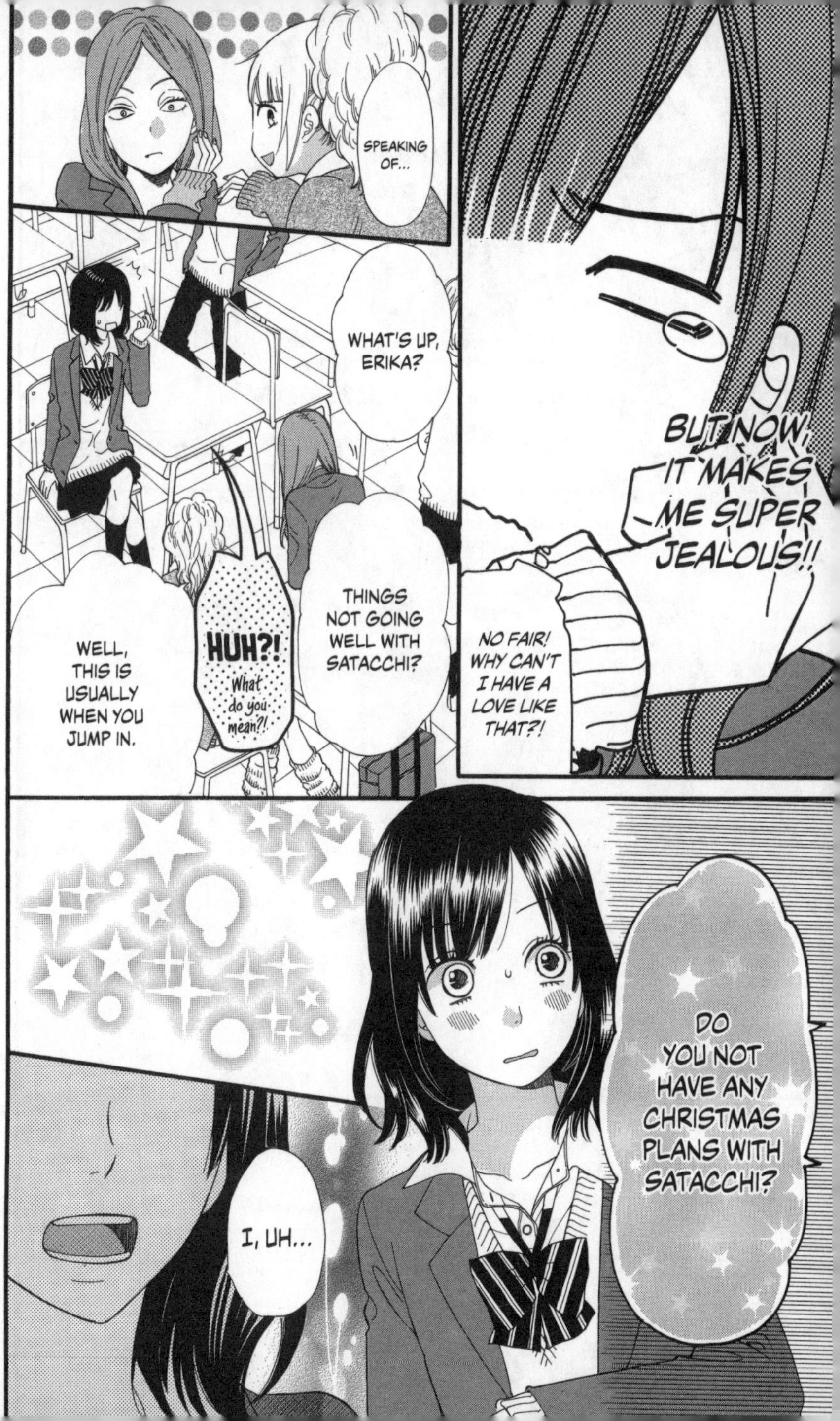
BUT NOW, IT MAKES ME SUPER JEALOUS!!
NO FAIR! WHY CAN'T I HAVE A LOVE LIKE THAT?!
SPEAKING OF...
WHAT'S UP, ERIKA?
THINGS NOT GOING WELL WITH SATACCHI?
HUH?! What do you mean?!
WELL, THIS IS USUALLY WHEN YOU JUMP IN.
DO YOU NOT HAVE ANY CHRISTMAS PLANS WITH SATACCHI?
I, UH...

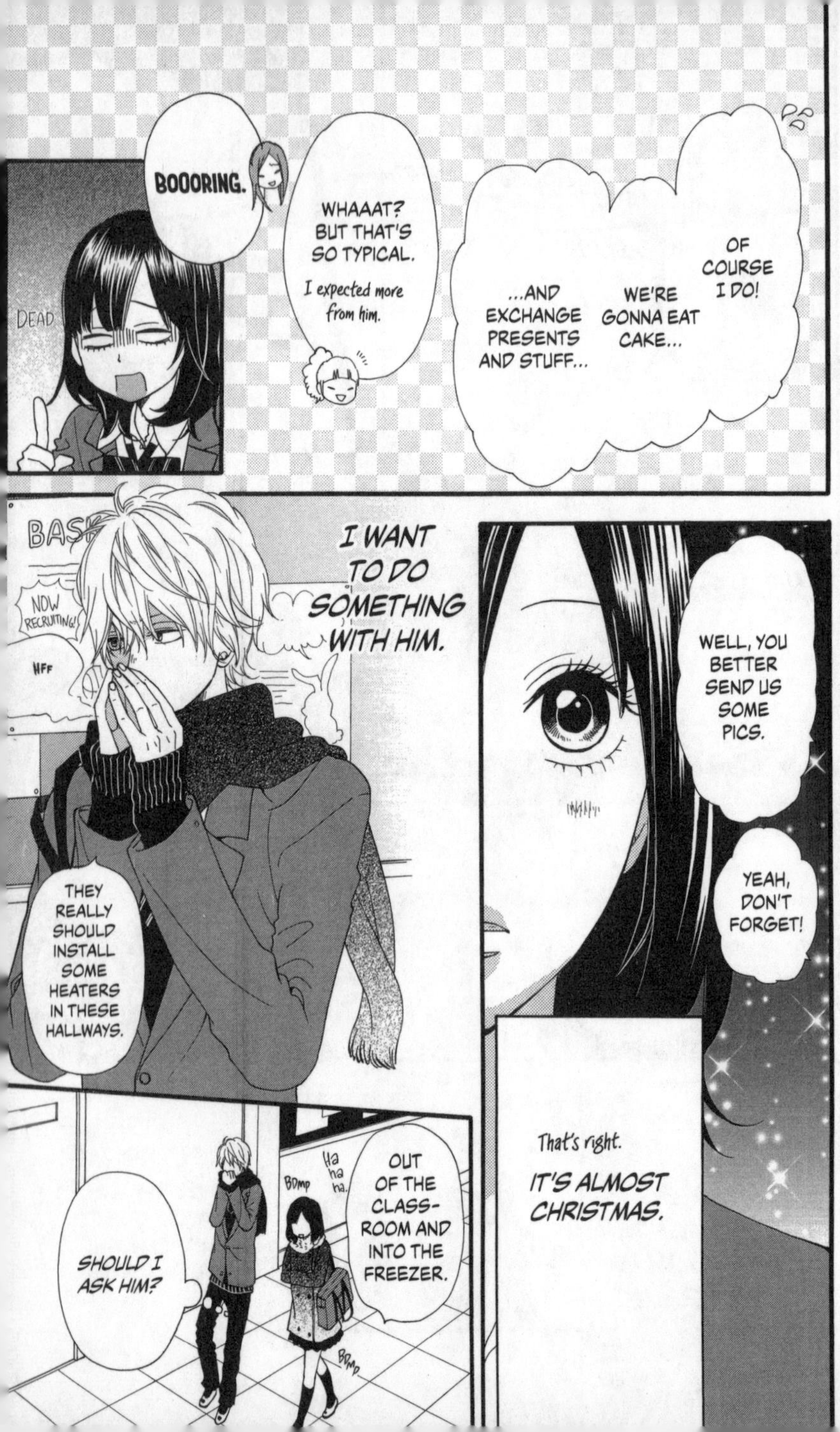
OF COURSE I DO!
WE'RE GONNA EAT CAKE...
...AND EXCHANGE PRESENTS AND STUFF...
WHAAAT? BUT THAT'S SO TYPICAL.
I expected more from him.
BOOORING.
DEAD
WELL, YOU BETTER SEND US SOME PICS.
YEAH, DON'T FORGET!
I WANT TO DO SOMETHING WITH HIM.
BAS
NOW RECRUITING!
HFF
THEY REALLY SHOULD INSTALL SOME HEATERS IN THESE HALLWAYS.
That's right.
IT'S ALMOST CHRISTMAS.
OUT OF THE CLASS-ROOM AND INTO THE FREEZER.
Ha ha ha.
BDMP
SHOULD I ASK HIM?
BDMP

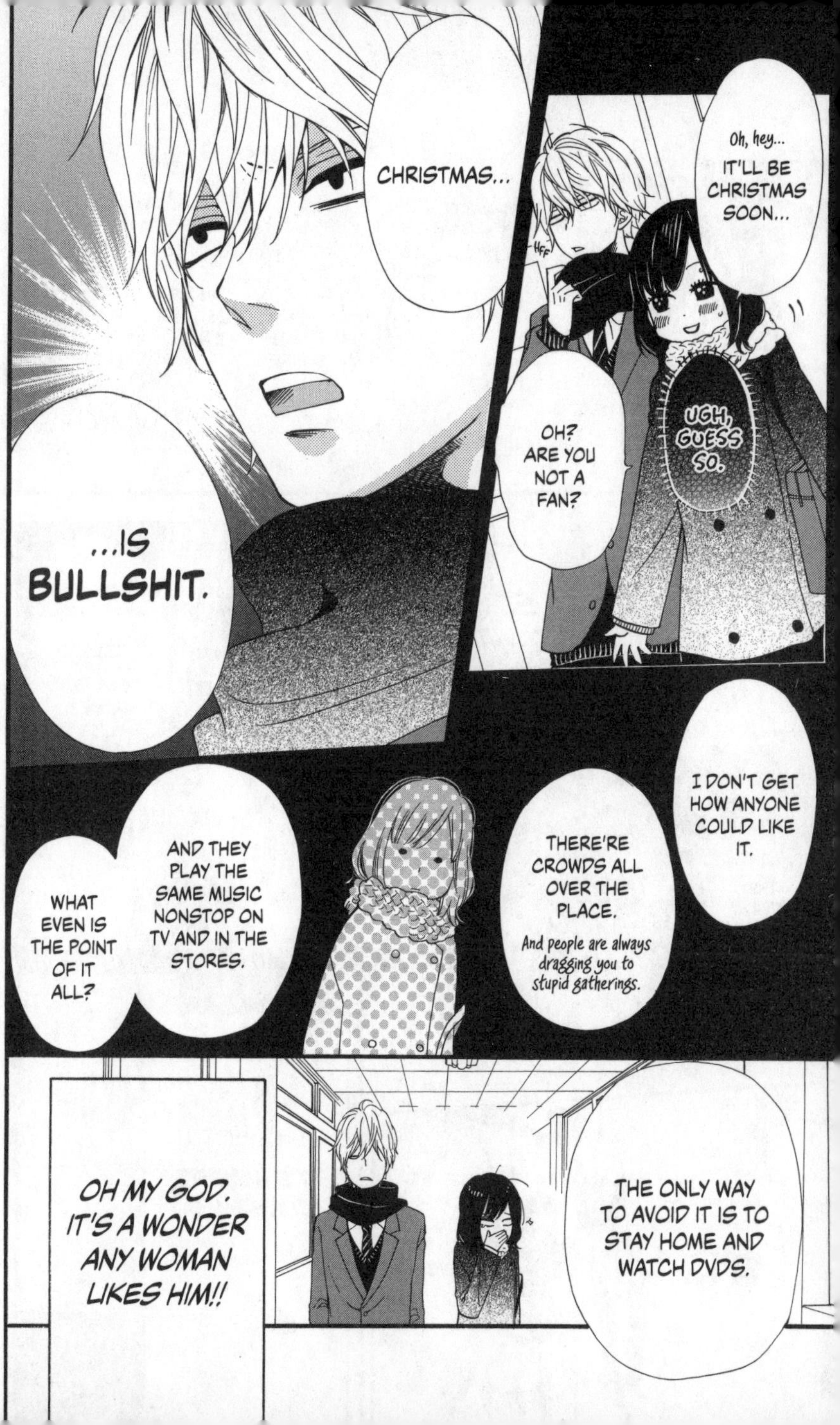
Oh, hey...
IT'LL BE CHRISTMAS SOON...
HFF
UGH, GUESS SO.
OH? ARE YOU NOT A FAN?
CHRISTMAS...
...IS BULLSHIT.
I DON'T GET HOW ANYONE COULD LIKE IT.
THERE'RE CROWDS ALL OVER THE PLACE.
And people are always dragging you to stupid gatherings.
AND THEY PLAY THE SAME MUSIC NONSTOP ON TV AND IN THE STORES.
WHAT EVEN IS THE POINT OF IT ALL?
THE ONLY WAY TO AVOID IT IS TO STAY HOME AND WATCH DVDS.
OH MY GOD. IT'S A WONDER ANY WOMAN LIKES HIM!!

2

So recently, *Margaret* magazine asked me to give a talk at an event. Honestly, I was initially pretty apprehensive about it. I hate talking in front of people. I'm not especially charismatic either, so, like, what was I supposed to say?! But my editor and everyone else did their best to help me out. (Momoko Koda even came in from Tokyo!! OMG!!) It ended up being a lot of fun. I learned a lot myself. Plus, all the contributors were so refreshing to be around. In the end, I feel like I actually got the most out of the experience. What a sneak I am! I'm so glad that they contacted me.

All the girls who are drawing manga these days are so cute, though... I wasn't expecting that! I was scared stiff at the after-party. All the authors were so cute! And so fashionable! It was kind of overwhelming. I guess the image of female manga artists as frumpy is pretty outdated now. It's a new era.

Actually, things haven't changed all that much. Maybe other authors have always been like this. I'm the one who needs to stop buying into that stereotype! Dang it!! The ink is smudging again! I suppose even this G pen has a life expectancy. Oh yeah, I've been doing all my inking with mapping pens lately. I might stop that soon though. But whatever.

2011.12.

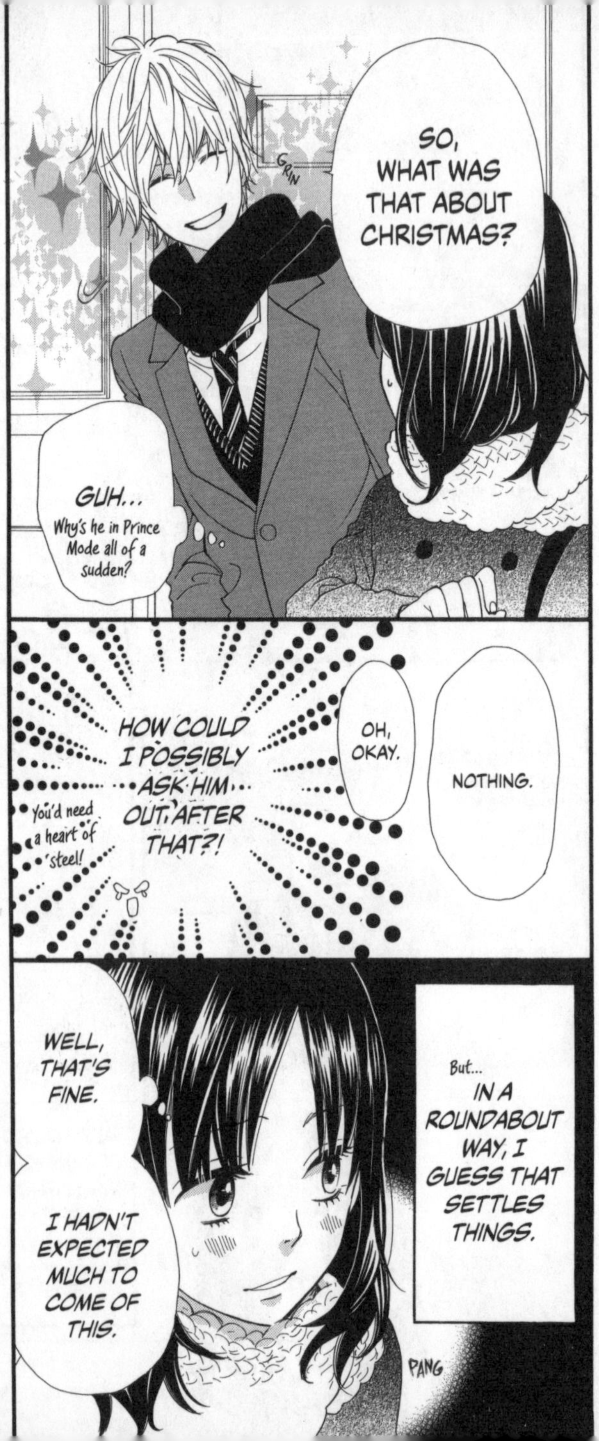
SO, WHAT WAS THAT ABOUT CHRISTMAS?
GRIN
GUH...
Why's he in Prince Mode all of a sudden?
NOTHING.
OH, OKAY.
HOW COULD I POSSIBLY ASK HIM OUT AFTER THAT?!
You'd need a heart of steel!
But... IN A ROUNDABOUT WAY, I GUESS THAT SETTLES THINGS.
WELL, THAT'S FINE.
I HADN'T EXPECTED MUCH TO COME OF THIS.
PANG

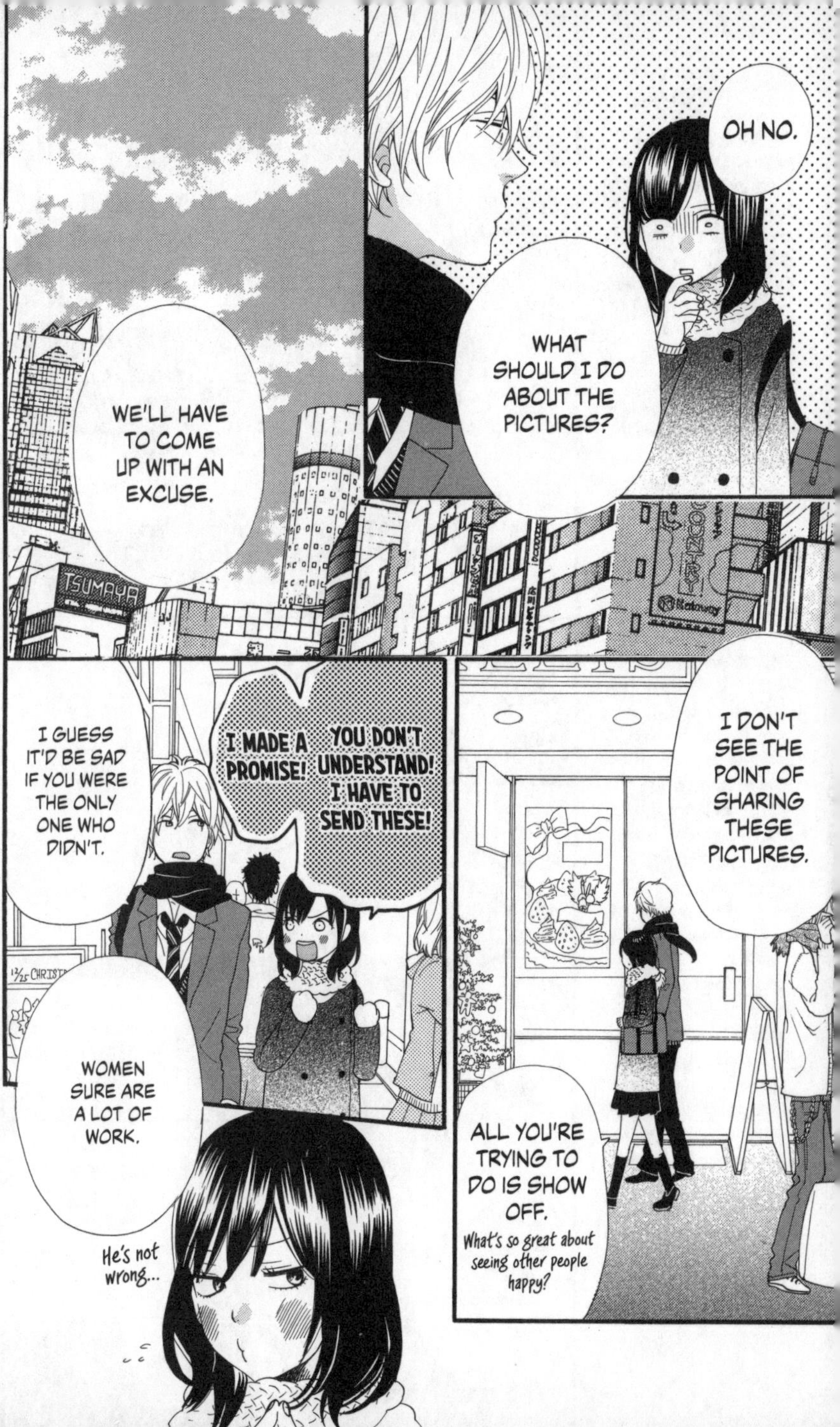
OH NO.
WHAT SHOULD I DO ABOUT THE PICTURES?
WE'LL HAVE TO COME UP WITH AN EXCUSE.
TSUMAYA
I DON'T SEE THE POINT OF SHARING THESE PICTURES.
ALL YOU'RE TRYING TO DO IS SHOW OFF.
What's so great about seeing other people happy?
YOU DON'T UNDERSTAND! I HAVE TO SEND THESE!
I MADE A PROMISE!
I GUESS IT'D BE SAD IF YOU WERE THE ONLY ONE WHO DIDN'T.
WOMEN SURE ARE A LOT OF WORK.
He's not wrong...

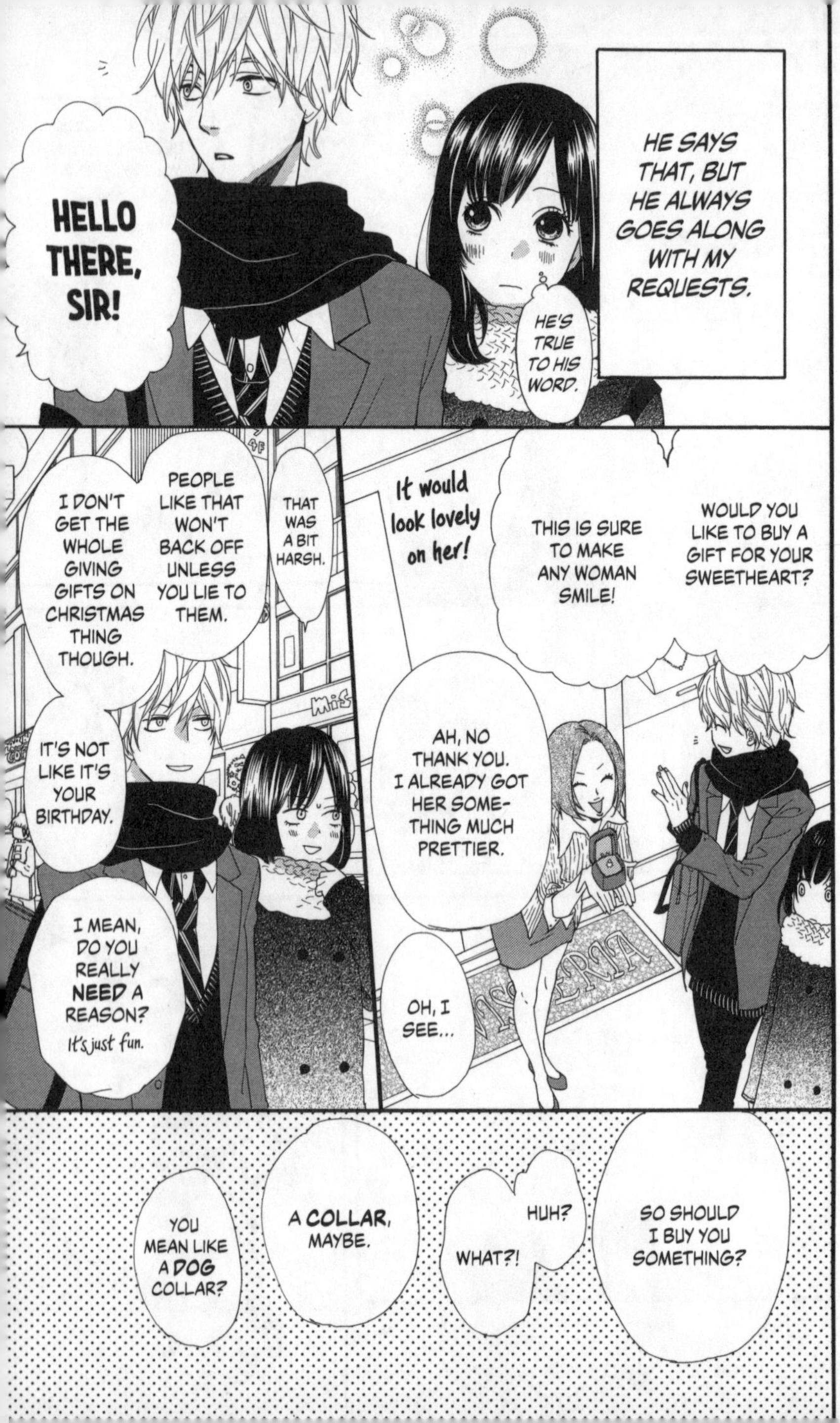
HE SAYS THAT, BUT HE ALWAYS GOES ALONG WITH MY REQUESTS.
HE'S TRUE TO HIS WORD.
HELLO THERE, SIR!
WOULD YOU LIKE TO BUY A GIFT FOR YOUR SWEETHEART?
THIS IS SURE TO MAKE ANY WOMAN SMILE!
It would look lovely on her!
AH, NO THANK YOU. I ALREADY GOT HER SOME-THING MUCH PRETTIER.
OH, I SEE...
THAT WAS A BIT HARSH.
PEOPLE LIKE THAT WON'T BACK OFF UNLESS YOU LIE TO THEM.
I DON'T GET THE WHOLE GIVING GIFTS ON CHRISTMAS THING THOUGH.
IT'S NOT LIKE IT'S YOUR BIRTHDAY.
I MEAN, DO YOU REALLY NEED A REASON?
It's just fun.
SO SHOULD I BUY YOU SOMETHING?
HUH?
WHAT?!
A COLLAR, MAYBE.
YOU MEAN LIKE A DOG COLLAR?

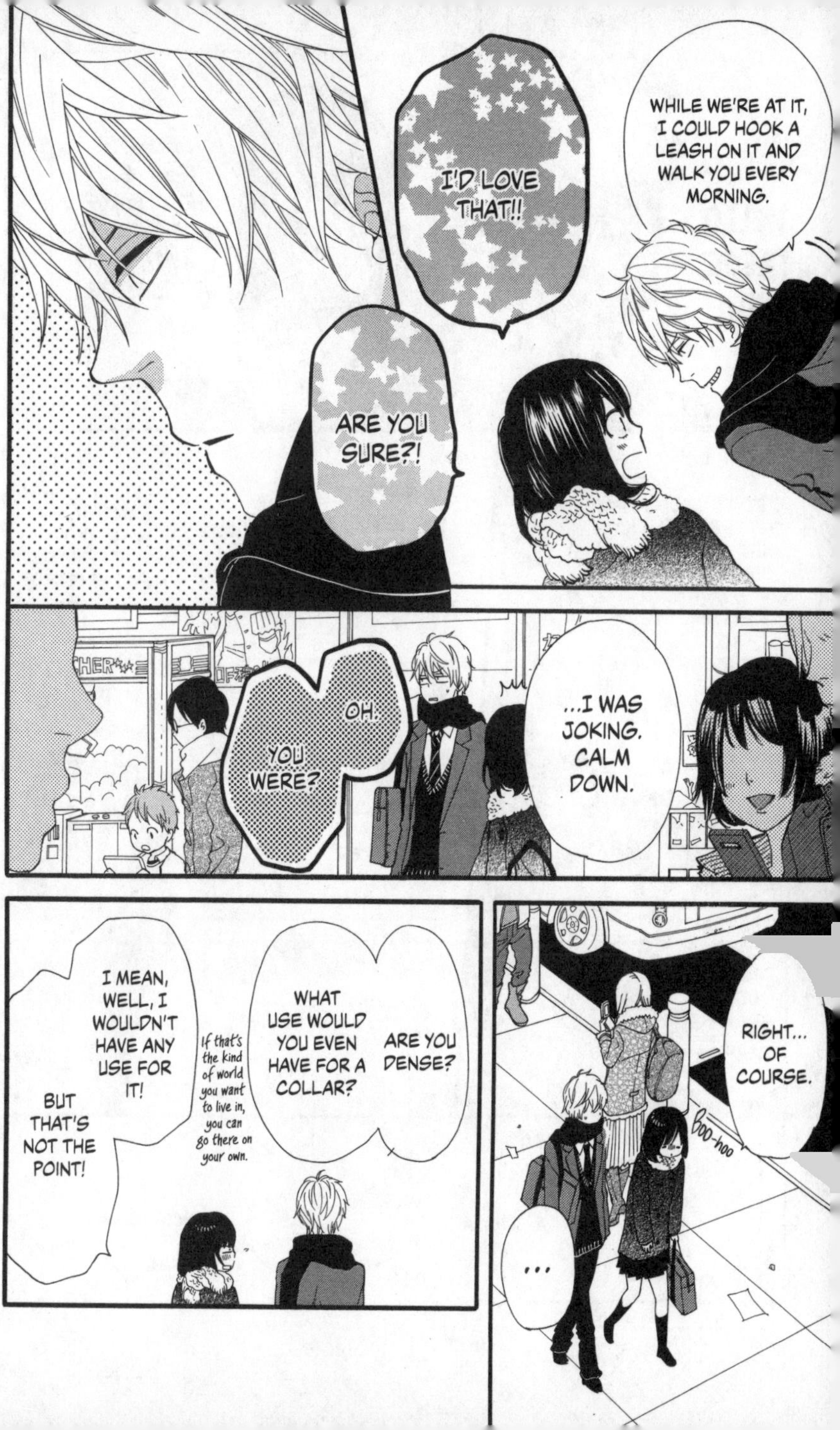
WHILE WE'RE AT IT, I COULD HOOK A LEASH ON IT AND WALK YOU EVERY MORNING.
I'D LOVE THAT!!
ARE YOU SURE?!
...I WAS JOKING. CALM DOWN.
OH.
YOU WERE?
RIGHT... OF COURSE.
Boo-hoo
...
ARE YOU DENSE?
WHAT USE WOULD YOU EVEN HAVE FOR A COLLAR?
If that's the kind of world you want to live in, you can go there on your own.
I MEAN, WELL, I WOULDN'T HAVE ANY USE FOR IT!
BUT THAT'S NOT THE POINT!

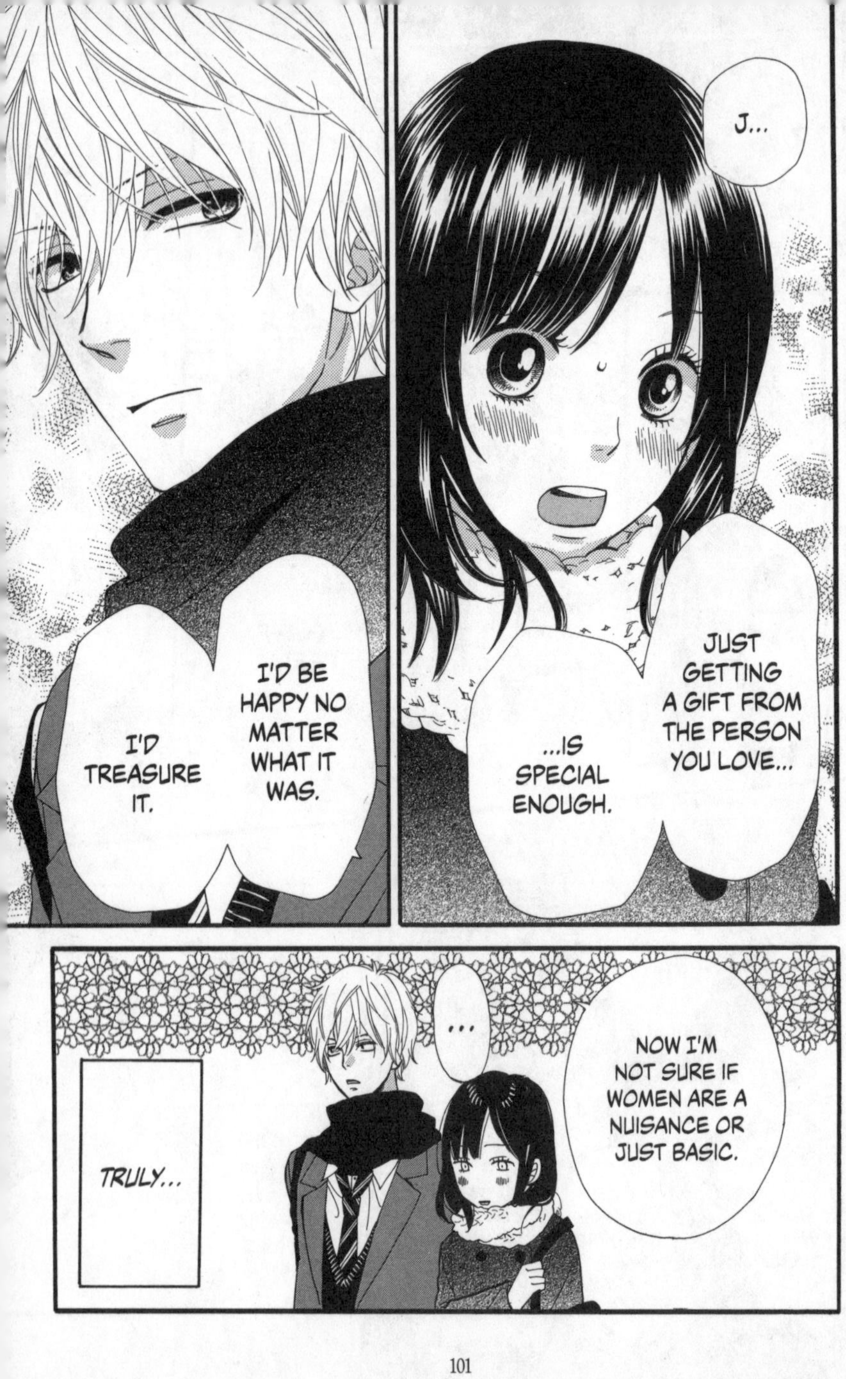
J...
JUST GETTING A GIFT FROM THE PERSON YOU LOVE...
...IS SPECIAL ENOUGH.
I'D BE HAPPY NO MATTER WHAT IT WAS.
I'D TREASURE IT.
NOW I'M NOT SURE IF WOMEN ARE A NUISANCE OR JUST BASIC.
...
TRULY...

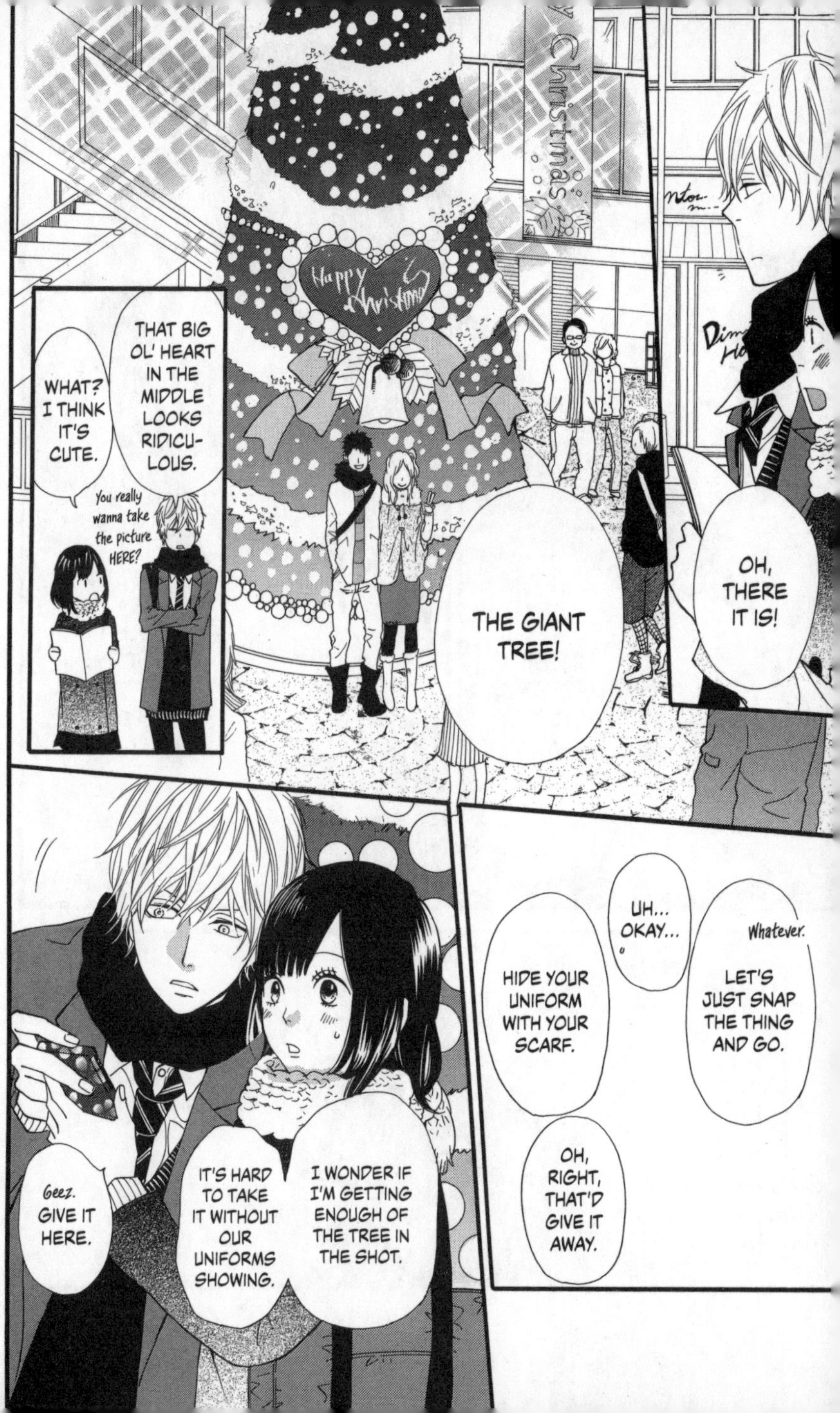
OH, THERE IT IS!
Christmas
Happy Christmas
THE GIANT TREE!
THAT BIG OL' HEART IN THE MIDDLE LOOKS RIDICULOUS.
WHAT? I THINK IT'S CUTE.
You really wanna take the picture HERE?
Whatever.
LET'S JUST SNAP THE THING AND GO.
UH... OKAY...
HIDE YOUR UNIFORM WITH YOUR SCARF.
OH, RIGHT, THAT'D GIVE IT AWAY.
I WONDER IF I'M GETTING ENOUGH OF THE TREE IN THE SHOT.
IT'S HARD TO TAKE IT WITHOUT OUR UNIFORMS SHOWING.
Geez. GIVE IT HERE.

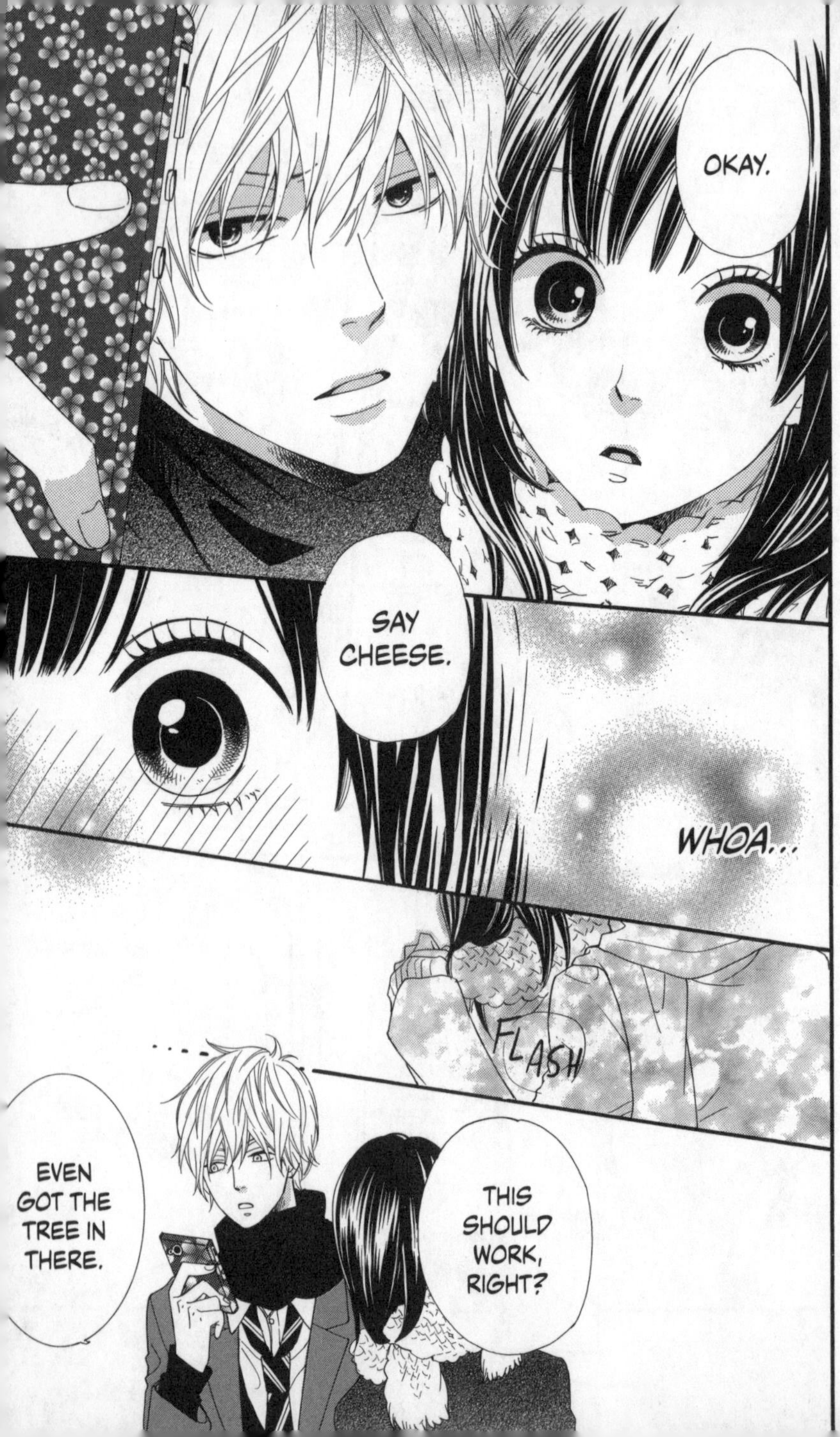
OKAY.
SAY CHEESE.
WHOA...
FLASH
THIS SHOULD WORK, RIGHT?
EVEN GOT THE TREE IN THERE.

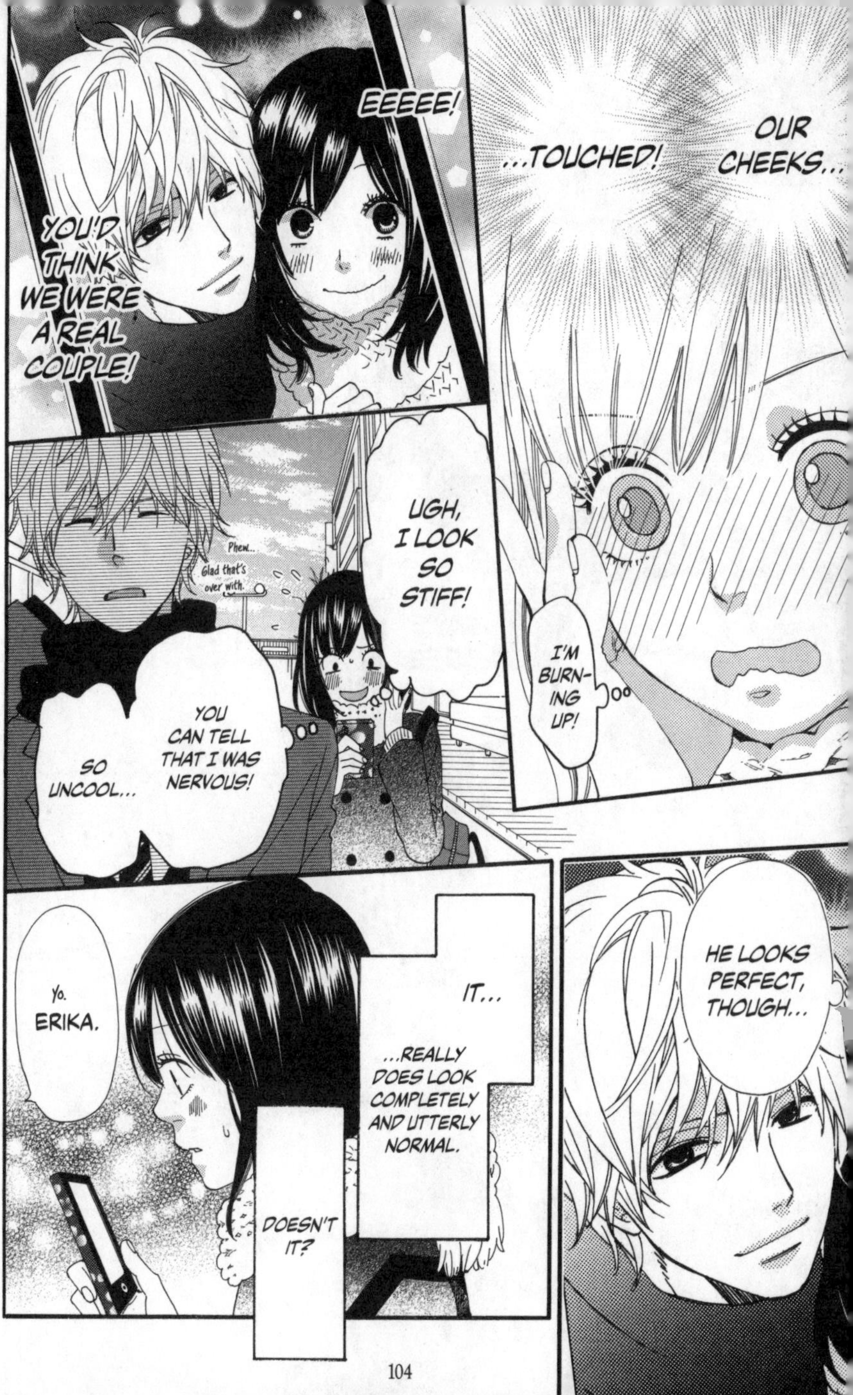
OUR CHEEKS...
...TOUCHED!
I'M BURNING UP!
EEEEE!
YOU'D THINK WE WERE A REAL COUPLE!
UGH, I LOOK SO STIFF!
Phew... Glad that's over with.
YOU CAN TELL THAT I WAS NERVOUS!
SO UNCOOL...
HE LOOKS PERFECT, THOUGH...
IT...
...REALLY DOES LOOK COMPLETELY AND UTTERLY NORMAL.
DOESN'T IT?
Yo. ERIKA.

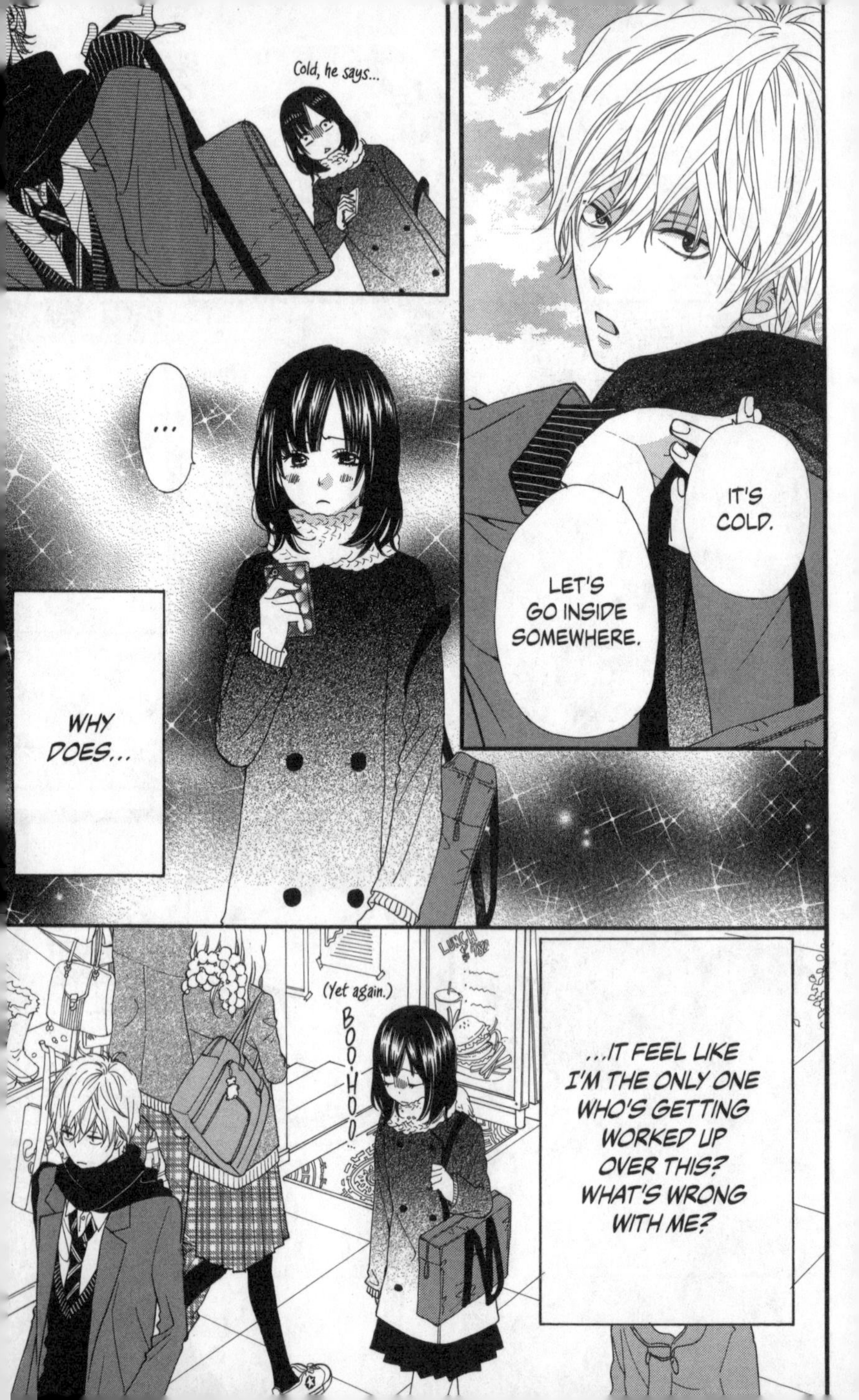
IT'S COLD.
LET'S GO INSIDE SOMEWHERE.
Cold, he says...
...
WHY DOES...
...IT FEEL LIKE I'M THE ONLY ONE WHO'S GETTING WORKED UP OVER THIS? WHAT'S WRONG WITH ME?
(Yet again.)
BOO-HOO...

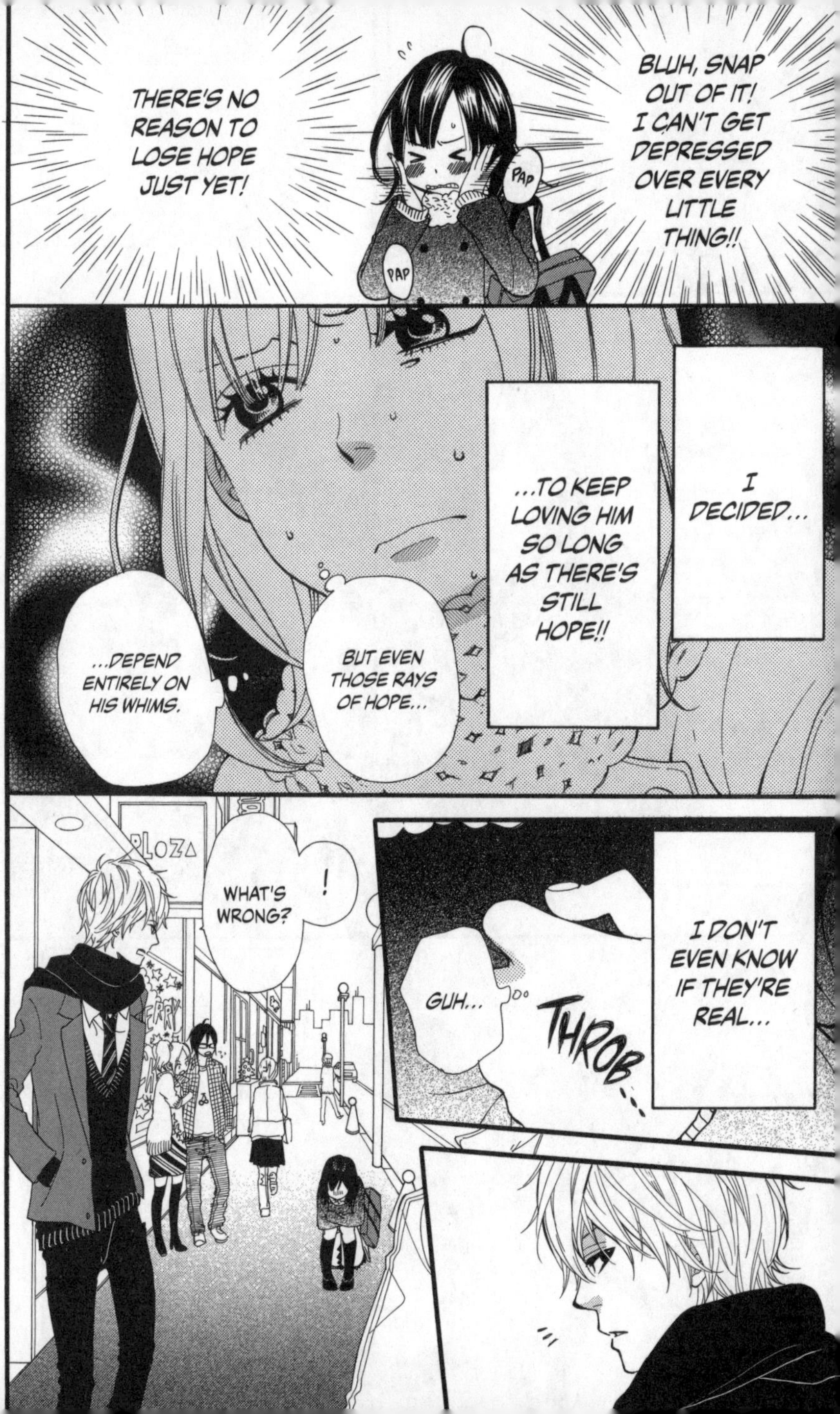
BLUH, SNAP OUT OF IT! I CAN'T GET DEPRESSED OVER EVERY LITTLE THING!!
PAP
PAP
THERE'S NO REASON TO LOSE HOPE JUST YET!
I DECIDED...
...TO KEEP LOVING HIM SO LONG AS THERE'S STILL HOPE!!
BUT EVEN THOSE RAYS OF HOPE...
...DEPEND ENTIRELY ON HIS WHIMS.
I DON'T EVEN KNOW IF THEY'RE REAL...
THROB...
GUH...
!
WHAT'S WRONG?
PLOZA

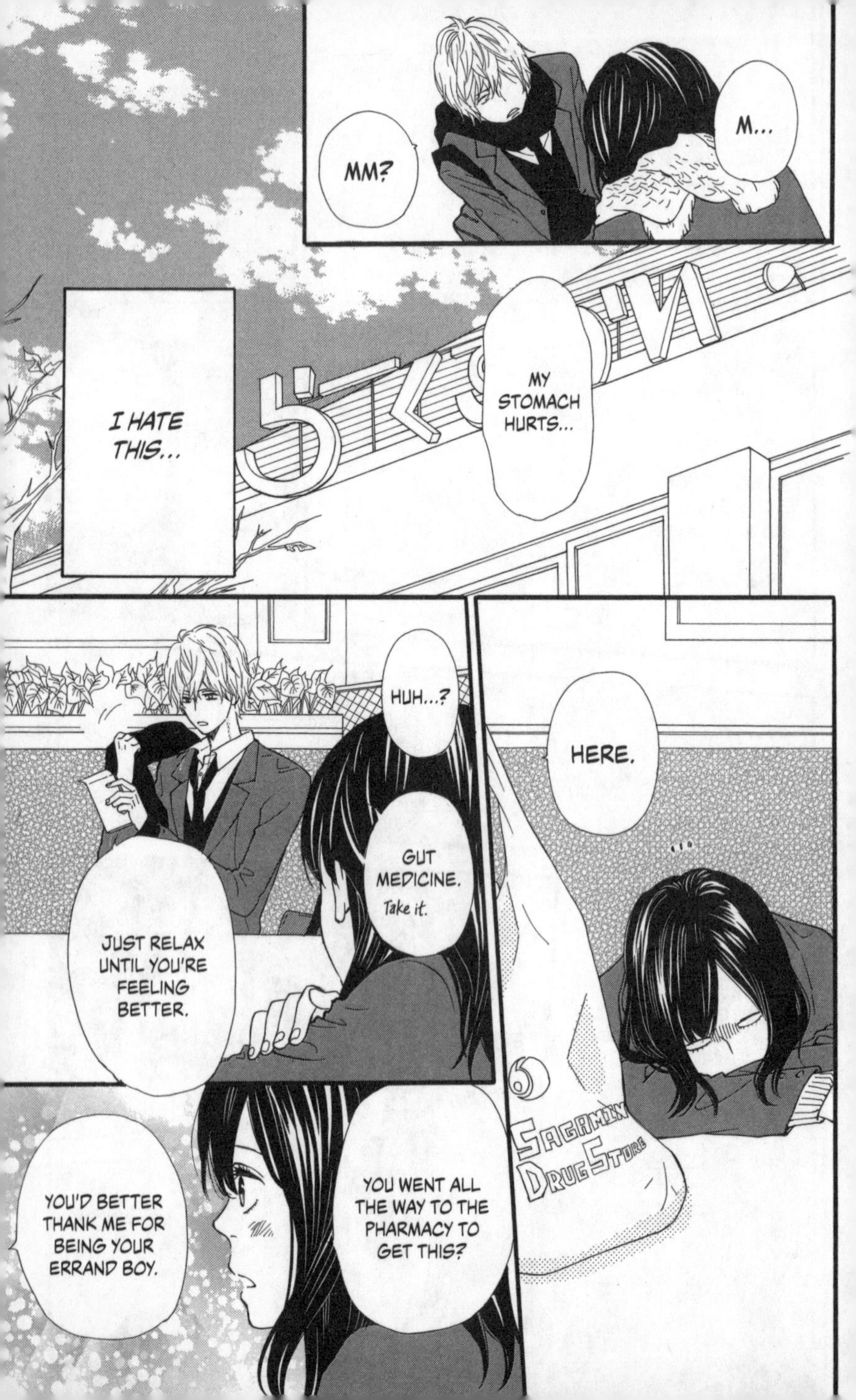
M...
MM?
MY STOMACH HURTS...
I HATE THIS...
HERE.
...
SAGAMIN
DRUG STORE
HUH...?
GUT MEDICINE. Take it.
JUST RELAX UNTIL YOU'RE FEELING BETTER.
YOU WENT ALL THE WAY TO THE PHARMACY TO GET THIS?
YOU'D BETTER THANK ME FOR BEING YOUR ERRAND BOY.

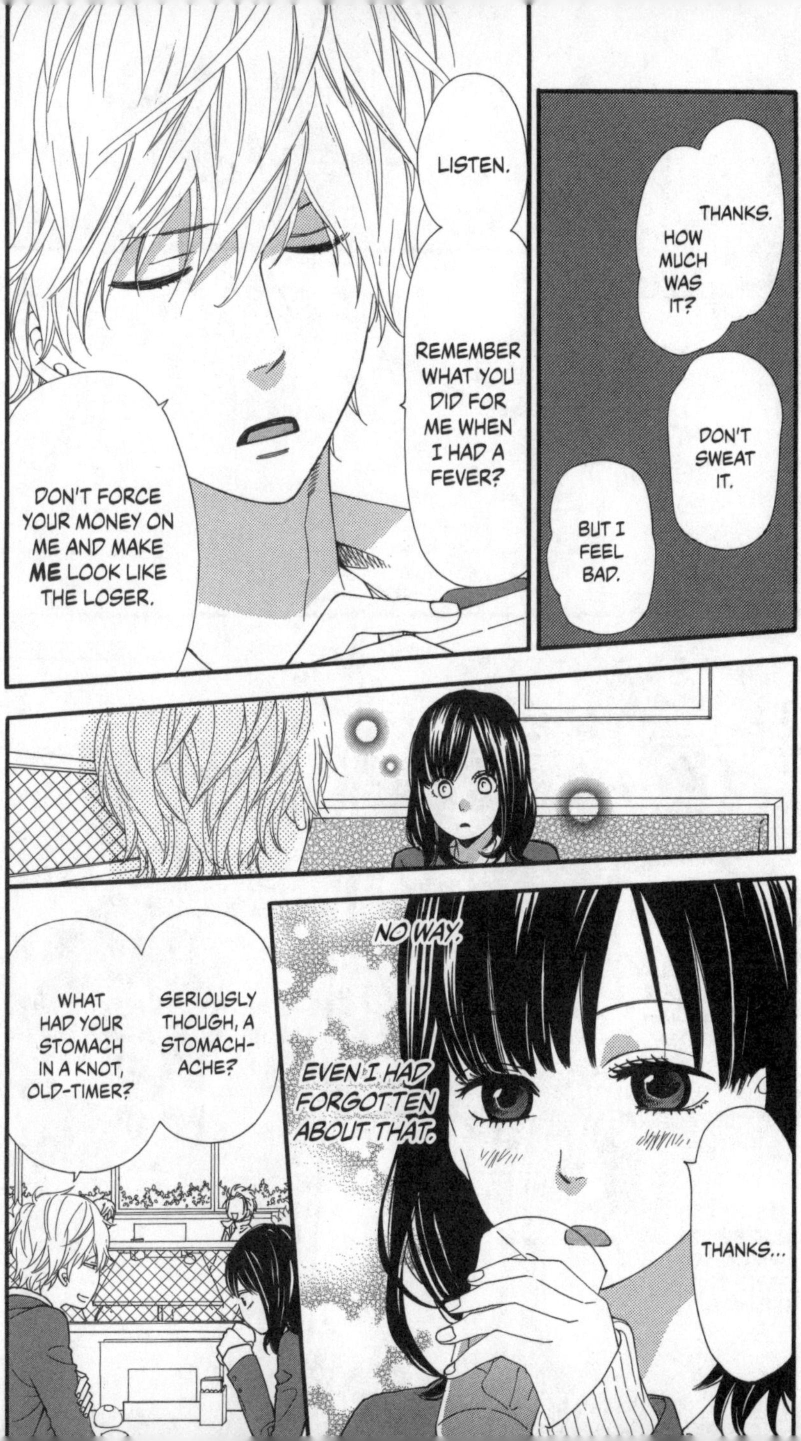
THANKS. HOW MUCH WAS IT?
DON'T SWEAT IT.
BUT I FEEL BAD.
LISTEN.
REMEMBER WHAT YOU DID FOR ME WHEN I HAD A FEVER?
DON'T FORCE YOUR MONEY ON ME AND MAKE **ME** LOOK LIKE THE LOSER.
NO WAY.
EVEN I HAD FORGOTTEN ABOUT THAT.
THANKS...
SERIOUSLY THOUGH, A STOMACH-ACHE?
WHAT HAD YOUR STOMACH IN A KNOT, OLD-TIMER?

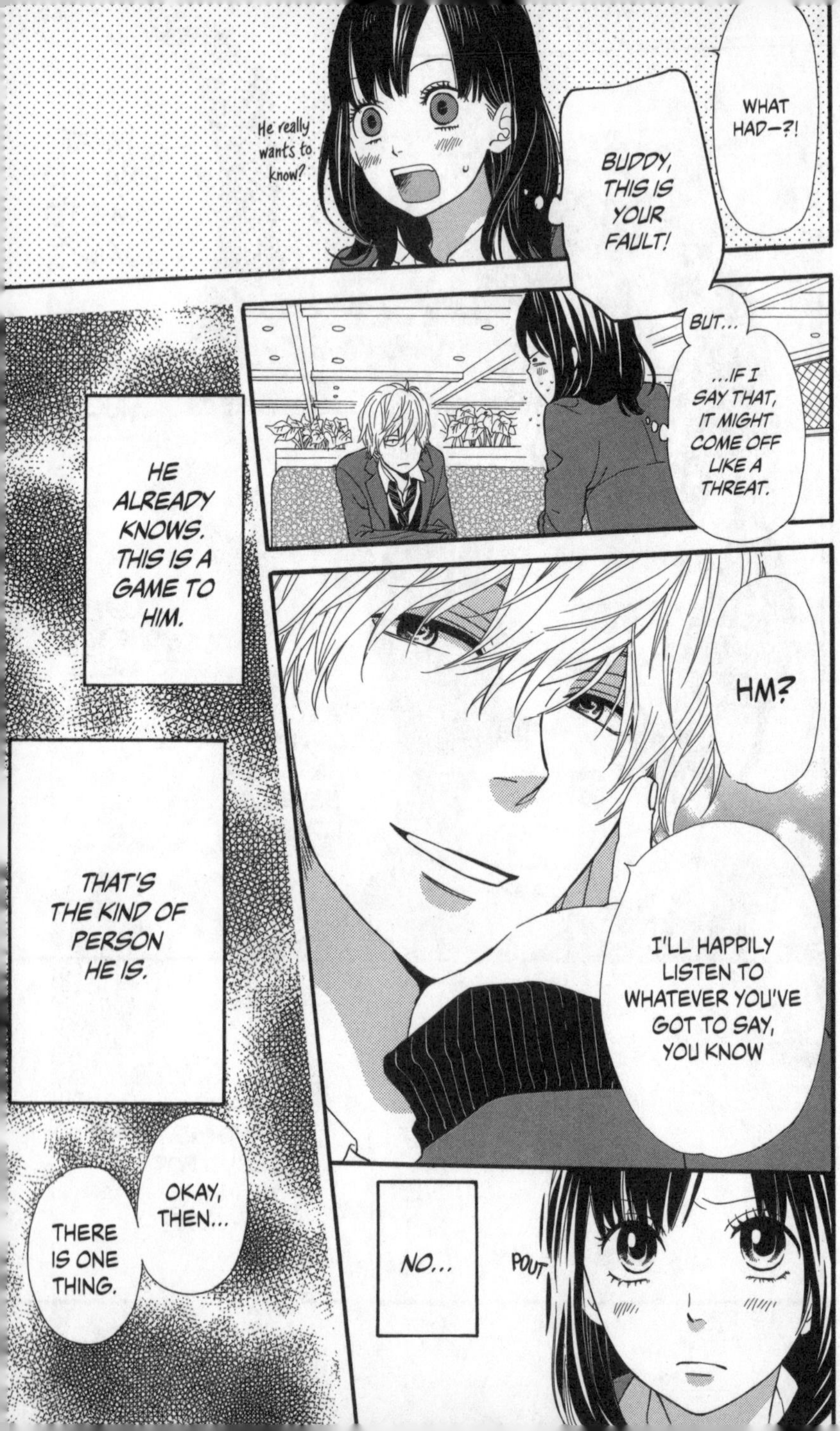
WHAT HAD—?!
BUDDY, THIS IS YOUR FAULT!
He really wants to know?
BUT...
...IF I SAY THAT, IT MIGHT COME OFF LIKE A THREAT.
HM?
I'LL HAPPILY LISTEN TO WHATEVER YOU'VE GOT TO SAY, YOU KNOW
HE ALREADY KNOWS. THIS IS A GAME TO HIM.
THAT'S THE KIND OF PERSON HE IS.
NO...
POUT
OKAY, THEN...
THERE IS ONE THING.

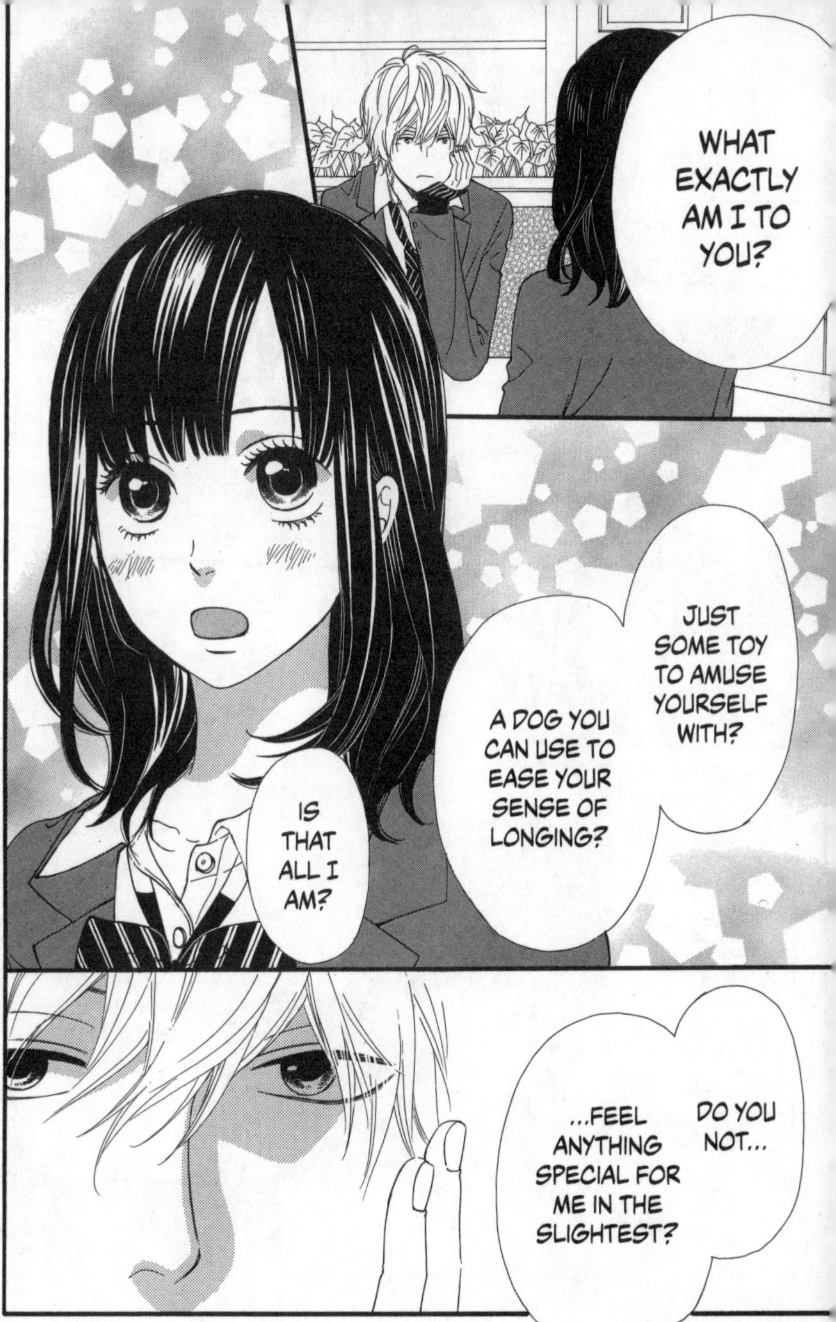
WHAT EXACTLY AM I TO YOU?
JUST SOME TOY TO AMUSE YOURSELF WITH?
A DOG YOU CAN USE TO EASE YOUR SENSE OF LONGING?
IS THAT ALL I AM?
DO YOU NOT...
...FEEL ANYTHING SPECIAL FOR ME IN THE SLIGHTEST?

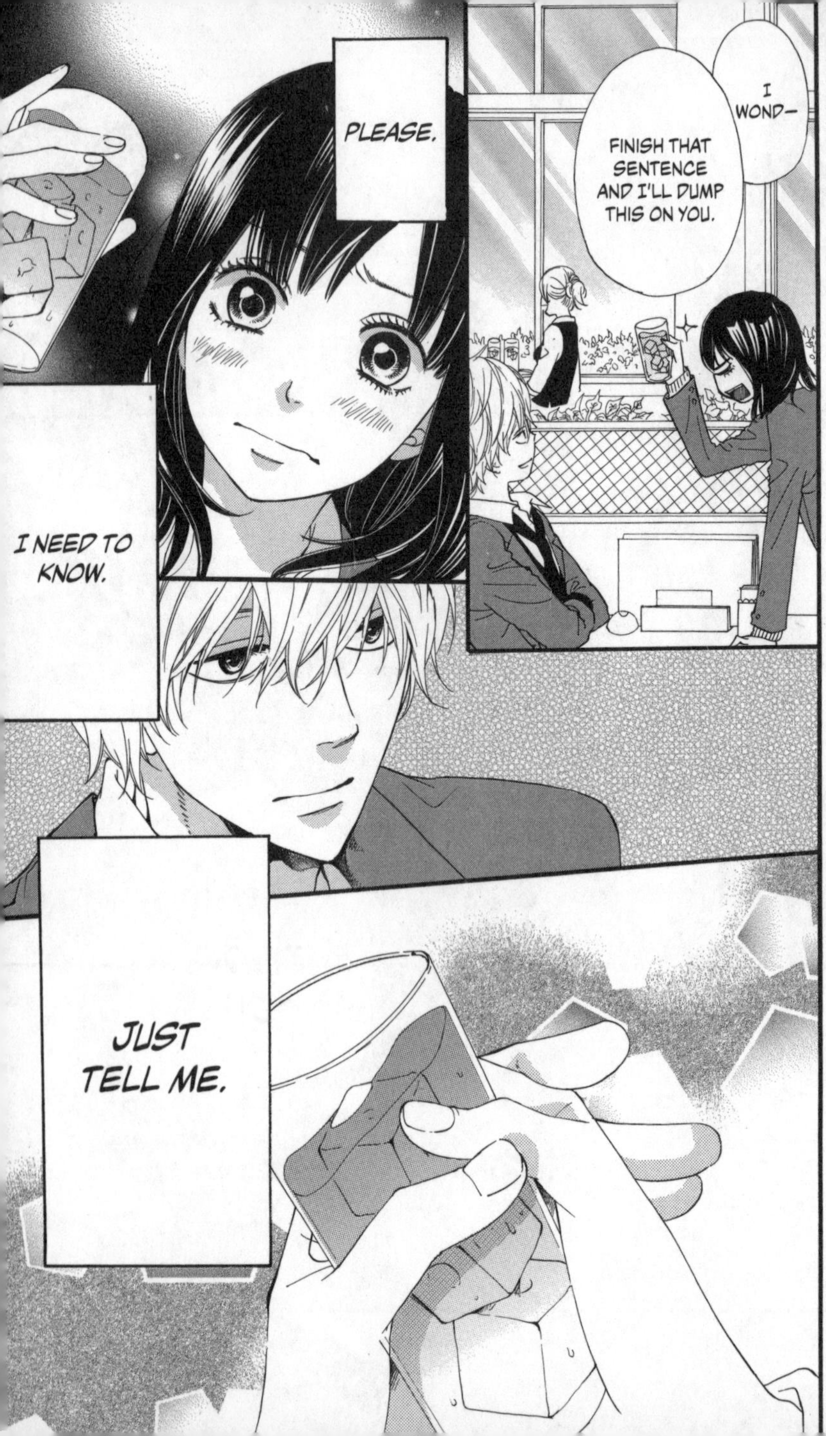
I WOND—
FINISH THAT SENTENCE AND I'LL DUMP THIS ON YOU.
PLEASE.
I NEED TO KNOW.
JUST TELL ME.

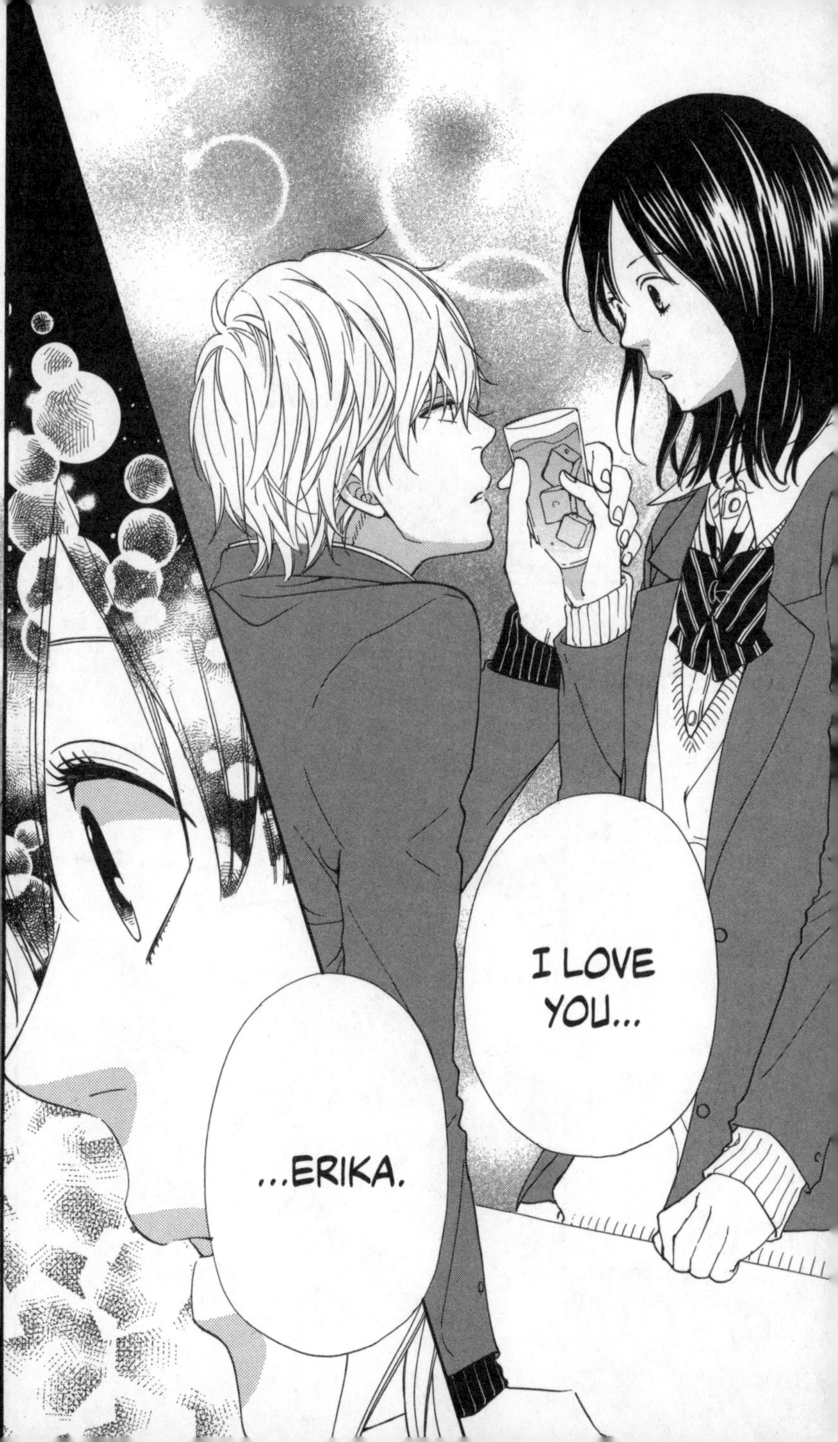
I LOVE YOU...
...ERIKA.

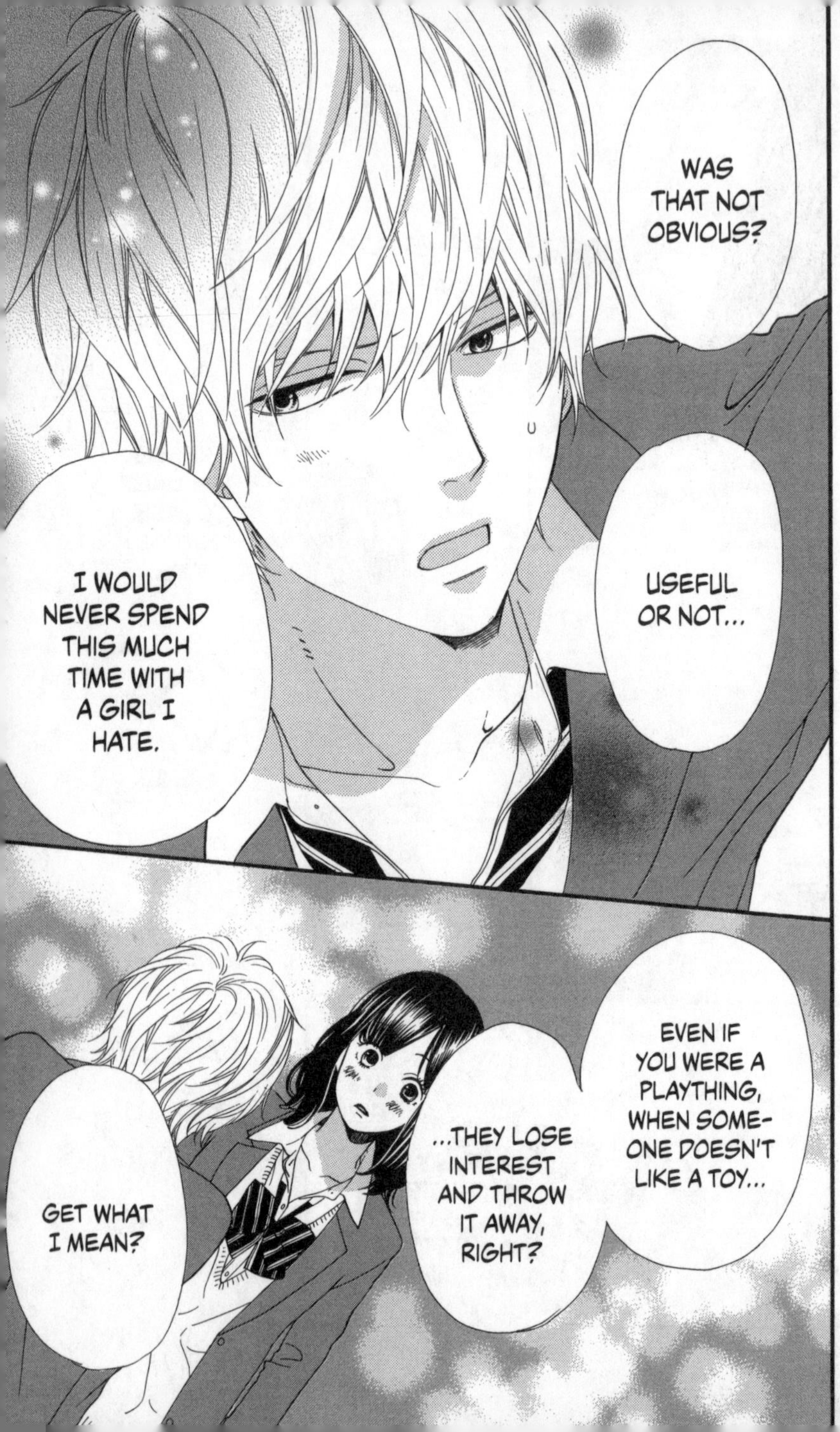
WAS THAT NOT OBVIOUS?
USEFUL OR NOT...
I WOULD NEVER SPEND THIS MUCH TIME WITH A GIRL I HATE.
EVEN IF YOU WERE A PLAYTHING, WHEN SOME-ONE DOESN'T LIKE A TOY...
...THEY LOSE INTEREST AND THROW IT AWAY, RIGHT?
GET WHAT I MEAN?

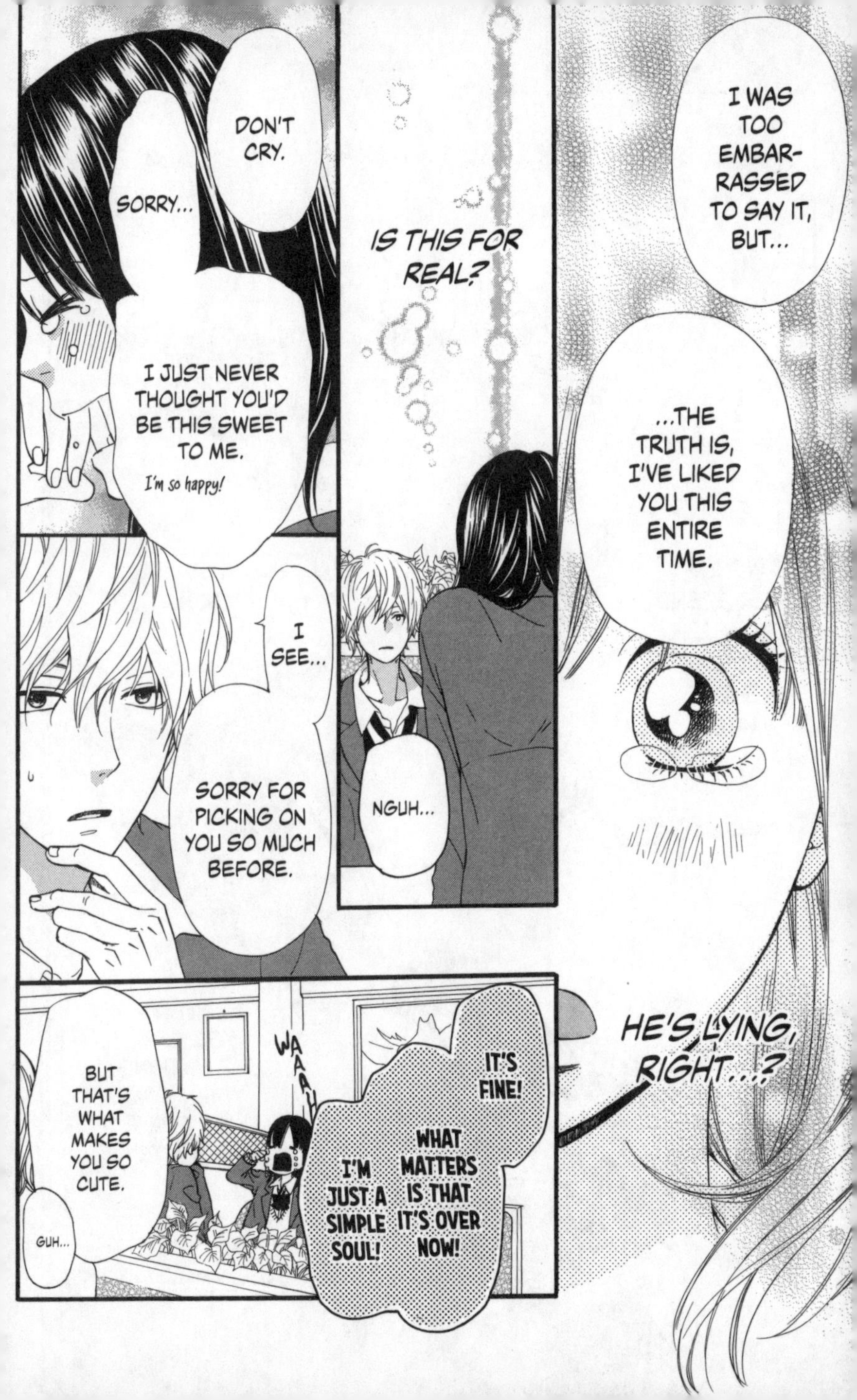
I WAS TOO EMBARRASSED TO SAY IT, BUT...
...THE TRUTH IS, I'VE LIKED YOU THIS ENTIRE TIME.
HE'S LYING, RIGHT...?
IS THIS FOR REAL?
NGUH...
DON'T CRY.
SORRY...
I JUST NEVER THOUGHT YOU'D BE THIS SWEET TO ME.
I'm so happy!
I SEE...
SORRY FOR PICKING ON YOU SO MUCH BEFORE.
IT'S FINE!
WHAT MATTERS IS THAT IT'S OVER NOW!
I'M JUST A SIMPLE SOUL!
WAAAH
BUT THAT'S WHAT MAKES YOU SO CUTE.
GUH...

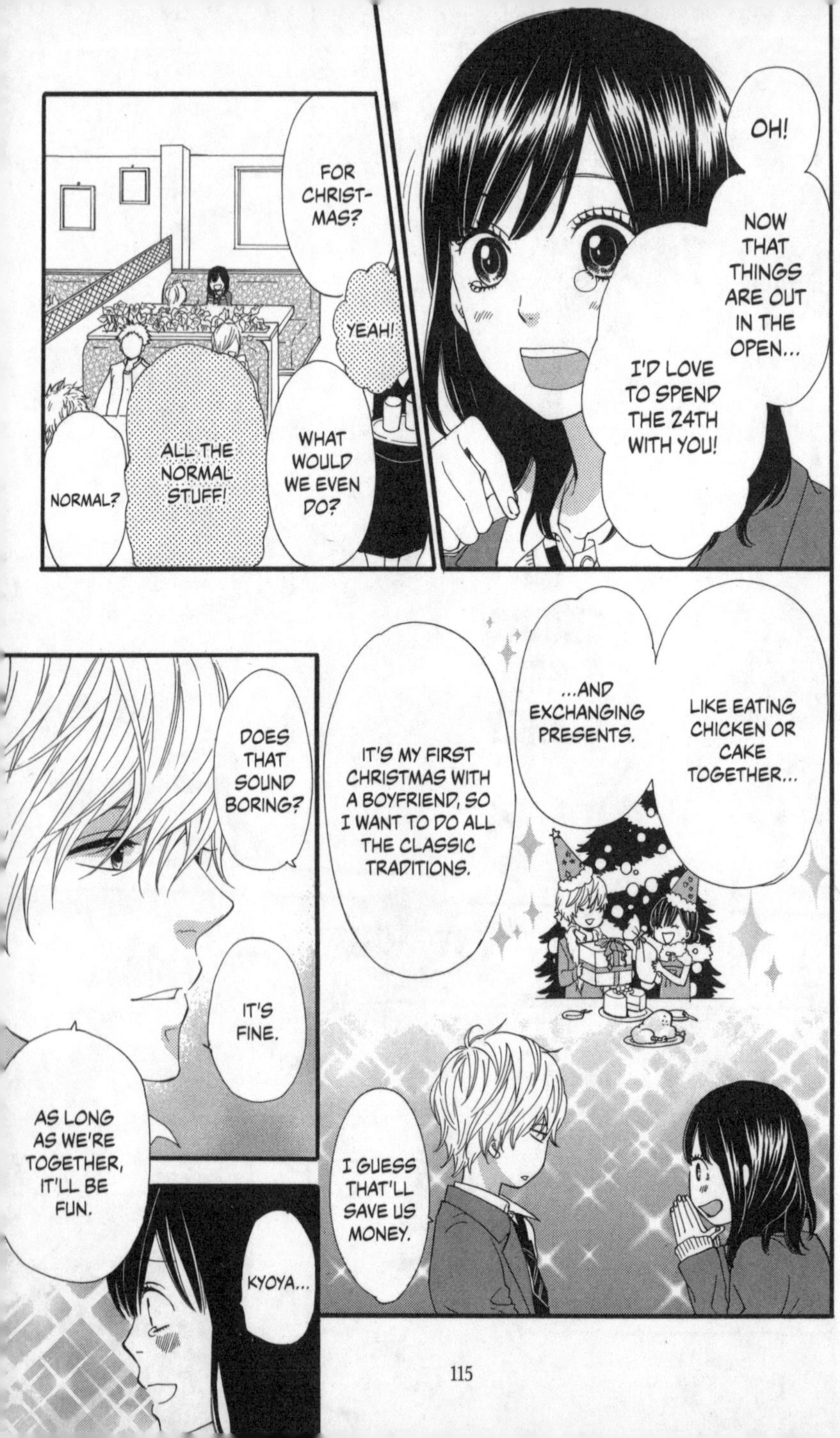
OH!
NOW THAT THINGS ARE OUT IN THE OPEN...
I'D LOVE TO SPEND THE 24TH WITH YOU!
FOR CHRISTMAS?
YEAH!
WHAT WOULD WE EVEN DO?
ALL THE NORMAL STUFF!
NORMAL?
LIKE EATING CHICKEN OR CAKE TOGETHER...
...AND EXCHANGING PRESENTS.
IT'S MY FIRST CHRISTMAS WITH A BOYFRIEND, SO I WANT TO DO ALL THE CLASSIC TRADITIONS.
I GUESS THAT'LL SAVE US MONEY.
DOES THAT SOUND BORING?
IT'S FINE.
AS LONG AS WE'RE TOGETHER, IT'LL BE FUN.
KYOYA...

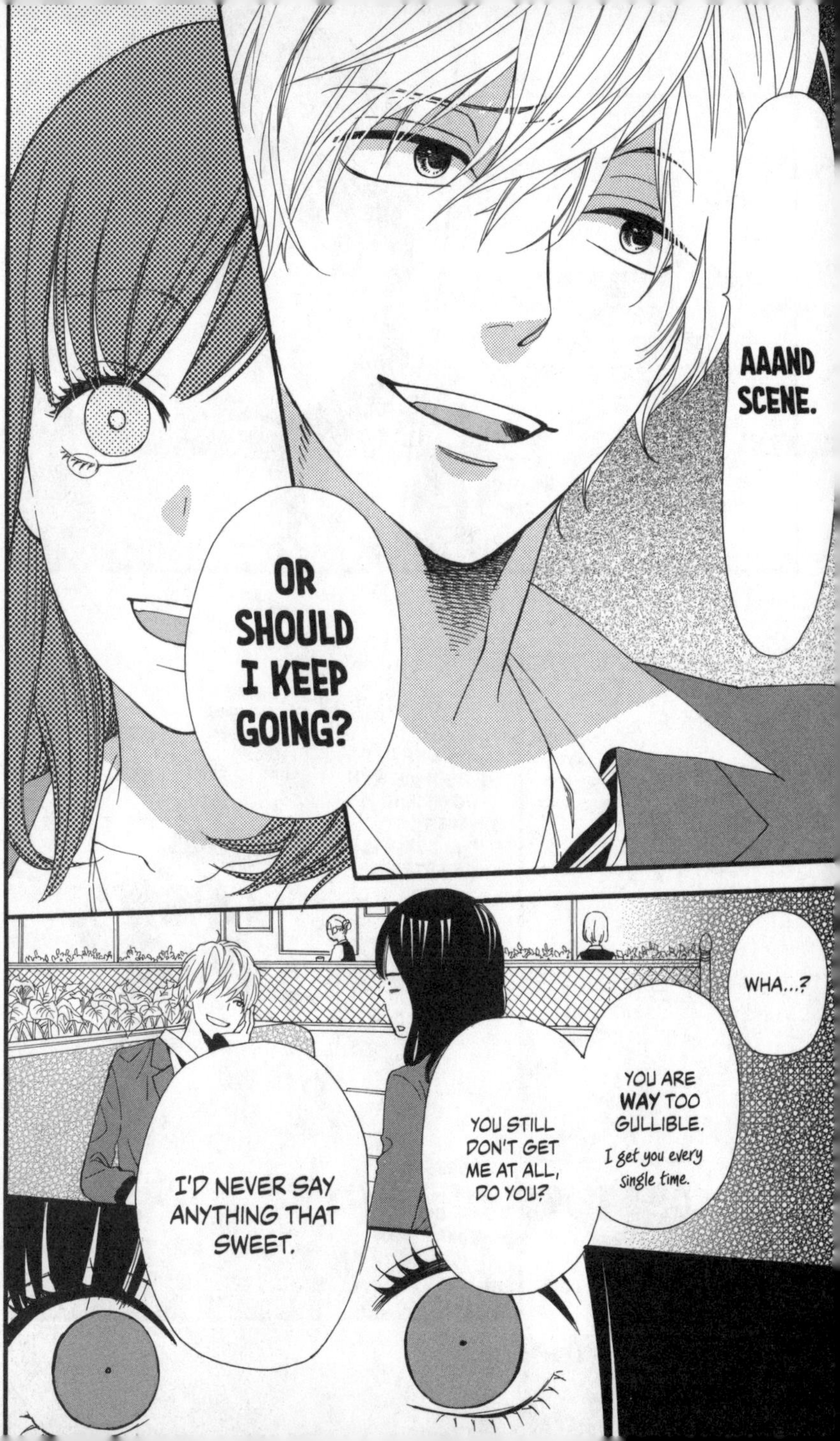
AAAND SCENE.
OR SHOULD I KEEP GOING?
WHA...?
YOU ARE WAY TOO GULLIBLE. I get you every single time.
YOU STILL DON'T GET ME AT ALL, DO YOU?
I'D NEVER SAY ANYTHING THAT SWEET.

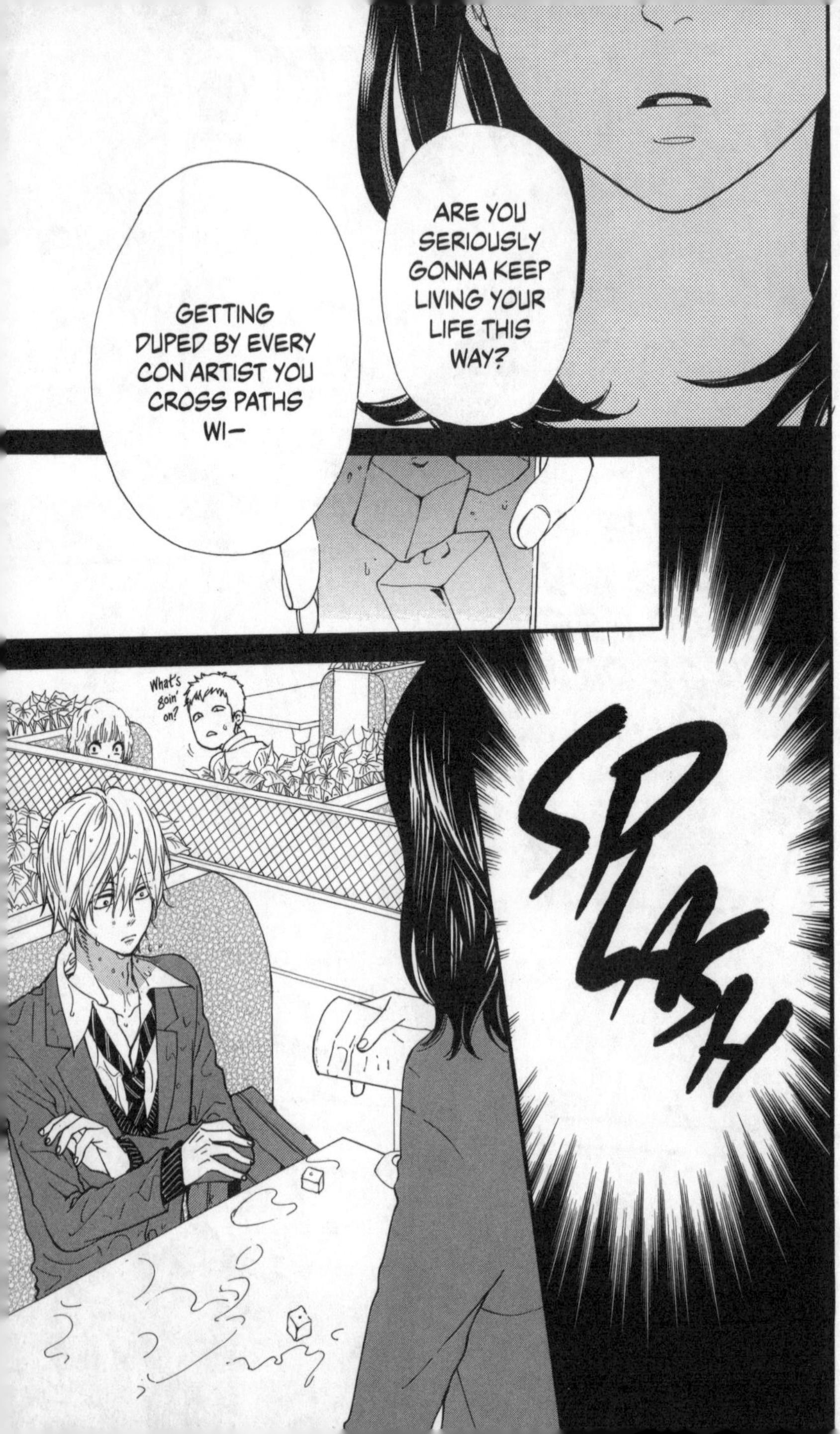
ARE YOU SERIOUSLY GONNA KEEP LIVING YOUR LIFE THIS WAY?
GETTING DUPED BY EVERY CON ARTIST YOU CROSS PATHS WI—
SPLASH
What's goin' on?

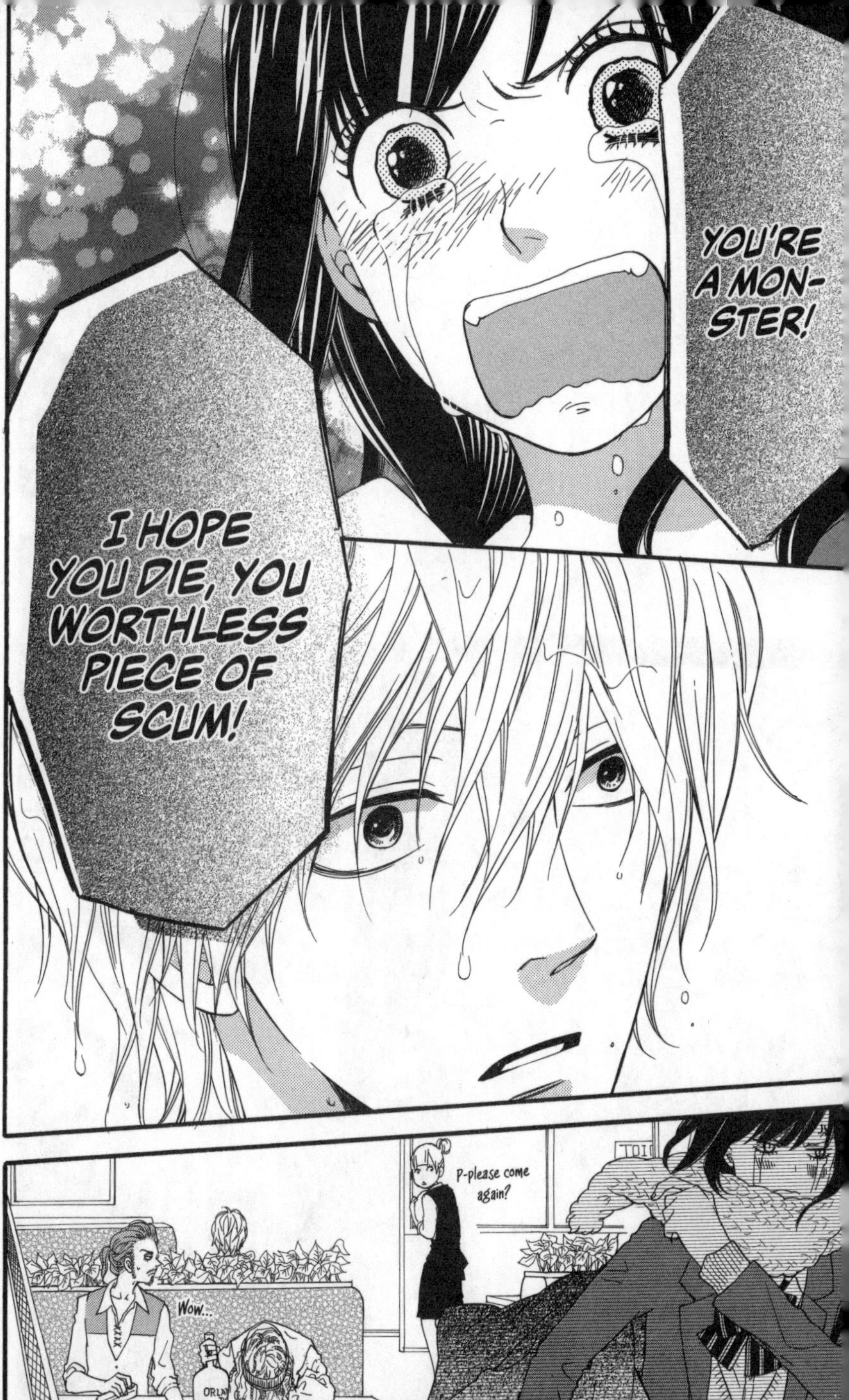
YOU'RE A MON- STER!
I HOPE YOU DIE, YOU WORTHLESS PIECE OF SCUM!
P-please come again?
Wow...

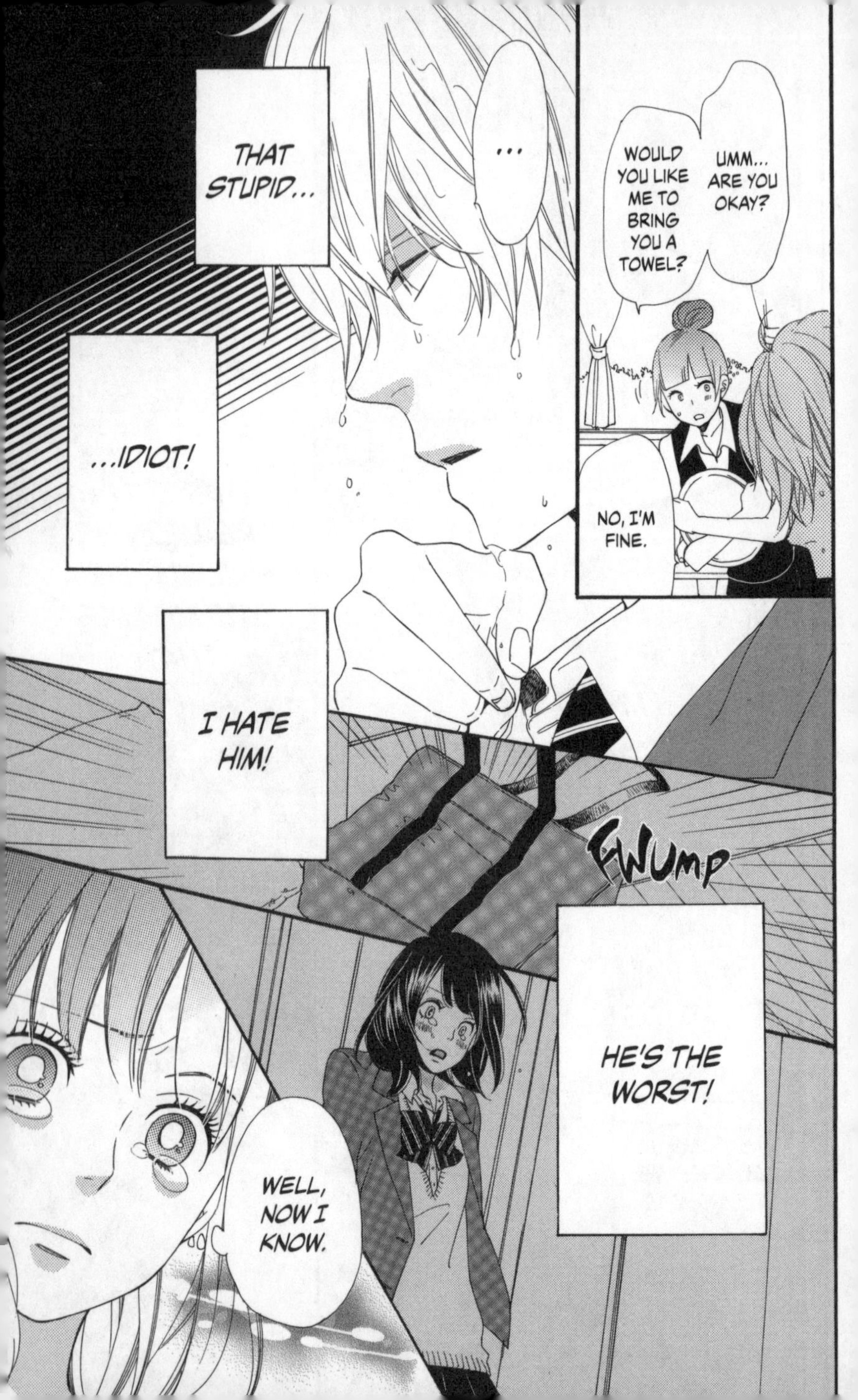
UMM... ARE YOU OKAY?
WOULD YOU LIKE ME TO BRING YOU A TOWEL?
NO, I'M FINE.
...
THAT STUPID...
...IDIOT!
I HATE HIM!
FWUMP
HE'S THE WORST!
WELL, NOW I KNOW.

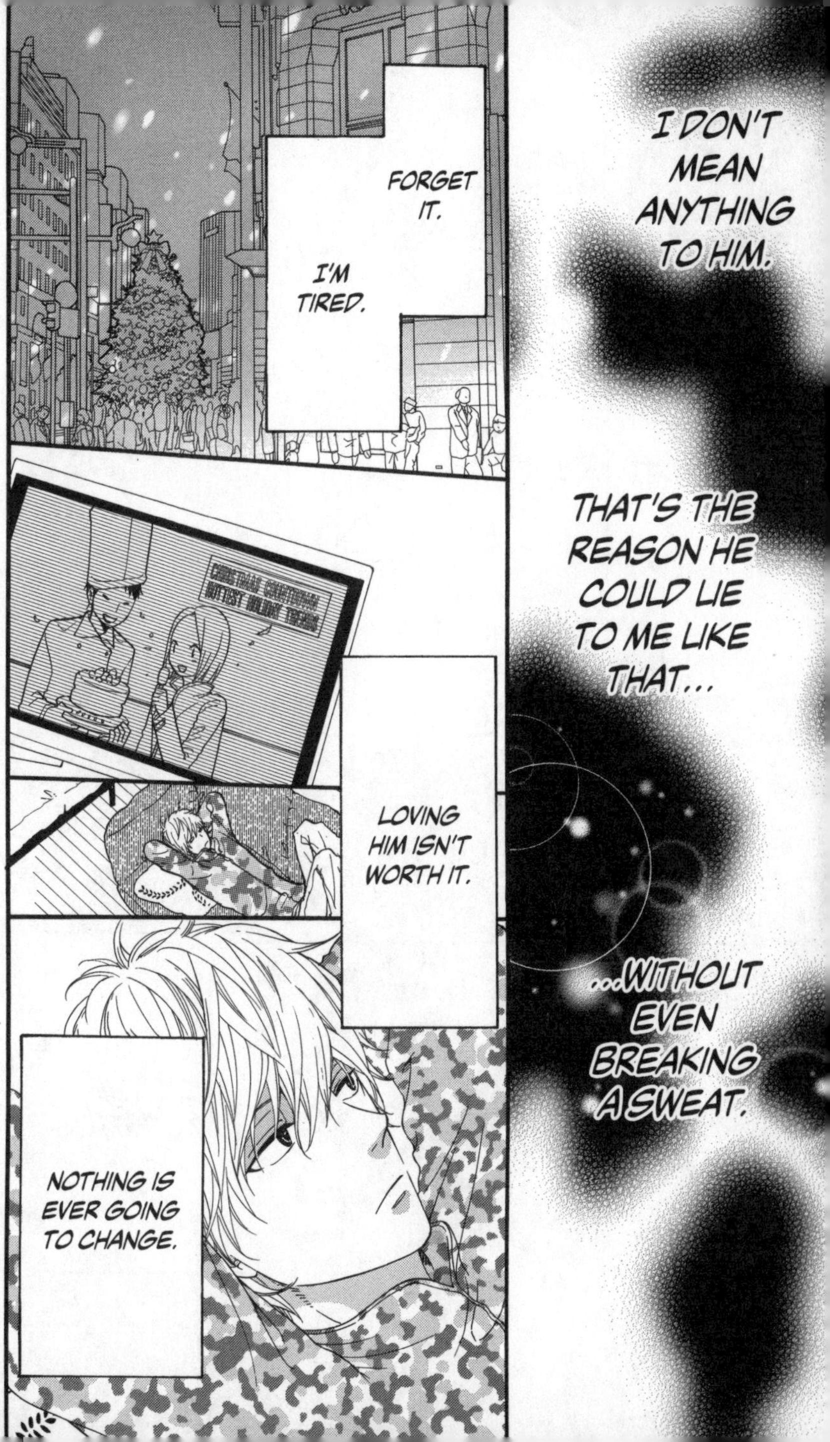
I DON'T MEAN ANYTHING TO HIM.
THAT'S THE REASON HE COULD LIE TO ME LIKE THAT...
...WITHOUT EVEN BREAKING A SWEAT.
FORGET IT.
I'M TIRED.
CHRISTMAS COUNTDOWN HOTTEST HOLIDAY TRENDS
LOVING HIM ISN'T WORTH IT.
NOTHING IS EVER GOING TO CHANGE.

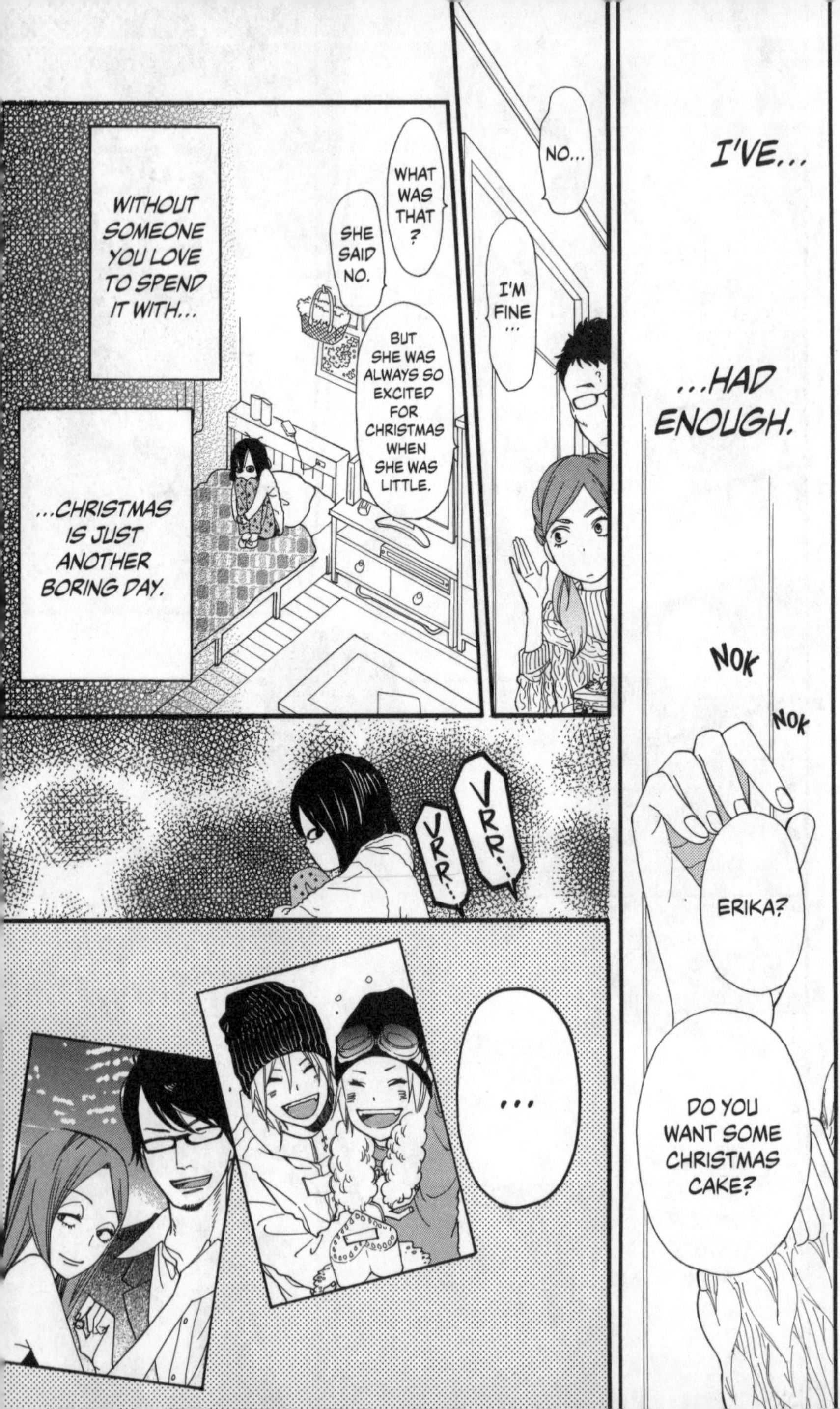
I'VE...
...HAD ENOUGH.
NOK
NOK
ERIKA?
DO YOU WANT SOME CHRISTMAS CAKE?
NO...
I'M FINE...
WHAT WAS THAT?
SHE SAID NO.
BUT SHE WAS ALWAYS SO EXCITED FOR CHRISTMAS WHEN SHE WAS LITTLE.
WITHOUT SOMEONE YOU LOVE TO SPEND IT WITH...
...CHRISTMAS IS JUST ANOTHER BORING DAY.
VRR...
VRR...
...

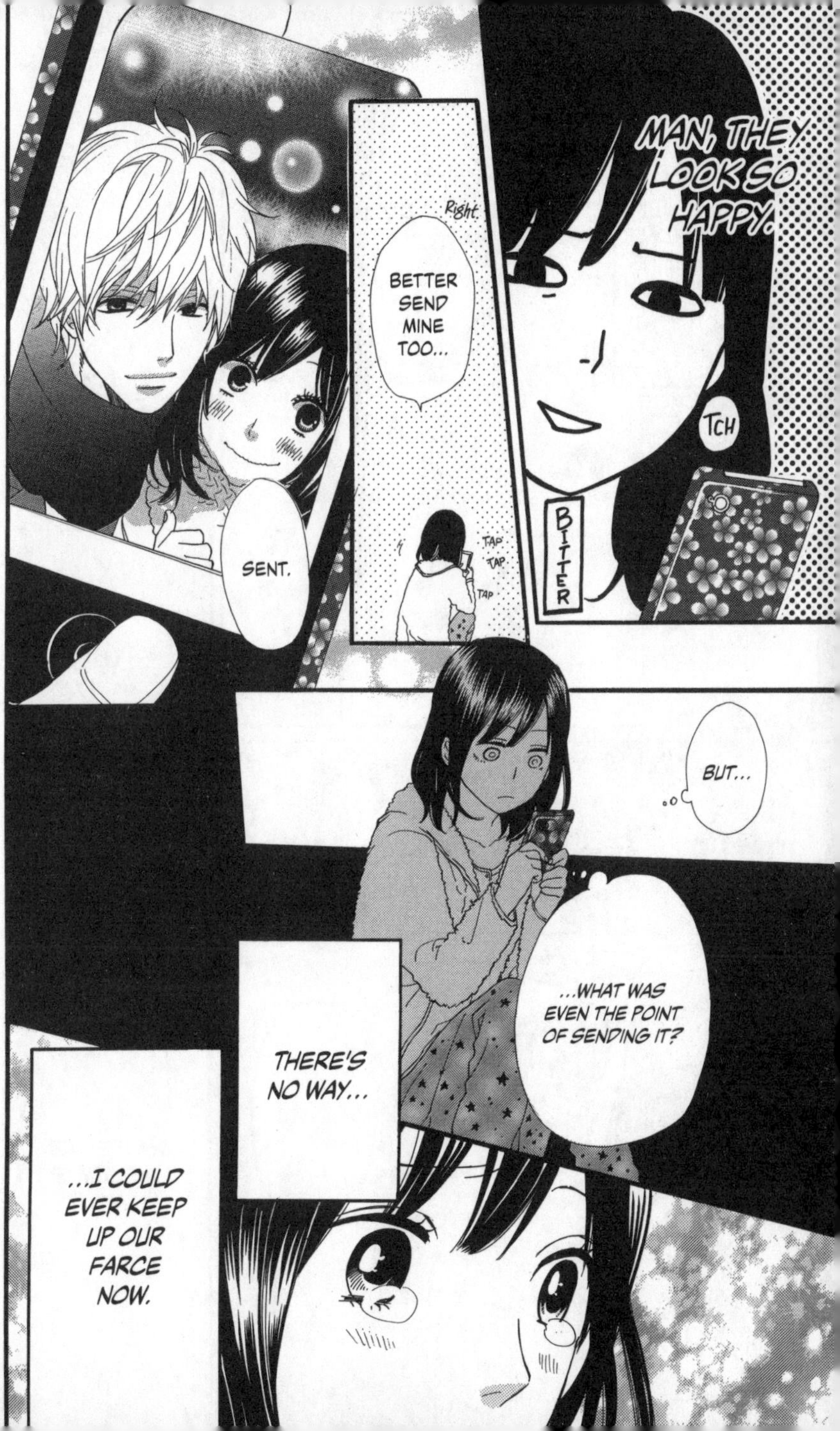
MAN, THEY LOOK SO HAPPY.
TCH
BITTER
Right.
BETTER SEND MINE TOO...
TAP TAP TAP
SENT.
BUT...
...WHAT WAS EVEN THE POINT OF SENDING IT?
THERE'S NO WAY...
...I COULD EVER KEEP UP OUR FARCE NOW.

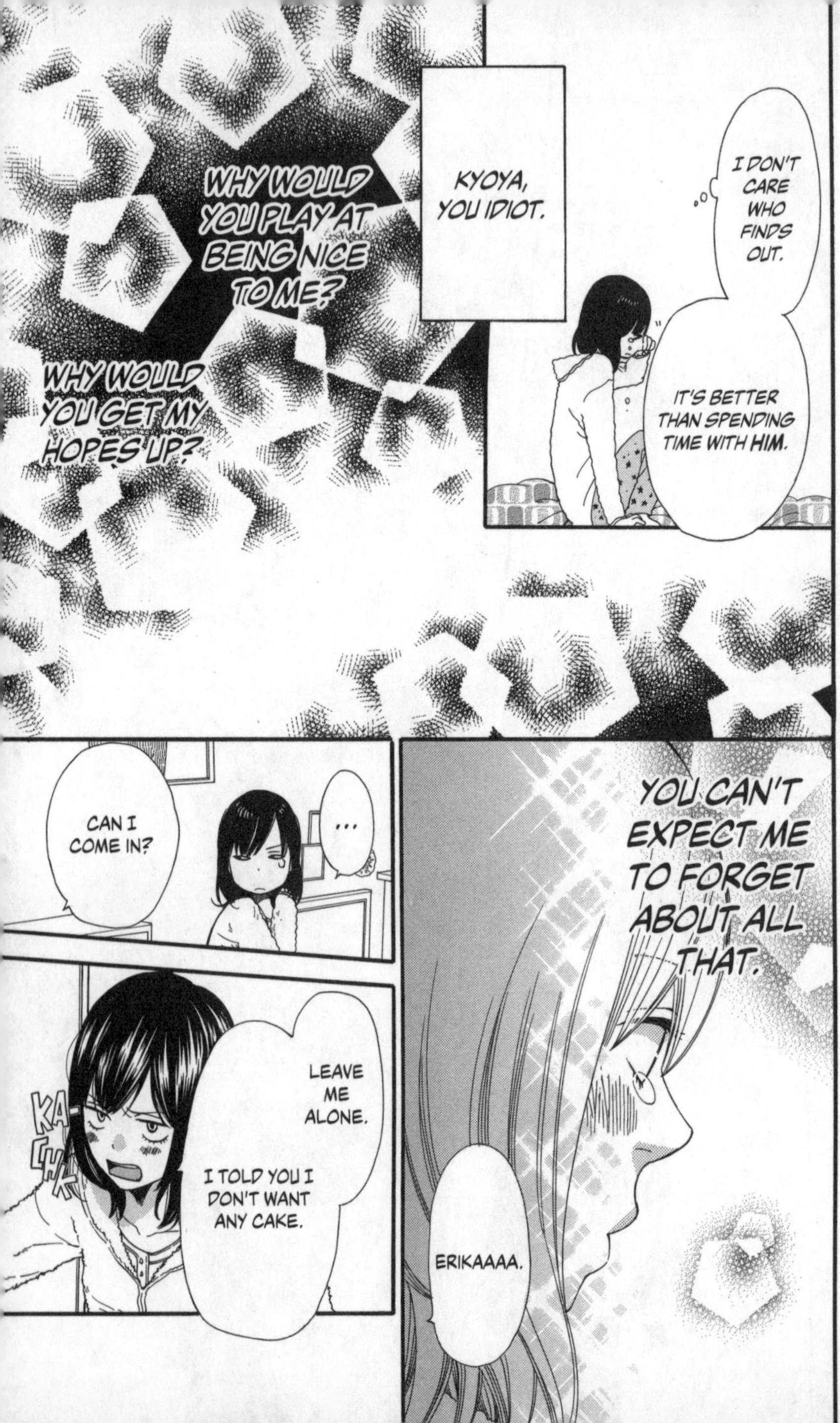
I DON'T CARE WHO FINDS OUT.
IT'S BETTER THAN SPENDING TIME WITH HIM.
KYOYA, YOU IDIOT.
WHY WOULD YOU PLAY AT BEING NICE TO ME?
WHY WOULD YOU GET MY HOPES UP?
YOU CAN'T EXPECT ME TO FORGET ABOUT ALL THAT.
ERIKAAAA.
...
CAN I COME IN?
KACHK
LEAVE ME ALONE.
I TOLD YOU I DON'T WANT ANY CAKE.

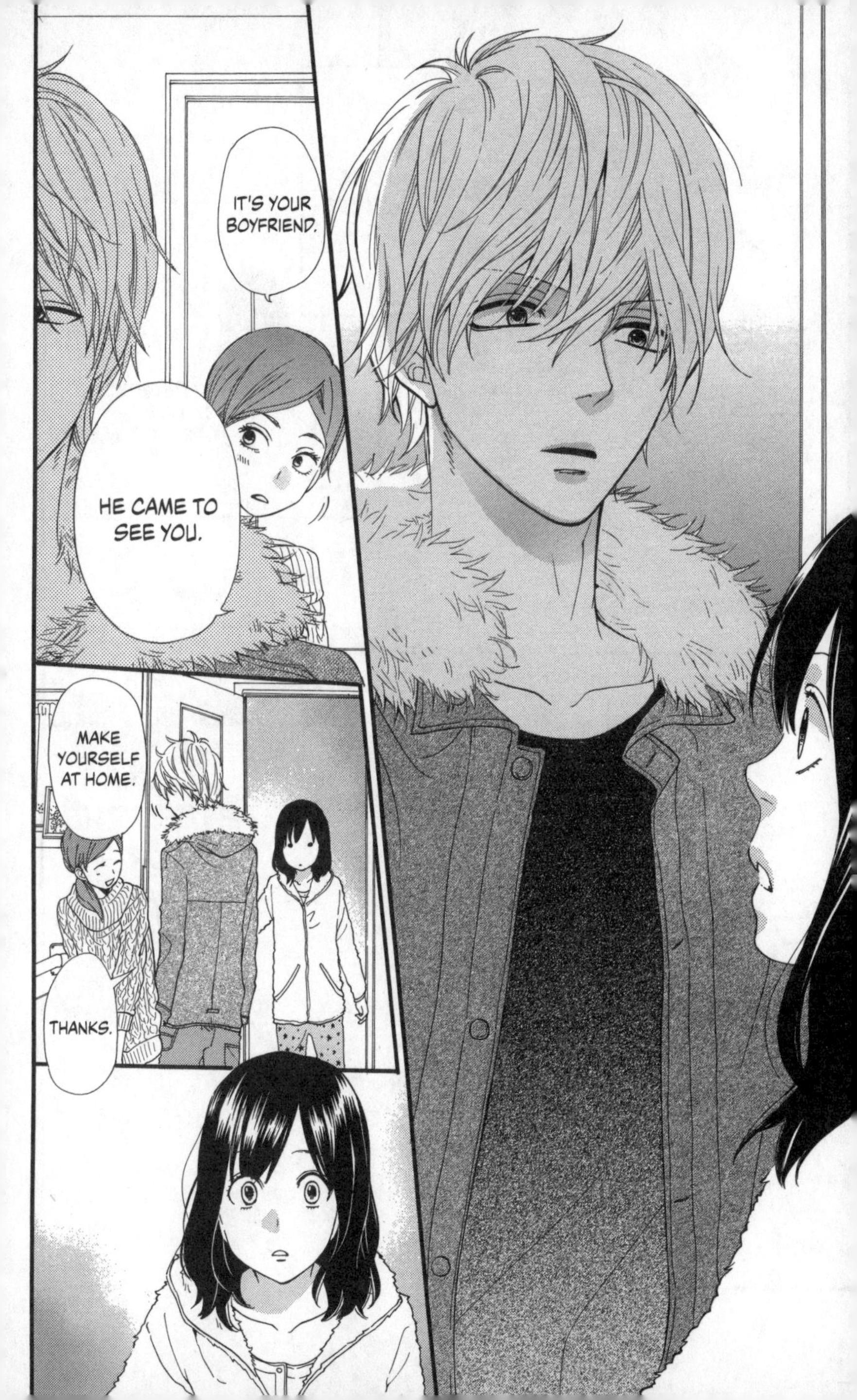
IT'S YOUR BOYFRIEND.
HE CAME TO SEE YOU.
MAKE YOURSELF AT HOME.
THANKS.

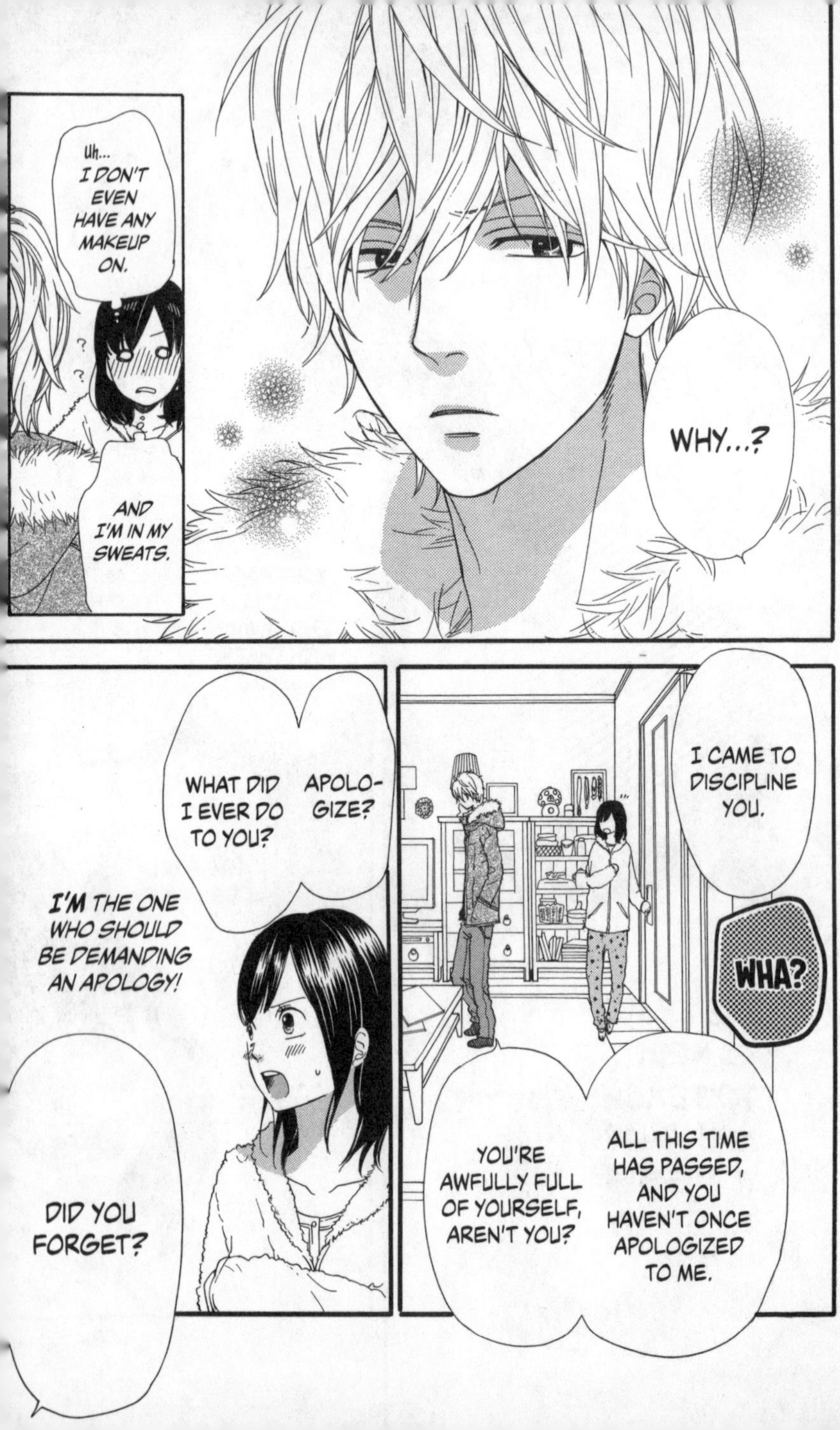
WHY...?
Uh... I DON'T EVEN HAVE ANY MAKEUP ON.
AND I'M IN MY SWEATS.
I CAME TO DISCIPLINE YOU.
WHA?
ALL THIS TIME HAS PASSED, AND YOU HAVEN'T ONCE APOLOGIZED TO ME.
YOU'RE AWFULLY FULL OF YOURSELF, AREN'T YOU?
APOLO-GIZE?
WHAT DID I EVER DO TO YOU?
I'M THE ONE WHO SHOULD BE DEMANDING AN APOLOGY!
DID YOU FORGET?

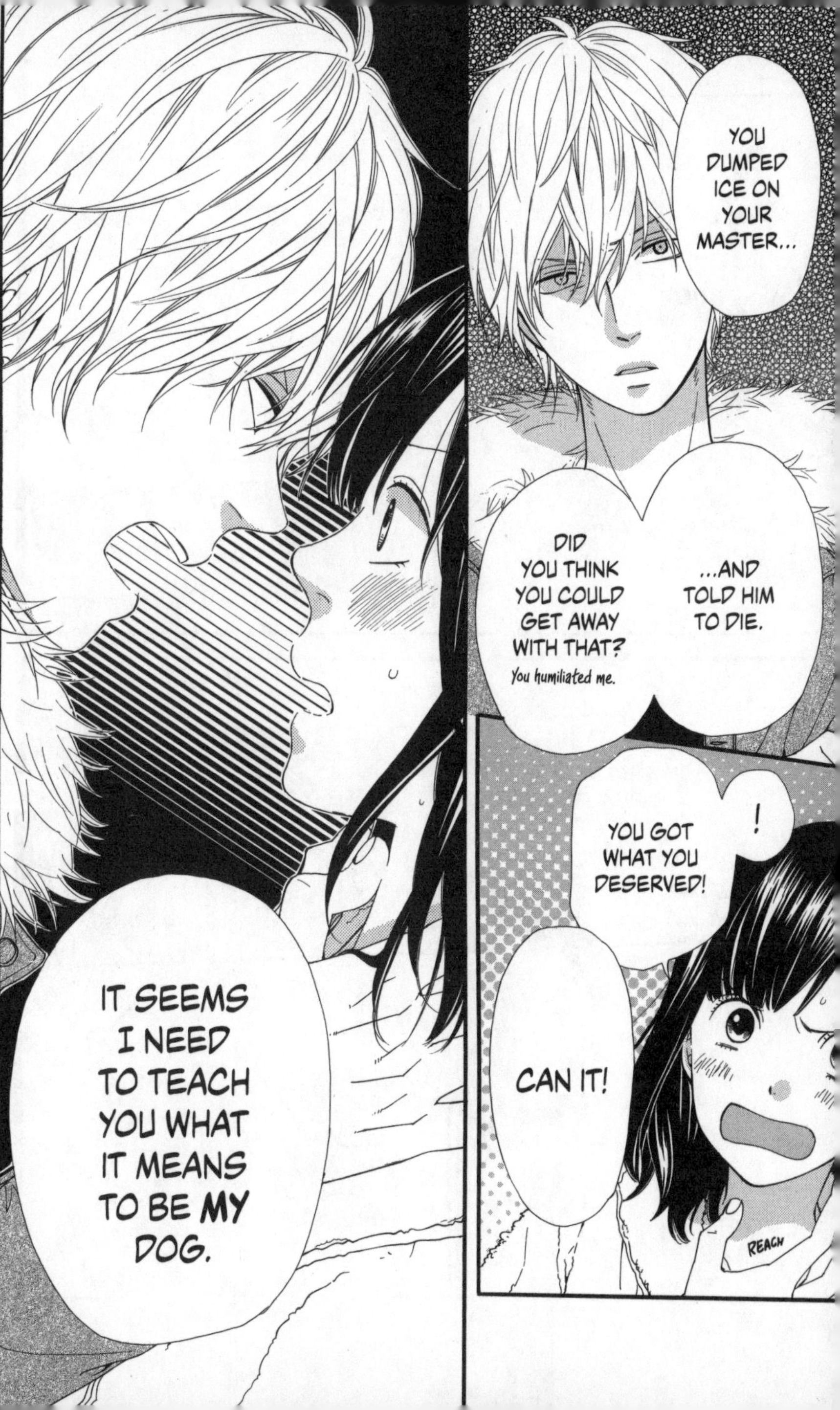
YOU DUMPED ICE ON YOUR MASTER...
...AND TOLD HIM TO DIE.
DID YOU THINK YOU COULD GET AWAY WITH THAT?
You humiliated me.
!
YOU GOT WHAT YOU DESERVED!
CAN IT!
REACH
IT SEEMS I NEED TO TEACH YOU WHAT IT MEANS TO BE MY DOG.

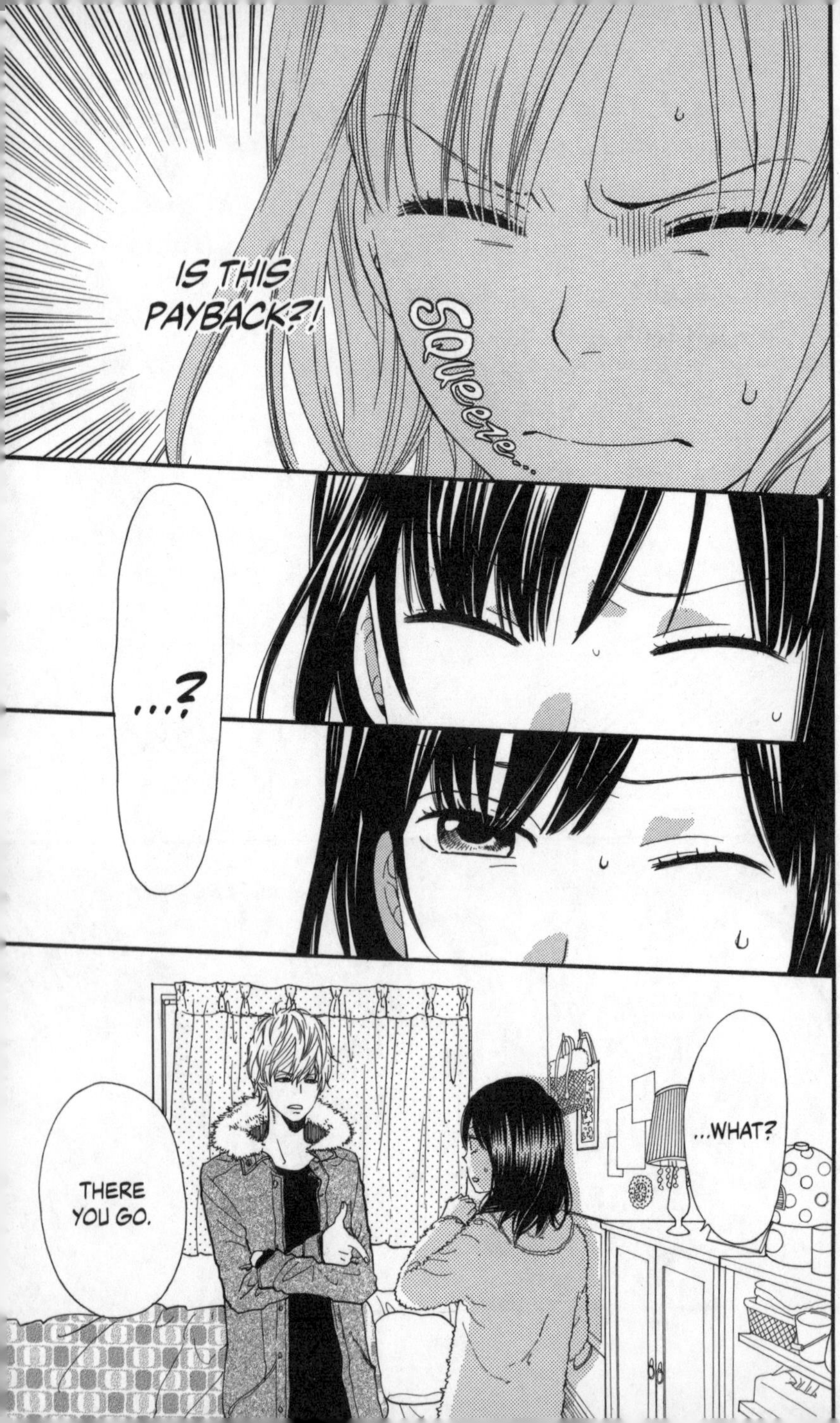
Squeeze...
IS THIS PAYBACK?!
...?
...WHAT?
THERE YOU GO.

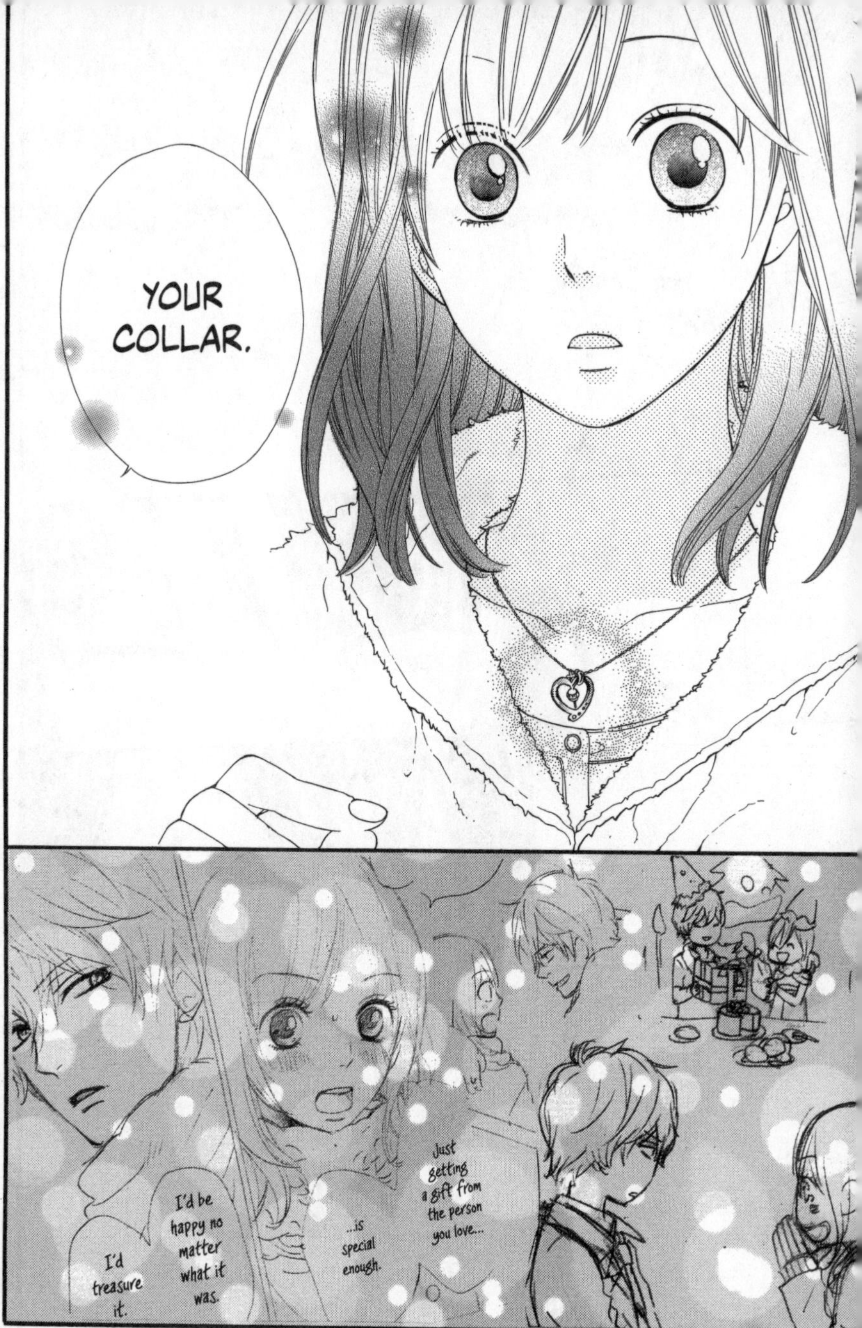
YOUR COLLAR.
Just getting a gift from the person you love...
...is special enough.
I'd be happy no matter what it was.
I'd treasure it.

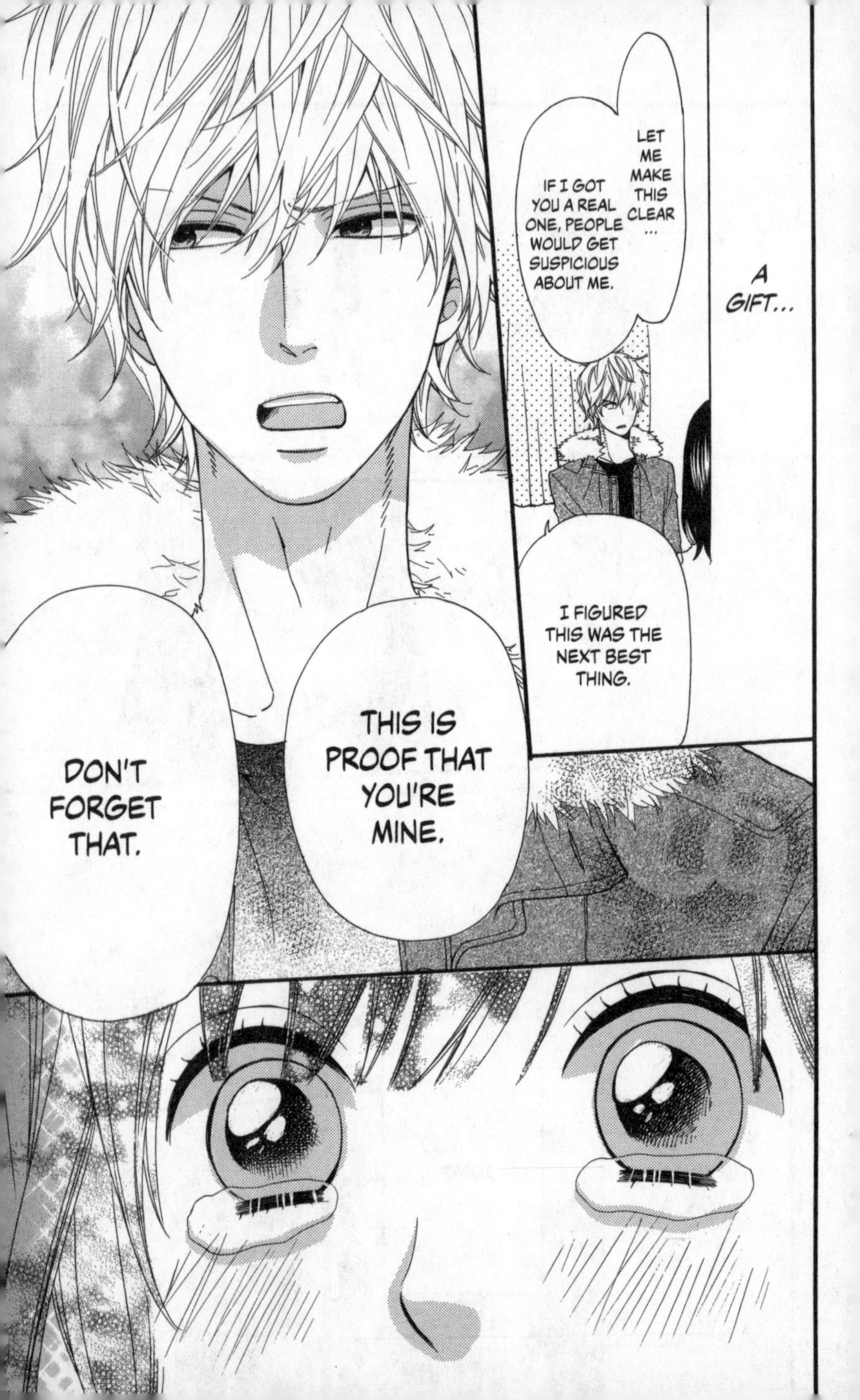
A GIFT...
LET ME MAKE THIS CLEAR...
IF I GOT YOU A REAL ONE, PEOPLE WOULD GET SUSPICIOUS ABOUT ME.
I FIGURED THIS WAS THE NEXT BEST THING.
THIS IS PROOF THAT YOU'RE MINE.
DON'T FORGET THAT.

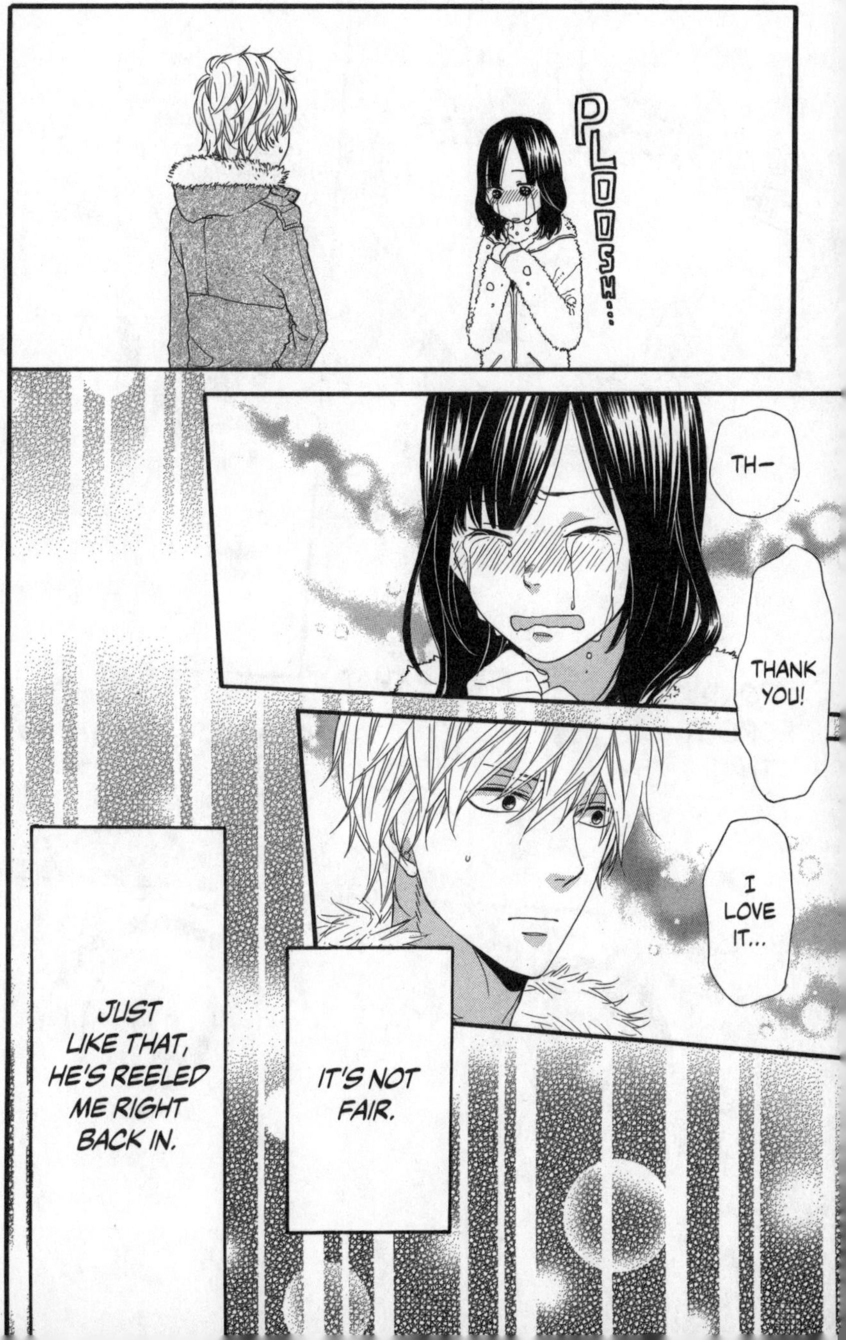
PLOOSH...
TH—
THANK YOU!
I LOVE IT...
IT'S NOT FAIR.
JUST LIKE THAT, HE'S REELED ME RIGHT BACK IN.

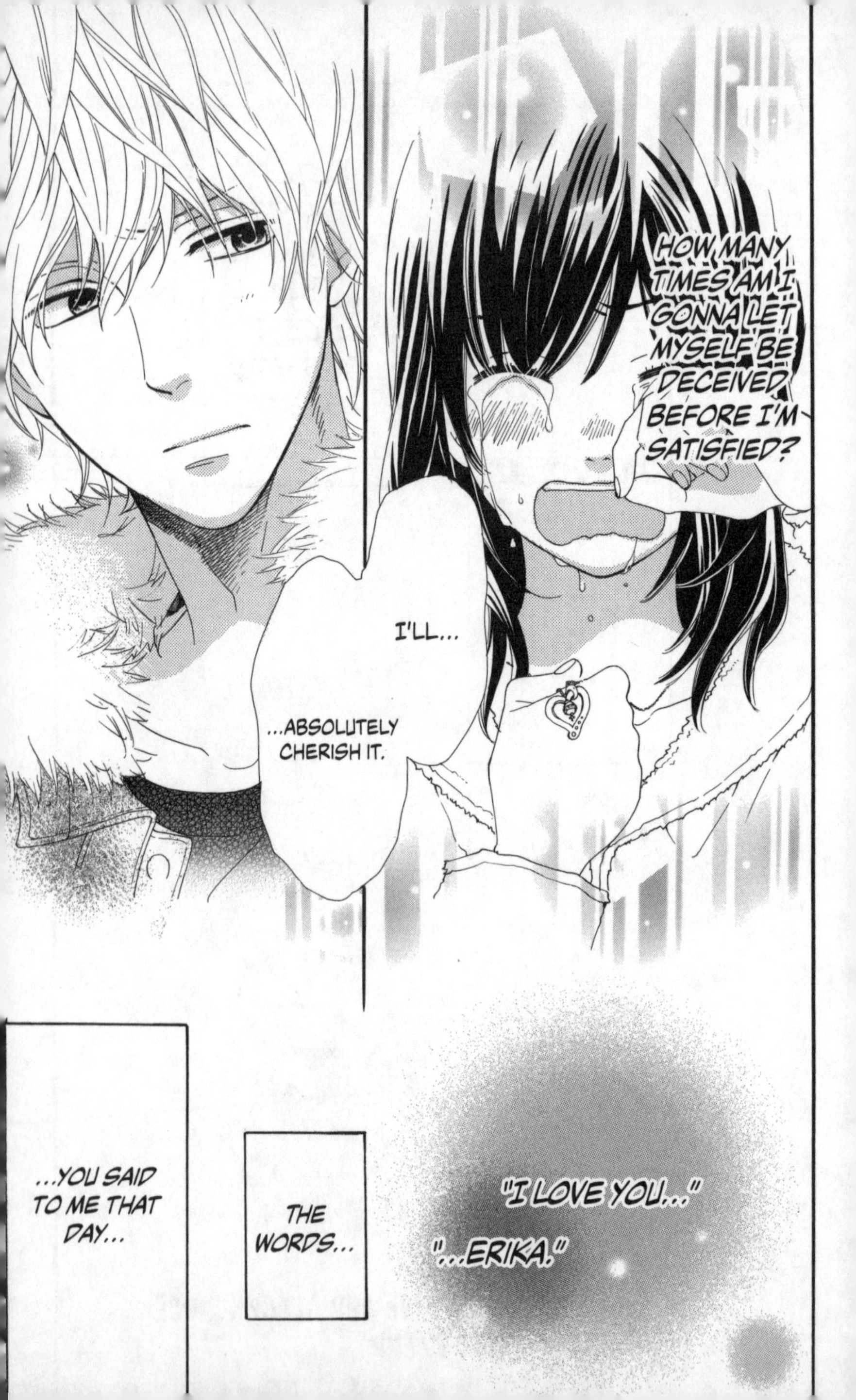
HOW MANY TIMES AM I GONNA LET MYSELF BE DECEIVED BEFORE I'M SATISFIED?
I'LL...
...ABSOLUTELY CHERISH IT.
"I LOVE YOU..."
"...ERIKA."
THE WORDS...
...YOU SAID TO ME THAT DAY...

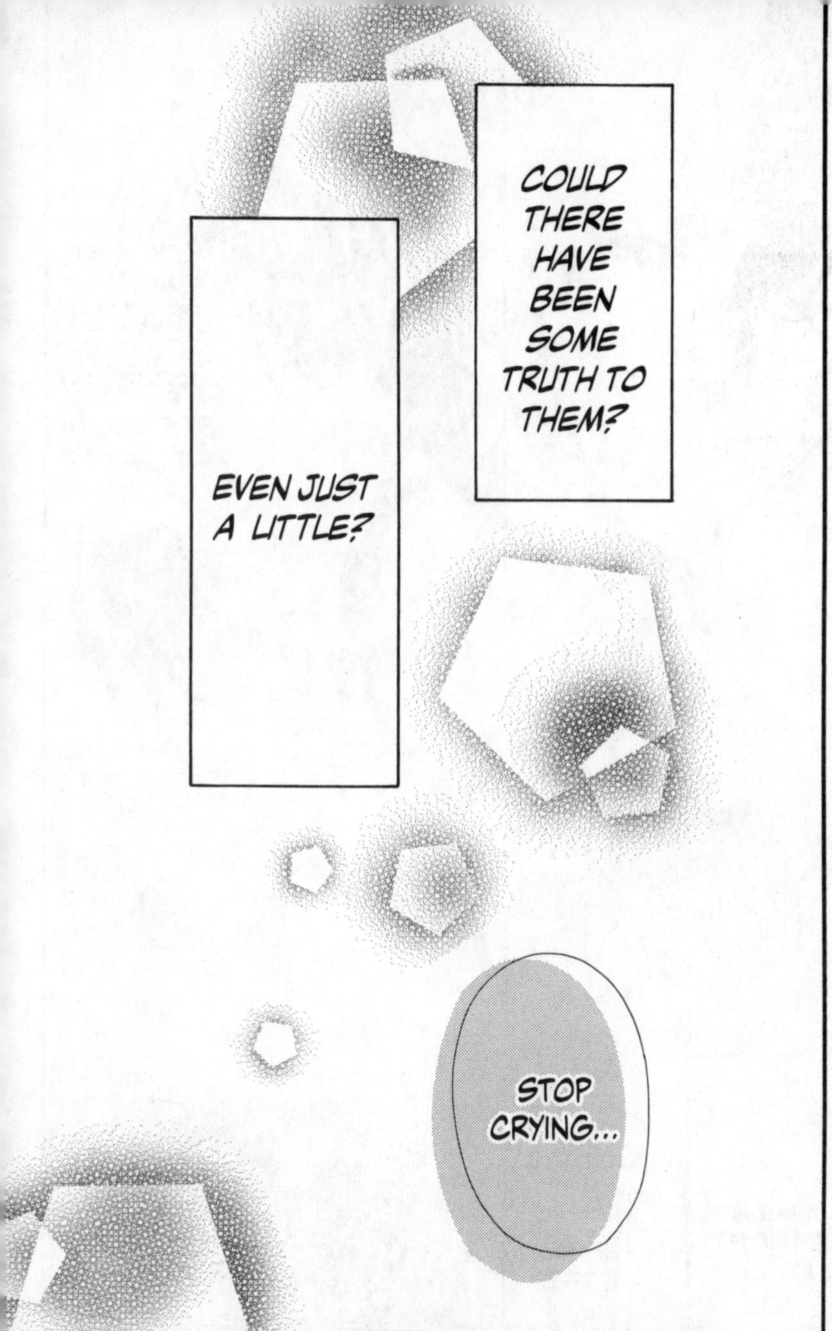
COULD THERE HAVE BEEN SOME TRUTH TO THEM?
EVEN JUST A LITTLE?
STOP CRYING...

WOLF GIRL AND BLACK PRINCE
VOL. 2/END

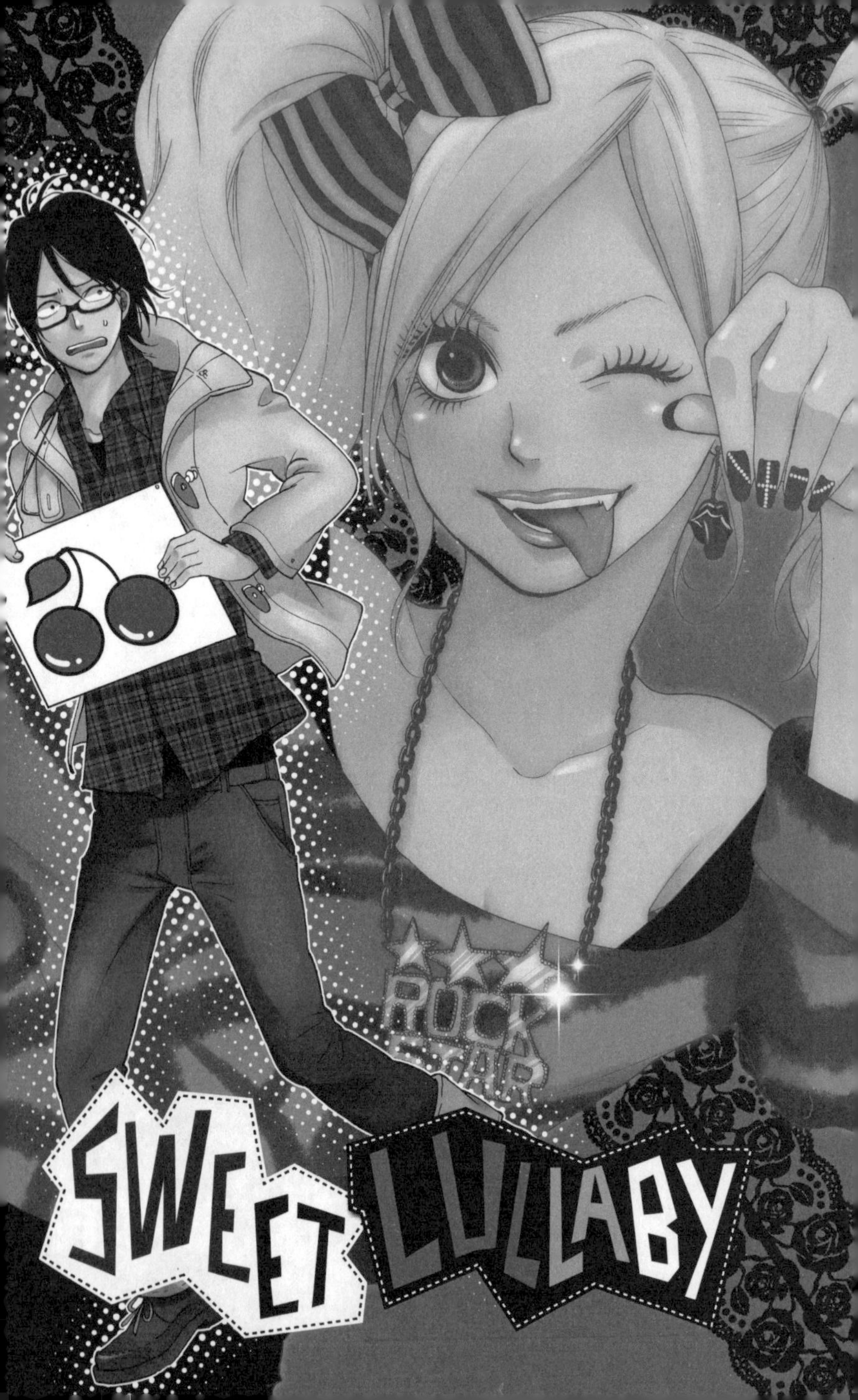
ROCK STAR
SWEET LULLABY

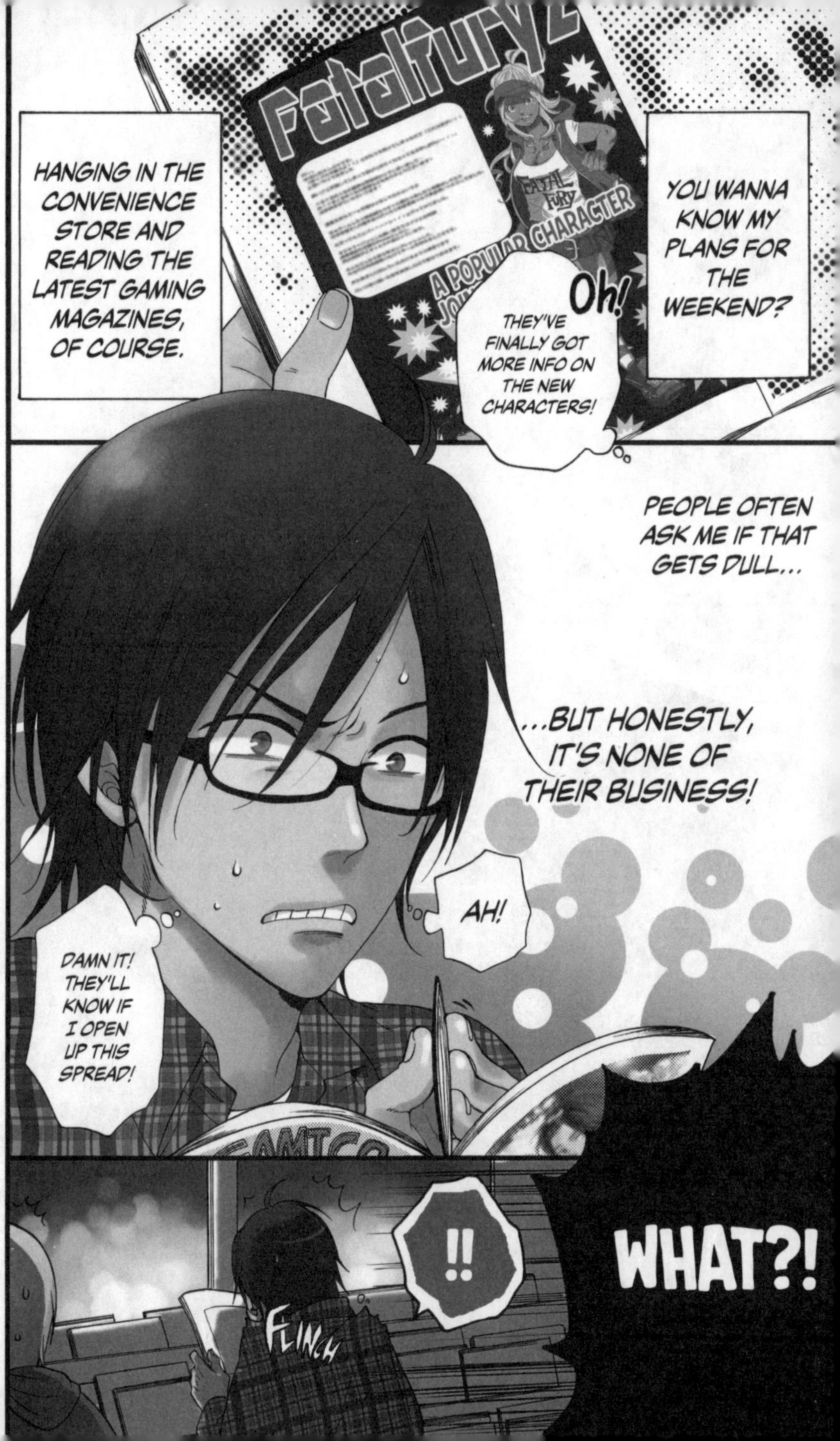
YOU WANNA KNOW MY PLANS FOR THE WEEKEND?
HANGING IN THE CONVENIENCE STORE AND READING THE LATEST GAMING MAGAZINES, OF COURSE.
Fatalfury2
A POPULAR CHARACTER
Oh!
THEY'VE FINALLY GOT MORE INFO ON THE NEW CHARACTERS!
PEOPLE OFTEN ASK ME IF THAT GETS DULL...
...BUT HONESTLY, IT'S NONE OF THEIR BUSINESS!
AH!
DAMN IT! THEY'LL KNOW IF I OPEN UP THIS SPREAD!
WHAT?!
!!
FLINCH

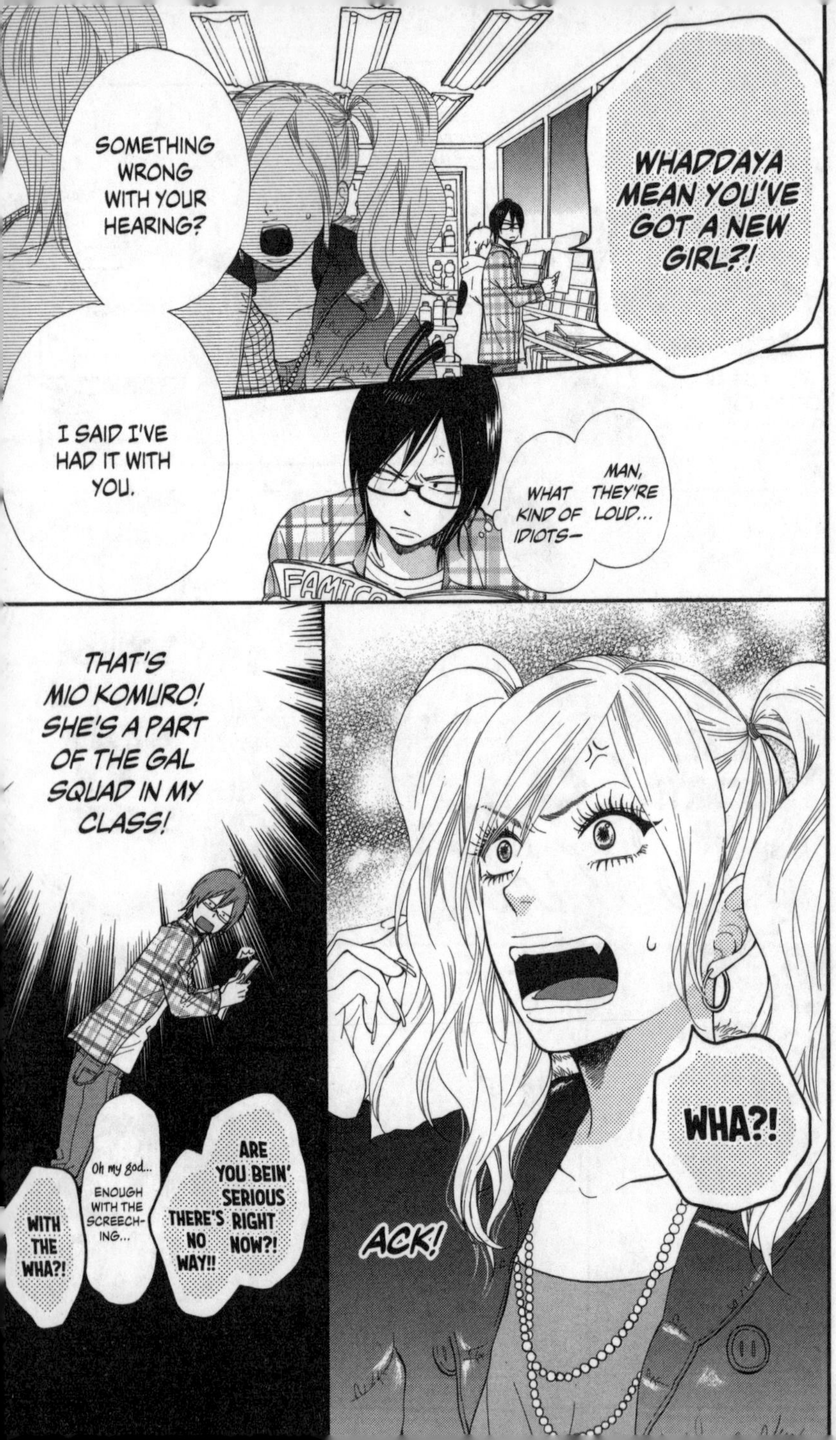
WHADDAYA MEAN YOU'VE GOT A NEW GIRL?!
SOMETHING WRONG WITH YOUR HEARING?
I SAID I'VE HAD IT WITH YOU.
MAN, THEY'RE LOUD...
WHAT KIND OF IDIOTS—
FAMICO
WHA?!
ACK!
THAT'S MIO KOMURO! SHE'S A PART OF THE GAL SQUAD IN MY CLASS!
ARE YOU BEIN' SERIOUS RIGHT NOW?!
THERE'S NO WAY!!
Oh my god... ENOUGH WITH THE SCREECHING...
WITH THE WHA?!

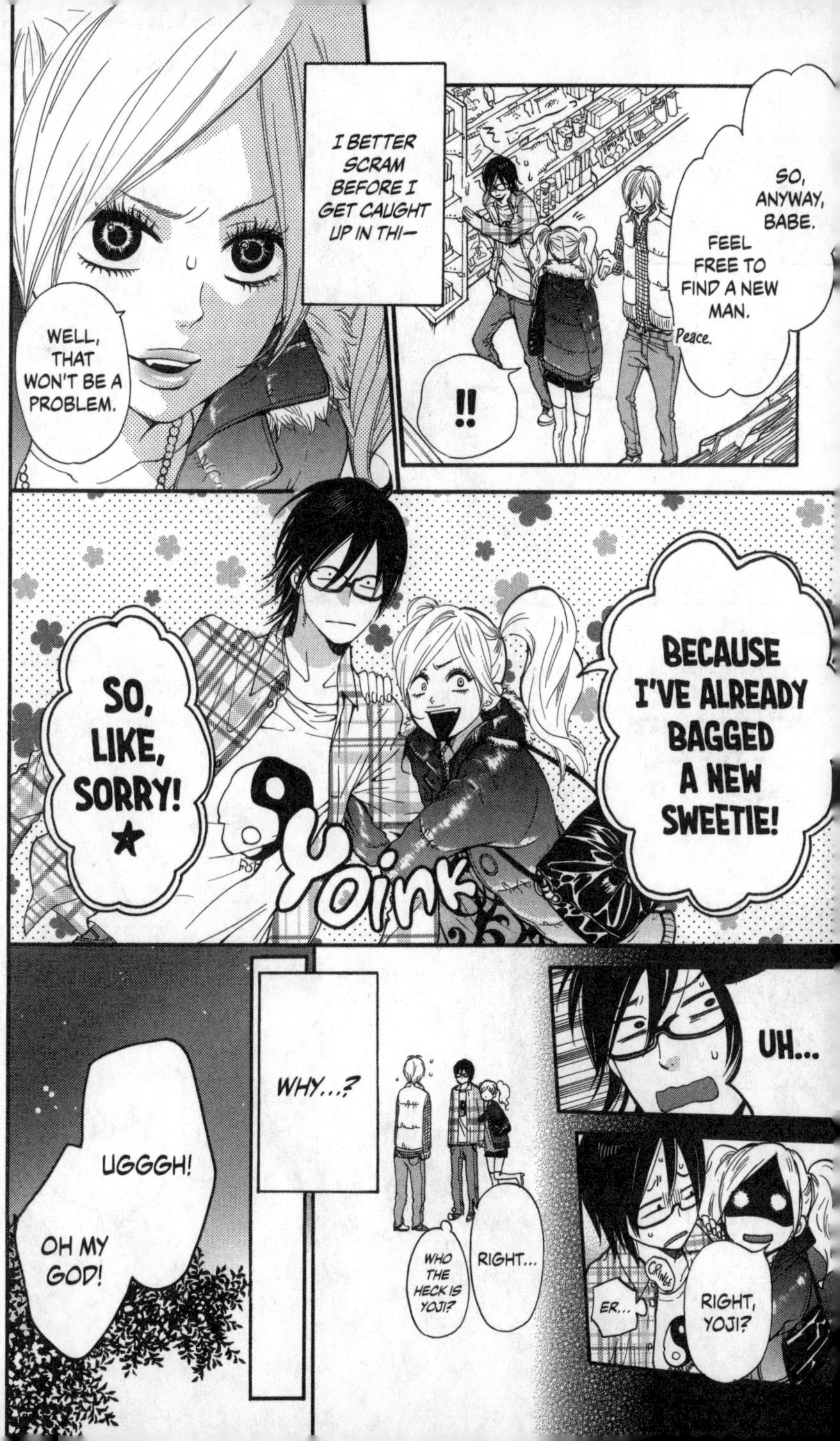
SO, ANYWAY, BABE.
FEEL FREE TO FIND A NEW MAN.
Peace.
!!
I BETTER SCRAM BEFORE I GET CAUGHT UP IN THI—
WELL, THAT WON'T BE A PROBLEM.
BECAUSE I'VE ALREADY BAGGED A NEW SWEETIE!
YOINK
SO, LIKE, SORRY! ★
UH...
RIGHT, YOJI?
CRINGE
ER...
WHY...?
RIGHT...
WHO THE HECK IS YOJI?
UGGGH!
OH MY GOD!

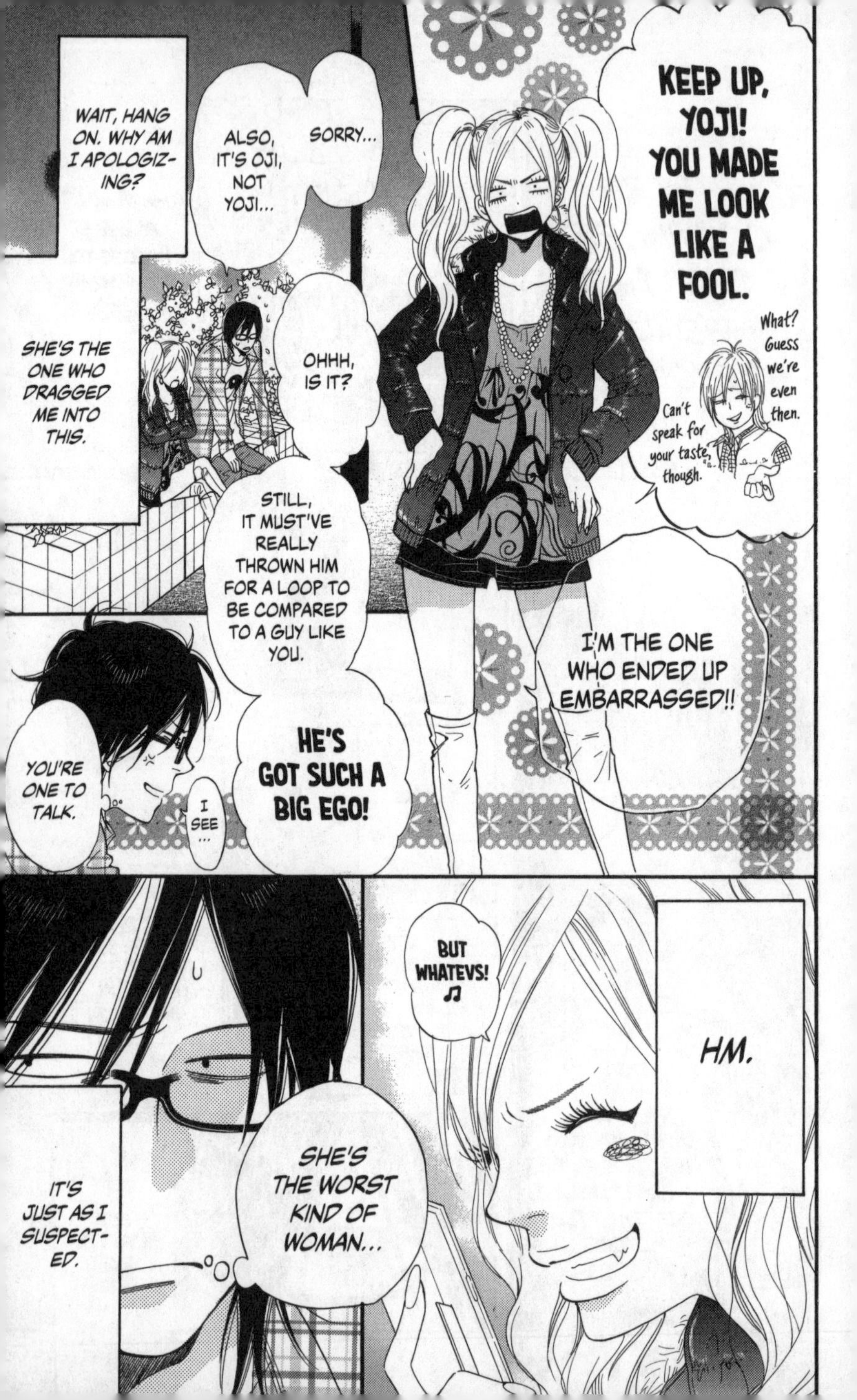
KEEP UP, YOJI! YOU MADE ME LOOK LIKE A FOOL.
What? Guess we're even then.
Can't speak for your taste, though.
SORRY...
ALSO, IT'S OJI, NOT YOJI...
WAIT, HANG ON. WHY AM I APOLOGIZING?
SHE'S THE ONE WHO DRAGGED ME INTO THIS.
I'M THE ONE WHO ENDED UP EMBARRASSED!!
OHHH, IS IT?
STILL, IT MUST'VE REALLY THROWN HIM FOR A LOOP TO BE COMPARED TO A GUY LIKE YOU.
HE'S GOT SUCH A BIG EGO!
I SEE...
YOU'RE ONE TO TALK.
HM.
BUT WHATEVS! ♫
SHE'S THE WORST KIND OF WOMAN...
IT'S JUST AS I SUSPECTED.

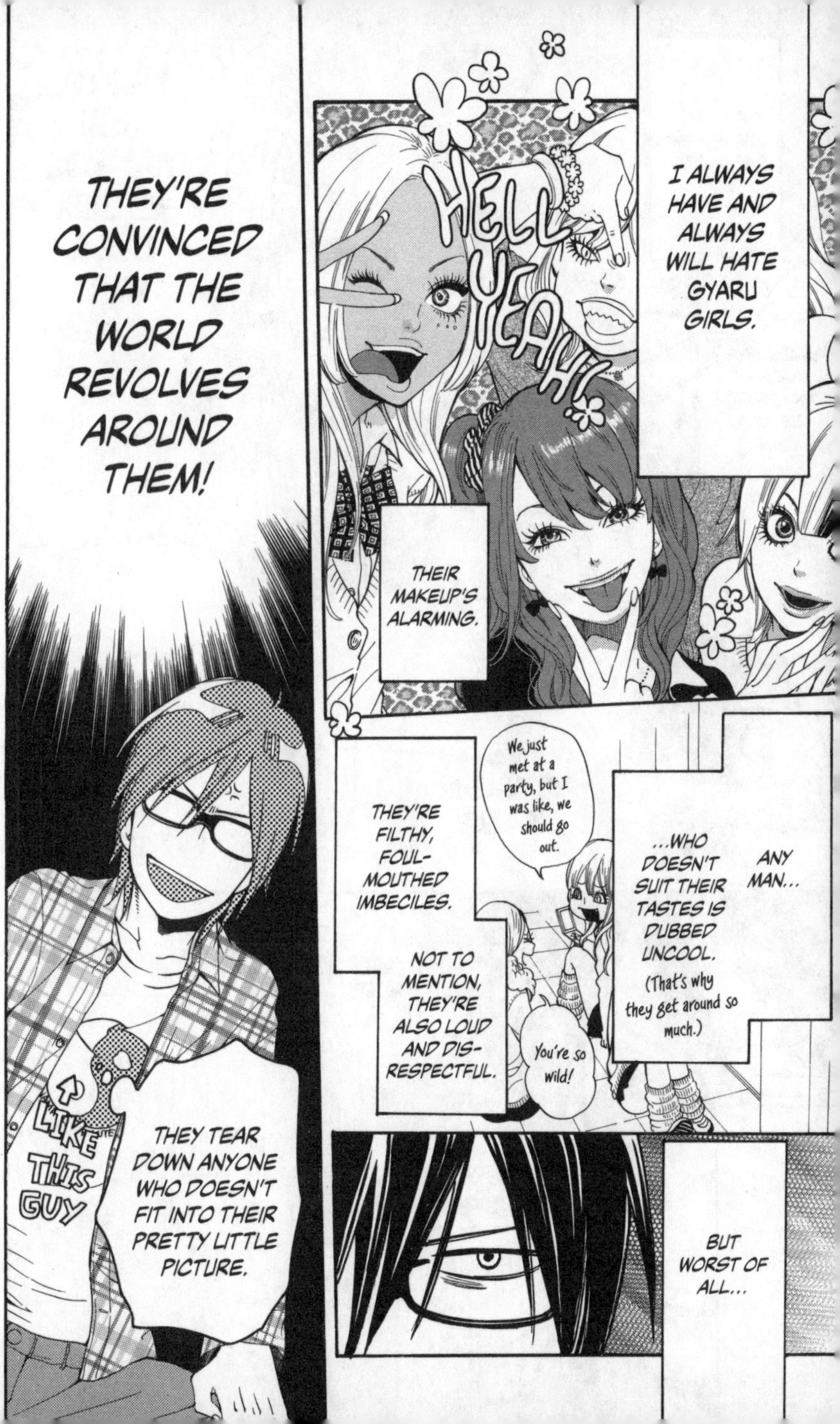
I ALWAYS HAVE AND ALWAYS WILL HATE GYARU GIRLS.
HELL YEAH!
THEIR MAKEUP'S ALARMING.
ANY MAN...
...WHO DOESN'T SUIT THEIR TASTES IS DUBBED UNCOOL.
(That's why they get around so much.)
We just met at a party, but I was like, we should go out.
THEY'RE FILTHY, FOUL-MOUTHED IMBECILES.
NOT TO MENTION, THEY'RE ALSO LOUD AND DIS-RESPECTFUL.
You're so wild!
BUT WORST OF ALL...
THEY'RE CONVINCED THAT THE WORLD REVOLVES AROUND THEM!
LIKE THIS GUY
THEY TEAR DOWN ANYONE WHO DOESN'T FIT INTO THEIR PRETTY LITTLE PICTURE.

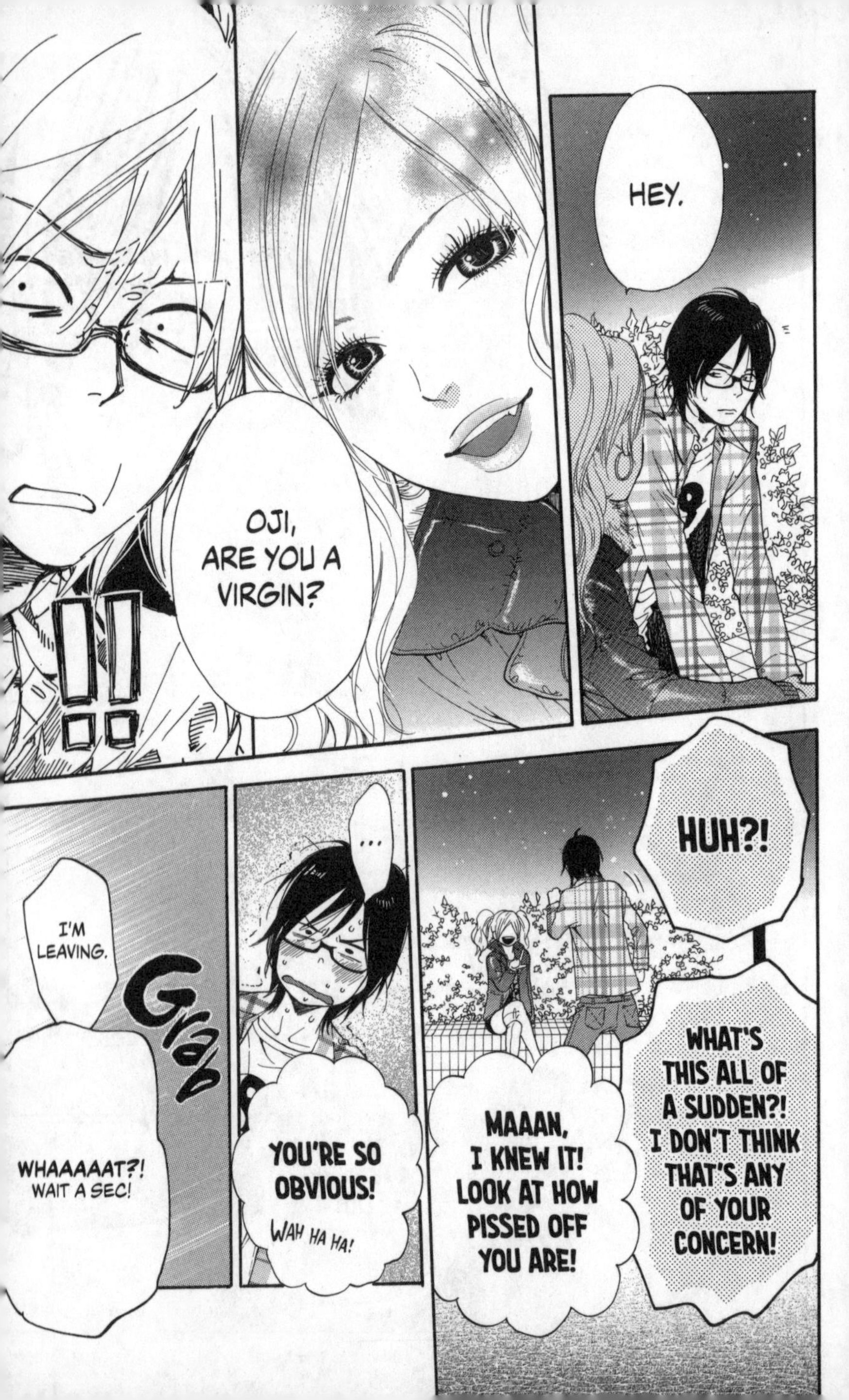
HEY.
OJI, ARE YOU A VIRGIN?
!!
HUH?!
WHAT'S THIS ALL OF A SUDDEN?! I DON'T THINK THAT'S ANY OF YOUR CONCERN!
MAAAN, I KNEW IT! LOOK AT HOW PISSED OFF YOU ARE!
...
YOU'RE SO OBVIOUS!
WAH HA HA!
I'M LEAVING.
Grab
WHAAAAAT?! WAIT A SEC!

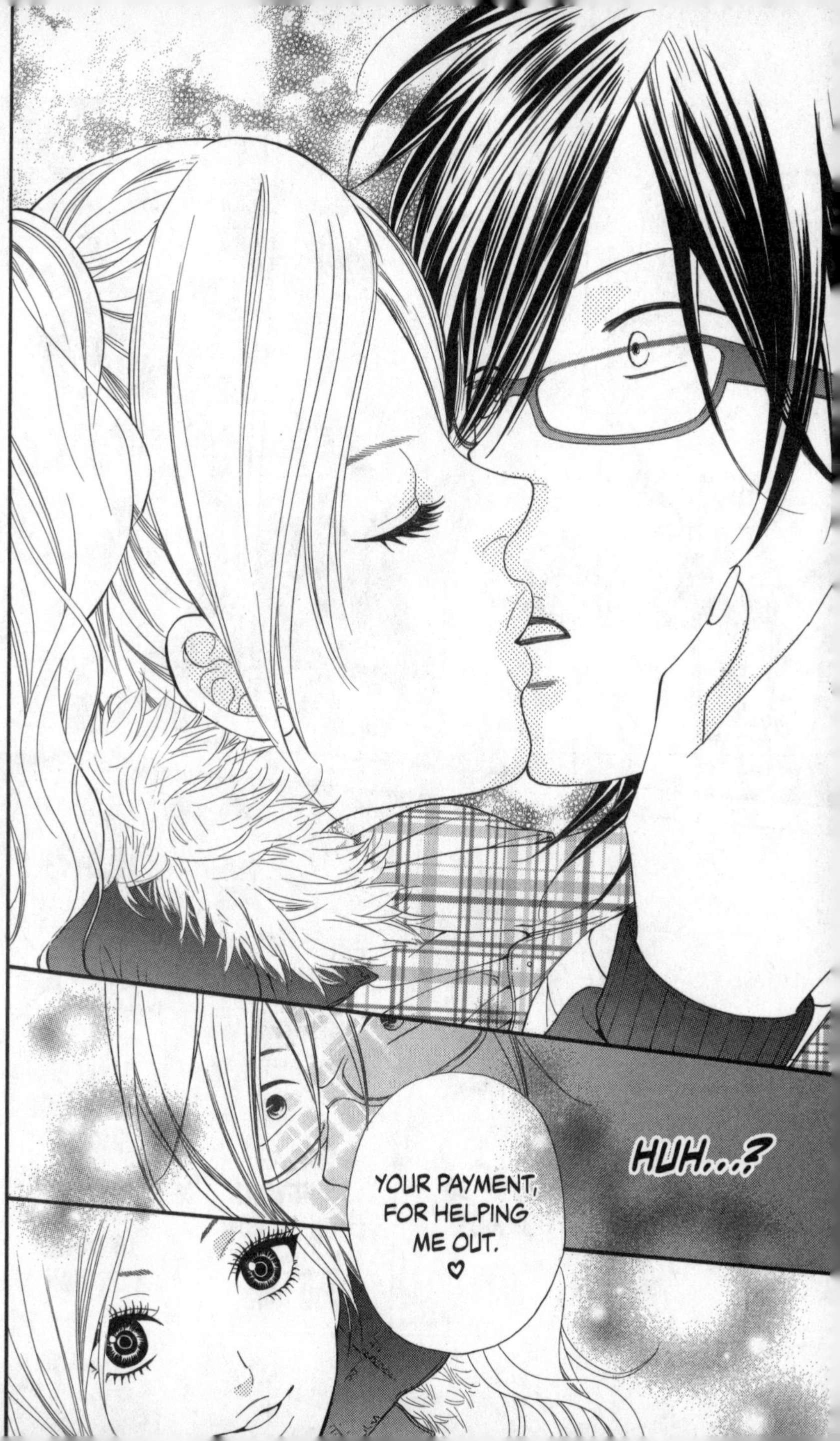
HUH...?
YOUR PAYMENT, FOR HELPING ME OUT. ♡

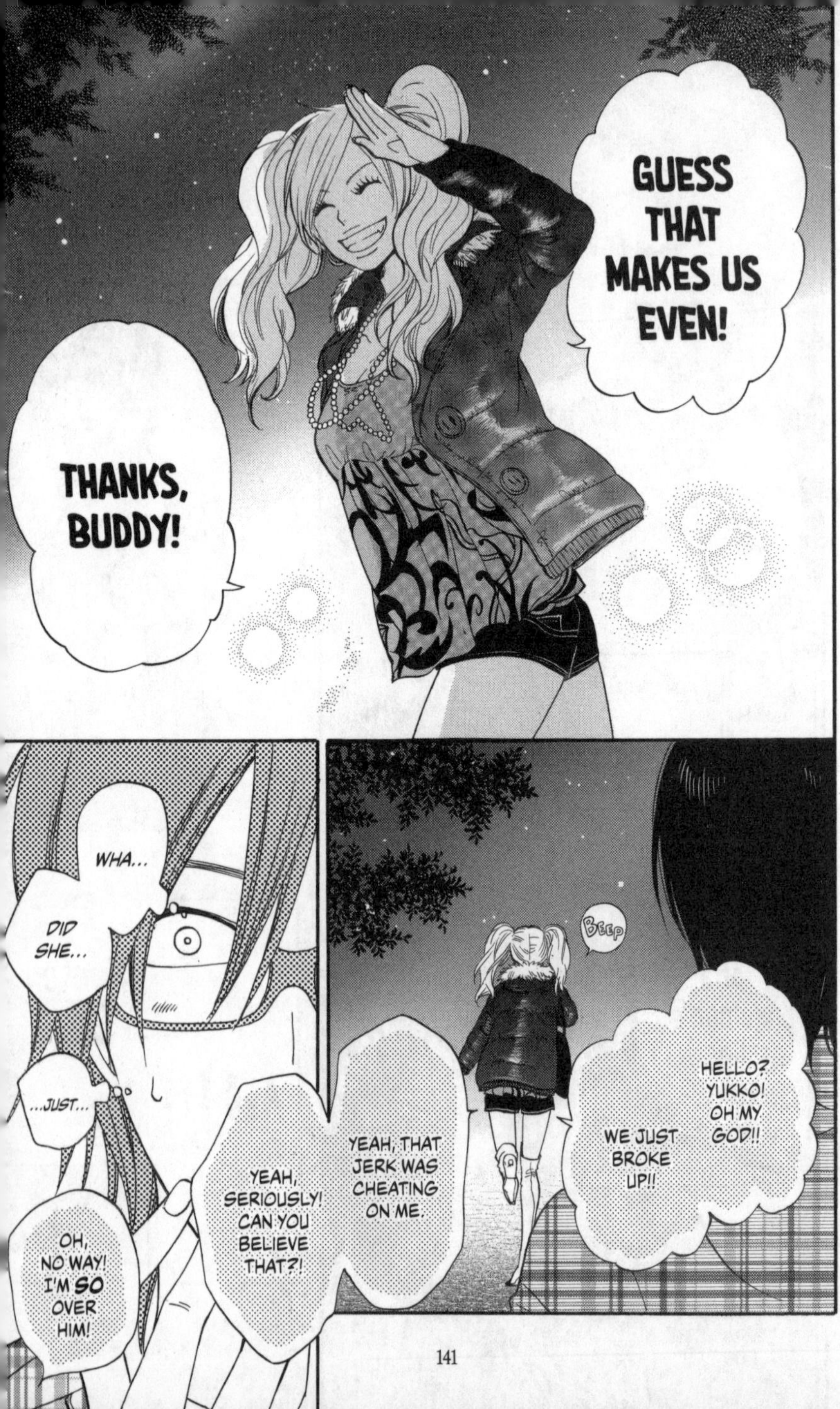
GUESS THAT MAKES US EVEN!
THANKS, BUDDY!
BEEP
HELLO? YUKKO! OH MY GOD!!
WE JUST BROKE UP!!
YEAH, THAT JERK WAS CHEATING ON ME.
YEAH, SERIOUSLY! CAN YOU BELIEVE THAT?!
OH, NO WAY! I'M SO OVER HIM!
WHA...
DID SHE...
...JUST...

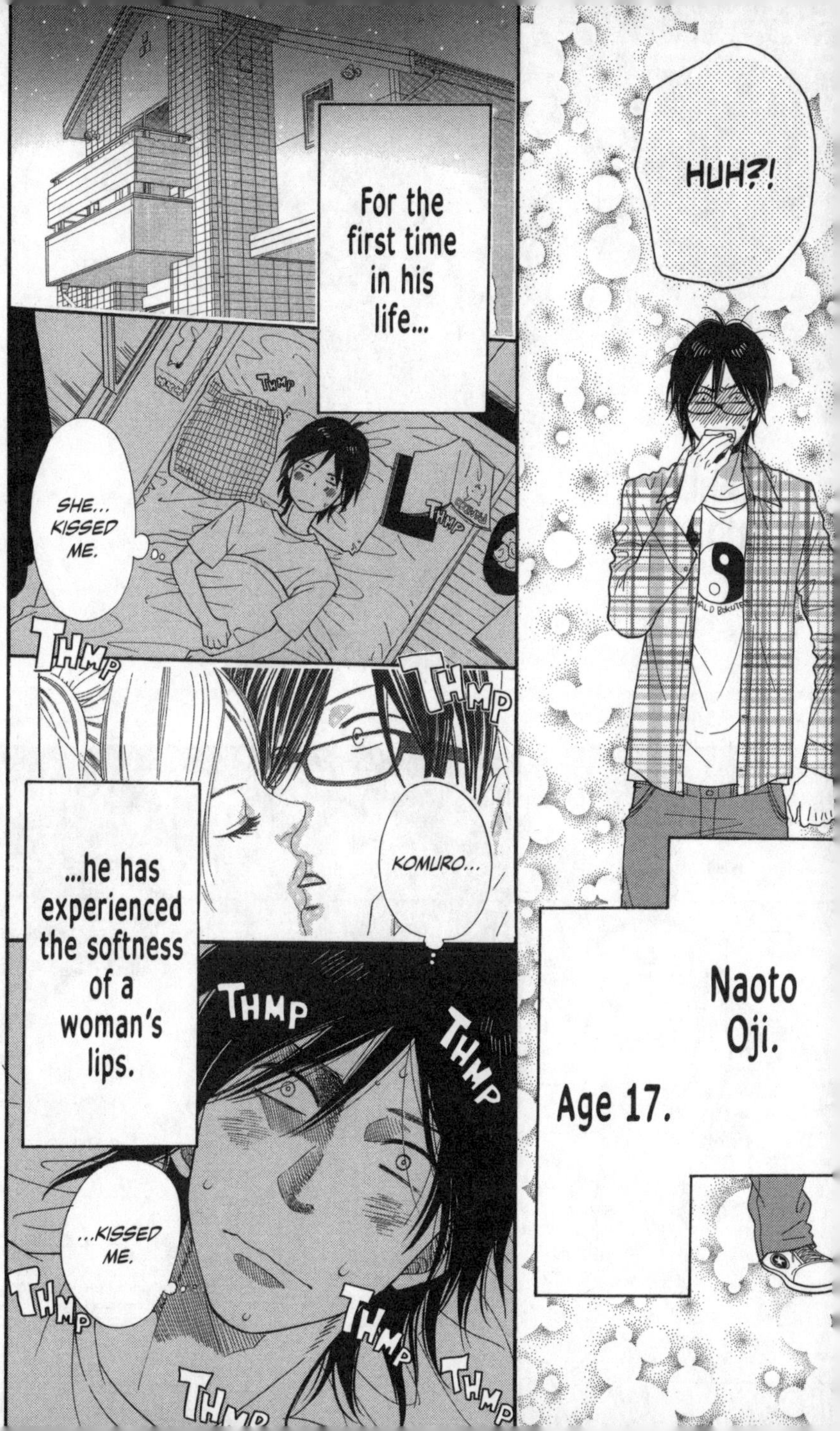
HUH?!
Naoto Oji.
Age 17.
For the first time in his life...
THMP
SHE... KISSED ME.
THMP
THMP
THMP
KOMURO...
...he has experienced the softness of a woman's lips.
THMP
THMP
...KISSED ME.
THMP
THMP
THMP
THMP

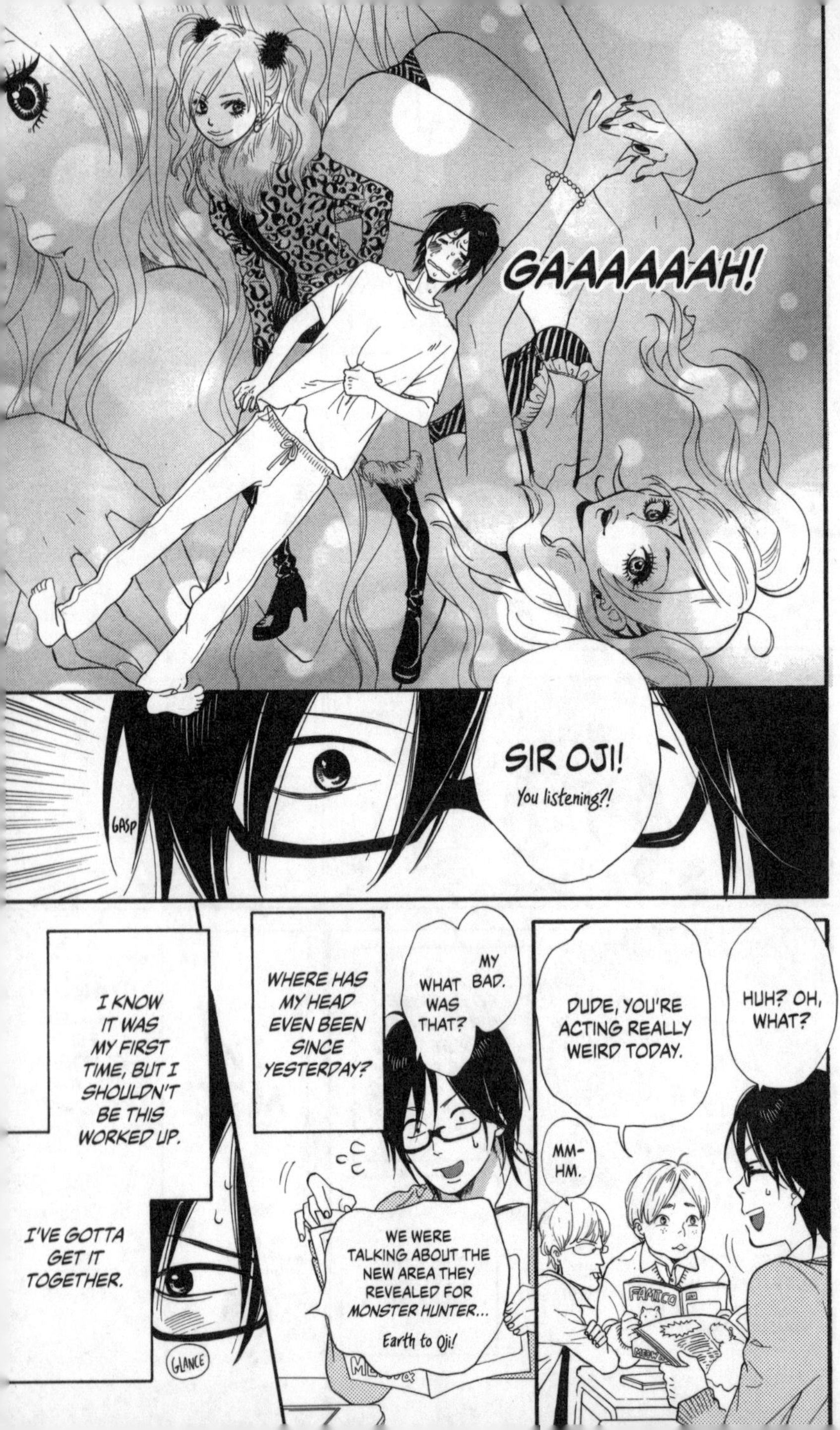
GAAAAAAH!
SIR OJI!
You listening?!
GASP
HUH? OH, WHAT?
DUDE, YOU'RE ACTING REALLY WEIRD TODAY.
MM-HM.
MY BAD.
WHAT WAS THAT?
WHERE HAS MY HEAD EVEN BEEN SINCE YESTERDAY?
WE WERE TALKING ABOUT THE NEW AREA THEY REVEALED FOR MONSTER HUNTER...
Earth to Oji!
FAMICO
I KNOW IT WAS MY FIRST TIME, BUT I SHOULDN'T BE THIS WORKED UP.
I'VE GOTTA GET IT TOGETHER.
GLANCE

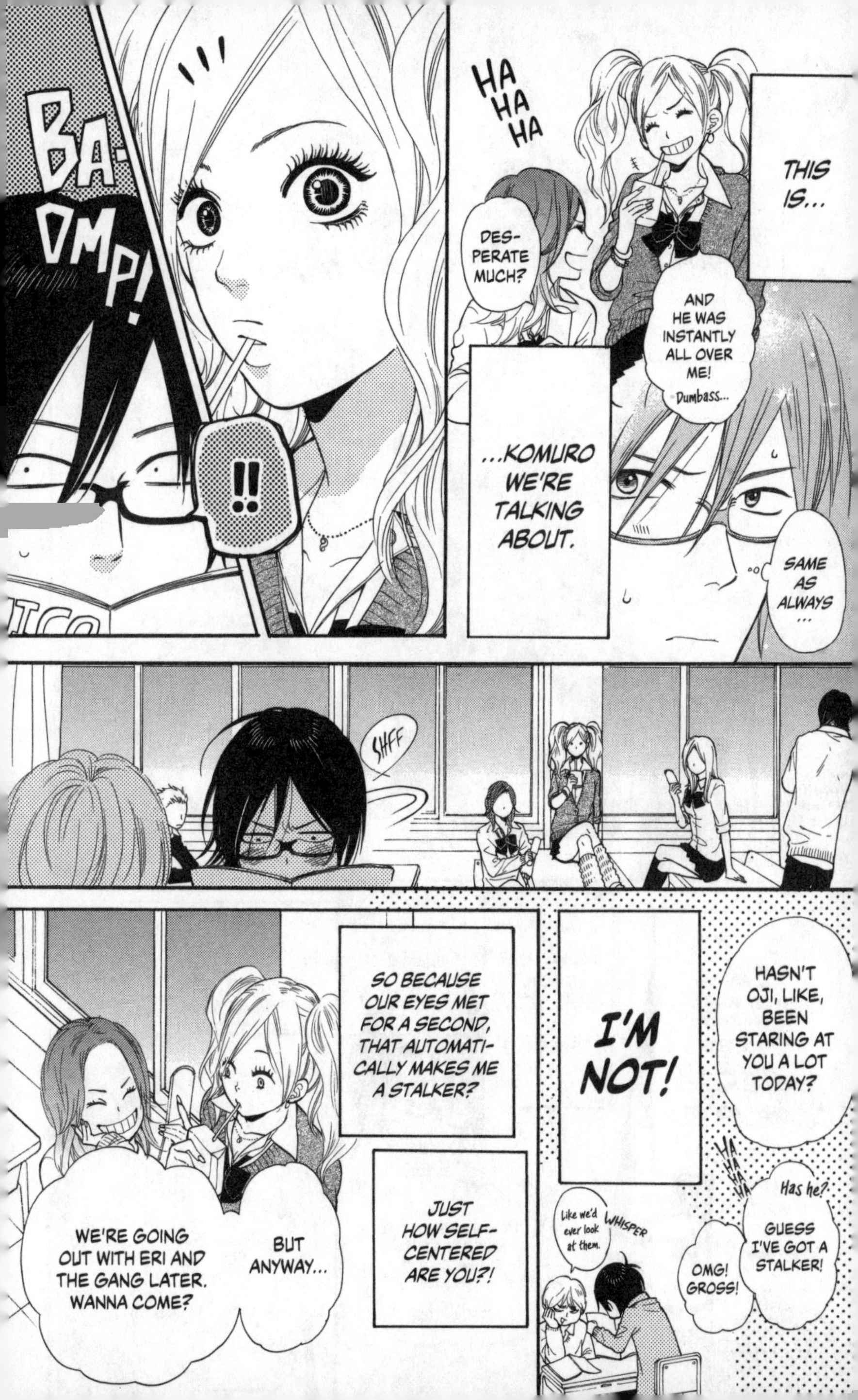
THIS IS...
HA HA HA
AND HE WAS INSTANTLY ALL OVER ME!
Dumbass...
DES-PERATE MUCH?
SAME AS ALWAYS...
...KOMURO WE'RE TALKING ABOUT.
BA-OMP!
!!
SHFF
HASN'T OJI, LIKE, BEEN STARING AT YOU A LOT TODAY?
HA HA HA
Has he?
GUESS I'VE GOT A STALKER!
OMG! GROSS!
WHISPER
Like we'd ever look at them.
I'M NOT!
SO BECAUSE OUR EYES MET FOR A SECOND, THAT AUTOMATI-CALLY MAKES ME A STALKER?
JUST HOW SELF-CENTERED ARE YOU?!
BUT ANYWAY...
WE'RE GOING OUT WITH ERI AND THE GANG LATER. WANNA COME?

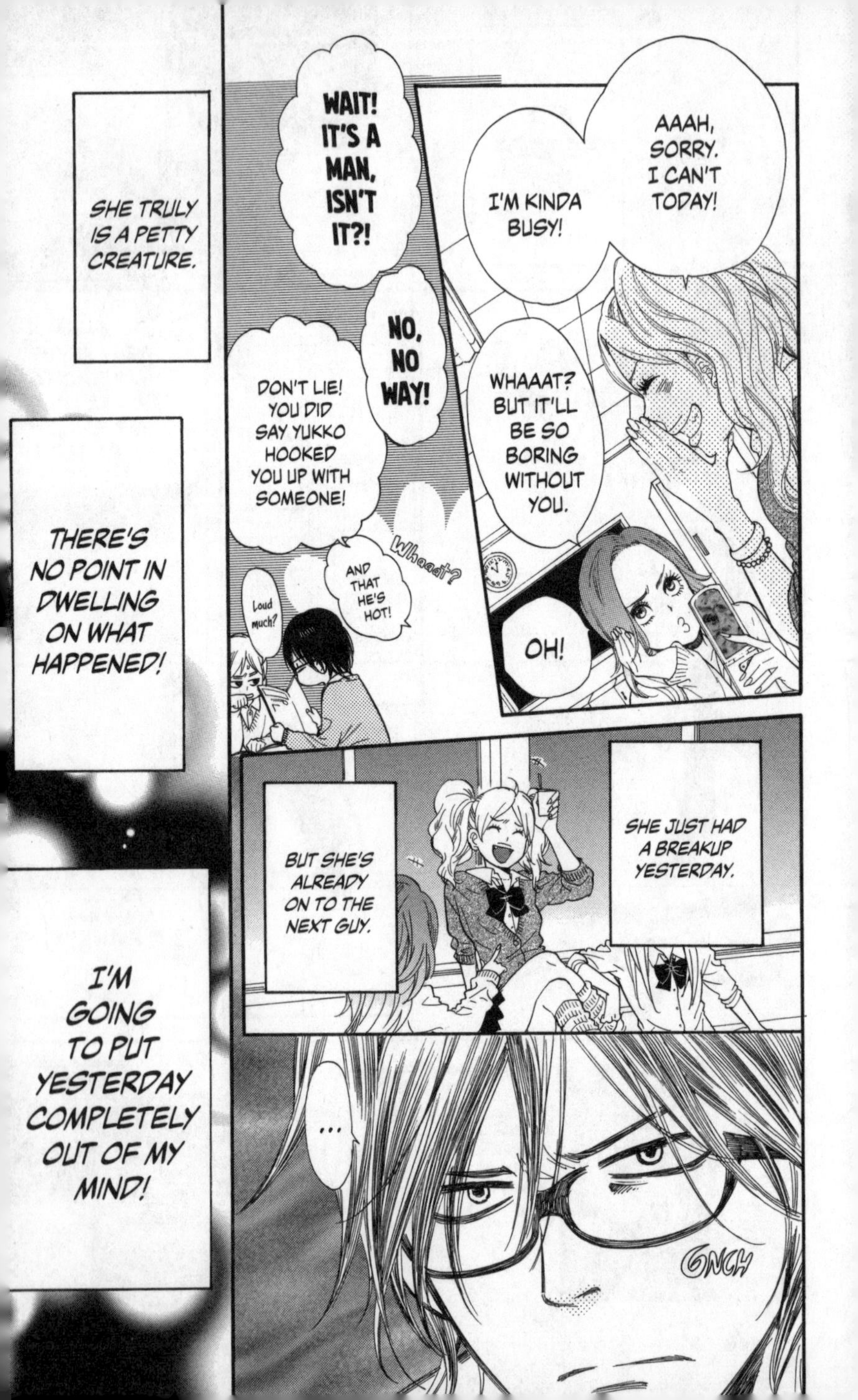
AAAH, SORRY. I CAN'T TODAY!
I'M KINDA BUSY!
WHAAAT? BUT IT'LL BE SO BORING WITHOUT YOU.
OH!
WAIT! IT'S A MAN, ISN'T IT?!
NO, NO WAY!
DON'T LIE! YOU DID SAY YUKKO HOOKED YOU UP WITH SOMEONE!
Whaaat?
AND THAT HE'S HOT!
Loud much?
SHE TRULY IS A PETTY CREATURE.
SHE JUST HAD A BREAKUP YESTERDAY.
BUT SHE'S ALREADY ON TO THE NEXT GUY.
THERE'S NO POINT IN DWELLING ON WHAT HAPPENED!
...
GNCH
I'M GOING TO PUT YESTERDAY COMPLETELY OUT OF MY MIND!

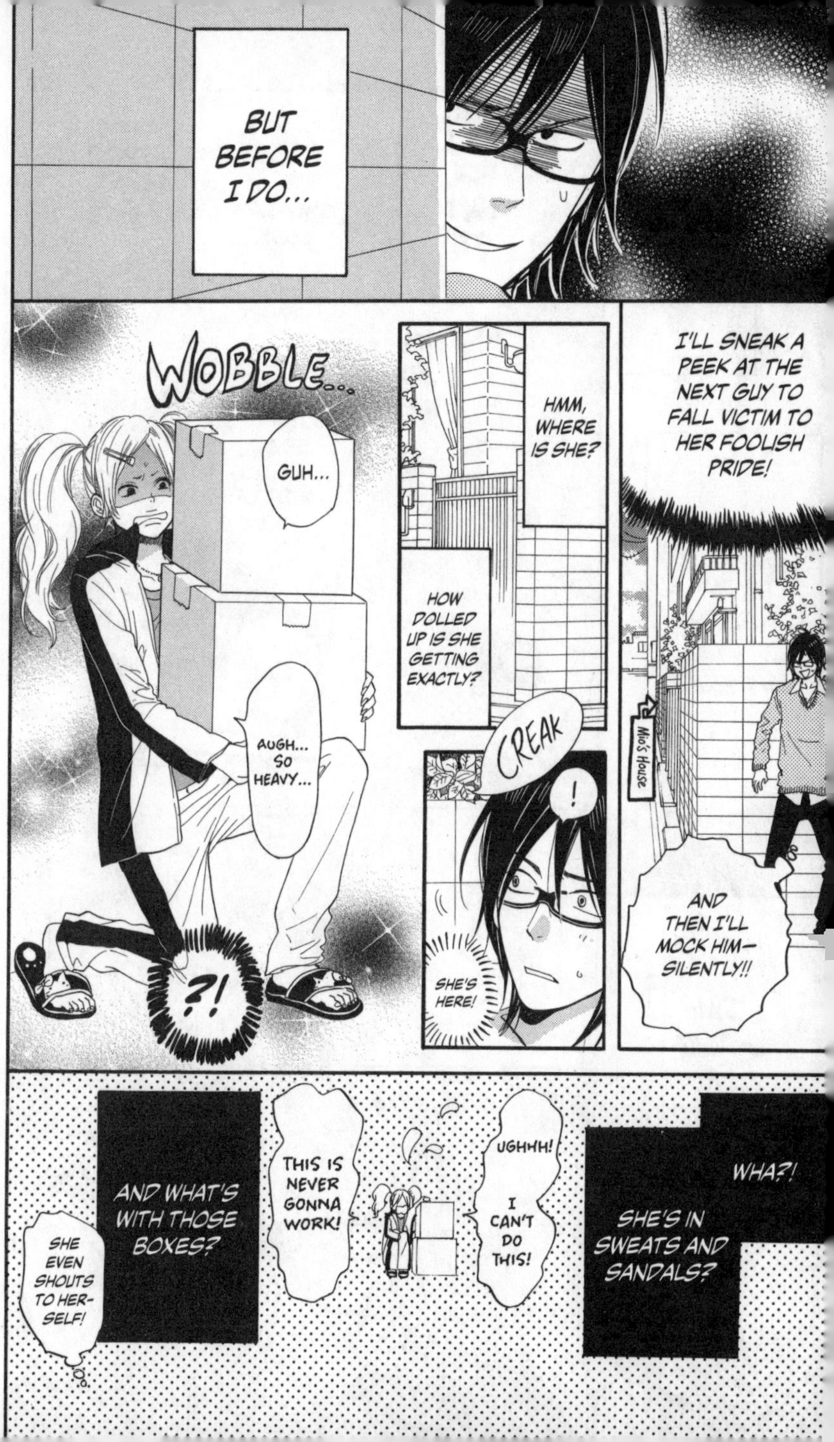
BUT BEFORE I DO...
I'LL SNEAK A PEEK AT THE NEXT GUY TO FALL VICTIM TO HER FOOLISH PRIDE!
Mio's House
AND THEN I'LL MOCK HIM—SILENTLY!!
HMM, WHERE IS SHE?
HOW DOLLED UP IS SHE GETTING EXACTLY?
CREAK
!
SHE'S HERE!
WOBBLE...
GUH...
AUGH... SO HEAVY...
?!
WHA?!
SHE'S IN SWEATS AND SANDALS?
UGHHH!
I CAN'T DO THIS!
THIS IS NEVER GONNA WORK!
AND WHAT'S WITH THOSE BOXES?
SHE EVEN SHOUTS TO HER-SELF!

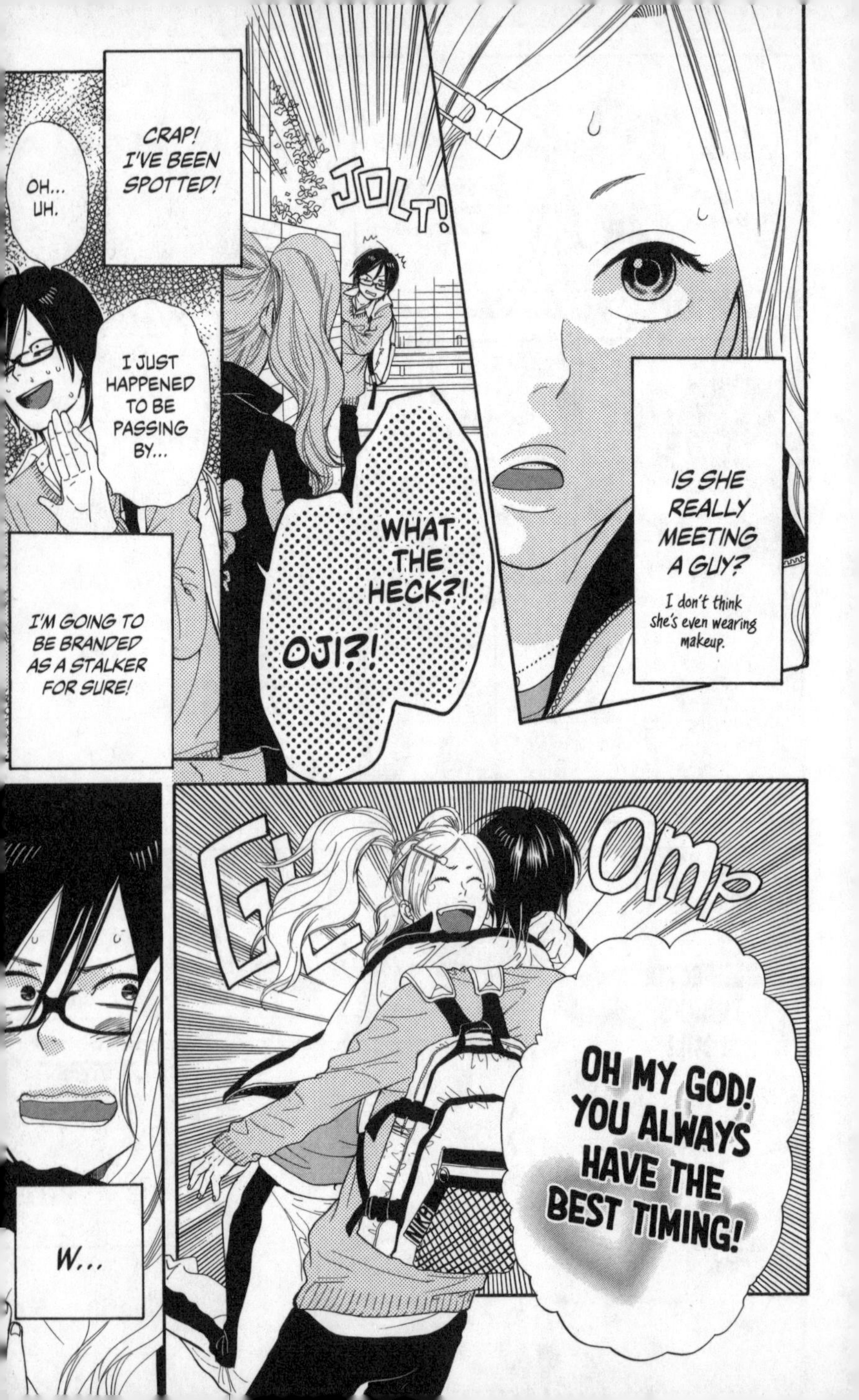
JOLT!
IS SHE REALLY MEETING A GUY?
I don't think she's even wearing makeup.
WHAT THE HECK?!
OJI?!
CRAP! I'VE BEEN SPOTTED!
OH... UH.
I JUST HAPPENED TO BE PASSING BY...
I'M GOING TO BE BRANDED AS A STALKER FOR SURE!
GLOMP
OH MY GOD! YOU ALWAYS HAVE THE BEST TIMING!
W...

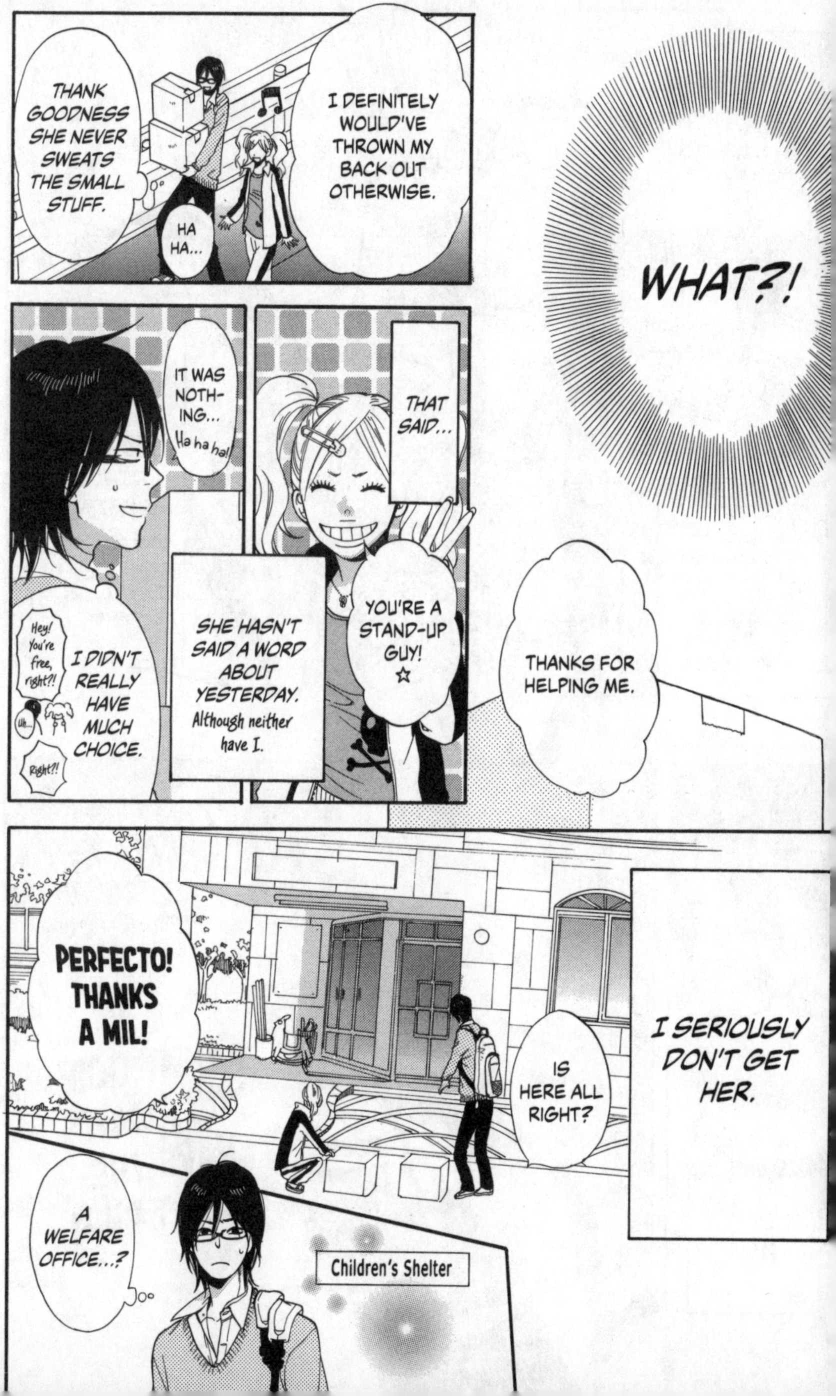
WHAT?!
I DEFINITELY WOULD'VE THROWN MY BACK OUT OTHERWISE.
THANK GOODNESS SHE NEVER SWEATS THE SMALL STUFF.
HA HA...
THANKS FOR HELPING ME.
THAT SAID...
YOU'RE A STAND-UP GUY! ☆
SHE HASN'T SAID A WORD ABOUT YESTERDAY. Although neither have I.
IT WAS NOTHING... Ha ha ha!
I DIDN'T REALLY HAVE MUCH CHOICE.
Hey! You're free, right?!
Uh...
Right?!
I SERIOUSLY DON'T GET HER.
IS HERE ALL RIGHT?
PERFECTO! THANKS A MIL!
A WELFARE OFFICE...?
Children's Shelter

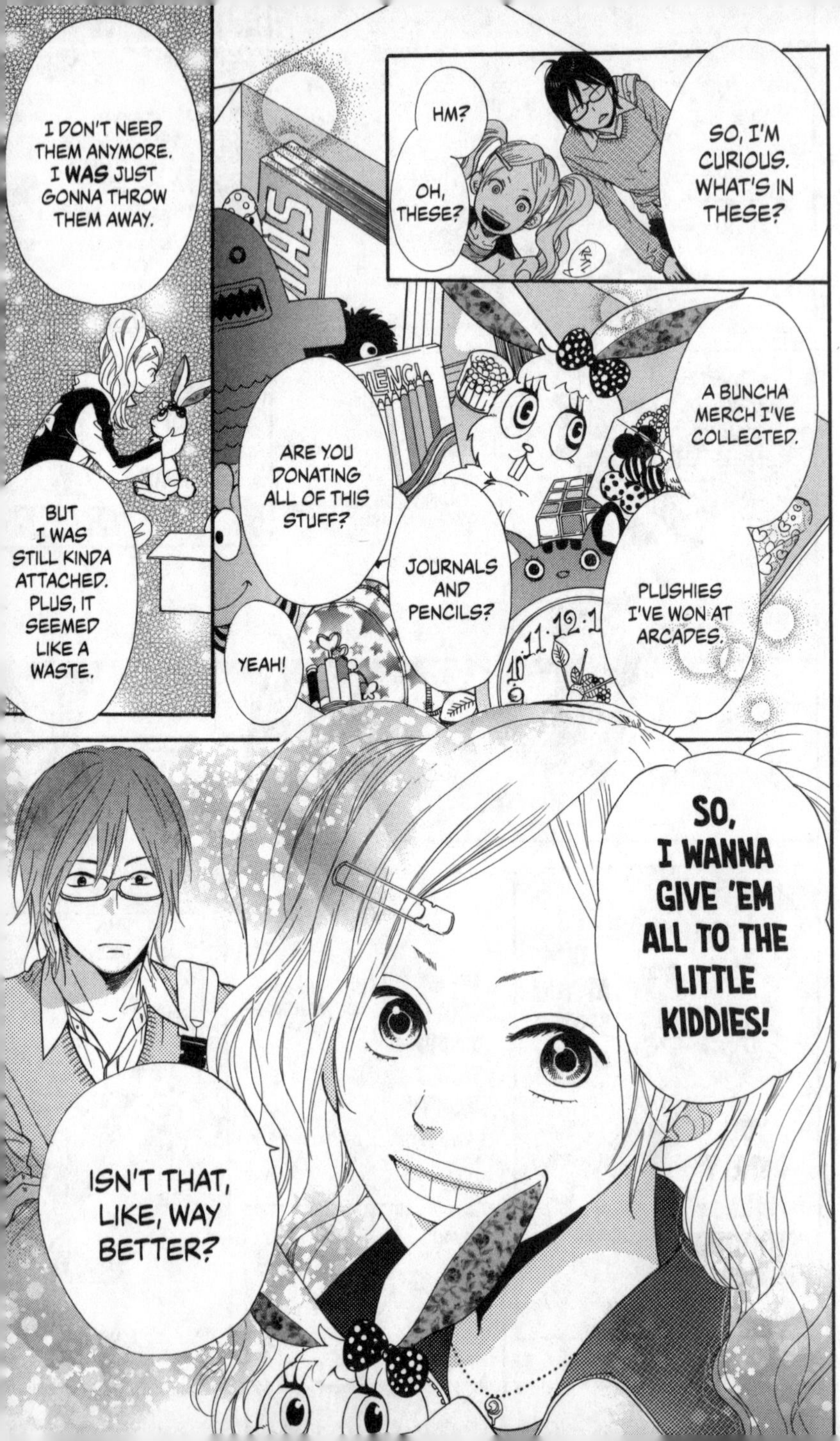
SO, I'M CURIOUS. WHAT'S IN THESE?
HM?
OH, THESE?
A BUNCHA MERCH I'VE COLLECTED.
PLUSHIES I'VE WON AT ARCADES.
JOURNALS AND PENCILS?
ARE YOU DONATING ALL OF THIS STUFF?
YEAH!
I DON'T NEED THEM ANYMORE. I WAS JUST GONNA THROW THEM AWAY.
BUT I WAS STILL KINDA ATTACHED. PLUS, IT SEEMED LIKE A WASTE.
SO, I WANNA GIVE 'EM ALL TO THE LITTLE KIDDIES!
ISN'T THAT, LIKE, WAY BETTER?

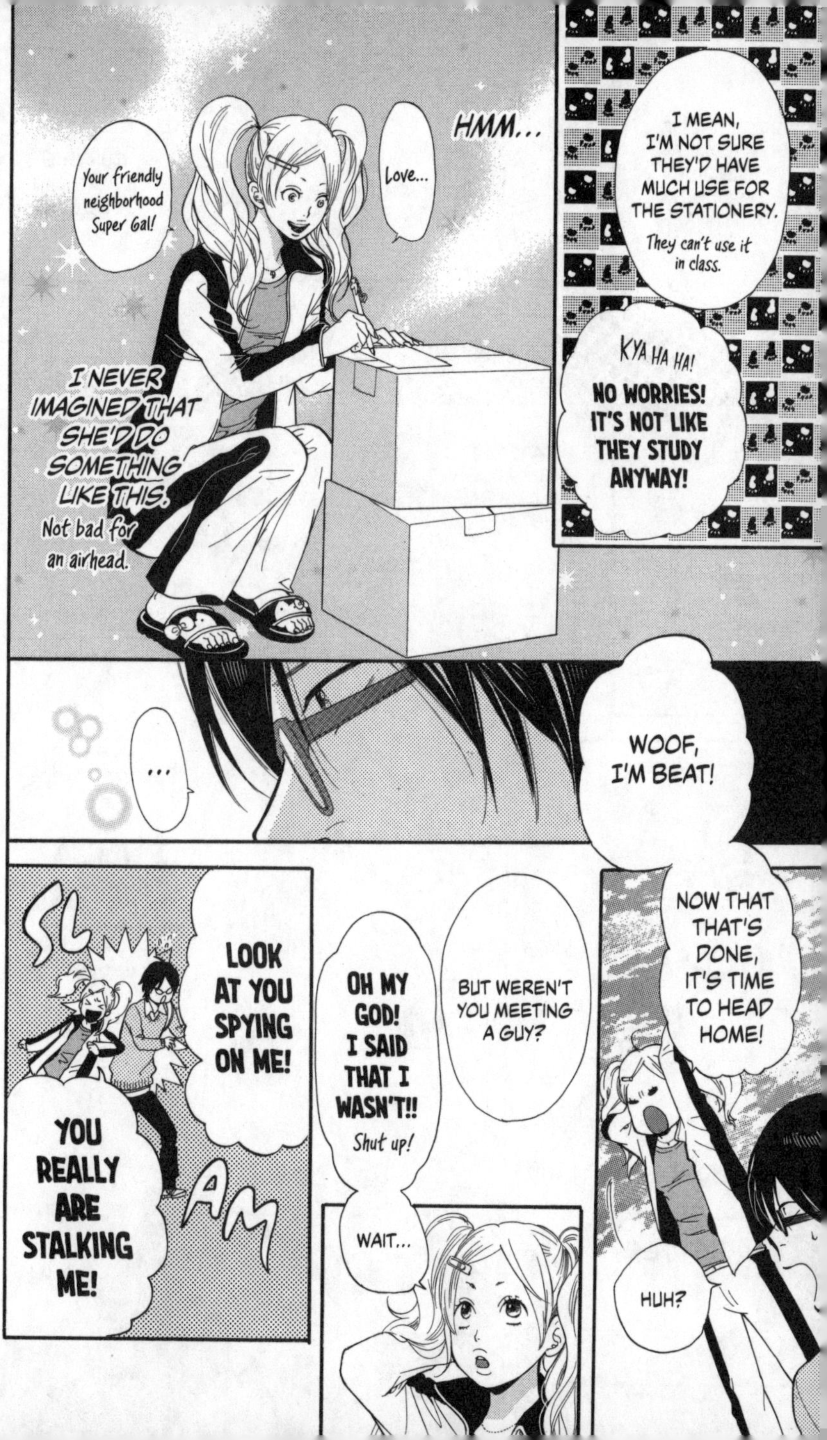
I MEAN, I'M NOT SURE THEY'D HAVE MUCH USE FOR THE STATIONERY.
They can't use it in class.
KYA HA HA!
NO WORRIES! IT'S NOT LIKE THEY STUDY ANYWAY!
HMM...
Love...
Your friendly neighborhood Super Gal!
I NEVER IMAGINED THAT SHE'D DO SOMETHING LIKE THIS.
Not bad for an airhead.
WOOF, I'M BEAT!
...
NOW THAT THAT'S DONE, IT'S TIME TO HEAD HOME!
HUH?
BUT WEREN'T YOU MEETING A GUY?
WAIT...
OH MY GOD! I SAID THAT I WASN'T!!
Shut up!
LOOK AT YOU SPYING ON ME!
SL
AM
YOU REALLY ARE STALKING ME!

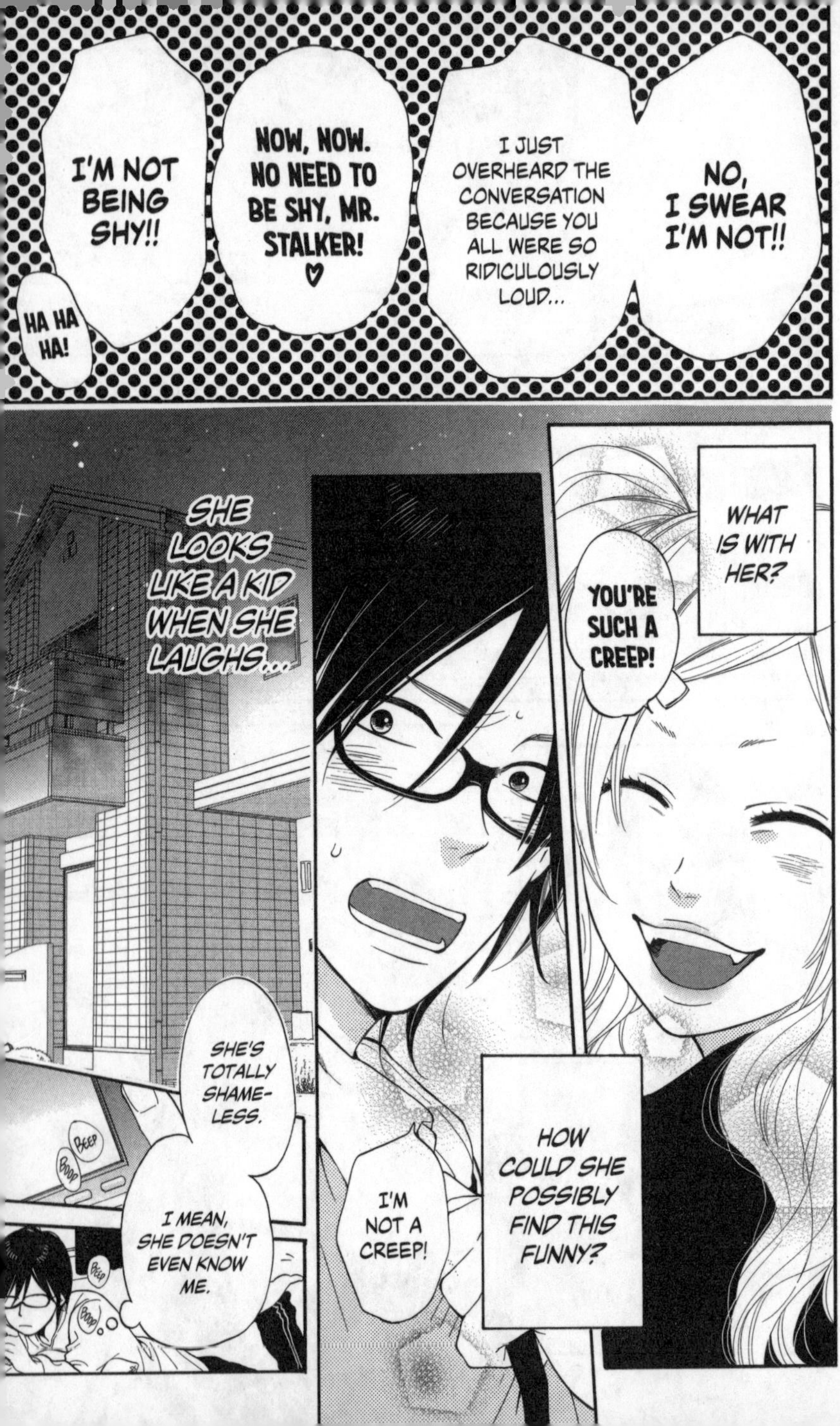
NO, I SWEAR I'M NOT!!
I JUST OVERHEARD THE CONVERSATION BECAUSE YOU ALL WERE SO RIDICULOUSLY LOUD...
NOW, NOW. NO NEED TO BE SHY, MR. STALKER! ♡
I'M NOT BEING SHY!!
HA HA HA!
WHAT IS WITH HER?
YOU'RE SUCH A CREEP!
HOW COULD SHE POSSIBLY FIND THIS FUNNY?
I'M NOT A CREEP!
SHE LOOKS LIKE A KID WHEN SHE LAUGHS...
SHE'S TOTALLY SHAME-LESS.
BEEP
BOOP
I MEAN, SHE DOESN'T EVEN KNOW ME.
BEEP
BOOP

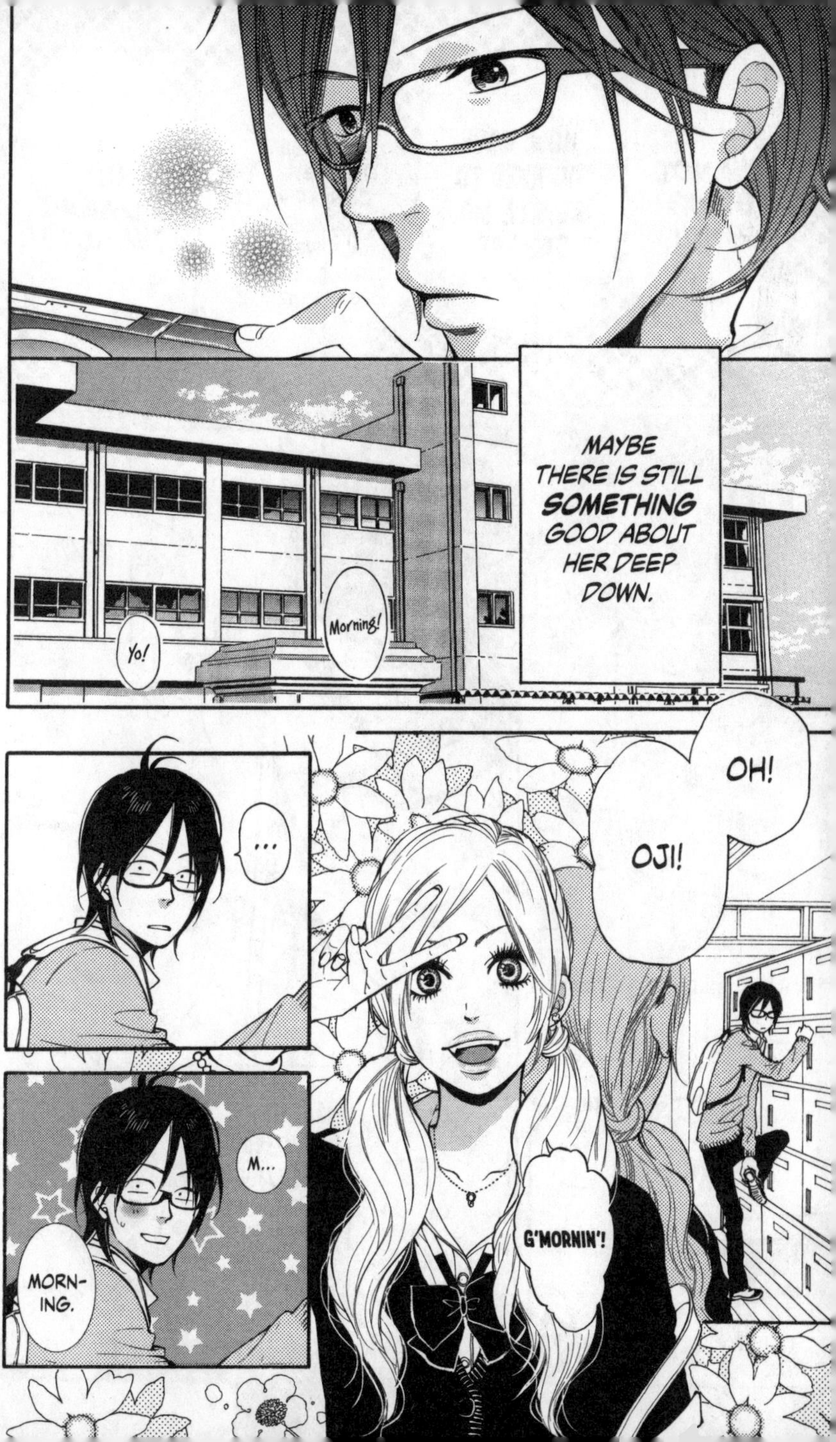

MAYBE THERE IS STILL SOMETHING GOOD ABOUT HER DEEP DOWN.
Morning!
Yo!
OH!
OJI!
G'MORNIN'!
...
M...
MORN-ING.

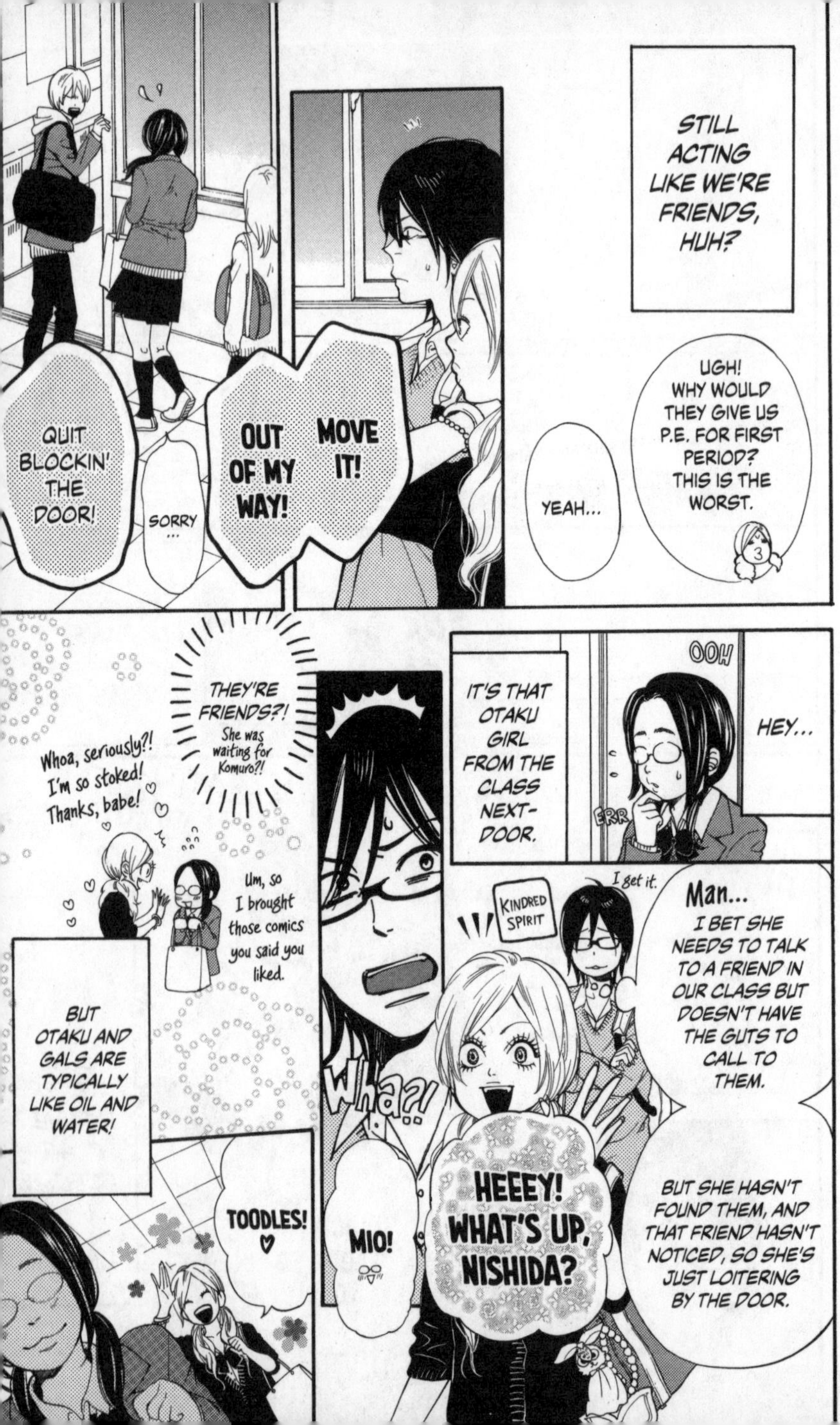
STILL ACTING LIKE WE'RE FRIENDS, HUH?
UGH! WHY WOULD THEY GIVE US P.E. FOR FIRST PERIOD? THIS IS THE WORST.
YEAH...
MOVE IT!
OUT OF MY WAY!
SORRY...
QUIT BLOCKIN' THE DOOR!
OOH
HEY...
ERR
IT'S THAT OTAKU GIRL FROM THE CLASS NEXT-DOOR.
Man... I BET SHE NEEDS TO TALK TO A FRIEND IN OUR CLASS BUT DOESN'T HAVE THE GUTS TO CALL TO THEM.
BUT SHE HASN'T FOUND THEM, AND THAT FRIEND HASN'T NOTICED, SO SHE'S JUST LOITERING BY THE DOOR.
I get it.
KINDRED SPIRIT
HEEEY! WHAT'S UP, NISHIDA?
MIO!
Wha?!
THEY'RE FRIENDS?!
She was waiting for Komuro?!
Um, so I brought those comics you said you liked.
Whoa, seriously?! I'm so stoked! Thanks, babe!
BUT OTAKU AND GALS ARE TYPICALLY LIKE OIL AND WATER!
TOODLES!

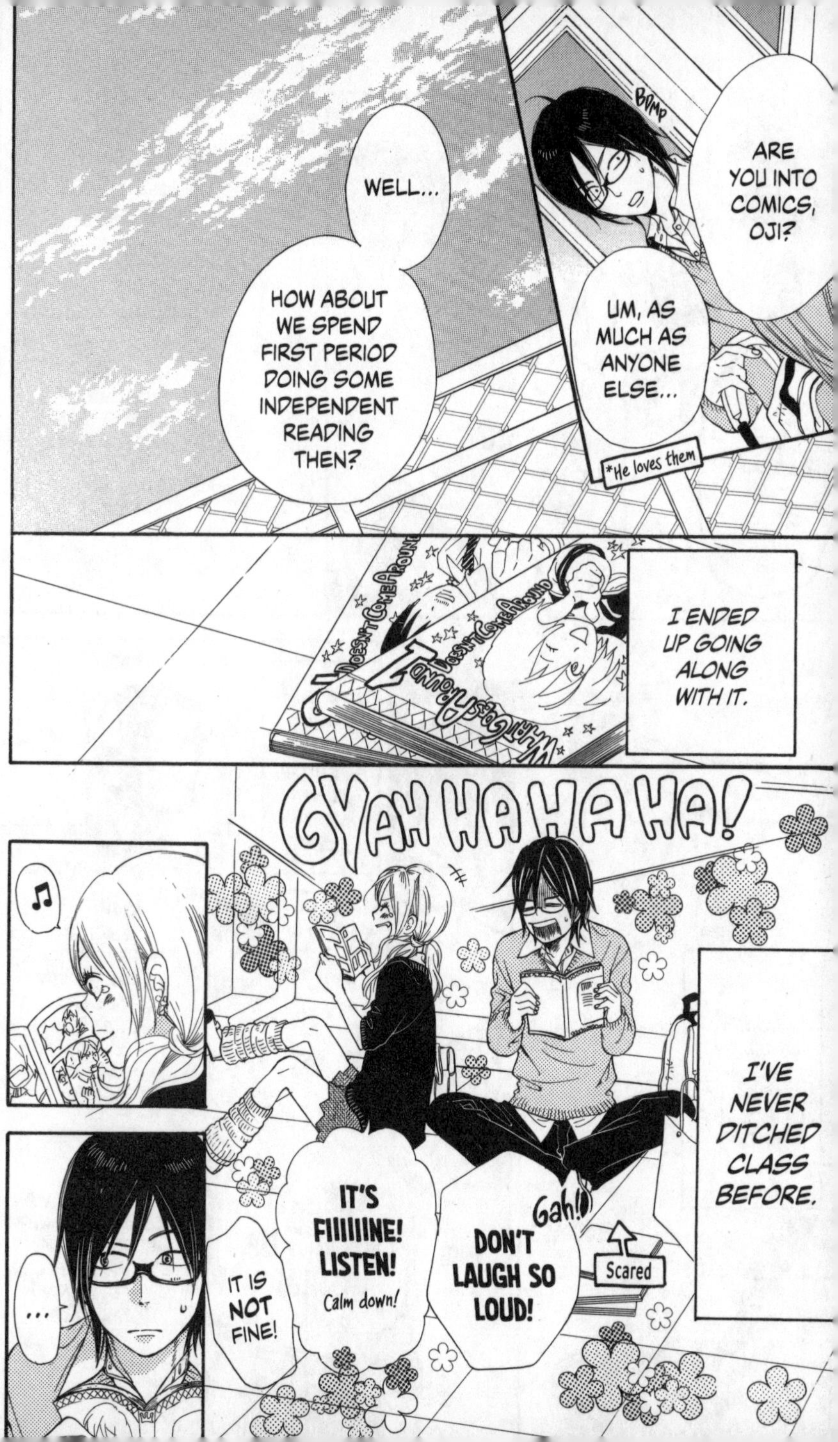
BDMP
ARE YOU INTO COMICS, OJI?
UM, AS MUCH AS ANYONE ELSE...
*He loves them
WELL...
HOW ABOUT WE SPEND FIRST PERIOD DOING SOME INDEPENDENT READING THEN?
I ENDED UP GOING ALONG WITH IT.
GYAH HA HA HA HA!
I'VE NEVER DITCHED CLASS BEFORE.
Gah!
DON'T LAUGH SO LOUD!
Scared
IT'S FIIIIIINE! LISTEN!
Calm down!
IT IS NOT FINE!
♪
...

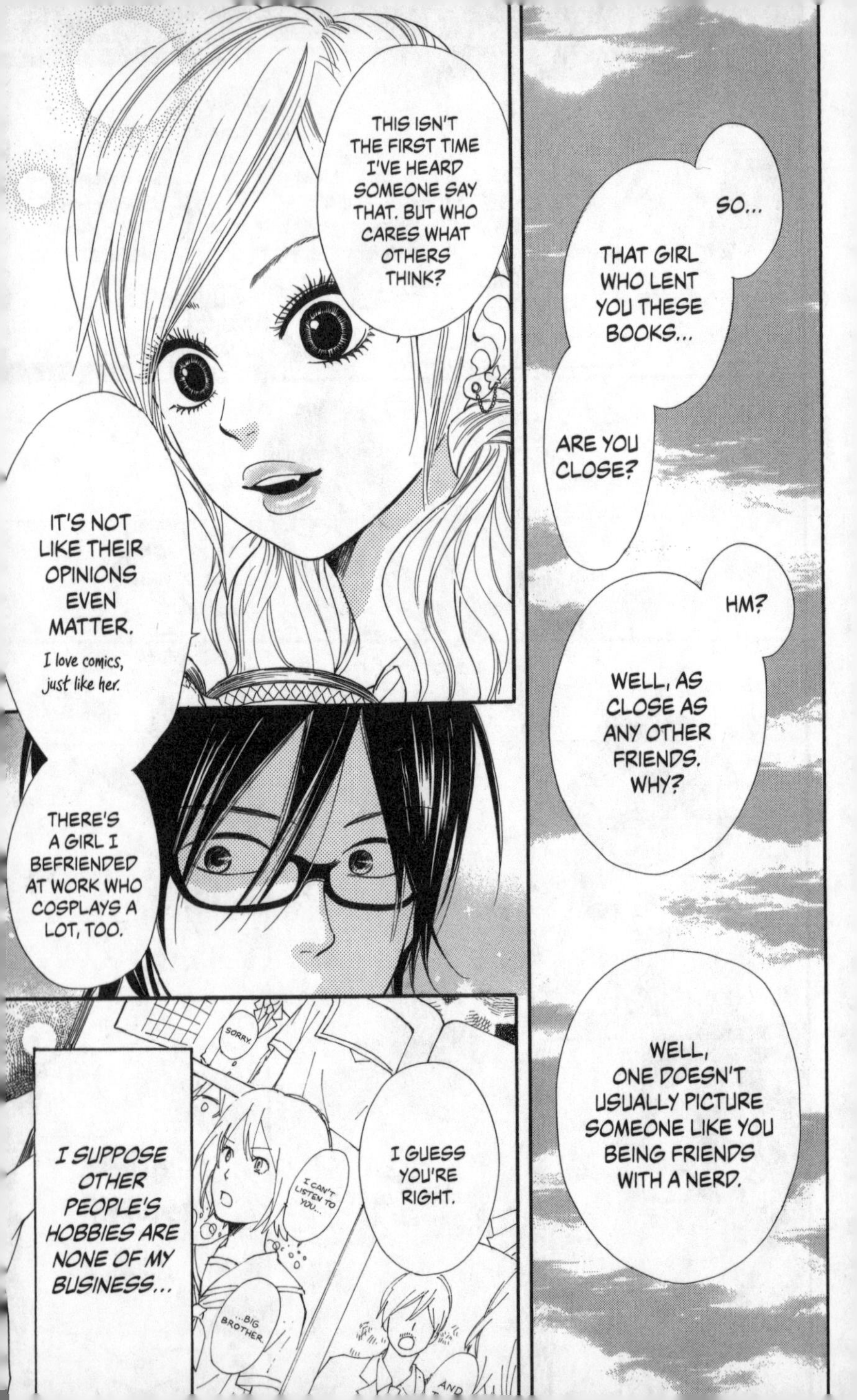
SO...
THAT GIRL WHO LENT YOU THESE BOOKS...
ARE YOU CLOSE?
HM?
WELL, AS CLOSE AS ANY OTHER FRIENDS. WHY?
WELL, ONE DOESN'T USUALLY PICTURE SOMEONE LIKE YOU BEING FRIENDS WITH A NERD.
THIS ISN'T THE FIRST TIME I'VE HEARD SOMEONE SAY THAT. BUT WHO CARES WHAT OTHERS THINK?
IT'S NOT LIKE THEIR OPINIONS EVEN MATTER.
I love comics, just like her.
THERE'S A GIRL I BEFRIENDED AT WORK WHO COSPLAYS A LOT, TOO.
I GUESS YOU'RE RIGHT.
SORRY.
I CAN'T LISTEN TO YOU...
...BIG BROTHER
I SUPPOSE OTHER PEOPLE'S HOBBIES ARE NONE OF MY BUSINESS...

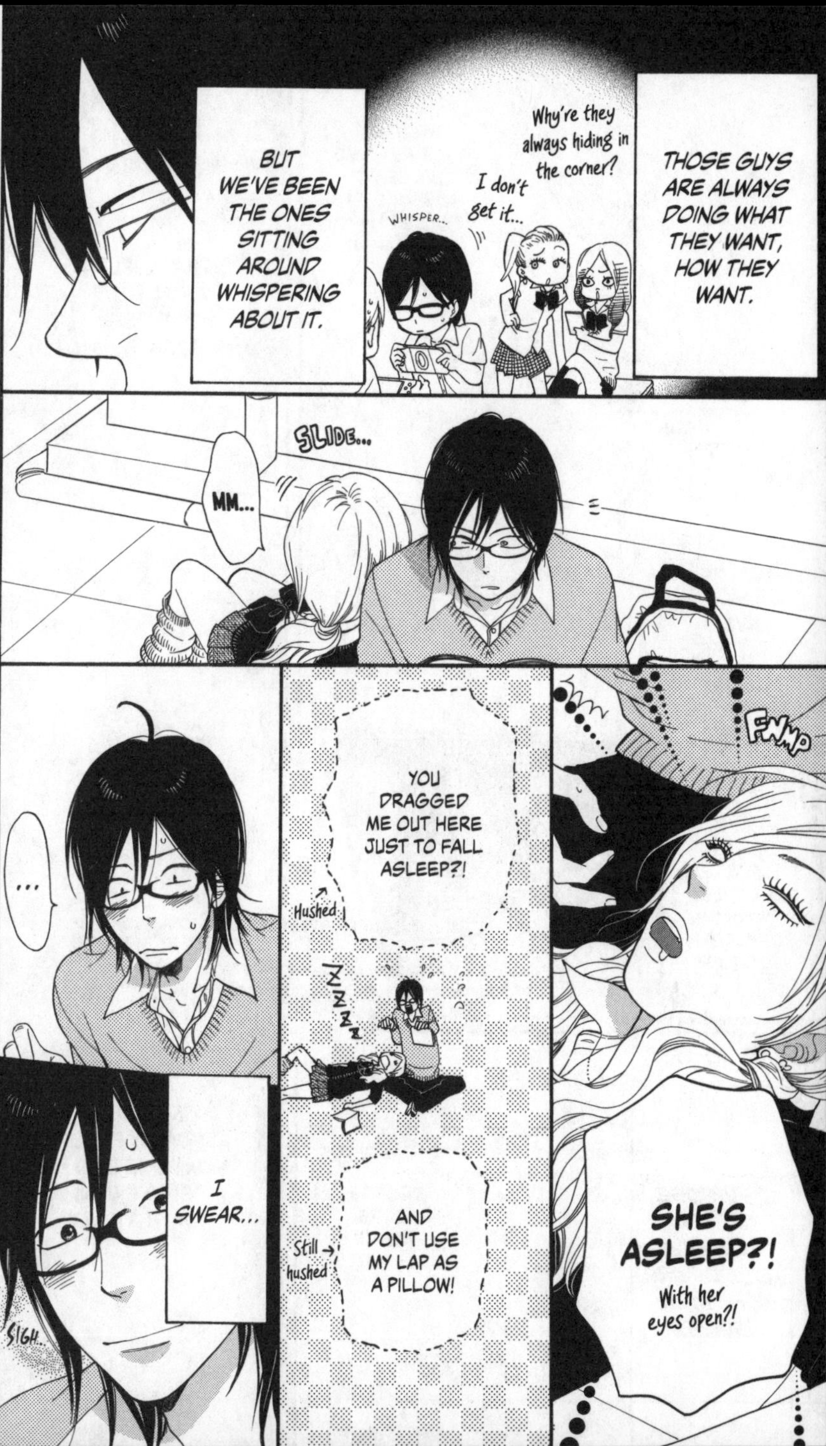
THOSE GUYS ARE ALWAYS DOING WHAT THEY WANT, HOW THEY WANT.
Why're they always hiding in the corner?
I don't get it...
WHISPER...
BUT WE'VE BEEN THE ONES SITTING AROUND WHISPERING ABOUT IT.
SLIDE...
MM...
FWMP
SHE'S ASLEEP?!
With her eyes open?!
YOU DRAGGED ME OUT HERE JUST TO FALL ASLEEP?!
Hushed
AND DON'T USE MY LAP AS A PILLOW!
Still hushed
...
I SWEAR...
SIGH...

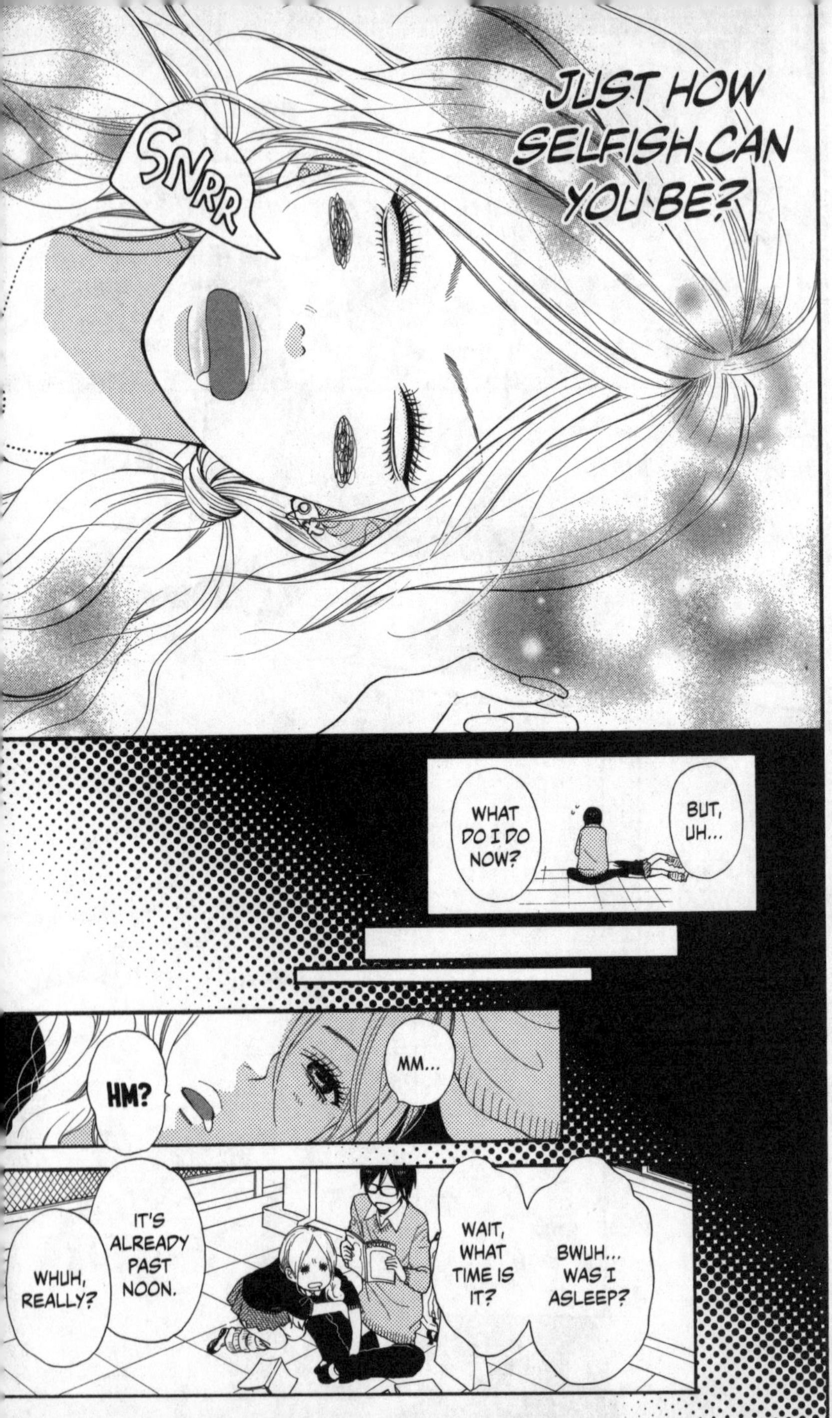
JUST HOW SELFISH CAN YOU BE?
SNRR
BUT, UH...
WHAT DO I DO NOW?
MM...
HM?
BWUH... WAS I ASLEEP?
WAIT, WHAT TIME IS IT?
IT'S ALREADY PAST NOON.
WHUH, REALLY?

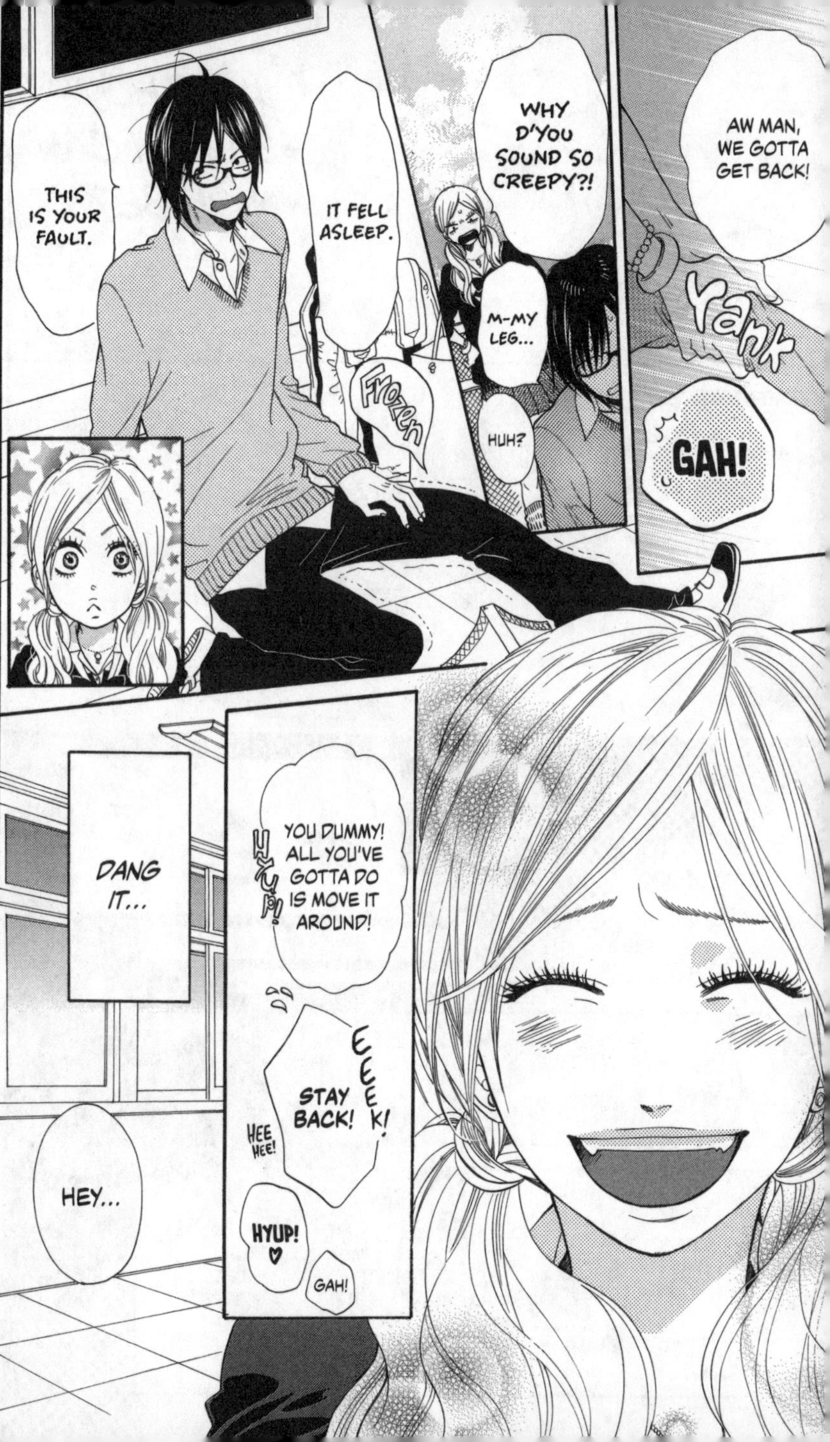
AW MAN, WE GOTTA GET BACK!
Yank
GAH!
WHY D'YOU SOUND SO CREEPY?!
M-MY LEG...
HUH?
IT FELL ASLEEP.
Frozen
THIS IS YOUR FAULT.
YOU DUMMY! ALL YOU'VE GOTTA DO IS MOVE IT AROUND!
Hyup!
EEEEK!
STAY BACK!
HEE HEE!
HYUP!
GAH!
DANG IT...
HEY...

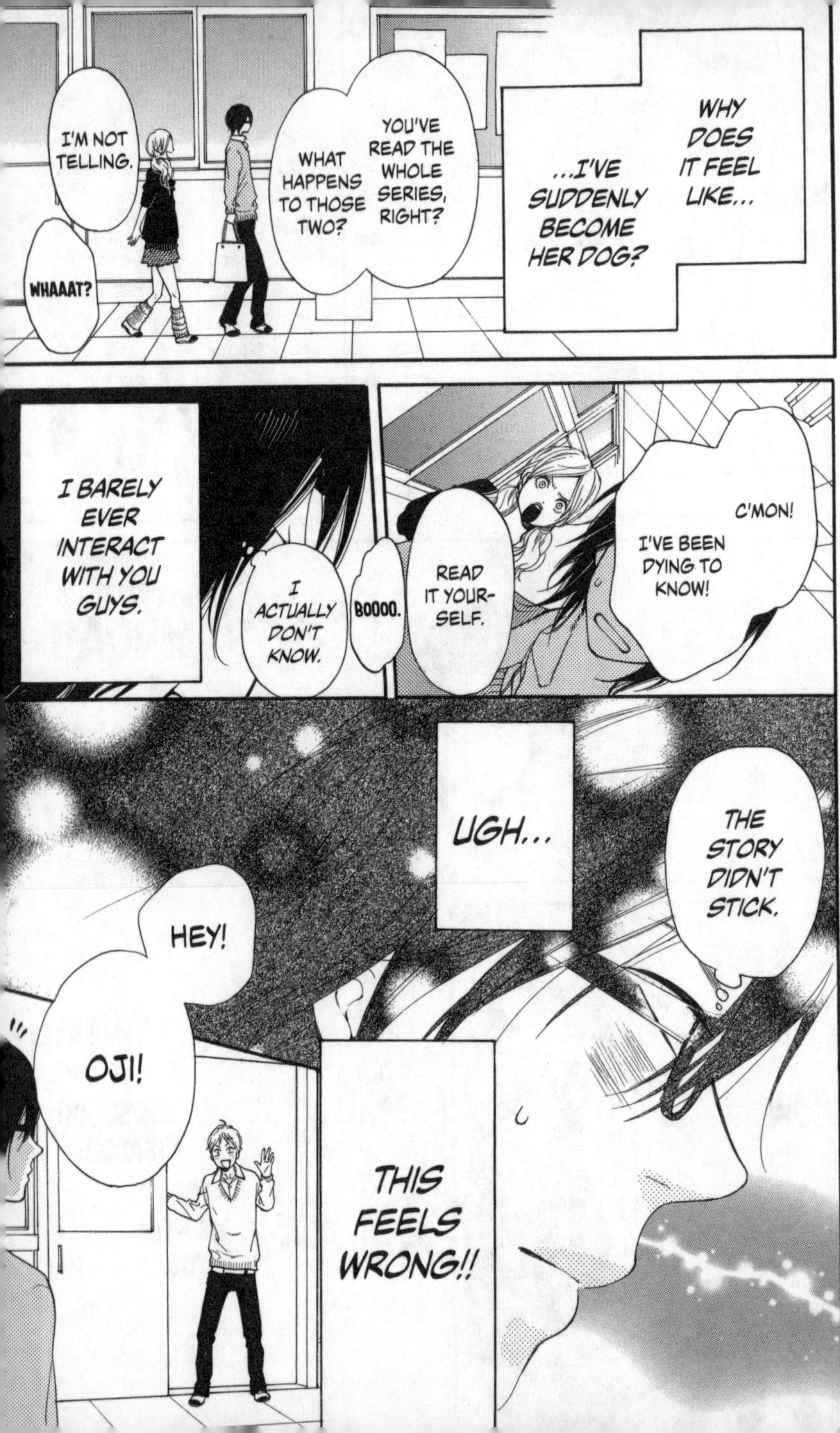
WHY DOES IT FEEL LIKE...
...I'VE SUDDENLY BECOME HER DOG?
YOU'VE READ THE WHOLE SERIES, RIGHT?
WHAT HAPPENS TO THOSE TWO?
I'M NOT TELLING.
WHAAAT?
C'MON!
I'VE BEEN DYING TO KNOW!
READ IT YOURSELF.
BOOOO.
I ACTUALLY DON'T KNOW.
I BARELY EVER INTERACT WITH YOU GUYS.
THE STORY DIDN'T STICK.
UGH...
THIS FEELS WRONG!!
HEY!
OJI!

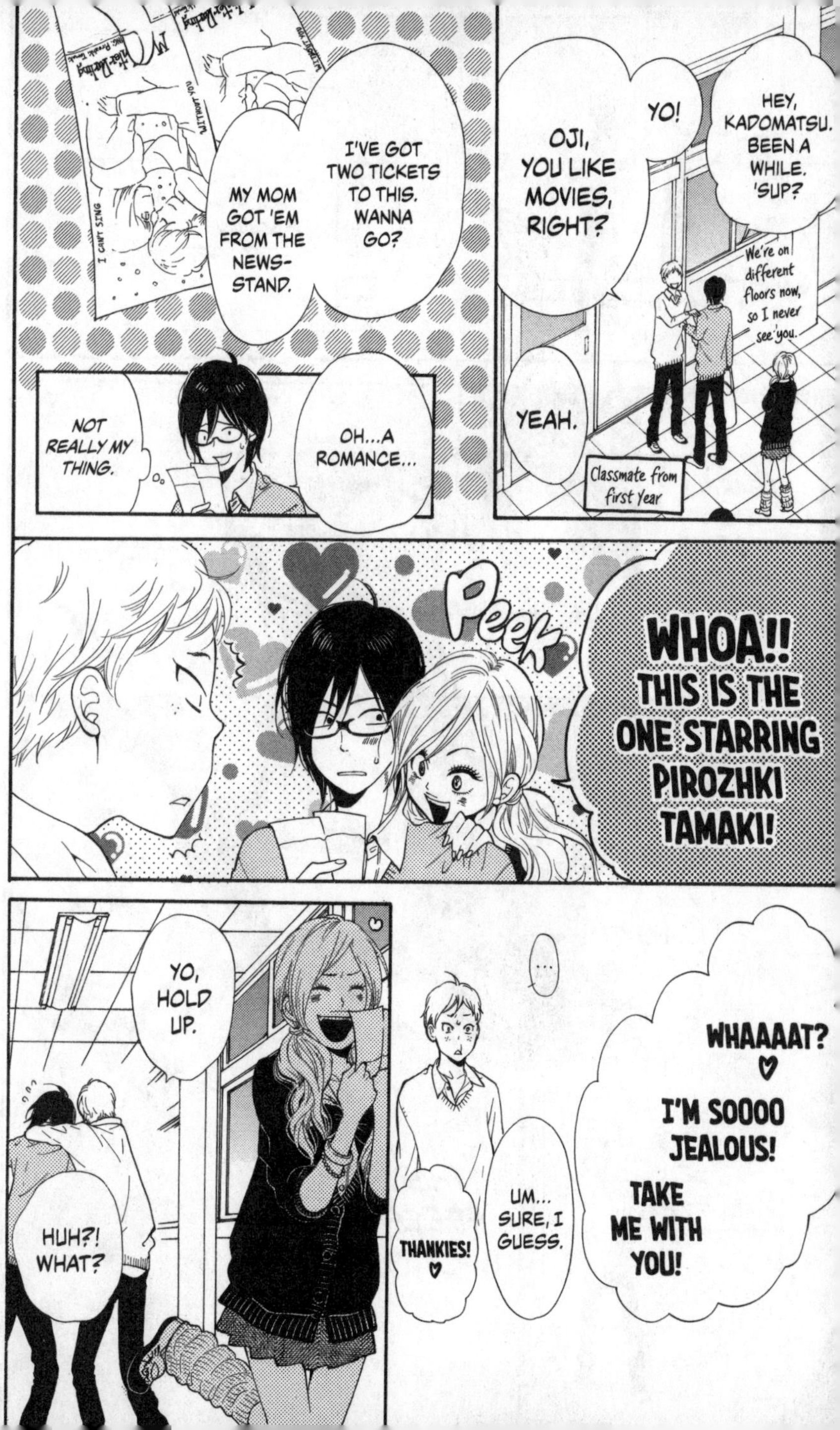
HEY, KADOMATSU. BEEN A WHILE. 'SUP?
YO!
OJI, YOU LIKE MOVIES, RIGHT?
We're on different floors now, so I never see you.
YEAH.
Classmate from first Year
I'VE GOT TWO TICKETS TO THIS. WANNA GO?
MY MOM GOT 'EM FROM THE NEWS-STAND.
OH...A ROMANCE...
NOT REALLY MY THING.
Peek
WHOA!! THIS IS THE ONE STARRING PIROZHKI TAMAKI!
WHAAAAT? ♡ I'M SOOOO JEALOUS! TAKE ME WITH YOU!
...
UM... SURE, I GUESS.
THANKIES! ♡
YO, HOLD UP.
HUH?! WHAT?

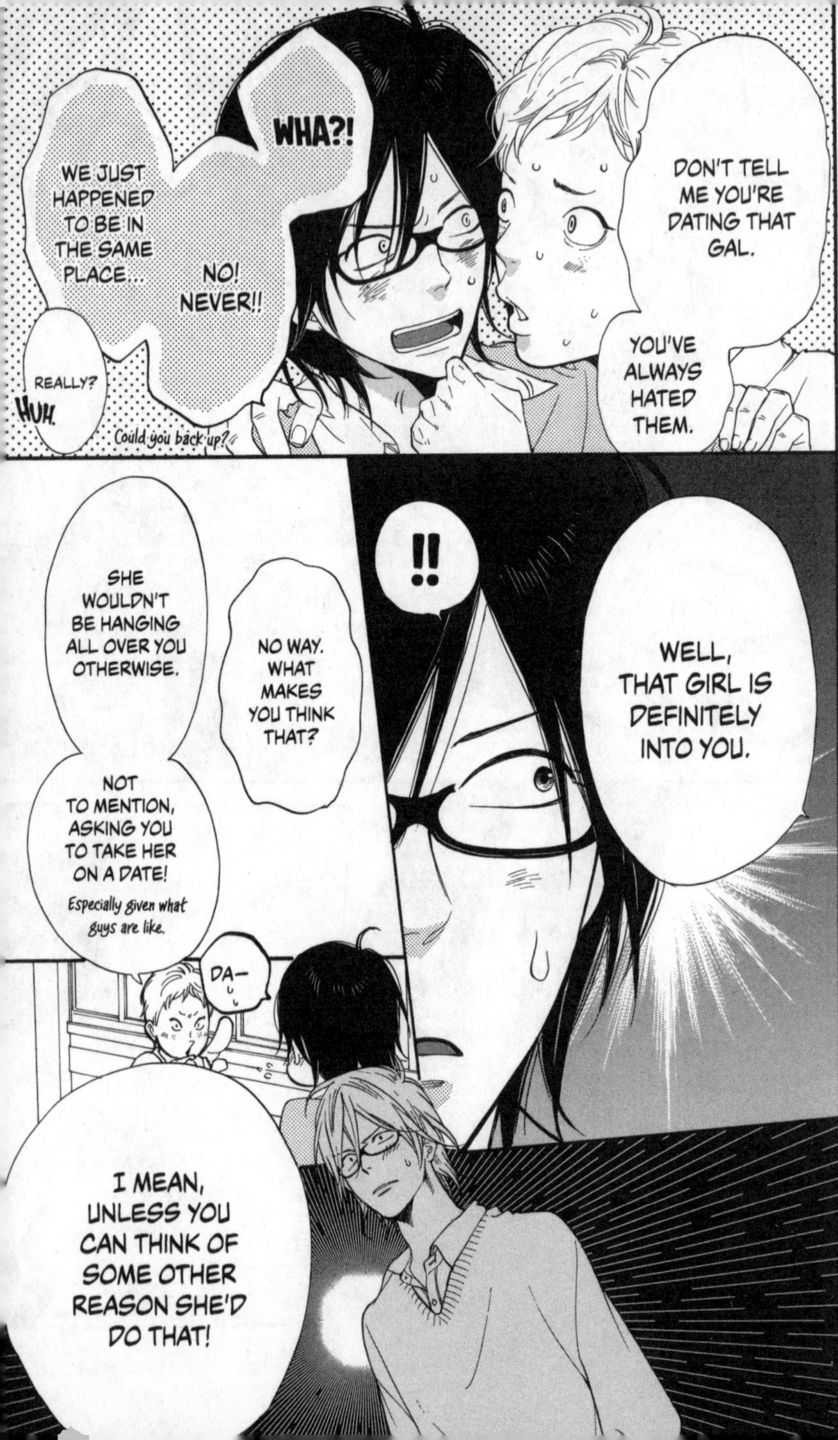
DON'T TELL ME YOU'RE DATING THAT GAL.
YOU'VE ALWAYS HATED THEM.
WHA?!
NO! NEVER!!
WE JUST HAPPENED TO BE IN THE SAME PLACE...
REALLY?
HUH.
Could you back up?
WELL, THAT GIRL IS DEFINITELY INTO YOU.
!!
NO WAY. WHAT MAKES YOU THINK THAT?
SHE WOULDN'T BE HANGING ALL OVER YOU OTHERWISE.
NOT TO MENTION, ASKING YOU TO TAKE HER ON A DATE!
Especially given what guys are like.
DA—
I MEAN, UNLESS YOU CAN THINK OF SOME OTHER REASON SHE'D DO THAT!

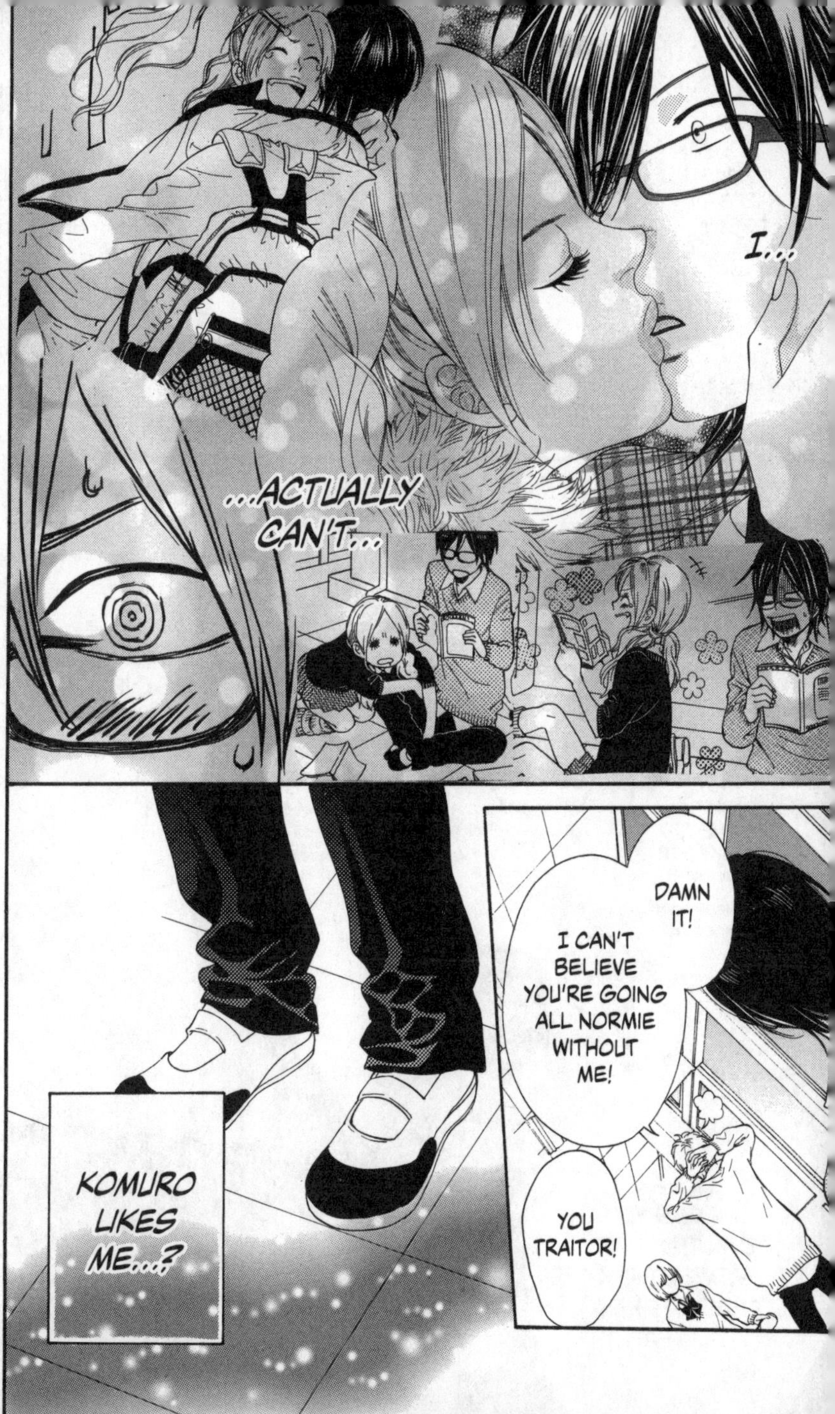
I...
...ACTUALLY CAN'T...
DAMN IT!
I CAN'T BELIEVE YOU'RE GOING ALL NORMIE WITHOUT ME!
YOU TRAITOR!
KOMURO LIKES ME...?

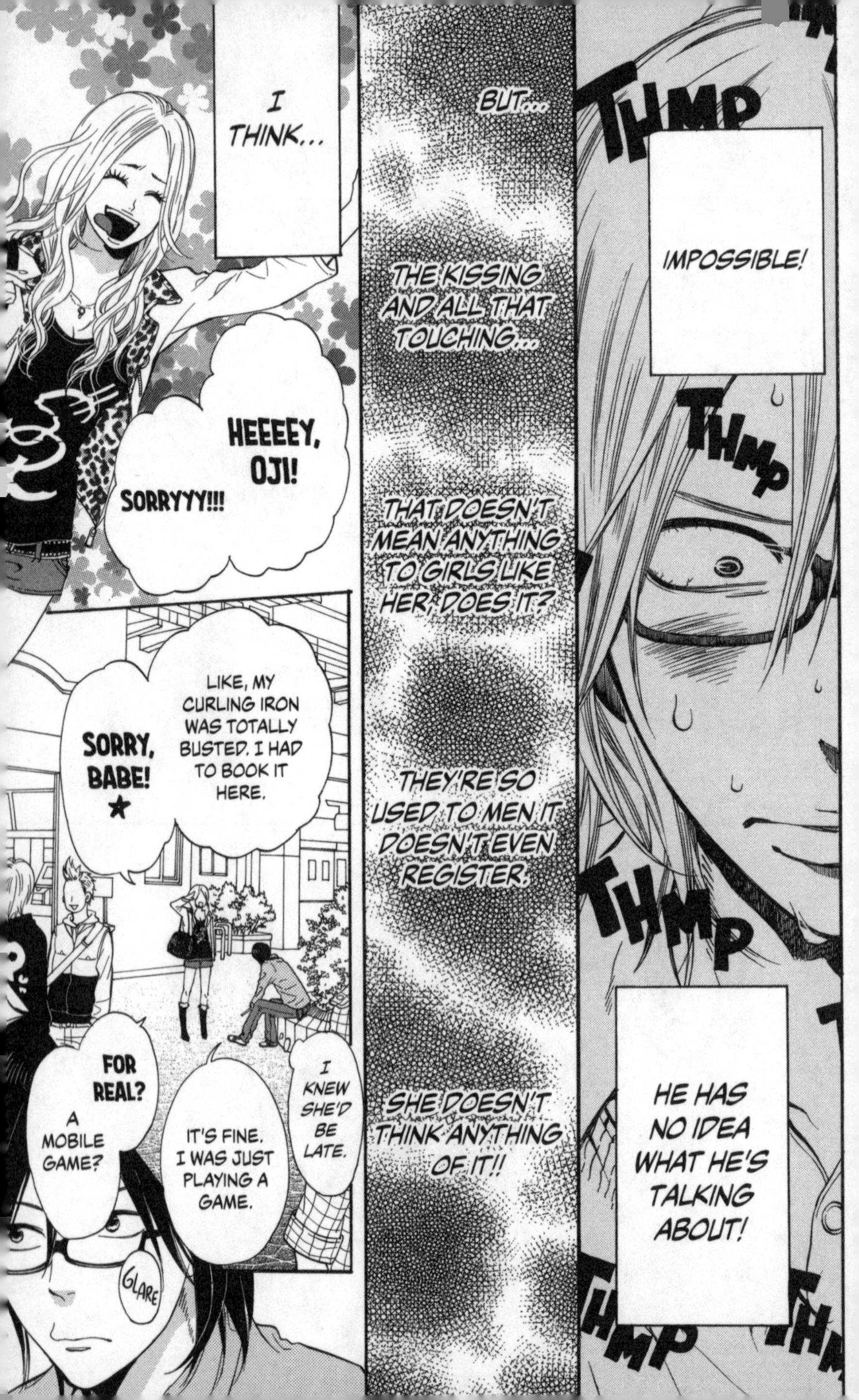
THMP
IMPOSSIBLE!
THMP
THMP
HE HAS NO IDEA WHAT HE'S TALKING ABOUT!
THMP
BUT...
THE KISSING AND ALL THAT TOUCHING...
THAT DOESN'T MEAN ANYTHING TO GIRLS LIKE HER, DOES IT?
THEY'RE SO USED TO MEN IT DOESN'T EVEN REGISTER.
SHE DOESN'T THINK ANYTHING OF IT!!
I THINK...
HEEEEY, OJI!
SORRYYY!!!
SORRY, BABE! ★
LIKE, MY CURLING IRON WAS TOTALLY BUSTED. I HAD TO BOOK IT HERE.
I KNEW SHE'D BE LATE.
IT'S FINE. I WAS JUST PLAYING A GAME.
FOR REAL?
A MOBILE GAME?
GLARE

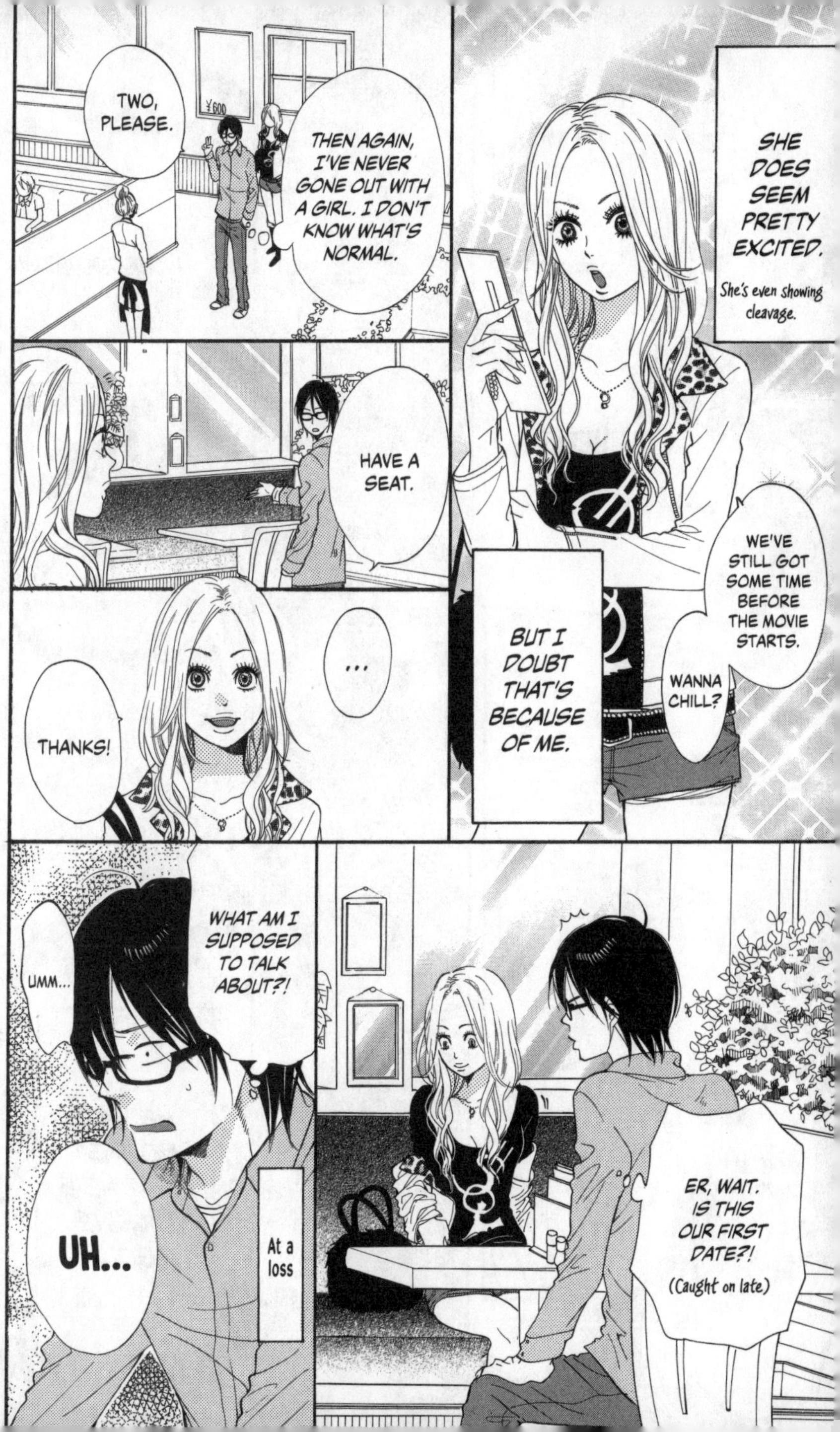
SHE DOES SEEM PRETTY EXCITED.
She's even showing cleavage.
WE'VE STILL GOT SOME TIME BEFORE THE MOVIE STARTS.
WANNA CHILL?
BUT I DOUBT THAT'S BECAUSE OF ME.
THEN AGAIN, I'VE NEVER GONE OUT WITH A GIRL. I DON'T KNOW WHAT'S NORMAL.
¥600
TWO, PLEASE.
HAVE A SEAT.
...
THANKS!
ER, WAIT. IS THIS OUR FIRST DATE?!
(Caught on late)
WHAT AM I SUPPOSED TO TALK ABOUT?!
UMM...
UH...
At a loss

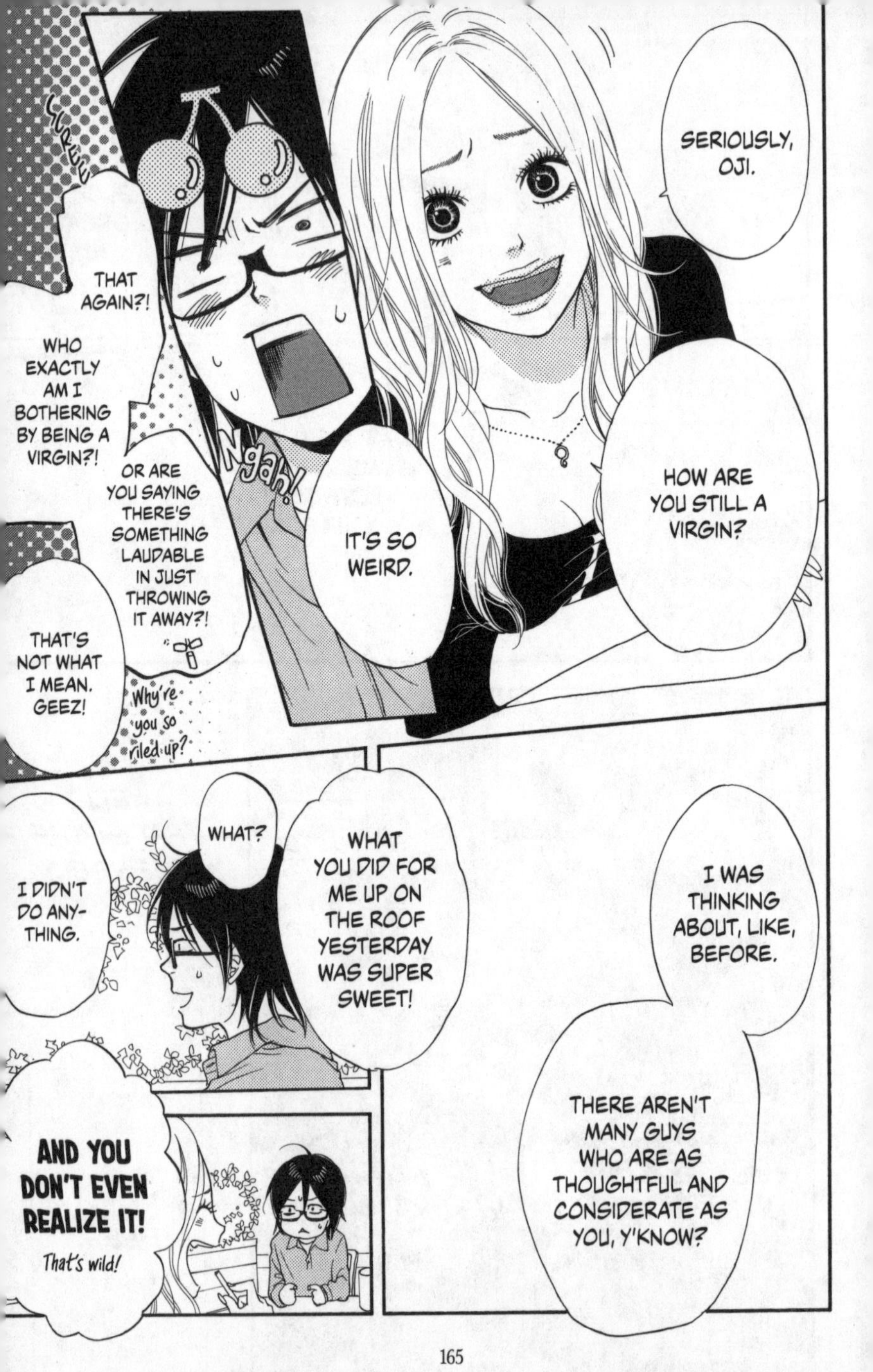
SERIOUSLY, OJI.
HOW ARE YOU STILL A VIRGIN?
IT'S SO WEIRD.
Ngah!
SCREEE
THAT AGAIN?!
WHO EXACTLY AM I BOTHERING BY BEING A VIRGIN?!
OR ARE YOU SAYING THERE'S SOMETHING LAUDABLE IN JUST THROWING IT AWAY?!
THAT'S NOT WHAT I MEAN. GEEZ!
Why're you so riled up?
I WAS THINKING ABOUT, LIKE, BEFORE.
THERE AREN'T MANY GUYS WHO ARE AS THOUGHTFUL AND CONSIDERATE AS YOU, Y'KNOW?
WHAT YOU DID FOR ME UP ON THE ROOF YESTERDAY WAS SUPER SWEET!
WHAT?
I DIDN'T DO ANY-THING.
AND YOU DON'T EVEN REALIZE IT!
That's wild!

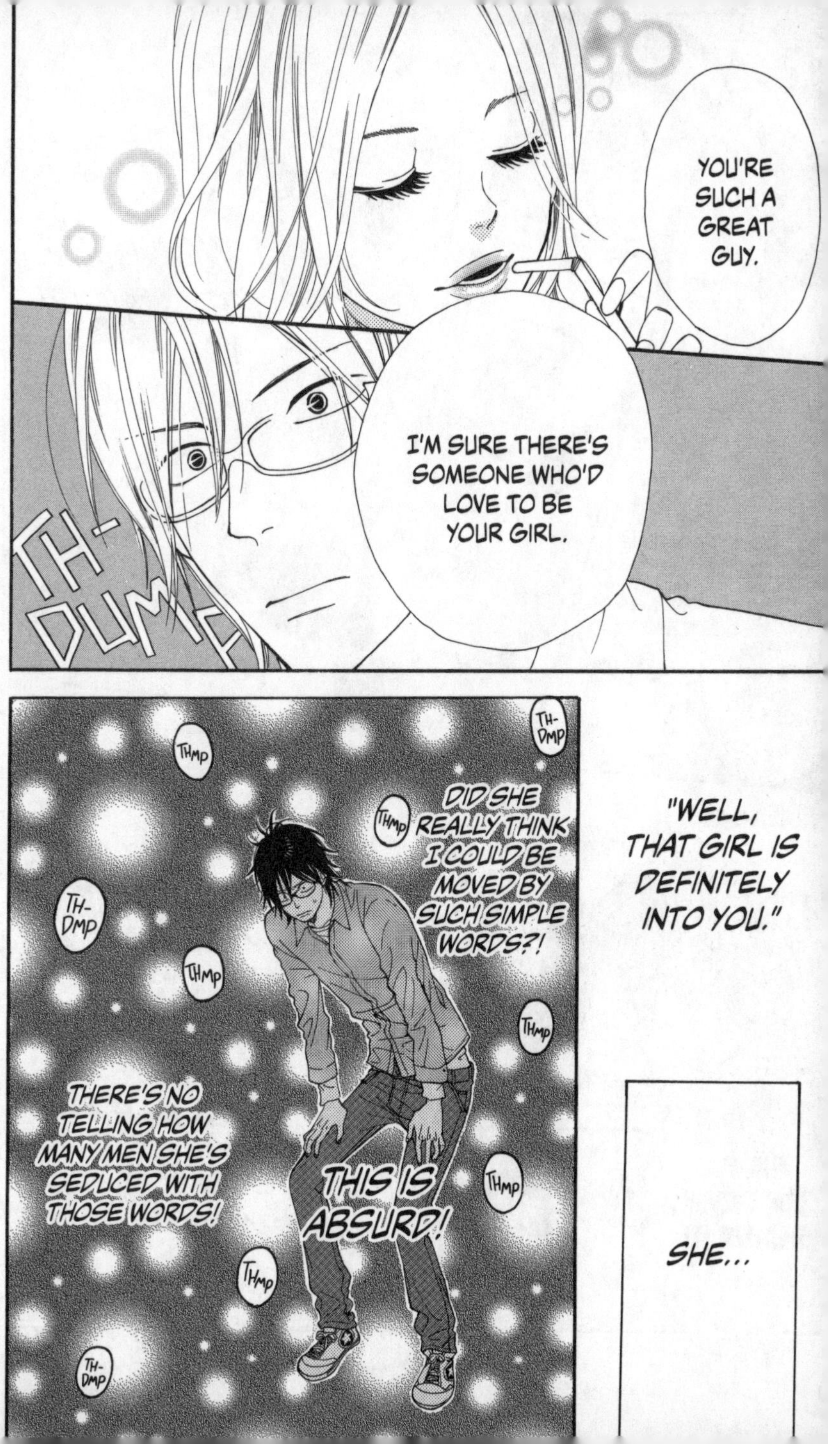
YOU'RE SUCH A GREAT GUY.
I'M SURE THERE'S SOMEONE WHO'D LOVE TO BE YOUR GIRL.
TH-DUMP
"WELL, THAT GIRL IS DEFINITELY INTO YOU."
SHE...
TH-DMP
THMP
THMP
DID SHE REALLY THINK I COULD BE MOVED BY SUCH SIMPLE WORDS?!
TH-DMP
THMP
THMP
THERE'S NO TELLING HOW MANY MEN SHE'S SEDUCED WITH THOSE WORDS!
THIS IS ABSURD!
THMP
THMP
TH-DMP

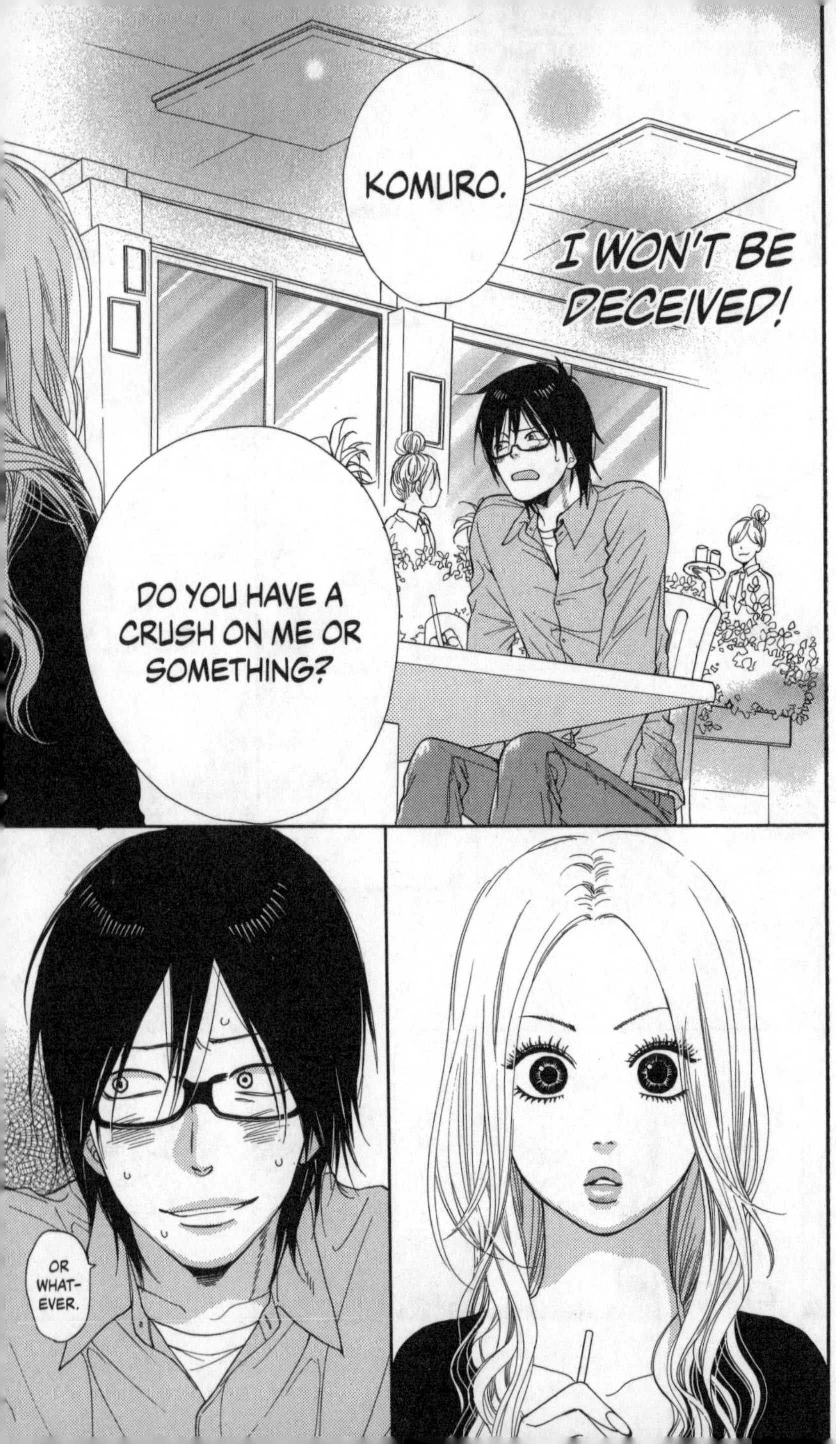
I WON'T BE DECEIVED!
KOMURO.
DO YOU HAVE A CRUSH ON ME OR SOMETHING?
OR WHAT-EVER.

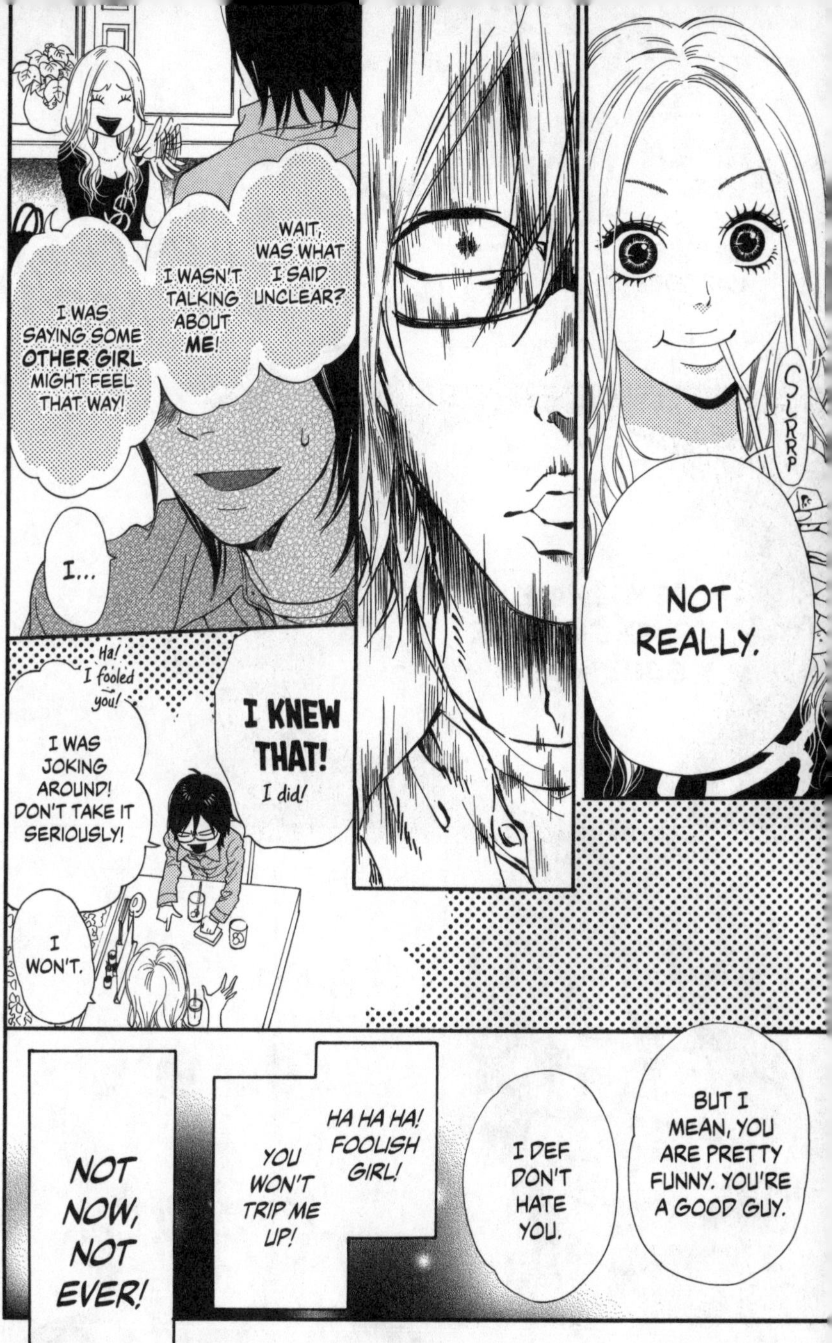
SLRRP
NOT REALLY.
WAIT, WAS WHAT I SAID UNCLEAR?
I WASN'T TALKING ABOUT ME!
I WAS SAYING SOME OTHER GIRL MIGHT FEEL THAT WAY!
I...
I KNEW THAT! I did!
Ha! I fooled you!
I WAS JOKING AROUND! DON'T TAKE IT SERIOUSLY!
I WON'T.
BUT I MEAN, YOU ARE PRETTY FUNNY. YOU'RE A GOOD GUY.
I DEF DON'T HATE YOU.
HA HA HA! FOOLISH GIRL!
YOU WON'T TRIP ME UP!
NOT NOW, NOT EVER!

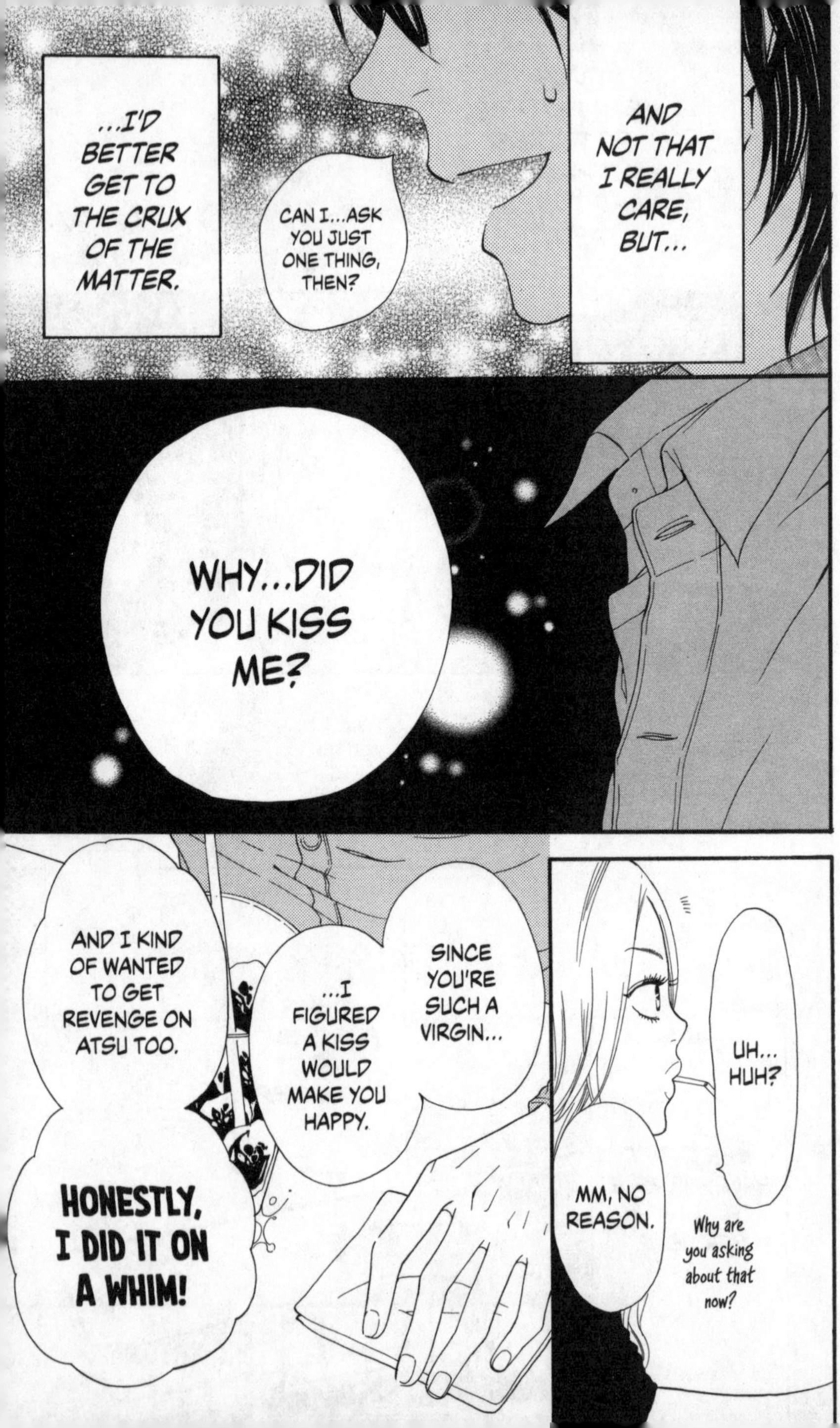
AND NOT THAT I REALLY CARE, BUT...
CAN I...ASK YOU JUST ONE THING, THEN?
...I'D BETTER GET TO THE CRUX OF THE MATTER.
WHY...DID YOU KISS ME?
UH... HUH?
Why are you asking about that now?
MM, NO REASON.
SINCE YOU'RE SUCH A VIRGIN...
...I FIGURED A KISS WOULD MAKE YOU HAPPY.
AND I KIND OF WANTED TO GET REVENGE ON ATSU TOO.
HONESTLY, I DID IT ON A WHIM!

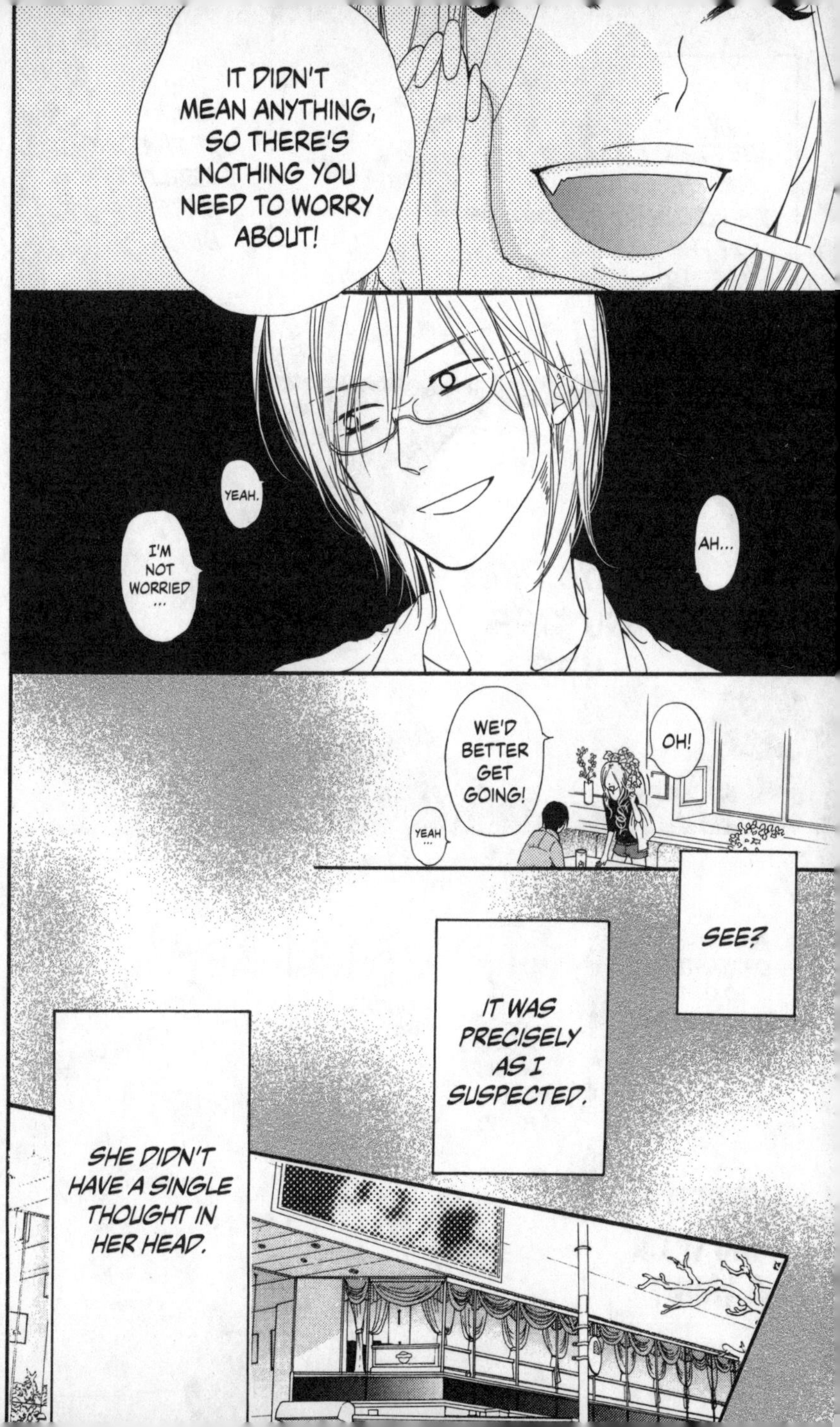
IT DIDN'T MEAN ANYTHING, SO THERE'S NOTHING YOU NEED TO WORRY ABOUT!
AH...
YEAH.
I'M NOT WORRIED ...
OH!
WE'D BETTER GET GOING!
YEAH ...
SEE?
IT WAS PRECISELY AS I SUSPECTED.
SHE DIDN'T HAVE A SINGLE THOUGHT IN HER HEAD.

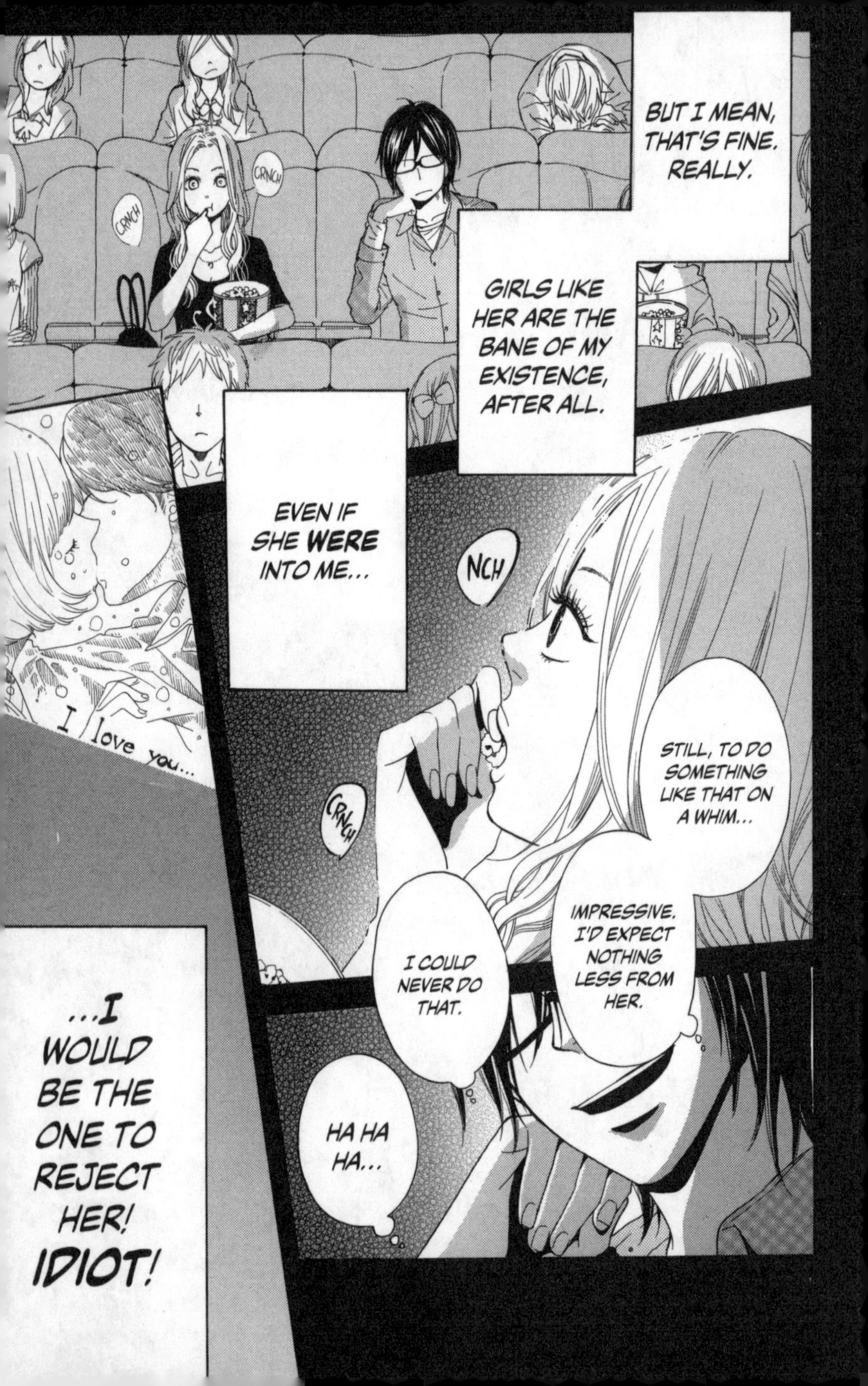
BUT I MEAN, THAT'S FINE. REALLY.
GIRLS LIKE HER ARE THE BANE OF MY EXISTENCE, AFTER ALL.
CRNCH
CRNCH
EVEN IF SHE WERE INTO ME...
NCH
STILL, TO DO SOMETHING LIKE THAT ON A WHIM...
CRNCH
I love you...
IMPRESSIVE. I'D EXPECT NOTHING LESS FROM HER.
I COULD NEVER DO THAT.
HA HA HA...
...I WOULD BE THE ONE TO REJECT HER! IDIOT!

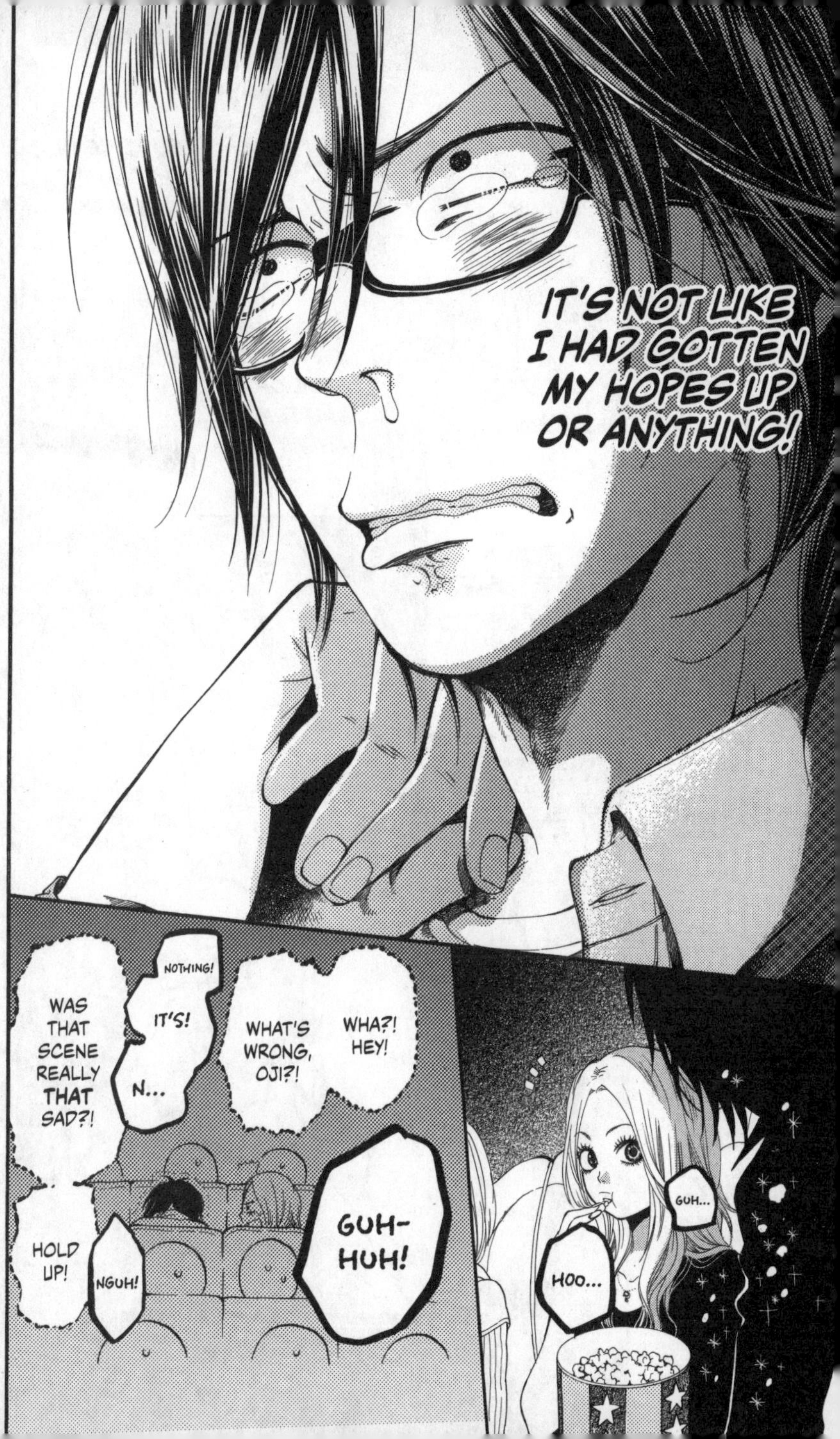
IT'S NOT LIKE I HAD GOTTEN MY HOPES UP OR ANYTHING!
GUH...
HOO...
WHA?! HEY!
WHAT'S WRONG, OJI?!
N... IT'S! NOTHING!
WAS THAT SCENE REALLY THAT SAD?!
GUH-HUH!
NGUH!
HOLD UP!

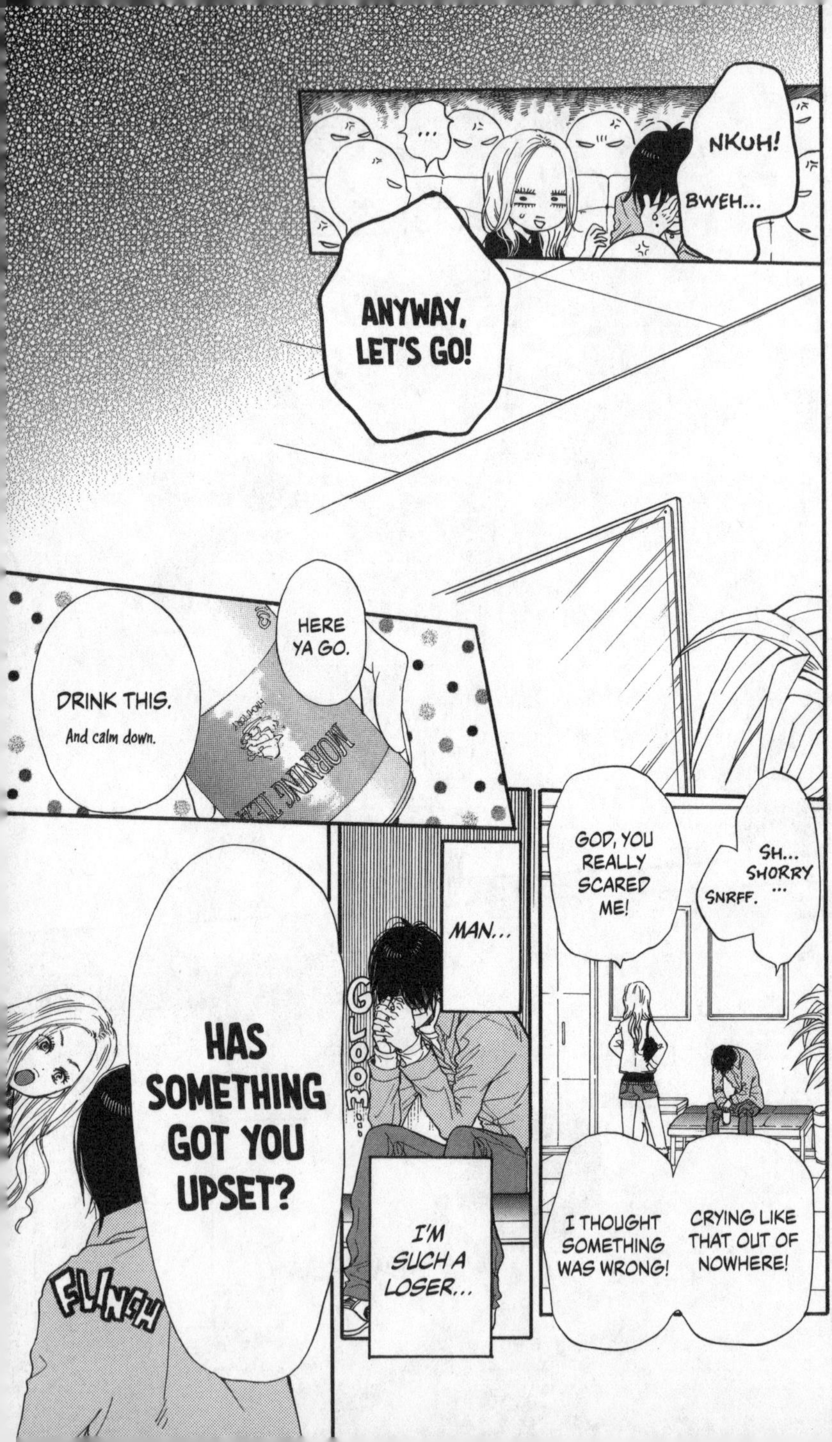
NKUH!
BWEH...
...
ANYWAY, LET'S GO!
HERE YA GO.
DRINK THIS.
And calm down.
SH... SHORRY...
SNRFF.
GOD, YOU REALLY SCARED ME!
CRYING LIKE THAT OUT OF NOWHERE!
I THOUGHT SOMETHING WAS WRONG!
MAN...
GLOOOM...
I'M SUCH A LOSER...
HAS SOMETHING GOT YOU UPSET?
FLINCH

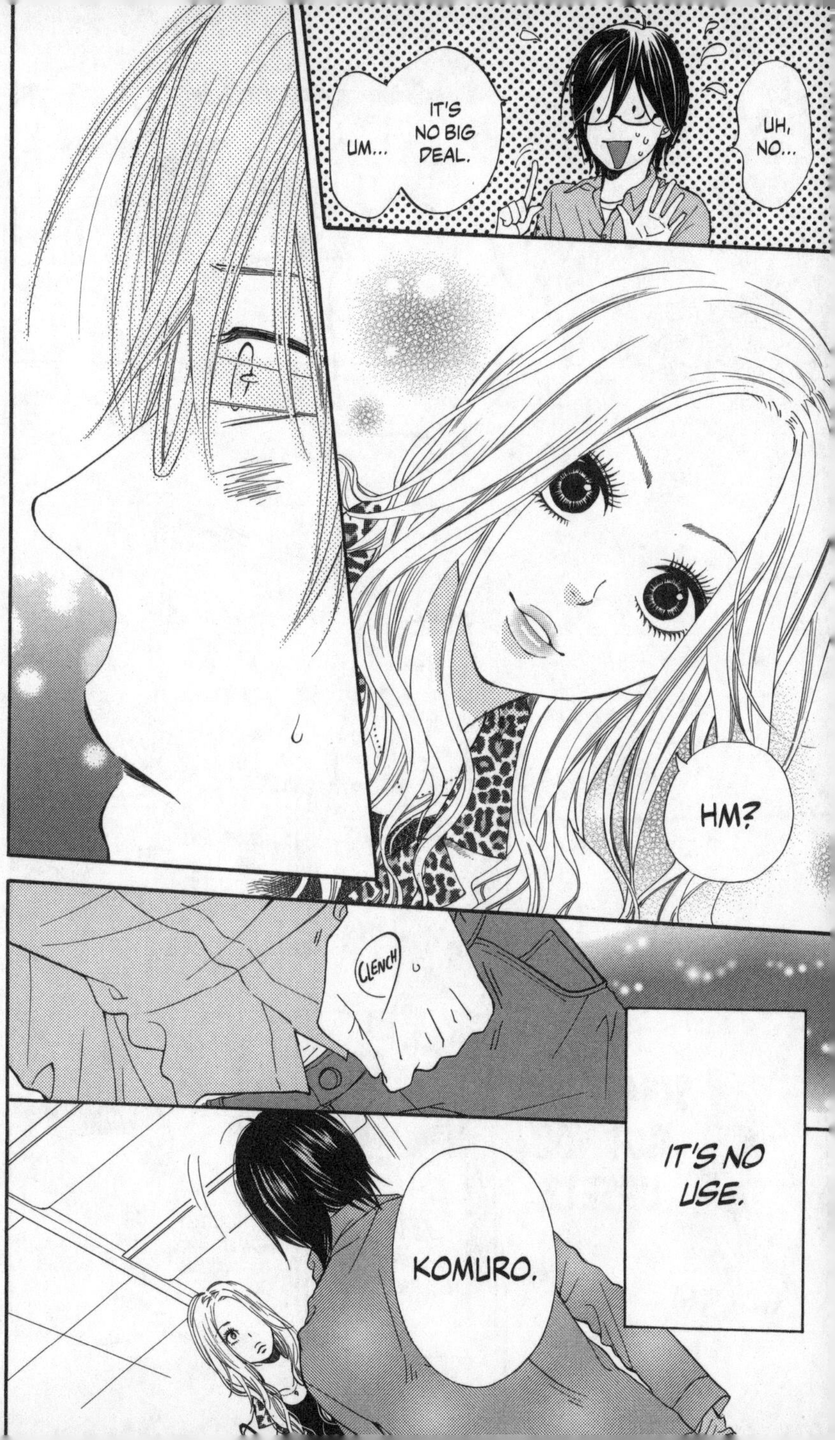

UH, NO...
UM... IT'S NO BIG DEAL.
HM?
CLENCH
IT'S NO USE.
KOMURO.

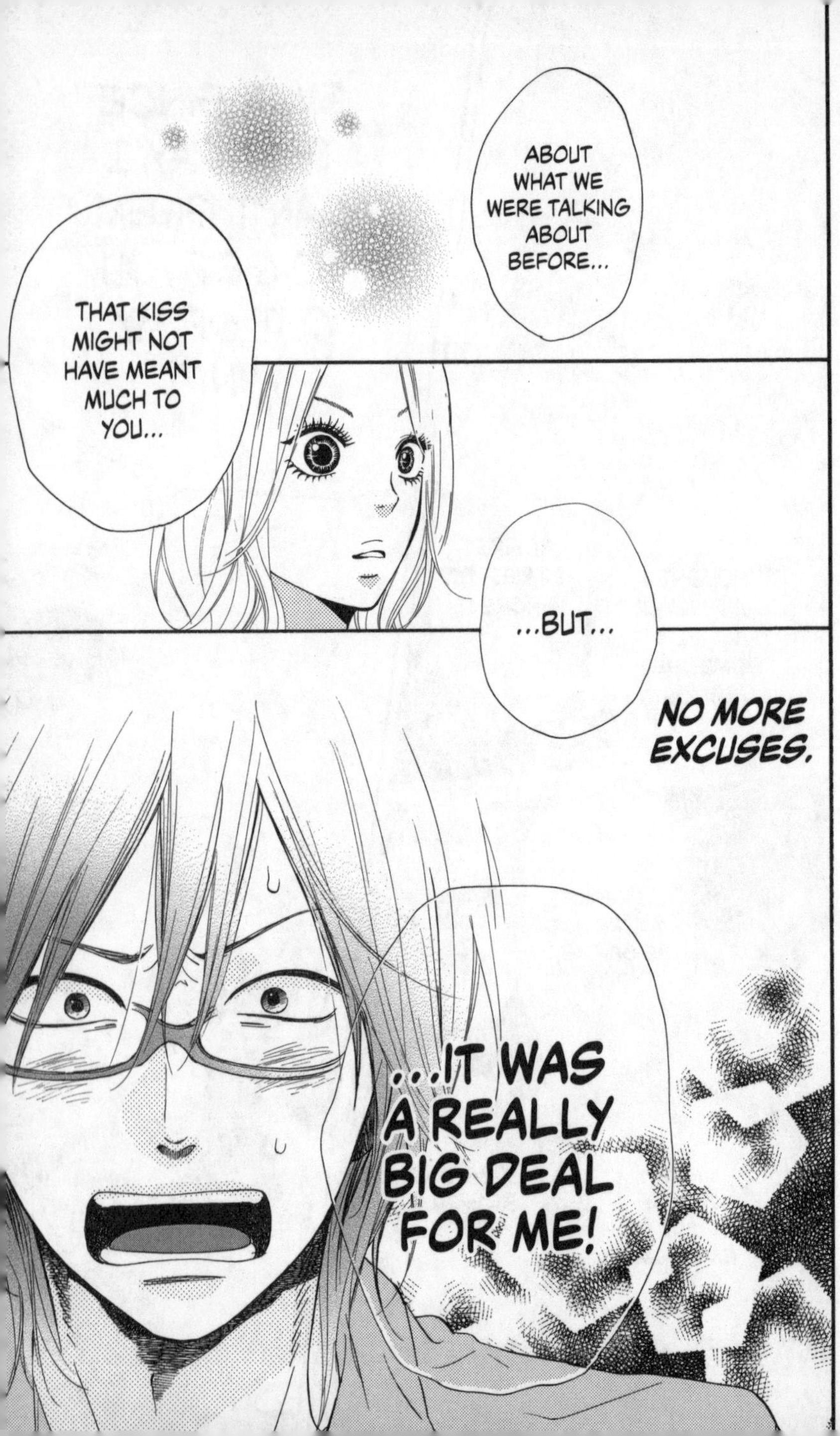
ABOUT WHAT WE WERE TALKING ABOUT BEFORE...
THAT KISS MIGHT NOT HAVE MEANT MUCH TO YOU...
...BUT...
NO MORE EXCUSES.
...IT WAS A REALLY BIG DEAL FOR ME!

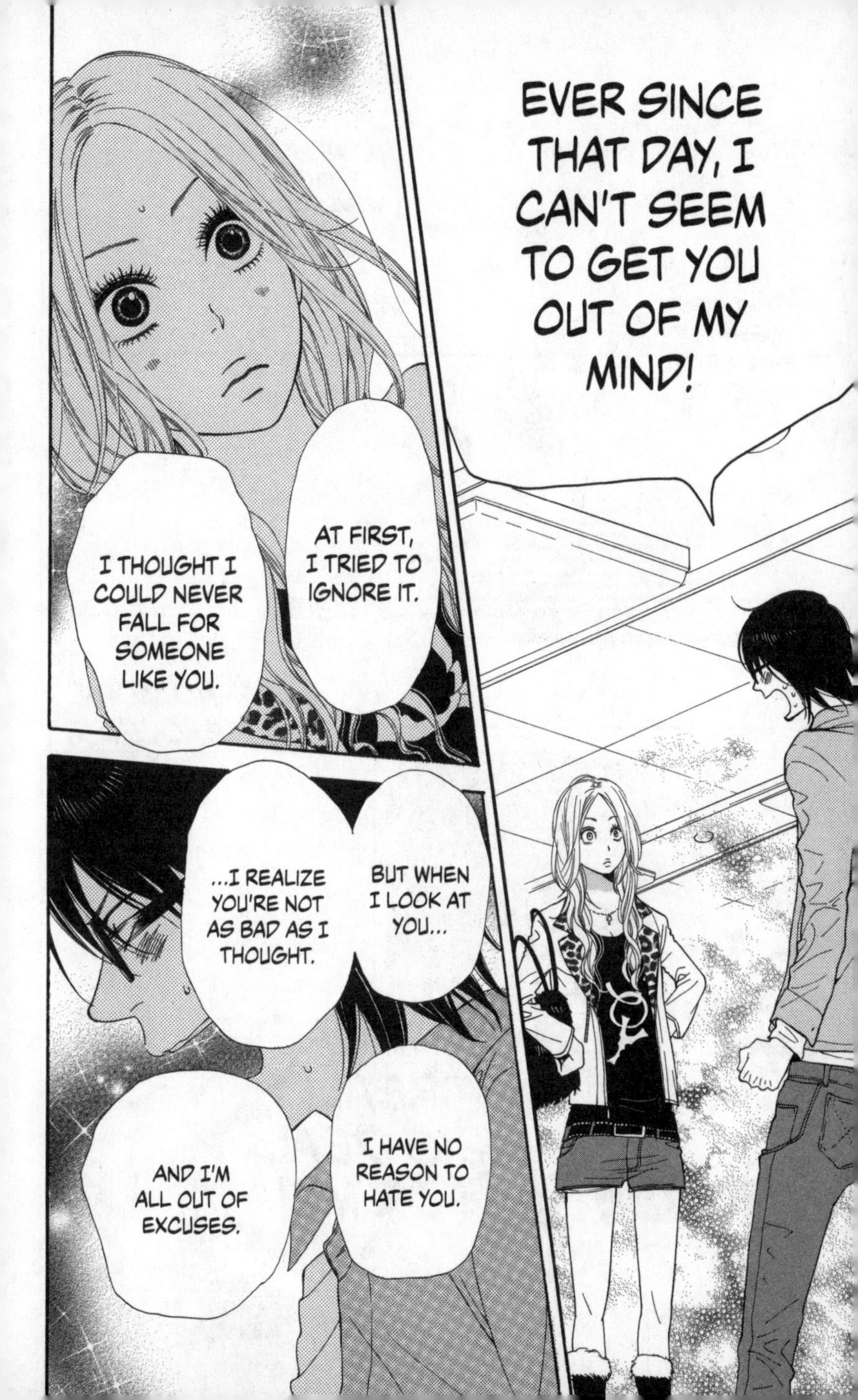
EVER SINCE THAT DAY, I CAN'T SEEM TO GET YOU OUT OF MY MIND!
AT FIRST, I TRIED TO IGNORE IT.
I THOUGHT I COULD NEVER FALL FOR SOMEONE LIKE YOU.
BUT WHEN I LOOK AT YOU...
...I REALIZE YOU'RE NOT AS BAD AS I THOUGHT.
I HAVE NO REASON TO HATE YOU.
AND I'M ALL OUT OF EXCUSES.

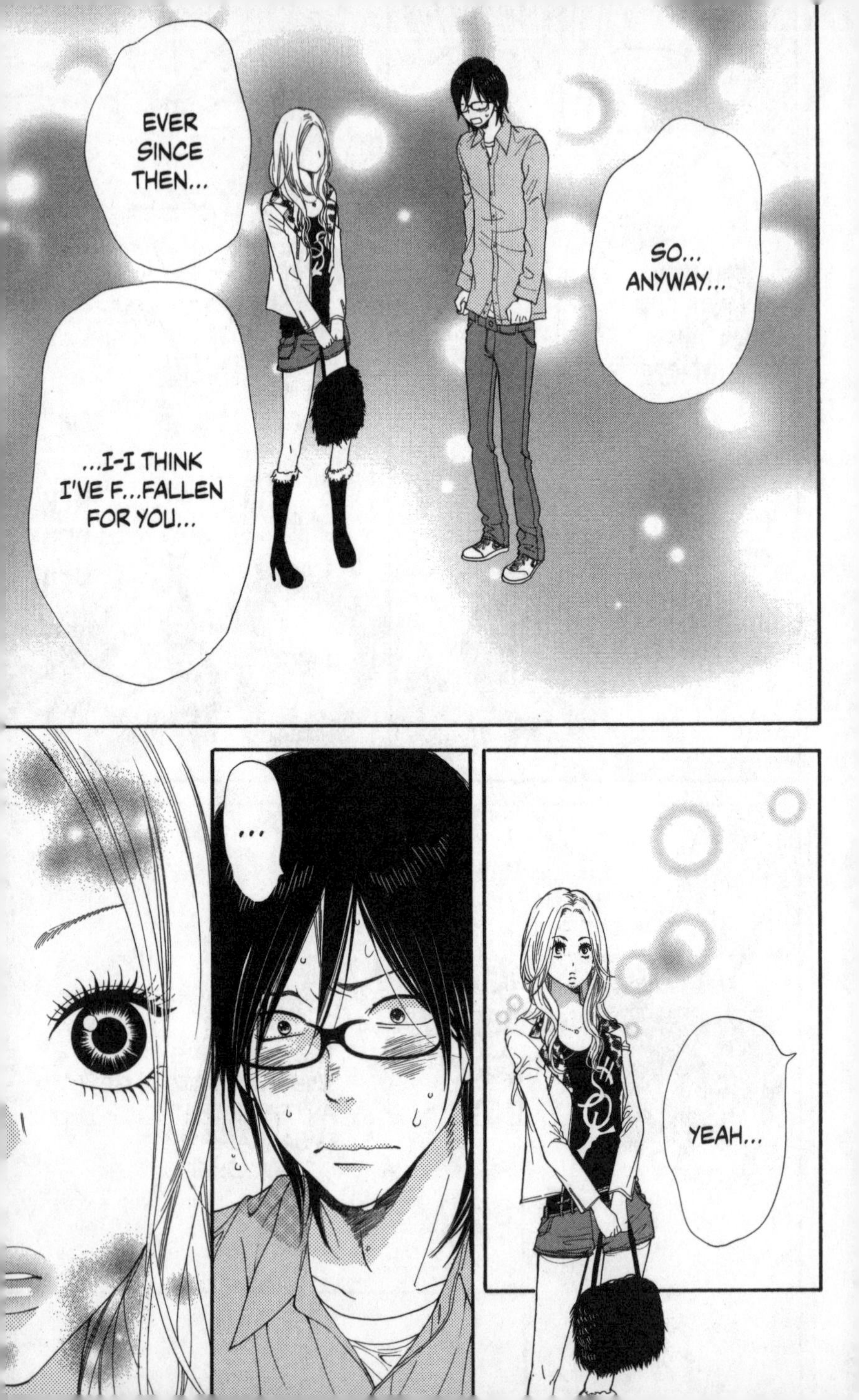
SO... ANYWAY...
EVER SINCE THEN...
...I-I THINK I'VE F...FALLEN FOR YOU...
YEAH...
...

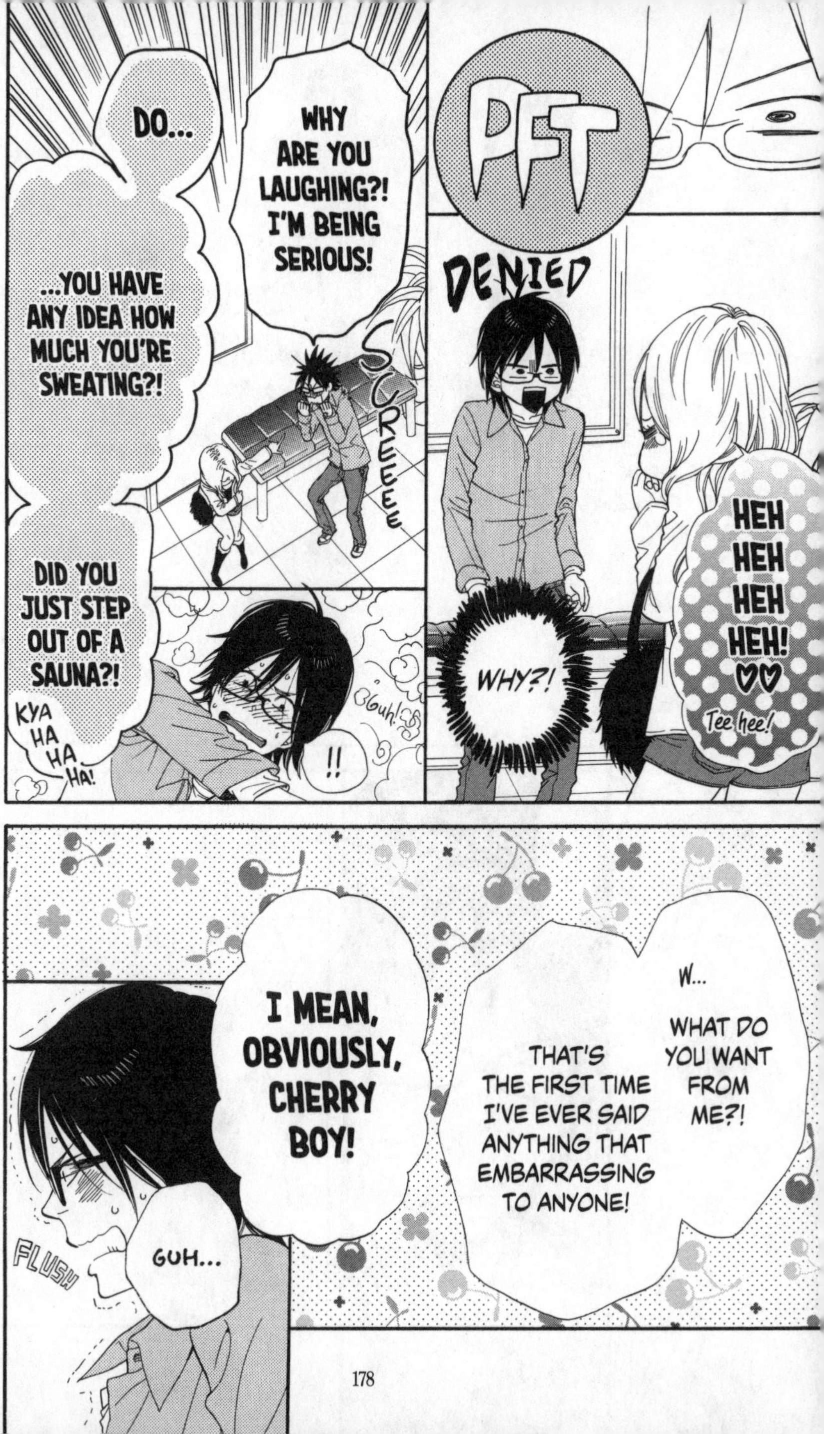
PFFT
DENIED
HEH HEH HEH HEH! ♡♡
Tee hee!
WHY?!
WHY ARE YOU LAUGHING?! I'M BEING SERIOUS!
SUREEEE
DO... ...YOU HAVE ANY IDEA HOW MUCH YOU'RE SWEATING?!
DID YOU JUST STEP OUT OF A SAUNA?!
KYA HA HA HA!
Guh!
!!
W... WHAT DO YOU WANT FROM ME?!
THAT'S THE FIRST TIME I'VE EVER SAID ANYTHING THAT EMBARRASSING TO ANYONE!
I MEAN, OBVIOUSLY, CHERRY BOY!
GUH...
FLUSH

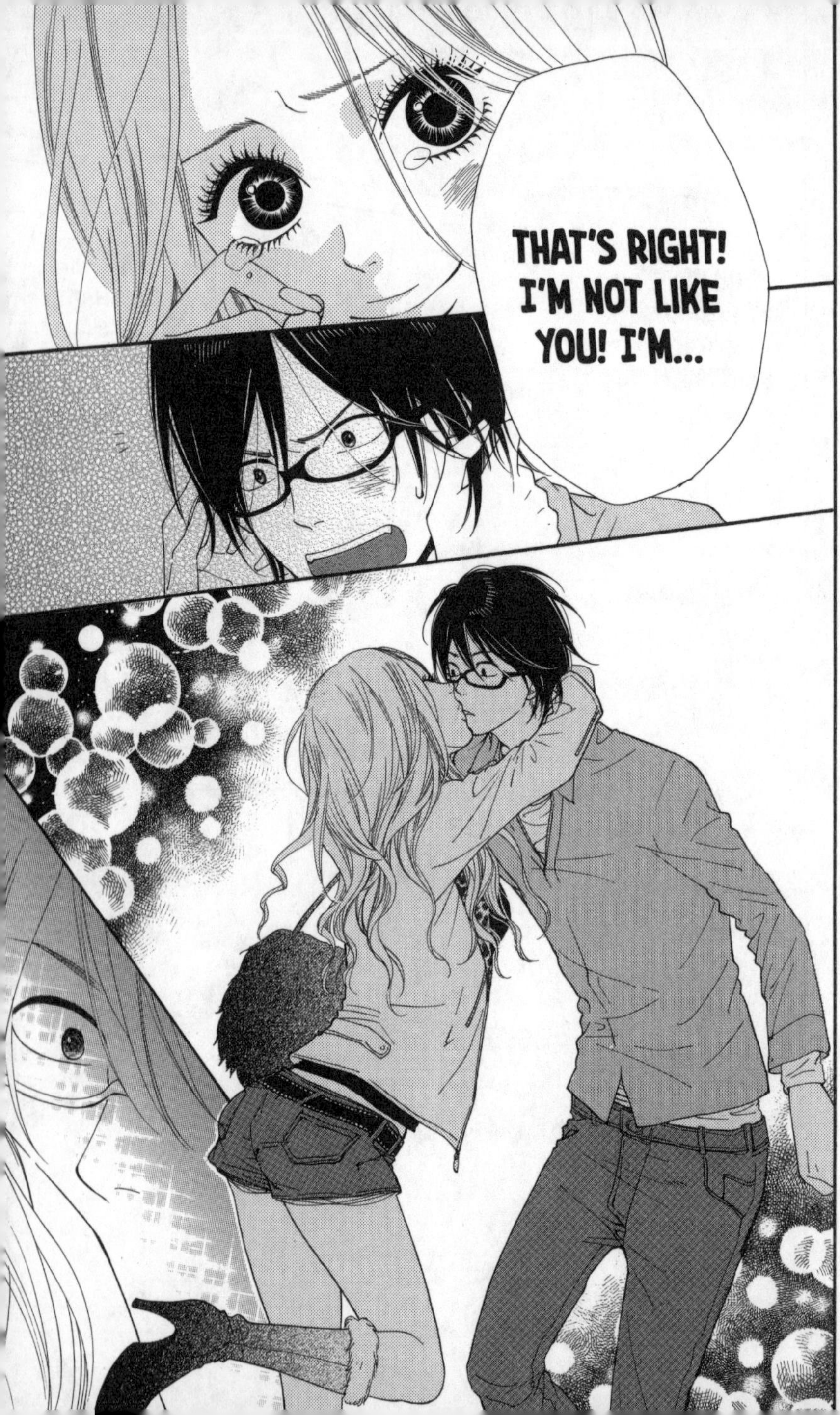
THAT'S RIGHT! I'M NOT LIKE YOU! I'M...

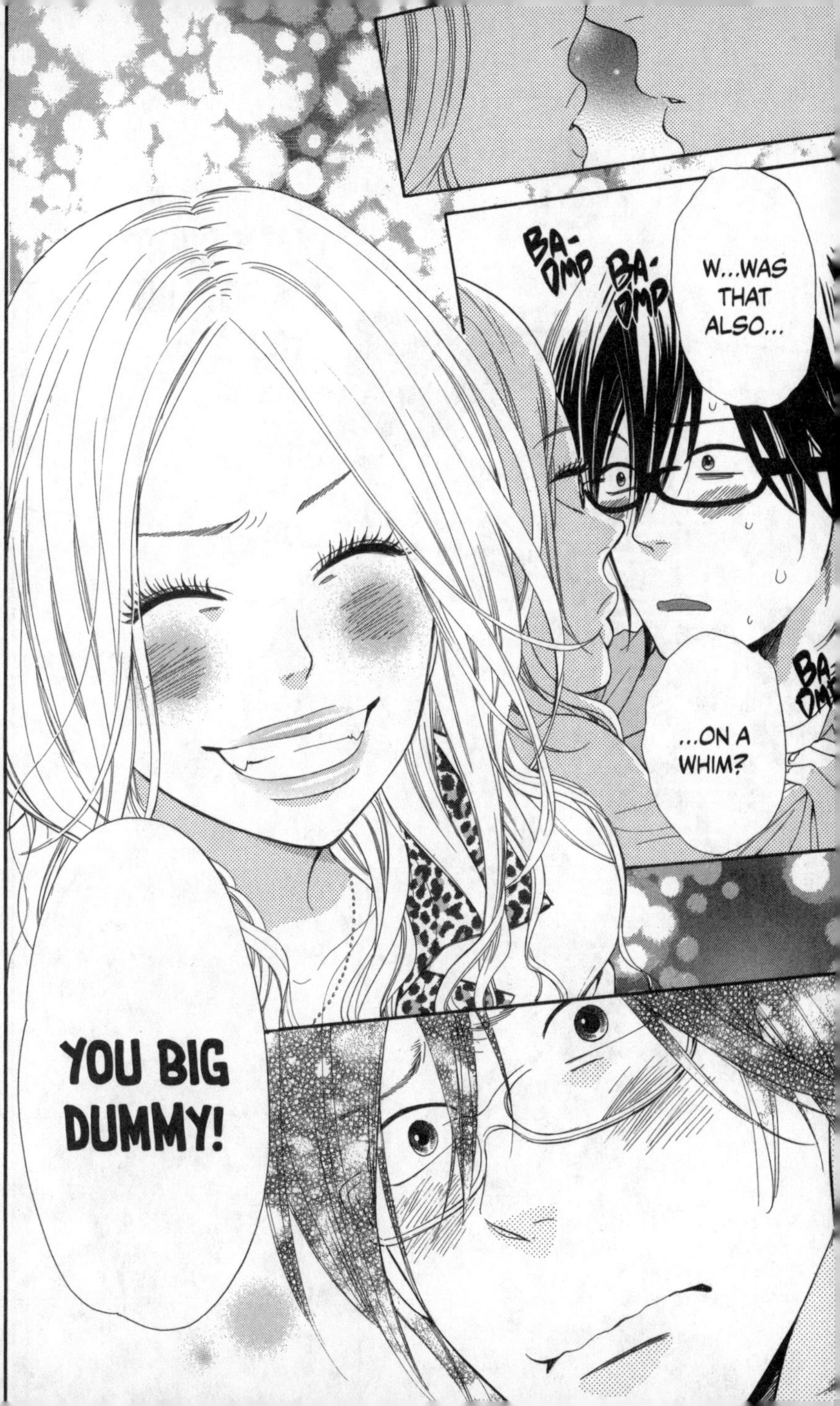
BA-DUMP BA-DUMP
W...WAS THAT ALSO...
...ON A WHIM?
YOU BIG DUMMY!

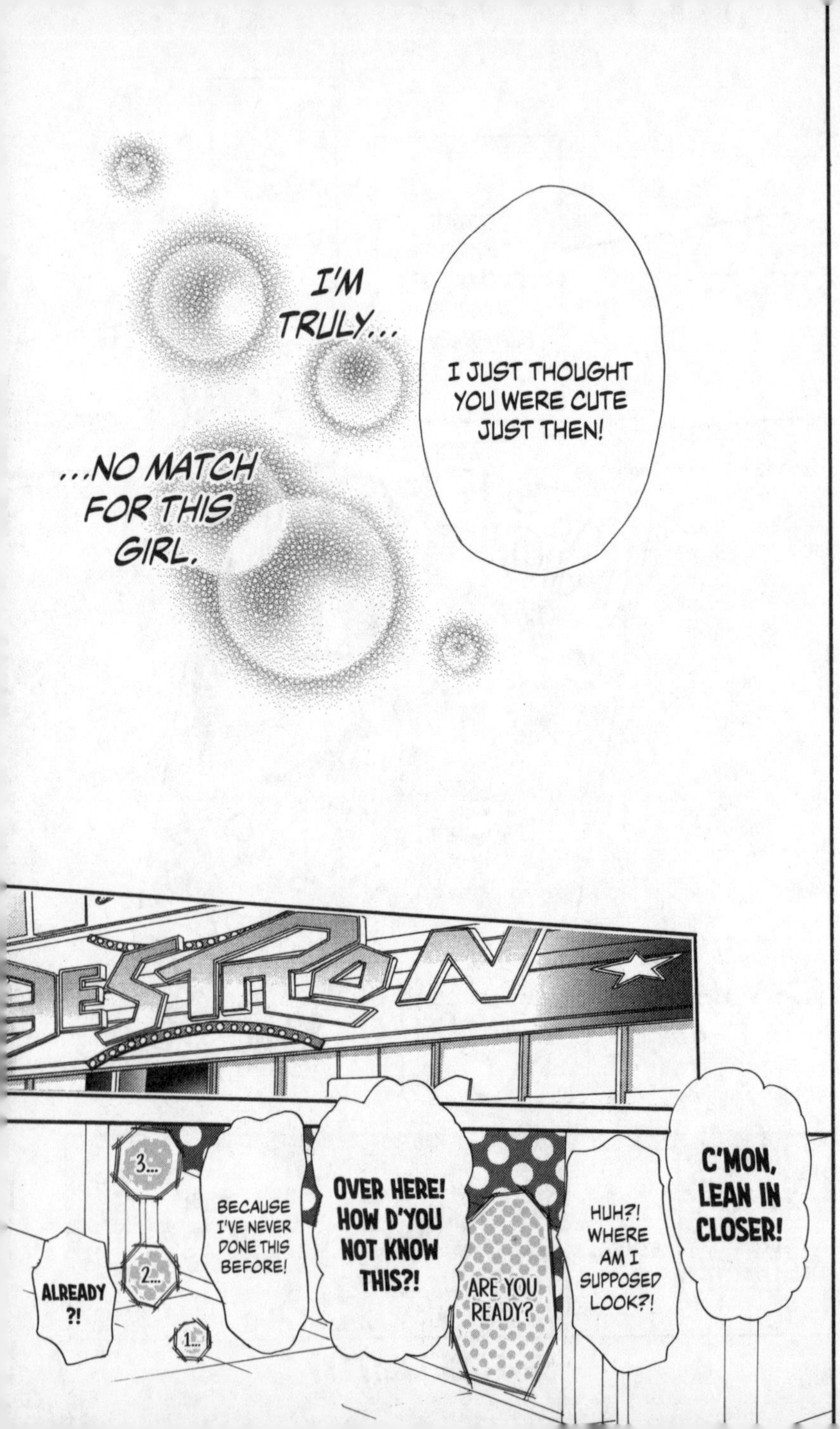
I JUST THOUGHT YOU WERE CUTE JUST THEN!
I'M TRULY...
...NO MATCH FOR THIS GIRL.
C'MON, LEAN IN CLOSER!
HUH?! WHERE AM I SUPPOSED LOOK?!
ARE YOU READY?
OVER HERE! HOW D'YOU NOT KNOW THIS?!
BECAUSE I'VE NEVER DONE THIS BEFORE!
3...
2...
1...
ALREADY ?!

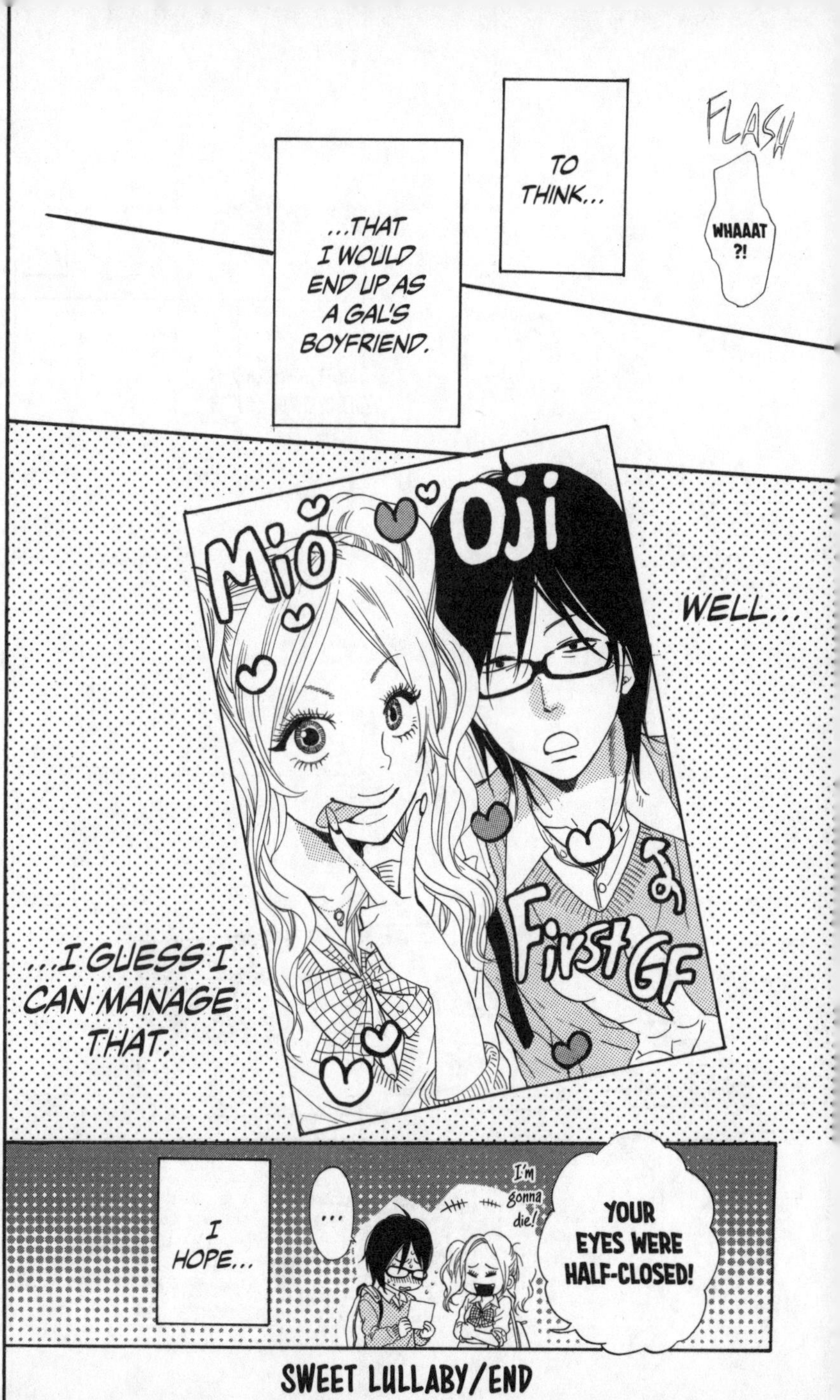
FLASH
WHAAAT?!
TO THINK...
...THAT I WOULD END UP AS A GAL'S BOYFRIEND.
Mio
Oji
First GF
WELL...
...I GUESS I CAN MANAGE THAT.
YOUR EYES WERE HALF-CLOSED!
I'm gonna die!
...
I HOPE...

SWEET LULLABY/END

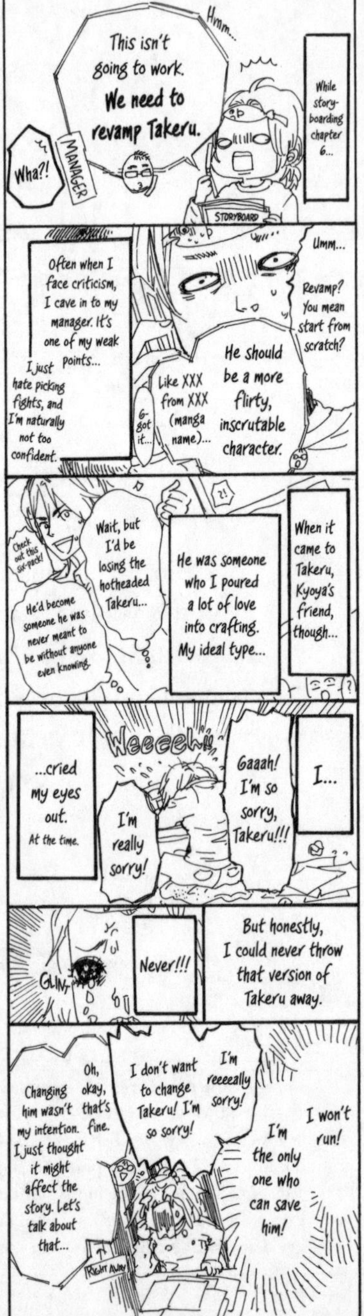
While storyboarding chapter 6...
Hmm...
This isn't going to work. We need to revamp Takeru.
MANAGER
Wha?!
STORYBOARD
Umm... Revamp? You mean start from scratch?
He should be a more flirty, inscrutable character.
Like XXX from XXX (manga name)...
G-got it...
Often when I face criticism, I cave in to my manager. It's one of my weak points...
I just hate picking fights, and I'm naturally not too confident.
When it came to Takeru, Kyoya's friend, though...
He was someone who I poured a lot of love into crafting. My ideal type...
Wait, but I'd be losing the hotheaded Takeru...
Check out this six-pack!
He'd become someone he was never meant to be without anyone even knowing.
I...
Gaaah! I'm so sorry, Takeru!!!
Weeeeeh!!
I'm really sorry!
...cried my eyes out. At the time.
But honestly, I could never throw that version of Takeru away.
Never!!!
GLINT
I won't run!
I'm the only one who can save him!
I'm reeeeally sorry!
I don't want to change Takeru! I'm so sorry!
Oh, okay, that's fine.
Changing him wasn't my intention. I just thought it might affect the story. Let's talk about that...
RIGHT AWAY

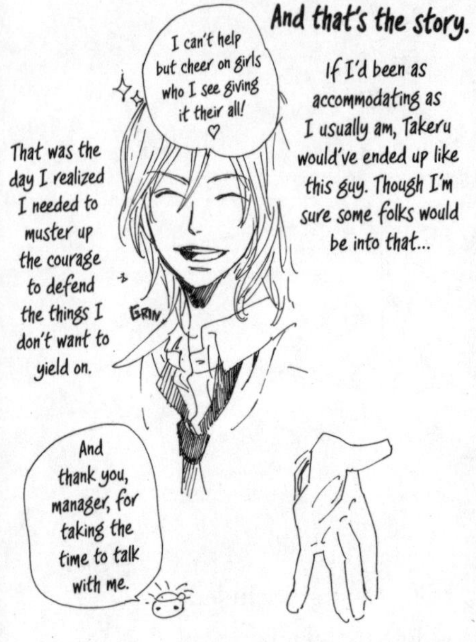
And that's the story.
If I'd been as accommodating as I usually am, Takeru would've ended up like this guy. Though I'm sure some folks would be into that...
I can't help but cheer on girls who I see giving it their all! ♡
That was the day I realized I needed to muster up the courage to defend the things I don't want to yield on.
GRIN
And thank you, manager, for taking the time to talk with me.

I'm a mess, but I'm still having a lot of fun drawing. Please look forward to *Wolf Girl and Black Prince* volume 3!

Ayuko Hatta

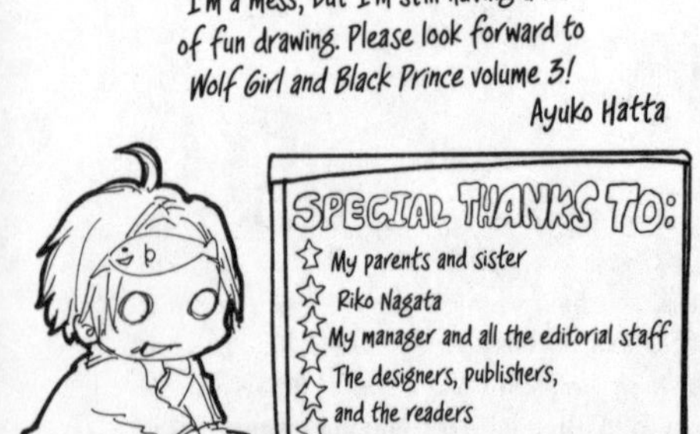
SPECIAL THANKS TO:
☆ My parents and sister
☆ Riko Nagata
☆ My manager and all the editorial staff
☆ The designers, publishers, and the readers
☆ Thank you very much!

Mio, the heroine of the one-shot included
in this volume, was modeled after my friend.
They're basically the same person.
She gets on my nerves sometimes, but that aside,
she's pretty cute. I wish her the world.

— AYUKO HATTA

Ayuko Hatta resides in the Kansai region of Japan. In 2007, she began her shojo manga career in *Deluxe Margaret* with *Order wa Boku de Yoroshii desu ka?* (Am I All You Wish to Order?). Since then, she has gone on to publish numerous works, including *Bye-Bye Liberty*, *Haibara-kun wa Gokigen Naname* (Haibara Is in a Bad Mood), and the popular hit series *Wolf Girl and Black Prince*. Her series *Ima Koi: Now I'm in Love* began serialization in 2019. She loves playing games and is generally acknowledged by those around her to be an innate gamer. She's also good at cooking and drawing caricatures.

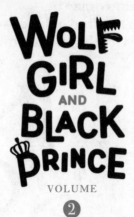

WOLF GIRL AND BLACK PRINCE

VOLUME

2

SHOJO BEAT EDITION

STORY AND ART BY
Ayuko Hatta

TRANSLATION — Diana Taylor
TOUCH-UP ART & LETTERING — Aidan Clarke
DESIGN — Alice Lewis
EDITOR — Karla Clark

Printed in Canada

Published by VIZ Media, LLC
P.O. Box 77010
San Francisco, CA 94107

10 9 8 7 6 5 4 3 2 1
First printing, July 2023

ratings.viz.com
RATED T+ OLDER TEEN

PARENTAL ADVISORY
WOLF GIRL AND BLACK PRINCE is rated T+ for Older Teen and is recommended for ages 16. This volume contains sexually suggestive themes and humor.

VIZ MEDIA
viz.com

Shojo Beat
shojobeat.com

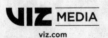